American Retrospectives

American Retrospectives:
Historians on Historians

Edited by
Stanley I. Kutler

The Johns Hopkins University Press
Baltimore and London

© 1995 The Johns Hopkins University Press
All rights reserved. Published 1995
Printed in the United States of America on acid-free paper
04 03 02 01 00 99 98 97 96 95   5 4 3 2 1

The Johns Hopkins University Press
2715 North Charles Street
Baltimore, Maryland 21218-4319
The Johns Hopkins Press Ltd., London

Library of Congress Cataloging-in-Publication Data will be found at the end of this book.

A catalog record for this book is available from the British Library.

ISBN 0-8018-5212-9
ISBN 0-8018-5213-7 (pbk.)

CONTENTS

ACKNOWLEDGMENTS

The contributors themselves, of course, made this volume possible. But Judith Kirkwood, Assistant Editor of *Reviews in American History*, superbly edited their work, undoubtedly enhancing it. Once again, it is a pleasure to acknowledge the support and contributions of Marie Hansen, Associate Director and Journals Manager at the Johns Hopkins University Press, and her fine staff.

The essays in this volume were published originally in *Reviews in American History*:

Bradford Perkins, "The Tragedy of American Diplomacy: Twenty-five Years After" 12, no. 1 (1984): 1–18; Martin Ridge, "Populism Redux: John D. Hicks and *The Populist Revolt*" 13, no. 1 (1985): 142–54; Stephen Botein, "Scientific Mind and Legal Matter: The Long Shadow of Richard B. Morris's *Studies in the History of American Law*" 13, no. 2 (1985): 303–15; Alan Brinkley, "Richard Hofstadter's *The Age of Reform*: A Reconsideration" 13, no. 3 (1985): 462–80; Donald B. Cole, "*The Age of Jackson*: After Forty Years" 14, no. 1 (1986): 149–59; David M. Kennedy, "Revisiting Frederick Lewis Allen's *Only Yesterday*" 14, no. 2 (1986): 309–18; Robert Dawidoff, "*The Growth of American Thought*: A Reconsideration" 14, no. 3 (1986): 474–86; Thomas K. McCraw, "The Challenge of Alfred D. Chandler, Jr.: Retrospect and Prospect" 15, no. 1 (1987): 160–78; Carol Lasser, "Century of Struggle, Decades of Revision: A Retrospective on Eleanor Flexner's Suffrage History" 15, no. 2 (1987): 344–54; James T. Kloppenberg, "Morton White's *Social Thought in America*" 15, no. 3 (1987): 507–19; Thomas P. Slaughter, "Merrill Jensen and the Revolution of 1787" 15, no. 4 (1987): 691–701; Robert M. Collins, "David Potter's *People of Plenty* and the Recycling of Consensus History" 16, no. 2 (1988): 321–35; Suzanne

Lebsock, "Reading Mary Beard" 17, no. 2 (1989): 324–39; Louis P. Masur, "Bernard DeVoto and the Making of *The Year of Decision: 1846*" 18, no. 3 (1990): 436–51; Jon Gjerde, "'Roots of Maladjustment' in the Land: Paul Wallace Gates" 19, no. 1 (1991): 142–53; Stephen J. Whitfield, "*The Image*: The Lost World of Daniel Boorstin" 19, no. 2 (1991): 302–12; Alex Lichtenstein, "*Industrial Slavery* and the Tragedy of Robert Starobin" 19, no. 4 (1991): 604–17; Aviam Soifer, "Willard Hurst, Consensus History, and *The Growth of American Law*" 20, no. 1 (1992): 124–44; Terrence J. McDonald, "Theory and Practice in the 'New' History: Rereading Arthur Meier Schlesinger's *The Rise of the City, 1878–1898*" 20, no. 3 (1992): 432–45; Daniel Feller, "Lee Benson and *The Concept of Jacksonian Democracy*" 20, no. 3 (1992): 591–601; James Campbell and James Oakes, "The Invention of Race: Rereading *White Over Black*" 21, no. 1 (1993): 172–83; Kenneth Cmiel, "Destiny and Amnesia: The Vision of Modernity in Robert Wiebe's *The Search for Order*" 21, no. 2 (1993): 352–68; Merton L. Dillon, "Gilbert H. Barnes and Dwight L. Dumond: An Appraisal" 21, no. 3 (1993): 539–52; David W. Blight, "Nathan Irvin Huggins, the Art of History, and the Irony of the American Dream" 22, no. 1 (1994): 174–90.

INTRODUCTION

The historian William Dodd once complained: "To write a good book may win one the approval of a few good friends and some others, but in ten years the best book has to be rewritten." Perhaps. Yet it seems sad, even wasteful, that good, innovative works are readily forgotten once they are "rewritten" by others. Of course, the new book itself is discarded, and, inevitably, the process repeats itself.

In his essay, "Vanitas and the Historian's Vocation," published in *Reviews in American History* in 1982, Michael Kammen took note of Dodd's lament. Kammen's essay was a celebration of historians and invoked great practitioners of the art from Edward Gibbon and Thomas Babbington Macaulay to a distinguished list of Americans in the nineteenth and twentieth centuries. Kammen's warm, gracious respect for those who had gone before him struck me as decidedly at odds with trends in the profession. To my mind, many historians are bent on making prophecy of Dodd's criticism. Increasingly, in books and articles, they seem to cite only the work of their peers and contemporaries, often failing to recognize how that work had evolved from apparently long-forgotten historians, some of whom *had* produced the pioneering inquiry on a subject.

For that reason, I commissioned a series of "Retrospective" essays for *Reviews in American History*, a series designed to remind historians of significant writers and books of the past, ones that had in various ways made present-day work understandable. What follows in this volume is a selection of some of the best of those essays. Obviously, they are essays that find merit in their subject, for one requirement of the essays was to explain the present vitality and usefulness of the work discussed. In addition, the essays explore the original reception and impact of the works and their utility through succeeding years.

I should confess that my selections reflect a personal journey of sorts, since many of the reexamined historians and their books profoundly influenced my own early training as a historian. They remain essential to my understanding of the American past—subject, of course, to the obvious caveat that their successors have ably enhanced and expanded their contributions. To be sure, the work of some historians is best forgotten. Still, we must be careful how we dismiss it: William Dunning's seminars of the 1890s, for example, produced pioneering monographs on that very recent phenomenon, Reconstruction. Despite their explicit racism and one-dimensional perspectives, those works had influence well into the 1960s, when a different time and outlook rejected their underlying assumptions.

I also hope that this collection might disabuse some historians of the notion that a sense of engagement, of political resonance, is of recent origin. I am well aware that historians who came of age during the era of the civil rights movement, Vietnam, and Watergate have brought a special perspective to their work. (Those events even affected those already "of age"!) But John D. Hicks on populism, Eleanor Flexner on women's suffrage, Gilbert Barnes and Dwight Dumond on abolitionism, and Nathan Huggins on the African-American experience certainly offered both engagement and commitment to their work and remind us that we are not so unique.

Alas! space does not permit the use of all the essays we published. I apologize to those writers whose splendid contributions I could not include here. But rather serendipitously, those included provide wonderful, chronological, topical, and methodological approaches. For the 1930s, we have essays on books by Richard Morris, Hicks, Frederick Lewis Allen, Barnes and Dumond, and Arthur Schlesinger, Sr. Representing succeeding decades are Merle Curti, Bernard DeVoto, Arthur Schlesinger, Jr., Mary Beard, and Morton White for their work in the 1940s; Merrill Jensen, James Willard Hurst, Richard Hofstadter, David Potter, Marvin Meyers, William Appleman Williams, and Flexner in the 1950s; F. Lee Benson, Daniel Boorstin, Alfred D. Chandler, Christopher Lasch, and Robert Wiebe for the 1960s; and Robert Starobin and Huggins in the 1970s. These writers offer an impressive coverage of historical periods and approaches: political, social, intellectual, economic, urban, agrarian, western, legal, diplomatic, women's and African-American history; and history written for scholars as well as for a larger audience. All in all, I believe, these essays offer a refreshing reminder of the variety, richness, and enduring quality of our craft.

Stanley I. Kutler

American Retrospectives

THE TRAGEDY OF AMERICAN DIPLOMACY: TWENTY-FIVE YEARS AFTER

Bradford Perkins

The influence of William Appleman Williams's *The Tragedy of American Diplomacy*, published a quarter century ago, is beyond challenge. An iconoclastic attack upon conventional wisdom, it is equally important because it framed arguments about its subject. In both ways it is very much like the study of the Constitution by Charles A. Beard, a scholar whom Williams reveres. And when historians finally escaped the conceptual fetters imposed by Beard and Williams they found that they could not — indeed, did not want to — ignore much that these figures suggested.

In 1959, *Tragedy* made a rather modest splash. The *New York Times* did review it, and the *Christian Science Monitor* denounced it as a Stalinist tract. But the *American Historical Review*, which then used smaller type and fewer words for reviews of minor publications, placed Williams's book in that category. Most reviewers praised the author's originality, then savaged his emphasis on economic factors. A political scientist, who suggested that the book was a mistake unlikely to be committed in his profession, believed it would be ignored: "The approach taken by Williams is no longer in the mainstream of international relations study."[1] But within only a few years *Tragedy* was definitely in the mainstream.

Reviewers concentrated on Williams's most persistent theme, that almost all Americans held "the firm conviction, even dogmatic belief, that . . . domestic well-being depends upon . . . sustained, ever-increasing overseas economic expansion."[2] Despite the decision to annex the Philippines, the preferred strategy of economic expansion was pursuit of the open door, the globalization of John Hay's China-oriented declarations of 1899 and 1900. As Williams phrased it, "When combined with the ideology of an industrial Manifest Destiny the history of the Open Door Notes became the history of American foreign relations . . . ."[3] Most policies, from McKinley onward, were determined by a desire to keep doors open, by open door imperialism designed to create informal empire.

Americans saw no contradiction between promoting their trade and improving the world by stimulating economic activity, or as Williams says, in putting "their self-interest to work to produce the well-being and the harmony of the world."[4] But although Americans professed to believe — even believed that they believed — that every nation had a right to determine its own path, in fact they felt, and came to insist, that the American way was the only one. They failed to see that the kind of economic activity they encouraged, in third world countries at least, was exploitative, that it institutionalized dependency and discouraged socioeconomic progress.[5] This blindness led the United States, with increasing activism, to pursue counterrevolutionary policies. Today's policies, in this view, represent "the final stage in the transformation of the open door from a utopian ideal into an ideology, from an intellectual outlook for changing the world into one concerned with preserving it in the traditional mold."[6] This argument meshes with and perhaps reinforces the economic one, and both emphasize expansionism, but the motivational priorities are strikingly different.

Second only to open door imperialism, the persistence of expansionism is the theme most often identified with *Tragedy*. Yet, although Williams included a brief, strained interpretation of James Madison's *Federalist #10* to suggest that America had been expansionist from the beginning, he really began his account toward the end of the nineteenth century.[7] *Tragedy* is an explanation for the overseas commercial expansion and ideological offensive of an industrialized America faced with the spectre of surplus production. Williams and others later pushed the expansionist theme backward, but there is little reason to identify the original version of *Tragedy* with this theme.[8]

In any case, the expansionist thesis expressed a near truism. At least until our time, American leaders have been committed to growth, economically and sometimes territorially. Early economic policy, limited in effect by limited power, sought to create an open door empire for agriculturists and shipowners. Still, although Williams would later object to the "question-begging" argument of those who insisted that he ought to define empire and expansion,[9] there surely is imprecision in comingling territorial expansion to control new areas of production with efforts to dispose of a surplus through expanded trade, to say nothing of a quest for ideological dominion.

In 1962 and again in 1972, Williams extensively revised *The Tragedy of American Diplomacy*. He increased its length by half, adding detail and extending the chronology. He also made scores of changes which hardened the arguments. In 1959 *Tragedy* described Hay's Open Door Notes as a "policy . . . for America's overseas expansion," a comment with which few would disagree; the third edition described it additionally as a policy "through which America's preponderant strength would enter and dominate all underdeveloped areas of the world."[10] The original edition stated that most of Wilson's opponents in the fight over the Treaty of Versailles "emphasized the need to continue economic expansion with greater vigor," while Williams later added that they also wished "to oppose . . . revolutions with more determination . . ." than Wilson.[11] Revised editions stressed, far more than the original, that the concept of an Axis menace in the 1930s predated any military threat. "It occurred instead," Williams wrote, "as those nations began to compete vigorously with American entrepreneurs in Latin America and Asia," and he also argued that "the strategy of the open door" — here used in the economic sense — "did lead to war."[12]

The changes reflected Williams's growing alienation. In 1959 he "seemed to imply that America could achieve a more humane and successful foreign policy by recognizing its former errors and only mildly reforming itself."[13] Then came America's violent reaction to the Castro revolution, and after that Vietnam. A new introduction began, "The tragedy of American diplomacy is aptly summarized, and defined for analysis and reflection, by the relations between the United States and Cuba" — intervention, exploitation, and counterrevolution, a paradigm of policies the world over. The new conclusion repeated an eloquent appeal for the tolerance of revolution but added that, for this to come about, "existing American society had to be changed."[14]

In 1959 *Tragedy* was a passionate essay. Later, in Jerald A. Combs's words, "colleagues and students applied [Williams's] theory in particular episodes in a harvest of monographs."[15] These were cycled back into revised versions of *Tragedy* as sources for new passages or footnotes to support sections which had inspired them in the first place. While revised editions are still thinly documented, the *ex post facto* apparatus of scholarship gives them a more traditional air.[16] Still, it is as a manifesto, not a monograph, that the book should be judged.

Writing on the "Open Door Interpretation" years later, Williams disclaimed sole responsibility for it. A group at the University of Wisconsin, he wrote, interacted to produce a mode of analysis of which *Tragedy* was the most general statement. Williams paid special tribute to "the particular genius of [Fred Harvey] Harrington."[17] Indeed, impressive works by the "Wisconsin school" were at least begun as dissertations under Harrington. But Harrington's views were less monothematic than Williams's. Two of his students, David F. Healy and Robert Freeman Smith, produced studies of relations with Cuba which were highly critical of American policy but did not insist that commercial considerations reduced others to insignificance.[18] Still, whether the product of Williams's conceptualizing or a synthesis of group ideas, *Tragedy* challenged traditional views and laid out alternatives.

One discussion of "William Appleman Williams and the 'American Empire'" sensibly distinguishes, as many fail to do, between those who share Williams's revisionism only in the general sense, as is the case with many cold war critics, and a true "school," those who essentially expand upon passages in *Tragedy*, which in practice usually means application of the concept of open door imperialism.[19] Most renowned of the latter is Walter LeFeber's *The New Empire*, which, although begun under Harrington, closely fits *Tragedy*'s mold. Unlike the latter, it concentrated only on the expansionist thrust prior to 1898, but the persistent theme was the search for markets to absorb an industrial surplus that seemed to threaten the economy. Tariff reciprocity, policy toward a Brazilian revolution, the quarrel with England over the boundary between British Guiana and Venezuela, and the coming of the Spanish-American War were all examined in light of their support of this theme. LaFeber's arguments were sometimes questionable or overdrawn, and he acknowledged that he had passed by episodes that did not fit his pattern. Still, *The New Empire*, an early elaboration of the market thesis, both showed the influence of *Tragedy* and seemed to support its claims.[20]

Subsequently, students of Williams, following his shift of emphasis into the period before 1898, produced a cluster of works which buttressed both *Tragedy* and *The Roots of the Modern American Empire*, the product of his new concern. Howard Schonberger maintained that farmers, merchants, and railroad-builders sought to improve access to overseas markets during the building spree after the Civil War, an argument more convincing if emphasized as a complement to rather than a substitute for interest in creation of a national market. Tom E. Terrill dismissed arguments over the tariff as essentially quibbles over tactics, since everyone was a commercial expansionist, thus blurring passionate disagreements and downplaying the success of protectionists. Edward P. Crapol emphasized the search for national economic independence and overseas markets. He argued, with only mild qualification, that Republicans won the election of 1896 because they convinced voters they knew "how best to foster overseas commercial expansion . . . ."[21]

Other works applied the market theme to the thirties and forties. Lloyd C. Gardner's *Economic Aspects of New Deal Diplomacy* ferreted out evidence that material considerations, not sentimental pan-Americanism or security-based or even ideological opposition to the Axis, lay at the heart of policy. In the introduction to a paperback edition in 1971 Gardner half-apologized for the lack of balance, but his ideas have found a modest place in later works on Rooseveltian diplomacy. More polemically, Dick Steward and David Green examined policy toward Latin America under Roosevelt and Truman, emphasizing the selfishness of tariff reciprocity. Frederick C. Adams made much the same point with reference to the Export-Import Bank.[22] All these books showed the danger, implicit in *Tragedy* itself, of pressing a single theme beyond its capacity to explain, of becoming uncritical pupils in a "school."

The open door argument proved more impressive when not made to deny the importance of other factors. Thus Thomas J. McCormick's *China Market:*

America's Quest for Informal Empire, 1893–1901, which dismissed ideological arguments as something "dipped into" to camouflage economic greed, was less satisfactory than Marilyn Blatt Young's *The Rhetoric of Empire, 1895–1901*, a study informed by Williams's concept but adding political and cultural factors. Similarly, Carl P. Parrini's *Heir to Empire: United States Economic Diplomacy, 1916–1923* suffered by comparison with Michael J. Hogan's *Informal Entente: The Private Structure of Cooperation in Anglo-American Economic Diplomacy, 1918–1928* because Parrini, too, was reluctant to go outside Williams's boundaries.[23]

These examples, even when supplemented by cold war literature, to which we will return, do not exhaust the possible list of works influenced by *Tragedy*. Still, large areas of study remain almost untouched by Williams's schema. No one has really applied his insights to policy in the early republic (the Monroe Doctrine would seem an inviting target) or expanded on Norman A. Graebner's argument, predating *Tragedy*, that a yearning for Far Eastern markets helps to explain the expansionism of the 1840s. Of course, historians continue to explore territorial expansion, especially the Louisiana Purchase and the acquisitions under Polk. Williams's distaste for expansionism may perhaps be detected in Alexander DeConde's *This Affair of Louisiana* (1976) and David M. Pletcher's *The Diplomacy of Annexation* (1973), but neither of these now standard works more specifically embraces his views.[24]

In 1975 Howard Schonberger proclaimed "the increasing domination of the historiography of American foreign policy by New Left scholars."[25] In fact, New Left history, to say nothing of Williams's particular brand, had not then approached domination. Nor did the open door interpretation continue to crest after 1975, by which date most of the monographs discussed above had been published. Critical studies have been and are numerous, but by no means do all bear the New Left mark, and narrow ones in the style of Crapol and Terrill are rare. Furthermore, most historians, both before and after 1959 or 1975, simply continued to work in traditional ways.

Tragedy of course stimulated — that is to say, influenced — critics as well as followers. One, in fact, provoked Schonberger's arrogant claim. William H. Becker published articles which powerfully challenged one of Williams's (and LaFeber's) basic assumptions, demonstrating that fears of a "glut" were not widespread in the years before World War I. Later he carried his attention down to 1921, examining government-business cooperation and concluding that "the expansion of the export of manufactured American goods between 1893 and 1921 is remarkable more for the lack of close government cooperation [with business] than for closer ties with business and government in the making of these sales." Equally critical, though not directed solely at Williams, was Alfred A. Eckes's article, "Open Door Expansionism Recon-

sidered: The World War II Experience." Eckes showed that, contrary to revisionist assertions, America's leaders did not believe that only expanded
exports could prevent a postwar depression and also showed that the
economic order they created was not designed with that consideration in
mind. Eckes later published a history of this structure which stressed its
political purposes and rebuked "economic determinists, [who,] in their quest
for synthesis, magnify economic factors at the expense of other policy objectives and thus wrench history out of perspective." [26]

Most impressive of several critiques of Williams's over-all approach was
Robert W. Tucker's *The Radical Left and American Foreign Policy*. Although
this book did not deal exclusively with Williams and was written with cold
war revisionism as its prime target, it provided an extensive, thoughtful
analysis of *Tragedy*'s conceptual base. Tucker saw an essential ambiguity in
Tragedy's central argument. As he phrased it, "the reader is never quite
clear — because Williams is never quite clear — whether America's institutions
necessitated expansion or whether America has been expansionist out of the
mistaken conviction that the well-being . . . of these institutions required
constant expansion." This was a valid point; Williams's position was opaque.
A careful reading, however, shows that he was unwilling to embrace determinism to the extent of making his argument absolutely dependent on it. And
wisely so. A determinist argument would have collided with obvious facts:
exports were, until recently, a small fraction of national output, and nations
subject to open door imperialism absorbed only a small part of that fraction.
In the end, Tucker rightly concluded that, despite ambiguity, Williams saw
policy "as largely responsive to a deeply rooted, although apparently
mistaken, conviction about the requirements of the nation's institutions." [27]

But, Tucker continued, if this was Williams's view, his argument did not
differ fundamentally from those of other critics, notably so-called realists,
who also argued that American policies were based on mistaken calculations.
"If," wrote Tucker, "the radical critique is understood to mean that we have
been expansionist out of mistaken conviction, . . . and that in expanding we
have sought to universalize American values . . . , then even if it is granted
that capitalism is the foremost of those values it is still not easy to see wherein
the critique is sharply distinguished from a more conventional criticism." [28]

America did want an American-style world. But, wrote Tucker, *Tragedy*
mistakenly defined this world, and American policy, in economic terms:
"America's interventionist and counterrevolutionary policy is the expected
response of an imperial power with a vital interest in maintaining an order
that, apart from the material benefits this order confers, has become
synonomous with the nation's vision of its role in history." [29] This statement,
accepting Williams's postulate of an expansionist America, was accompanied

by important qualifications. It referred to the cold war years; Tucker challenged Williams by pointing out how little, not how much, the United States had usually done before 1939 in response to threats to its kind of world. He also argued that "the method of indirect and informal empire," which Williams considered uniquely American and especially nefarious, "is not an American invention. It is not even a Capitalist invention." [30]

On balance, Tucker was highly critical of *Tragedy*. Nevertheless, he repeatedly praised Williams, and other radicals, for challenging the view, held even by nonradical critics who attacked policies without questioning motivation, that the country's basic outlook had been unselfish. "If nothing else," he concluded, "the radical critique has forced us to acknowledge the extent to which an obsessive self-interest has been central in American foreign policy." [31]

Another critic, J. A. Thompson, shared many of Tucker's conclusions and added others of his own. (He did not, however, credit Williams with useful demythologizing.) He objected that loose use of words such as "expansion" and "empire" allowed Williams to create a false impression of continuity. He argued that open door imperialism was so imprecisely defined that it comprehended "any political action [however weak] designed to promote foreign trade." Even more, he said, for those who accepted *Tragedy*'s argument, "'imperial expansion' seems to be synonomous with successful economic competition . . . ," even if the government did not act at all. [32] Thompson's essay, published in 1973, in effect summed up the arguments against *Tragedy*. That so much labor had gone into this reaction is itself proof of *Tragedy*'s influence.

Tragedy, then, had clearly made its mark. Williams had asserted the pervasiveness of national self-interest, reversing the realists' complaint and the patrioteers' boast that it had often been neglected. He had shown that national interest comprehended economic concerns as well as security interests. He had suggested a symbiosis between officials and businessmen. If predecessors had touched upon aspects of these things, Williams was first to synthesize them.

On the other hand, zeal carried him too far. In the 1972 edition of *Tragedy*, Williams deplored the attitude which "defines history as a stockpile of facts to be requisitioned on the basis of what is needed to prove a conclusion decided upon in advance." [33] But he himself had done exactly that, selecting and organizing the data not only to prove a conclusion but also to isolate it from competing ideas. Furthermore, he had postulated consistency, even effectiveness, where a less committed observer would have found hesitation, contradiction, and variety.

These failings, when added to the shortcomings pointed out by such people as Becker and Tucker, led many to reject Williams's interpretations out of hand, often dismissing them as simplistic Marxism. But Williams is neither Marxist nor simple.[34] Those who read him carefully, who refused to serve as post hoc footnoters or members of a scholarly Inquisition, moved his influence to a new level.

Critical was the incorporation of economic motivation into any account of American policy, not as an afterthought but as an integrated part of the whole. Critical, too, was an awareness of the relationship between business and government, although these historians pointed out that the relationship was by no means without friction. They gave ideology a major role, including a commitment to capitalism which was deep, not hypocritical. And they added other factors, notably bureaucratic politics, that Williams had ignored.

Hankerers after paradigms and models objected to the new eclecticism. Recently, Thomas J. McCormick, whose *China Market* was an early product of the Wisconsin school, objected that so-called postrevisionist students of the cold war, and by extension all those who viewed history as complex and uncertain, worked on "The operative premise . . . that multiplicity, rather than articulation, is equivalent to sophistication. Systematicism is not their strong suit."[35] He and others have suggested a "corporatist" structure which would transcend the narrowness of Williams and the anarchy of postrevisionists and those who think like them. The corporatist approach may be loosely defined as a recognition of causal multiplicity, always including ideological factors, with, however, a heavy emphasis on economic factors. However employed, the approach is heavily in debt to Williams.

Much work in this vein, often undertaken before the label was invented, has dealt with World War I and its aftermath. The authors agree that an activist nation sought world power, largely through the use of economic weapons. Often they are very critical of Williams and his followers, who, Melvyn Leffler complained, fail "to weigh and to balance the relative importance of commercial considerations vis-à-vis other economic, fiscal, strategic, and political factors . . . ." Some time later, Leffler produced an impressive study which sought to restore the balance without denying importance to "commercial considerations." In *Informal Empire*, Michael Hogan gave prominent place to ambitions for trade and stressed collaboration between government and private interests, but he argued, too, that leaders sought a stable world through as much as for economic growth. Singly and together, such authors have raised Williams's approach to a more complex level, but his influence is clear.[36] Whether this approach will work as well for periods of intense political crisis and military confrontation remains to be seen.

N. Gordon Levin sensitively employed *Tragedy* in a different fashion in his study of Woodrow Wilson. Although Levin especially thanked Louis Hartz, a conservative, and Hartz's concept of American exceptionalism informed the book, the preface to *Woodrow Wilson and World Politics* paid homage to Williams and other radicals. Levin defined Wilson's goal as "the attainment of a liberal capitalist world order . . . , safe both from traditional imperialism and revolutionary socialism, within whose stable liberal confines a missionary America could find moral and economic pre-eminence."[37] Like Williams, he showed that Wilson vigorously sought trade expansion, particularly through the strategy of the open door. And Levin believed, like Williams, that Wilson's United States was an expansionist nation seeking to establish and lead a world system based in large part on capitalist values.

But Levin joined these themes, drawn from *Tragedy*, with Hartzian ones to create a sophisticated whole. He stressed Wilson's conviction that American political and social values were the finest in the world and that their acceptance by all nations would assure peace and progress. He took great pains to make clear that Wilson not only did not see but could not conceive that his two purposes — expanded trade and an Americanized world — might conflict with one another. The intellectual impressiveness of *Woodrow Wilson and World Politics* is further confirmation of the wisdom of viewing *Tragedy* as what it is, a stimulus and not a blueprint.

No other book is more closely identified with cold war revisionism than *The Tragedy of American Diplomacy*. Although only about one-fourth of the 1959 edition dealt with the period after World War II, earlier pages had prepared the ground for its treatment of the recent period, not only by staking out arguments but, more broadly, by establishing the critical thrust that is the heart of revisionism. Still, for various reasons, the nature and extent of *Tragedy*'s influence is difficult to establish.

In the first place, cold war revisionism was very diverse, in marked contrast to the conceptual unity of the literature on open door imperialism in earlier periods. Revisionists agreed with Williams, of course, that the United States bore chief responsibility for the tense confrontation with the Soviet Union. Beyond that they varied greatly, often disputatiously.[38] Obviously, all critics of cold war policies, even those who acknowledge their debt to Williams's spirit, cannot be identified as disciples, although careless writers have been tempted to do so.[39]

It is tempting, particularly since Gabriel Kolko came to share the leadership of revisionism, to identify him as a follower of Williams. There are of course similarities, particularly of spirit. But there are also differences, for example, in analyzing Soviet policy or motives for the Marshall Plan, which reflect dissimilar assumptions. Kolko brought to his study of the cold war approaches developed in earlier, critical treatments of Progressive reform. He was far more rigorous in analysis than Williams, more Marxist, and the acknowledgment in *The Politics of War* of obligations to Arno Mayer and Barrington Moore reflected this. Kolko joined the revisionist crusade initiated by *Tragedy*, and he forced his way to its front rank, but he cannot be considered Williams's disciple except in the most general sense.[40]

That the nature of *Tragedy*'s arguments changed when it examined the cold war also complicates matters. Here, Williams's treatment was unusual in that, for almost the only time, he evaluated the policies of another nation. *Tragedy*'s logic did not require such an excursus, and the sympathetic discussion of Russian motives and actions sounded like special pleading. In 1959, reminding Americans that the Soviet Union emerged from World War II in a weakened state and that many Soviet policies were defensive was fresh and important. It was questionable to describe the Soviet Union as an essentially pluralistic society – a pluralistic oligarchy, if you will – and to view Stalin's actions as solely a response to American aggressiveness. Most revisionists embraced the first set of arguments but rejected or ignored the second.[41]

Such arguments weakened *Tragedy* as a whole, allowing critics to charge that it was a pro-Soviet tract. In the first chapter of an attack on the New Left treatment of cold war origins, Robert J. Maddox savaged Williams, at one time his teacher, as he did all the authors with whom he dealt. He pointed to real and, more often, dubious examples of their misuse of sources, endeavoring to show a pro-Soviet bias. Maddox's vituperative tone and narrow concentration on policy toward Eastern Europe in 1945 and 1946 severely limited his effectiveness. Even historians critical of Williams objected that Maddox presented "a surfeit of innuendo and a paucity of hard evidence." They also objected, quite rightly, that "in his zeal to expose Williams's imprecision, Maddox loses sight of Williams's scope." Although Maddox's spleen was unique, Williams's gratuitous comments on Soviet behavior diverted others, as well, from the scheme and philosophy that was *Tragedy*'s chief claim to attention.[42]

The last section of *Tragedy* also differed from earlier portions in that the economic theme was muted. Williams continued to present evidence that American leaders sought foreign markets, and he saw this as a major factor in policy toward the Third World. He argued that, especially at Potsdam, the United States fought for Eastern European and Far Eastern markets. Still, in these pages economic expansionism played a small part, at least by comparison with the emphasis given it in earlier parts of the book.

Instead, Williams stressed "the ideology of the open door . . . ." Open door expansionism became in essence an aggressive crusade to propagate American values across the world: "As far as American leaders were concerned," he wrote, "the philosophy and practice of open door expansionism had become, in both its missionary and economic aspects, *the* view of the world." Williams refused to "assign priorities to the various facets of the *Weltanschauung*," economic or other, only asserting rather lamely that "the open-door outlook was based on an economic definition of the world . . . ." Still, in his view, the employment of American power "in keeping with the traditional policy of the open door crystalized the cold war." [43]

Thus the open door concept was extended to accommodate almost any interpretation stressing American aggressiveness. As Mark Stoler has written, "While Williams's Open Door approach theoretically provided a general framework of analysis, the framework proved to be so broad that its numerous adherents could apply either a rigid economic determinism or virtually ignore economics and economic issues and concentrate instead on vaguely related political beliefs and actions." [44] Whereas the first three-quarters of *Tragedy* provided a clear guide for those who wished to follow it, the treatment of the cold war was a more diffuse *cri de coeur*.

Perhaps predictably, since *Tragedy* abandoned the single focus on markets, few who can be identified as Williams's followers applied that theme to the cold war years, certainly not to the extent of obscuring others. Books by two men who had been at Wisconsin with Williams and had written market-centered monographs illustrate this point. While Lloyd C. Gardner's *Architects of Illusion*, a study of policymakers who led America toward a false goal, stressed economic considerations, Gardner did not minimize ideological ones, as he had in *New Deal Diplomacy*. Walter LaFeber's *America, Russia, and the Cold War* (1967) differed even more from his earlier book. LaFeber's study is sometimes described, usually with the qualification that it is temperate, as economic determinist. In fact, although economic factors were examined, others received more stress, particularly the desire for an open door world in the broadest sense. (A theologian, Reinhold Niebuhr, rather than a businessman, was most often cited as spokesman of the American consensus.) LaFeber deplored the effort to Americanize the world, but he avoided Williams's extravagances. When published in 1967, LaFeber's work seemed very revisionist; today it is widely perceived as the best survey of its subject, an indication of how much of revisionism (and *Tragedy*'s spirit) has been absorbed.

Yet it was also possible to reach conclusions broadly similar to LaFeber's without sharing his orientation. In a study of the early cold war, Thomas G. Paterson also described the pursuit of an American-style, American-dominated world — in *Tragedy*'s jargon, an open door world. America's "often haughty, expansionist, and uncompromising" policies, Paterson wrote, drove a hesitant (but not innocent) Soviet Union to forceful reactions of its own. But he denied that economic goals were important and even that a capitalist outlook dominated America's world view. Economic power was the frequently misused weapon of political diplomacy, not its goal, Paterson argued. Thus he distanced himself from Williams's followers, although *Soviet-American Confrontation* levied the same basic charges against Washington policymakers.[45]

It was equally possible simultaneously to embrace and to reject key parts of Williams's argument. Bruce Kuklick, author of *American Policy and the Division of Germany*, described himself as "parasitic" on Williams but devoted pages to an attack on him. Kuklick agreed that the United States, by its aggressive policies, produced the division of Germany. But he denied that the open door had dominated policy since at least the 1890s. To so argue, he insisted, was "deeply ahistoric"; it suggested a nonexistent consistency in American aims, whereas postwar policy toward Germany was determined by time-bound conditions. Although he used different terms, when Kuklick described the goals of policy they differed little from those *Tragedy* suggested — liberal democracy, American influence, and world trade expansion. Provocative though he thought these goals, Kuklick insisted they were more than self-serving. Leaders expected benefits for their country, but also the world. Like N. Gordon Levin, Kuklick maintained that the American vision "simultaneously embraces moral commitment and politico-economic interest."[46] This endorsed rather than challenged much of what Williams had written, though not what both critics and simplifiers read into *Tragedy*.

These examples suggest that the influence of *Tragedy*, "the first important scholarly revision of recent American diplomacy . . . ," has been inspirational rather than specific. It is ridiculous to argue that other revisionist studies are "little more than extended footnotes on interpretations Williams first put forward."[47] Few have applied the open door concept in quite the same way, even granted that, dealing with the cold war, Williams shifted his definition. Few have viewed the Soviet system as sympathetically as Williams did in 1959, and few have drawn the conclusion, added in revision, that "developments after 1952 [Stalin's death in 1953?] in Russia, and . . . the events of 1956 in Poland and Hungary . . ." indicated a softening of that system.[48]

For about a decade after 1965, historians did battle over the cold war. Not only books and articles but historiographical essays abounded.[49] Then the battle moderated. Differences remained, but few revisionists any longer denounced their opponents as mere apologists for the State Department, nor were they denounced in reply as perpetrators of academic fraud moved by Communist sympathies. Moreover, the site of battle, so to speak, shifted. Almost no historian any longer wrote on the cold war with the purpose of holding Joseph Stalin guilty before the bar of history. The last major effort in this style was the work of a British pair, Sir John Wheeler-Bennett and

Anthony Nicholls, published in 1972. A useful barometer of change is provided by new editions of John W. Spanier's survey, which, without abandoning the hard line of the original, have progressively incorporated revisionist ideas.[50]

Some, particularly those who identify themselves as postrevisionists, suggest that a Hegelian dialectic has taken place: orthodox thesis challenged by revisionist antithesis has produced the higher truth of postrevisionist synthesis. Yet it can be argued that postrevisionists, although they concede American failings, really aim to destroy revisionism. It can also be argued, by those who hanker after philosophical clarity, that they merely present a potpourri, not a synthesis. As Warren Kimball complains, "leaving no reason unturned is not the same as developing a new thesis." Moreover, just as the revisionist label blurs the variety within that camp, so postrevisionists differ greatly in tone and conclusion. There is a world of difference between John Lewis Gaddis's pioneering postrevisionist study, *The United States and the Origins of the Cold War*, often critical of American policy but harsher on the Soviets, and Daniel Yergin's dramatic book on the same subject, so negative toward the Americans that Jerald Combs, for example, can describe it as a "moderate revisionist account."[51]

Whether or not labeled postrevisionists, a large majority of those now writing on the cold war owe substantial debts to Williams and other revisionists. They recognize economic factors, largely ignored by orthodox historians of the past, and they agree with Williams in placing policies aimed at trade expansion within a broader context. While they do not endorse *Tragedy*'s view of Stalin's Russia, they almost unanimously argue that Soviet leaders, though grasping and brutal, had no blueprint for world revolution. And they agree, most of all, that it is misleading to view American policies as purely defensive rather than at least in part as efforts to extend American interests and influence. Many find useful the concept of empire, though often blanching at the term itself, and at least since the tragedy of Vietnam began to unfold a chorus of voices has criticized the overextension of that empire.[52]

Of course, some of these conclusions seem obvious, and some had been argued before Williams wrote. At least since George F. Kennan's famous lectures in 1950, realists had condemned the overextension of American interest and the overcommitment of power, although they did not consider these to be inevitable products of the *Weltanschauung* and usually exempted policy toward Western Europe (but not the Truman Doctrine's hyperbole) from their criticism. This view was developed in surveys of the cold war by Norman A. Graebner in 1962, before revisionism took hold, and by Ronald Steel, then outside the revisionist camp, in 1967.[53] Still, granting the point, it remains true that what seemed obvious to realists had not really been absorbed until argued — perhaps overargued — by revisionists, for whom William A. Williams was the bellwether.

A dozen years have passed since Robert W. Tucker pondered on the extent of "the influence exerted by the radical critique. That it has exerted an influence is clear," he concluded. "What is not clear is the extent of this influence . . ."; indeed, any effort to gauge it was, in Tucker's view, unlikely to succeed.[54] In a precise sense, this is true, not least because influence is so difficult to define. Need only the spirit or must the specifics of Williams's account be adopted if influence is to be claimed? How much of either? Moreover, regarding *Tragedy*, the effort to establish influence is particularly difficult because, as has been argued, the book makes two different, though reconcilable, arguments. Later writers can reject or ignore one or the other of them, perhaps apply one to a period in which for Williams it was a lesser theme, yet draw inspiration from *Tragedy*.

Assessing *Tragedy*'s influence on histories of the cold war is especially difficult. The mere passage of time, the realist critique of moralism and extravagance, Gabriel Kolko's strident determinism, and the brutal education provided by Vietnam all contributed to the tide of criticism. *Tragedy*, nevertheless, was the first fundamental assault on the merits of American objectives. If few works in its direct descent have won the acceptance extended to LaFeber's history of the cold war (and LaFeber is much readier to see the world in all its complexities), most revisionists are deeply beholden to *Tragedy* in a more general but fundamental sense.

It is clearer that the heyday of the open door imperialist argument — the theme, concentrating on trade expansion, for which Williams is best known — has passed. Few now see *Tragedy* as the best, certainly not the only, guide to pre–World War II diplomacy. Those books most narrowly applying its theme, whether to the late nineteenth century or a later time, are sometimes credited with adding a minor dimension to understanding, no more, and the stream of new studies is nearly dry.

What survives is the influence of *The Tragedy of American Diplomacy* on those who receive it intelligently and selectively. When Tucker wrote, the debate was a battle, not a dialogue. Most disputants, although not Tucker, argued either that *Tragedy* was a sacred writing, true and all-explaining, or a mere tissue of lies and distortions. As the combatants became exhausted, progress began. Historians recognized that too little attention had been paid to factors emphasized by Williams. Although they varied greatly in the extent to which they allowed this recognition to influence them and often rejected important parts of his arguments, they produced better history. Studies of the 1920s and works on the cold war lumped together under the postrevisionist label are but two examples of this process.

Whether a new schema, a structure as complete as Williams's, will result is questionable. Postrevisionism can be a mish-mash of contending judgments, and the corporatist thesis is both vague and insufficiently tested. Historians today — and not merely historians of American diplomacy — often rather self-consciously seek for some system into which all eras and events may be fitted. These searches may fail, as Williams's did. But no comprehensive scheme, no broad generalizations, and few but the narrowest studies of episodes in American foreign relations will be written, if they are to shine, without an awareness of and an accommodation to William Appleman Williams's *Tragedy of American Diplomacy.*

Bradford Perkins, Department of History, University of Michigan, is the author of a prize-winning trilogy on Anglo-American diplomacy and is a former president of the Society of Historians of American Foreign Relations.

1. Charles A. McClelland, review, *American Political Science Review* 53 (1959), p. 1196.

2. William Appleman Williams, *The Tragedy of American Diplomacy,* rev. ed. (1962), p. 11. (Hereafter cited as *Tragedy 1962.*) The phrasing, although not the idea, is new in the 1962 edition.

3. William Appleman Williams, *The Tragedy of American Diplomacy* (1959), pp. 39–40. (Hereafter cited as *Tragedy.*)

4. Ibid., p. 64.

5. Williams did not so much disagree with as ignore classical economic theory, which denied that trade was "a zero-sum game in which American export sales corresponded to foreign losses. . . . [G]lobal trade was a positive-sum game in which all participants gained — [though] not necessarily equally . . ." (Alfred E. Eckes, Jr., "Open Door Expansionism Reconsidered: The World War II Experience," *Journal of American History* 59 [1972–73], p. 914). On the other hand, even in revisions, Williams did not incorporate "dependency theory," although its thrust would have reinforced his arguments. (See especially André Gunder Frank, *Capitalism and Underdevelopment in Latin America* [1967].)

6. *Tragedy,* p. 150.

7. But see William Appleman Williams, "The Age of Mercantilism: An Interpretation of the American Political Economy, 1763–1828," *William & Mary Quarterly,* 3rd Series, 15 (1958): 419–37.

8. Contrast *Tragedy,* p. 25, with William Appleman Williams, *The Tragedy of American Diplomacy,* 2nd rev. ed. (1972), p. 25. (Hereafter cited as *Tragedy 1972.*) In *Tragedy 1972* Williams inserted a long passage (pp. 23–27) incorporating arguments from his *The Roots of the Modern American Empire* (1969) that agriculturists contributed first and perhaps most to expansionism of the later nineteenth century.

9. *Tragedy 1972,* p. 55. How far the expansionist theme can be carried has recently been demonstrated by Emily S. Rosenberg, *Spreading the American Dream: American Economic and Cultural Expansion, 1890–1945* (1982). Rosenberg describes overseas economic activities of the American government and business, but she also includes missionary activity, philanthropy, the Office of War Information, and a wide variety of overseas activity. The result is a diffuse eclecticism.

10. *Tragedy,* p. 35; *Tragedy 1972,* p. 45.

11. *Tragedy,* p. 63; *Tragedy 1972,* p. 93.

12. *Tragedy 1972,* pp. 173, 185. Williams thanks Lloyd C. Gardner for exchanging notes and ideas on the Roosevelt period (p. 177n), but his account is even less nuanced than Gardner's *Economic Aspects of New Deal Diplomacy* (1964).

13. Jerald A. Combs, *American Diplomatic History* (1983), p. 257.

14. *Tragedy 1972*, pp. 1, 307. For the same thought, see also Williams, *Roots*, pp. 451–53, where the noncapitalist but non-Marxist prescription is endorsed. Initially, *Tragedy* concentrated on the drive to increase manufactured exports, but now agricultural interests are seen as equally involved. Reform, as opposed to fundamental change, is thus a less likely answer.

15. Combs, *American Diplomatic History*, p. 256.

16. Williams also cited unpublished student papers, conversations and exchanges of research notes with colleagues. The exchange of notes, frequently mentioned by Williams's students, offers obvious problems, since the donor has already screened the sources.

17. William Appleman Williams, "Open Door Interpretation," Alexander Deconde, ed., *Encyclopedia of American Foreign Policy* (1978), p. 708.

18. David F. Healy, *The United States and Cuba, 1898–1902* (1963); Robert Freeman Smith, *The United States and Cuba: Business and Diplomacy, 1917–1960* (1962). Healy minimized the influence of businessmen on Cuban policy, and in a later work, *U.S. Expansionism: The Imperialist Urge of the 1890s* (1970), he downplayed economic considerations. Smith viewed policy toward Mexico in much the same spirit in *The United States and Revolutionary Nationalism in Mexico, 1916–1932* (1972). Both Healy and Smith, like Fred Harvey Harrington, in *God, Mammon and the Japanese* (1944), a study of relations with Korea, devoted much attention to developments in the target country. An unfortunate legacy of *Tragedy*, not considered in this essay, is the emphasis on the sources of American policy at the expense of diplomatic history as a study of interaction.

19. J. A. Thompson, "William Appleman Williams and the 'American Empire,'" *American Studies* 7 (1975), p. 1n.

20. Walter LaFeber, *The New Empire* (1963). Just as LaFeber buttressed Williams's argument after it appeared, so Ernest A. Paolino, in *The Foundations of the American Empire* (1973), a study of William H. Seward's expansionism, documented, on the basis of manuscript research, what LaFeber argued on the basis of limited published materials.

21. Howard Schonberger, *Transportation to the Seaboard* (1971); Tom E. Terrill, *The Tariff, Politics, and American Foreign Policy* (1973); Edward P. Crapol, *America for Americans* (1973).

22. Lloyd C. Gardner, *Economic Aspects of New Deal Diplomacy*, paperback ed. (1971), pp. xi–xiii; Dick Steward, *Trade and Hemisphere* (1975); David Green, *The Containment of Latin America* (1971); Frederick C. Adams, *Economic Diplomacy: the Export-Import Bank and American Foreign Policy* (1976).

23. Thomas J. McCormick, *China Market: America's Quest for Informal Empire, 1893–1901* (1967), p. 9; Marilyn Blatt Young, *The Rhetoric of Empire, 1895–1901* (1968); Carl P. Parrini, *Heir to Empire* (1969); Michael J. Hogan, *Informal Entente* (1977). McCormick's study began as a dissertation under Harrington.

24. Norman A. Graebner, *Empire on the Pacific* (1955). Two textbooks applying *Tragedy's* approach do cover the entire chronology: Lloyd C. Gardner, Walter F. LaFeber, and Thomas J. McCormick, *Creation of the American Empire* (1973), and William Appleman Williams, ed., *From Colony to Empire* (1972). In the latter, however, chapters on the transcontinental sweep are by Richard W. VanAlstyne, whose criticisms of American aggressiveness long precede *Tragedy*. See also Thomas G. Paterson, J. Garry Clifford, and Kenneth J. Hagan, *American Foreign Policy* (1977), which much less rigorously follows the Williams model.

25. Howard Schonberger, "William H. Becker and the New Left Revisionists: A Rebuttal," *Pacific Historical Review* 44 (1975), p. 249. Thomas J. McCormick, himself an early revisionist, estimates that between 25 and 30 percent of works published in the 1970s and 10 to 15 percent of those appearing in the early 1980s might be categorized as revisionist ("Drift or Mastery? A Corporatist Synthesis for American Diplomatic History," *Reviews in American History* 10 [1982], p. 318).

26. William H. Becker, "American Manufacturers and Foreign Markets, 1870–1900," *Business History Review* 47 (1975): 466–81; "Foreign Markets for Iron and Steel, 1893–1913," *Pacific Historical Review* 44 (1975): 233–48; *The Dynamics of Business-Government Relations*

(1982), p. xiv; Eckes, "Open Door Expansionism"; Alfred A. Eckes, Jr., *A Search for Solvency* (1975), p. 275.

27. Robert W. Tucker, *The Radical Left and American Foreign Policy* (1971), pp. 56, 14.

28. Ibid., p. 70.

29. Ibid., p. 111.

30. Ibid., p. 81.

31. Ibid., p. 148.

32. Thompson, "Williams and the 'American Empire,'" p. 103. For a recent restatement, see Richard A. Melanson, "The Social and Political Thought of William Appleman Williams," *Western Political Quarterly* 31 (1978): 392–409.

33. *Tragedy 1972*, p. 207.

34. For a lucid Marxist critique of Williams's *Contours of American History*, see Herbert Aptheker, "American Development and Ruling-Class Ideology," *Studies on the Left* 3, 1 (1963): 97–105.

35. McCormick, "Drift or Mastery?," p. 319.

36. Melvyn P. Leffler, "The Origins of Republican War Debt Policy, 1921–1923," *Journal of American History* 59 (1972–73): 601; Melvyn P. Leffler, *Elusive Quest* (1979); Hogan, *Informal Entente*. See also Burton I. Kaufmann, *Efficiency and Expansion* (1974), and, though centering on Europe, Stephen A. Schuker, *The End of French Predominance in Europe* (1976).

37. N. Gordon Levin, Jr., *Woodrow Wilson and World Politics* (1968), p. vii.

38. See, e.g., Michael Leigh, "Is There a Revisionist Thesis on the Origins of the Cold War?," *Political Science Quarterly* 89 (1974): 101–16.

39. For example, Denna Frank Fleming began work on his revisionist study, *The Cold War and Its Origins*, 2 vols. (1961) in 1947, did not include Williams in a long list of acknowledgments, and only briefly mentioned the open door thesis, yet is identified as a disciple by Richard A. Melanson ("Social and Political thought of Williams," p. 392).

40. Gabriel Kolko, *The Politics of War* (1968), p. vii. (Kolko also thanked N. Gordon Levin.) Joyce and Gabriel Kolko's *The Limits of Power* (1972) includes an extended discussion of the Marshall Plan. For Kolko's earlier views, see especially *The Triumph of Conservatism* (1963).

41. However, for an argument similar to Williams's, see William O. McCagg, Jr., *Stalin Embattled, 1943–1948* (1978).

42. Robert James Maddox, *The New Left and the Origins of the Cold War* (1973); Richard A. Melanson, "Revisionism Subdued? Robert James Maddox and the Origins of the Cold War," *Political Science Reviewer* 7 (1977): 270, 266.

43. *Tragedy*, pp. 180, 150, 163–64, 151. Williams later denied that he had claimed that "the United States started or caused the cold war." He merely maintained, he said, that American policy "hardened the natural tensions . . . into bitter antagonisms and inflexible positions" (*Tragedy 1972*, pp. 206–7). This rather fine distinction is a rare softening of the 1959 version. For a similar statement, see Lloyd C. Gardner, *Architects of Illusion* (1970), p. x.

44. Gerald K. Haines and J. Samuel Walker, eds., *American Foreign Relations: A Historiographical Review* (1981), p. 198.

45. Thomas G. Paterson, *Soviet-American Confrontation* (1973), p. 260. Economic goals are similarly minimized in Thomas G. Paterson, *On Every Front: The Making of the Cold War* (1979), especially in ch. 4.

46. Bruce Kuklick, *American Policy and the Division of Germany* (1972), pp. 237, 239, 4.

47. Melanson, "Revisionism Subdued?," p. 23; Maddox, *New Left and the Cold War*, p. 13.

48. *Tragedy 1972*, p. 288.

49. For the latter, see Richard Dean Burns, ed., *Guide to American Foreign Relations since 1700* (1983), pp. 709–12. All but five of the listed items appeared before 1975.

50. Sir John Wheeler-Bennett and Anthony Nicholls, *The Semblance of Peace* (London: MacMillan London Ltd., 1972); John W. Spanier, *American Foreign Policy since World War II* (1960; 7th ed., 1977).

51. John Lewis Gaddis, "The Emerging Post-Revisionist Synthesis on the Origins of the Cold

War," *Diplomatic History* 7 (1983): 171–90; Warren F. Kimball, "Comment," ibid., p. 199; John Lewis Gaddis, *The United States and the Origins of the Cold War, 1941–1947* (1972); Daniel Yergin, *Shattered Peace: The Origins of the Cold War and the National Security State* (1977); Combs, *American Diplomatic History*, p. 331.

52. Gaddis, "Post-Revisionist Synthesis," pp. 180–81, makes the most of these points, although the bulk of this article is devoted to a criticism of revisionism for errors of omission and commission.

53. George F. Kennan, *American Diplomacy, 1900–1950* (1951); Norman A. Graebner, *Cold War Diplomacy* (1962); Ronald Steel, *Pax Americana* (1967).

54. Tucker, *Radical Left and American Foreign Policy*, pp. 146–47.

POPULISM REDUX:
JOHN D. HICKS AND *THE POPULIST REVOLT*

Martin Ridge

"*The Populist Revolt* made its initial appearance in print while I was in Cambridge," John D. Hicks noted in his autobiography. "Among my colleagues, Arthur Schlesinger and Paul Buck read it approvingly, while from Henry Steele Commager, whom I hardly knew, I received a heartening letter."[1] Hicks did not mention that the *New York Times Book Review* devoted more than a full page to his book, that its reviewer said *The Populist Revolt* was "far and away the best account of populism that we have and one not likely to be replaced,"[2] or that scholarly reviewers were abundant in their praise of his work.[3]

Two reviewers found *The Populist Revolt* timely since it was published in 1931 as the Great Depression deepened. Roscoe D. Martin, who had recently completed a pioneering study of Texas populism,[4] began his review rather poignantly: "In these days of 'hard times,' when unemployment and agricultural surpluses combine to make the lot of the workingman seem hard, when the leaders of bygone days arise once more to champion the cause of the people . . . the memory of students of American history, economics and politics goes back forty years to the agrarian uprising at the end of the last century."[5] And Benjamin Kendrick, whose incisive review seemed scarcely able to suppress his rage at a society wracked by depression, had little doubt but that had the farmers "enjoyed a great victory . . . American history in the last three decades might have been fundamentally altered."[6] Reviewers of *The Populist Revolt* commended Hicks for his judicious and objective treatment of a complex subject and praised not only his style but also his careful synthesis of the existing literature.

The Populist Revolt was welcomed by the profession and quickly assimilated into the scholarly literature for many reasons. Hicks had set his book in the context of the Turner thesis, which took it out of the tradition of simple narration, and he linked the Populist platform to subsequent national legislation. Moreover, he wrote with remarkable sympathy for the plight of southern farmers and demonstrated how the complexities of the race issue influenced reform efforts in the South. Despite his essentially dispassionate tone and apparent objectivity, Hicks was clearly within the Progressive tradition of both politics and history. And, finally, the book was read when the tragedy of the drought and the Great Depression was probably the prevailing concern among most American scholars. Hicks's straightforward explanation of farmers' problems in the 1880s and 1890s put the issues of the 1920s and 1930s in a clearer perspective.

In addition, the book was unusually acceptable in scholarly ways, especially Hicks's exceedingly skillful use of both contemporary and secondary works. His bibliography indicated that he had mined the literature of Populism, and he generously acknowledged his debt to the works of other scholars — even to the extent of dedicating the book to his graduate students. He also included an annotated bibliography, which at times was candid: for example, he identified an article by Sidney Dillon on "The West and the Railroads" as the work of the president of the Union Pacific. If most of the annotations were terse or even superficial, they were doubtless helpful to readers who wanted a quick and informed guide to a large literature that was popular, scholarly, and often unfamiliar. *The Populist Revolt* was a model monograph about a topic as current and controversial to that generation as the cold war is today.

Hicks found the origins of Populism in the farmers' alliance movement in both the West and the South. The post Civil War years, especially the late 1870s and early 1800s, witnessed remarkable population growth and economic development in the prairie plains states that was followed by drought, depression, and disillusionment. The South, during the same period, saw a steady transformation of its society, with increasing rates of farm tenancy and the steady spread of the crop lien and share crop systems. Hicks believed that these distressed agrarian economies, which engendered protest organizations, demands for monetary reform, and political agitation, made Populism a unique social and political movement that transcended one region of the country. The South, he postulated, both because of the impact of the Civil War and the character of cotton production and distribution, was very much like the capital-starved, underdeveloped prairie plains frontier. Despite many sectional differences the Middle West and the South shared economic problems that made them especially receptive to social organization and political action. Although Hicks later retreated from his view that with Populism had begun "the last phase of a long and perhaps a losing struggle . . . to save agricultural America from the devouring jaws of industrial America . . . ," this was the essential phenomenon that he saw linking the Middle West and the South together, and it was a vital theme of his book.[7]

As Hicks described it, the opening of the farmers' frontier on the prairie plains produced an era of railroad building, land speculation, town founding, and increased indebtedness for social overhead purposes, all of which reached a climax in the mid-1880s when poor harvests and cyclical depression resulted in a business collapse. The promise of prosperity yielded to the reality of low farm prices, staggering debts, unacceptable freight rates, high interest charges, foreclosed mortgages, farm tenancy, and exposure to price structures devised by emerging trusts and monopolies. Making their lives more dismal was the farmers' belief that the agricultural frontier — the opportunity to take up cheap virgin land that had been available to American farmers for three centuries — was now gone. They believed that there was no place to try again. "They suffered," Hicks wrote, "or at least thought they suffered, from the trusts and middlemen, from the money lenders and bankers, and from the muddled currency." [8] Little wonder, as Hicks saw it, that agrarian spokesmen fulminated against those individuals and those corporations they believed acted without regard for the welfare of agricultural America. Hicks did not attempt a critical analysis of Populist rhetoric as social criticism.

He saw a direct causal relationship between the growth of rural organizations and the economic condition of the farmers. By the early 1880s, he observed, "a whole new crop of farm orders appeared." Of these the most important were the National Farmers' Alliance, with its membership located primarily in the upper Mississippi Valley, and the National Farmers' Alliance and Industrial Union, which originated in Texas but spread throughout the South by steadily linking itself to smaller orders. Hicks judged the Northern Alliance "the first really effective organization," and praised its founder, Milton George, a Chicago journalist, for laying the groundwork of a membership that reached 100,000 by 1882. Although the Northern Alliance faltered during the early 1880s, by 1890, with wheat prices tumbling, the reports of Alliance historians who stated that membership was increasing at a rate of 1000 per week seemed valid to Hicks. He was less expansive about the Southern Alliance and its founder, Dr. C. W. Macune, placing the blame for the failure of the two alliances to merge in 1889 at the door of the southerners, although the programs of the two groups were quite similar. Hicks gave great credit to Leonidas L. Polk of North Carolina, who assumed leadership of the Southern Alliance and pushed ahead by capturing membership in Kansas and the Dakotas, and the areas as "far west as Washington, Oregon, and California [and] as far east as Ohio, Pennsylvania, and New York." [9] Hicks noted that the Southern Alliance stressed the cooperative movement, called attention to the weaknesses of cooperatives in an undercapitalized economy (not to mention one where hostile wholesalers and retailers fought them), and drew a clear connection between the cooperative movement in the Southern Alliance and its later advocacy of the subtreasury scheme for marketing nonperishable farm products. But for Hicks the logical sequence of the movement placed the subtreasury plan in the context of the political rather than the cooperative side of the Alliance.

Hicks was clearly at his best in explaining the political dimension of the farmers' movement. He captured the excitement of the outdoor political rallies, the rhetoric of the radical farm press, and the dramatic effectiveness of Populism's orators: the much-ridiculed "Sockless" Jerry Simpson; the dedicated if pedestrian James B. Weaver; the fearless Leonidas L. Polk; the colorful Mary Elizabeth (reputed to have said "raise less corn and more *Hell*") Lease; the indefatigable Ignatius Donnelly; as well as the cynical but effective Tom Watson. Beside describing campaigns and spectacles Hicks turned his attention to what happened after the elections of 1890, 1892, and 1894, indicating how and why legislative sessions developed as they did, where the Populist program was advanced or sacrificed, and how compromises sent fusion candidates to state houses or Congress. He traced the rise of the Peoples party from its inception to its crisis among the electorate in 1894. He presented the first balanced explanation of the capture of the Peoples party convention by the party's silverite wing in 1896 and the Bryan nomination that led to ultimate fusion with the Democrats.

Hicks treated silver as a genuine issue (and accepted the mining interests as Populists, albeit dominated by mining moguls), although he indicated that there were significant differences between the prosilver group and the old line greenbackers in the Peoples party, who were an important part of its membership. Hicks never doubted that the Republican party's leadership and the conservative business community recognized in silver a serious threat to the nation's economy and that they responded accordingly. When he chronicled their efforts he did not describe the "Battle of the Standards" as a sham. He saw the election of 1896 as being of criticial importance not only because it determined the direction the nation would take but also because of what it did to the Peoples party. To Hicks 1896 was a significant election year, in the sense that political scientists might define it as a critical election, because he thought that it rearranged voting habits for a generation.

Hicks outlined the party's troubled course during the campaign of 1896, and the confusion of interests and factions that followed in its wake. He ended with Populism's pathetic fade-out. He did not trace the final years of party activity as a constructive effort but rather only to emphasize the disappointment of leaders and followers alike. Yet his assessment was not negative: he concluded that "populistic doctrines showed an amazing vitality."[10]

Hicks paid only passing attention to blacks in the alliance movement. He indicated that courageous efforts toward racial unity on the economic issues of the day evoked the most hostile responses in the South and led ultimately to black disfranchisement. He probably believed that he had handled the matter evenhandedly. *The Populist Revolt*, however, was authored by a man very much a creature of his time: Hicks presented blacks in terms of southern stereotypes. In discussing the crop lien system which required that only cotton be raised, even though it almost invariably resulted in creating impoverished and dependent farmers, Hicks wrote: "The Negroes possibly preferred cotton culture to anything else because of the greater opportunity it gave them for the satisfaction of their gregarious instincts. Perhaps too their characteristic shiftlessness was less damaging to cotton than it might have been to other crops." He saw blacks as attracted to the Alliance "by the ritual as well as by the possible economic benefit of the order . . . ."[11] In the 1930s, when *The Populist Revolt*, appeared these observations were ignored by reviewers who commented favorably on Hicks's effectiveness in showing the corrosive influence of race in the 1890s drive for reform.[12]

In his closing chapter Hicks speaks to his reader from the Progressive tradition in assessing Populist contributions. Of these, woman suffrage, the Australian ballot, primary elections, and the initiative and referendum were only a few of the most obvious. Hicks was quite sympathetic to the Populist platform's financial planks, pointing out that what had at one time been denounced as the rantings of lunatics and the ideas of country bumpkins had resulted in serious revisions of the nation's banking laws. Hicks felt too that Populism, in its quest for economic and political remedies for the grievances of many Americans, forecast a goodly share of enlightened federal legislation. The Populists had, he believed, been in measure vindicated. In *The Populist Revolt*, Hicks effectively demonstrated Populism's democratic symbolism when he described its struggle for impartial, independent, and clean politics and, above all, in its enlightened interpretation of the general welfare. He closed his book noting: "one must recognize that when old Populist panaceas can receive the enthusiastic support of Hooverian Republicans and Al-smithian Democrats these once startling demands are no longer radical."[13]

The Populist Revolt was an instant success, despite the fact that it was markedly revisionist. Although Hicks proclaimed the Turnerian frontier tradition, his sympathy for the soft money views of the Populists placed him at odds with Frederick Jackson Turner as well as with such standard historians of American finance as Davis R. Dewey and James L. Laughlin.[14] As a Progressive historian, he implicitly accepted economics as the basis of politics. Hicks challenged the orthodox interpretation of American history, best exemplified by John Spencer Bassett's 1000 page tome, *A Short History of the United States: 1492–1928* (1932), that devoted less than two pages to the Peoples party and none to it as a social movement. Hicks placed Populism and its platform proposals in the Progressive tradition by insisting that it was neither an aberrant nor a false dawn of twentieth-century American liberalism. Moreover, the book was surprisingly analytical. It was a convenient paradigm for others working in the period. C. Vann Woodward, who dissented from Hicks's interpretation in many ways, relied on it in his classic *Tom Watson: Agrarian Rebel* (1938).

Challenges and revision of Hicks began in the 1950s and came from three quite different sources. In 1955 Allan G. Bogue published *Money at Interest: The Farm Mortgage on the Middle Border.* That same year Richard Hofstadter brought out *The Age of Reform from Bryan to FDR.* And in 1963, E. P. Thompson published *The Making of the English Working Class.* The impact of Bogue and Thompson on Populist historiography was ultimately profound but less immediately evident than that of Hofstadter, which proved highly evocative.

Richard Hofstadter, an unusually gifted intellectual historian and brilliant writer who sought an explanation for the American reform tradition, raised serious questions about Populist ideology and context that Hicks had not asked. *The Age of Reform* reflected not only Hofstadter's critical reading of authors associated with the Populist cause and an awareness of sociological theory but also his knowledge of transnational intellectual trends, especially the reactionary nature of most agrarian movements in Europe. His treatment, which embraced his deep suspicion of agrarianism, hypothesized that the angry farmers in the South and Middle West were hard-pressed Protestants and petty capitalists unable to come to terms with the realities of a world-wide market economy and turned — as did other groups with declining status — to xenophobia and antisemitism.[15] The Populist platforms of the 1890s notwithstanding, Hofstadter's followers argued, Populism had a dark side that could be seen as contributing to America's authoritarian and xenophobic tradition. These ideas were popular among sociologists and political theorists, who had a field day providing idiosyncratic interpretations of Populist writers and reading history backward to fit the Populist cause into their theories of authoritarian trends. All of this work, including Hofstadter's, was in a sense tainted because prudent readers could not determine how these critics defined "populism": was it a party or a pejorative term for a mass movement? It was soon evident that Hofstadter's major contribution had little to do with Populism; he was raising questions about the nature of American political history. Would historians continue in a Progressive mode, emphasizing economic factors, or would they look to other issues, such as religion, status, group anxiety, and ethnicity as critical variables?

This dialogue in intellectual history engendered by Hofstadter was sparkling. It led to vitriolic book reviews and verbal fireworks at historical conventions. Arguing about what Populists meant by what they said, of course, proved futile — the exegetical work of Norman Pollack and Oscar Handlin to the contrary notwithstanding.[16] The critical dimension of this debate was its deductive nature, its argument by analogy, and its rhetoric of persuasion. "Proof," as the word was used by other historians, eluded the participants.

It is on this point of proof that the Hofstadter hypothesis regarding Populism collapsed. Much that had been written by historians as matters of judgment and acts of faith could be readily tested by inductive methods and empirical research. The best early model of this kind of research was Bogue's *Money at Interest*, which challenged some of the key assumptions of the Populists: that money lending was profitable, interest rates outrageous, and farm tenancy oppressive. Bogue did not address himself to Hofstadter's questions but his work was groundbreaking both because of what he found and, more important, because of the way he asked historians to think about Populism.[17] His students as well as others who considered themselves social and behavioral scientists began testing prevailing interpretations in Populist historiography.

Space limitations preclude discussing the legion of books in this neo-positivist convention but two deserve to be singled out. Walter T. K. Nugent's *The Tolerant Populists: Kansas Populism and Nativism* (1962) *proved* that Kansas Populists were often themselves immigrants and Catholics and that Hofstadter's reading of a few publicists could hardly be considered valid. Nugent, like Bogue, heralded the winds of change. Stanley Parsons, one of Bogue's students, deserves special mention. In *The Populist Context: Rural versus Urban Power on a Great Plains Frontier* (1973) Parsons showed how measurable behavior could identify group traits and spatial distribution. Parsons's work was a model monograph on how to test a thesis. Most members of this generation of scholars who turned to the use of quantitative methods proved to be equally comfortable with traditional literary sources. They have not yet resolved to their own satisfaction, or that of others, whether race, economics, power, or the ethnocultural factor is most important in Populist political behavior.[18]

But one interesting aspect of much of the quantitative research is that while it tests many variables in different contexts, it has never been able to ignore the importance of economic factors. As a result much of the work tends to refine, clarify, and underscore many of the conclusions initially put forward by Hicks. Many of these scholars feel that it is still significant to read Hicks first. It is worth noting that in a recent essay on what made some men Populists a revisionist concluded that Hicks may not have been far off the mark.[19]

E. P. Thompson has markedly influenced American scholarship. His *The Making of the English Working Class*, a sophisticated Marxist analysis of English society between the 1780s and 1840s, has led to some reassessments of nineteenth-century American history. These studies were based not only on Thompson's theories regarding class but also on his methods and use of sources. Thompson wrote about what he saw as members of an emerging working class, who were not victims of industrialization but participants in a process and whose values and culture were threatened and revised. The experience and interaction of working people during the industrialization of England is a vital part of Thompson's thesis. Although Thompson eschewed quantitative methods, his work fits well within the context and methods of the new social history. Thompson was concerned with working people — artisans and craftsmen — and his ideas have had their most profound impact in this area of research, but his ideas were equally applicable to rural America, especially in the South, where major changes resulting from the Civil War and the transportation revolution altered the status of the rural work force, both black and white. A neo-Thompsonian might well ask if, during the late nineteenth century, an American working class was in the making in the American South and Middle West.

Lawrence Goodwyn's *Democratic Promise: The Populist Movement in America* (1976), which displays Thompson's influence, is the first overall treatment of Populism since Hicks. It is an important book partly because it demonstrates how a social organization evolves, develops a network, and spreads, and partly because it views Populism as a cultural phenomenon derived from, and also a part of, the industrialization of America. Where Hicks depicted the South and the West as regions of capital-starved agrarian entrepreneurs who were eager to use the most modern methods, crops, and tools, and were determined to break the stranglehold of eastern bankers and transportation magnets so they could participate in the world-wide market economy, Goodwyn's Populists are, in a sense, like Thompson's artisans — men and women from whom the tools of production and distribution were being stripped and who sought through cooperation and the use of government to reclaim or reestablish a republican commonwealth, in the seventeenth-century egalitarian sense, where the industrialization of the nation would not leave them a dependent class. For this reason the cooperative movement and the subtreasury plan loom large in Goodwyn's treatment as explanatory factors, since both would have freed the farmers from merchants and bankers. To Hicks, however, these were essentially unworkable (cooperatives) and visionary (the subtreasury) schemes, especially outside of the cotton South.

The disagreements in interpretation could be spelled out at great length, but in essence Hicks is explaining the economic origin of a third party well within the traditional framework of the American political system, and Goodwyn is setting out a "movement culture" that he believes held out the promise of a cooperative society that would have preserved the values and sense of community that characterized rural America. Hicks rejoices in those elements of Populism enacted into law by the major parties; Goodwyn laments the last chance for Americans to accept a solution to modern problems that derives from the folk traditions. Hicks explains Populism's charismatic leaders; Goodwyn, like Thompson, takes pride in rescuing from the dustbin of history lesser-known persons who came out of the depressed farming (working) class in order to save their way of life and offered viable solutions to the acute problems of industrializing America.

Goodwyn's study received some laudatory reviews.[20] His interpretation is increasingly popular in textbooks, is mentioned in bibliographies, and some writers see in it a new orthodoxy. Bruce Palmer's *"Men over Money": The Southern Critique of American Capitalism*, published in 1980 and also in the Thompson tradition, provides a brilliant underpinning for Goodwyn, while Steven Hahn's analysis in *The Roots of Southern Populism*, although heavily indebted to Palmer, makes the best empirically tested case for the existence of a humane rural culture among the petty-capitalist landholders in Georgia's uplands and provides an argument for the presence of a "movement culture" among these people in the Populist era.[21] Hahn in many ways validates Goodwyn, especially his evidence that the small landowning farmer in the uplands was content and probably would have preferred to remain outside of the larger market economy that was forced on the region with the economic reorientation that followed the Civil War.[22] He also makes a strong case for Populist dissent embracing a republican spirit. Hahn is aware that there are as yet many unanswered questions, perhaps the most important of which is why a political movement of such power failed. He implicitly rejects Goodwyn's explanation, and suggests that kinship ties, the basis of social stability in the uplands, again became paramount, and the organizational strength that grew out of the "movement culture" faded.[23]

Democratic Promise did not receive universal acclaim. Theodore Saloutos felt the emphasis on cooperatives was exaggerated and underresearched. He also insisted that Goodwyn had not fully explicated his thesis. More interesting, Saloutos referred to Anna Rochester's slim, old-line Marxist analysis of Populism as having a better grasp of economic issues.[24] Gilbert Fite, after praising the book as one scholars must read, went on to say "Goodwyn has weakened his study by accepting agrarian rhetoric too literally and giving too much emphasis to cooperation." Fite insisted that Goodwyn "strain[ed] credulity" by asking his readers to believe that Populism was America's last chance.[25]

The most severe indictment came from Robert W. Cherny. Goodwyn, to make his point that Texas was the heartland of Populism, that cooperatives were the measure of the true Populist spirit, and that the Populists succumbed because of a "shadow movement" of politicians who were unfamiliar with or hostile to the cooperative movement and who were willing to fuse with the Democrats merely to put honest men in office, denied that the Nebraska Populists were ideologically sound because they were the group most responsible for Populist-Democratic fusion in 1896. If the "shadow movement" was widespread, its main presence was in Nebraska. Cherny's critique of *Democratic Promise* finds Goodwyn's facts about Nebraska Populism completely wrong. Cherny argues that Goodwyn simply overlooked or ignored research that would have contradicted his opinions, that he offered reasons for party policies without evidence for his judgments, and that the portions of the *Democratic Promise* dealing with Nebraska are riddled with both large and petty errors. He insists that Goodwyn's history of Nebraska Populism is *wie es eigenlich sein sollte* rather than *wie es eigenlich gewesen ist*, and he argues that Goodwyn invents his history by misreading or extrapolating from general works while ignoring the basic books in the field. Even more damaging is Cherny's evidence that Nebraska not only pioneered cooperatives, which were far more widespread there than Goodwyn states, but also that Nebraska Populists supported the most radical dimensions of the cause. To his parade of horribles (errors) in Goodwyn, Cherny adds that Goodwyn is hostile to the work of behavioral historians and has fallen victim of a "reductive fallacy," assessing the success or failure of the movement on the basis of a single criterion.[26] Since Goodwyn placed so much stress on Nebraska and the idea of a "shadow movement." Cherny's work deserves careful reading.

Cherny made brief reference to another criticism prepared by a team of scholars led by Stanley Parsons, which was later published in the *Journal of American History*.[27] Parsons's team set out to test empirically the controlling assumptions of the Goodwyn thesis: "the cooperative movement recruited American farmers, and their subsequent experience within the cooperatives radically altered their political consciousness."[28] The team program postulated three verifiable questions: was the cooperative structure large enough to reach an adequate population to account for the size of the movement, was the sequence of events from the formation of the cooperatives to the development of the party correct or were there anachronisms, and did the dialogue on a cooperative commonwealth in the vehicles of communication in the movement prove Goodwyn's assertions about the magnitude of the issue. All three questions could be answered statistically. In each case,

Parsons's team found that Goodwyn was wrong. In fact, evidence was not only lacking to sustain the argument but also indicated that the opposite was true. The Parsons team, which felt that its research had destroyed the crux of Goodwyn's argument, concluded that the basic elements in *The Populist Revolt* (excluding the theory of a vanishing frontier), as refined by the generation of historians after Bogue, remain intact.[29]

In retrospect, it is now clear that *The Populist Revolt*, far from being the last word on Populism, proved to be an evocative book that produced a variety of valuable case studies.[30] That parts of *The Populist Revolt* have been rejected, revised, retained, and still subject to debates does credit to John D. Hicks's scholarship and insight. After fifty years, his work has held up rather well. That does not mean the profession does not need a new treatment of Populism. So much has been written that even a summary of the literature pointing out where scholars disagree would be of value. Whether it is possible to provide a statement that will achieve a consensus is highly debatable. Ideological and methodological cleavages are far wider and deeper than they were in the 1920s, when Hicks was at work. It is unlikely that any future author of a national treatment will enjoy the widespread acceptance that both Hicks and Goodwyn received, although the critiques of Goodwyn's work have begun to erode its following. But the complexity and subtlety required of a new study of Populism should be more of a challenge than a deterrent to scholars in the field. Whoever takes up the challenge and is successful stands a chance of producing a book that may last for another half-century. Meanwhile the profession must make do with two overall studies that have been challenged or revised.

Martin Ridge, Senior Research Associate, Henry E. Huntington Library, is coauthor of Westward Expansion *(1982).*

1. John D. Hicks, *My Life with History: An Autobiography* (1968), p. 145.

2. William MacDonald, "When Populism Swept the Farm Lands of the Country," *New York Times Book Review*, October 18, 1931.

3. For example, see Benjamin Kendrick, *North Carolina Historical Review* 10 (1933), p. 83; David S. Muzzey, *North Dakota Historical Review* 6 (1932), p. 170; and Lester B. Shippee, *Mississippi Valley Historical Review* 18 (1931), p. 417.

4. Roscoe D. Martin, *Peoples Party in Texas* (1933).

5. *Southwest Historical Quarterly* 35 (1932), p. 320.

6. Kendrick, p. 85.

7. Hicks, p. 146.

8. Hicks, p. 95.

9. Hicks, pp. 96, 98, 127.

10. Hicks, p. 404.

11. Hicks, pp. 47, 115.

12. See Kendrick, p. 85.

13. Hicks, p. 422.

14. In his seminal essay, "The Significance of the Frontier in American History," (*Frontier in American History*, 1920, p. 32) Frederick Jackson Turner denounced the western proclivity for soft money. Davis Rich Dewey, *Financial History of the United States* (1928); James L. Laughlin, *Money and Prices* (1919).

15. A humane man, John D. Hicks took personally and deeply resented the implication that since he had not mentioned the antisemitic rhetoric of some Populist authors that he condoned it.

16. Norman Pollack, "Hofstadter on Populism: A Critique of the 'Age of Reform,'" *Journal of Southern History* 26 (1960): 478–500; "Fear of Man: Populism, Authoritarianism, and the Historian," *Agricultural History* 39 (1965): 59–67; and Oscar Handlin, "Reconsidering the Populists," *Agricultural History* 39: 68–74.

17. Allan Bogue, of course, was not the only or the first scholar to think in these terms, but he was the most active in encouraging his students to examine the problems of Populism and to address them himself. It is worth noting also that Lee Benson published *Merchants, Farmers, and Railroads: Railroad Regulation and New York Politics, 1850–1887* in 1955.

18. The works of Peter Argersinger, Sheldon Hackney, Richard Jensen, James Wright, Gerald H. Gaither, Frederick Leubke, Paul Kleppner, Walter T. K. Nugent, Steven Hahn, and Robert Cherny illustrate the conflicting strands of analysis. These and other factors have not been overlooked by scholars relying on more traditional sources and methodologies as the excellent work of O. Gene Clanton, David Trask, and Ivy Hair, to mention only three, indicates. This list could be extended greatly to include scholars who have accepted one or more variables in sequence or simultaneously.

19. James Turner, "Understanding the Populists," *Journal of American History* 67 (1980): 354–73, takes virtually every author on Populism to task for failing to address the key question of why only some people became Populist in depressed areas and others did not. He concludes in part, "John D. Hicks may not have been far off the mark, after all, when he explained Populism as a product of the frontier" (p. 370).

20. Robert C. McMath, writing in the *American Historical Review* 82 (1977): 753–54, said, "this is an important book," although he also said that it did not answer a host of questions; Henry C. Dethloff called it the "best effort to date to comprehend the essence of Populism," in a review in *Agricultural History* 52 (1978): 216–17; and Charles A. Cannon, in the *Journal of Southern History* 43 (1977): 471–72, said that it was the "definitive work." Walter T. K. Nugent was cautious but felt it demonstrated "vigor and fresh research," *Journal of American History* 62 (1977): 464–65.

21. Both Bruce Palmer and Steven Hahn also express a debt to Eugene Genovese, who influenced their thinking, and to the support and guidance of C. Vann Woodward at different points in their work.

22. Steven Hahn's work is not only important because of its scope and meticulous research but also because it offers a revisionist view of much of the period from 1850 to 1890.

23. It may be ironic, but one could read Steven Hahn, especially his recognition of the upland folk as petty capitalists, and conclude in contrast to his views that Hicks was right all along — parts of the South were like the West, replete with areas within one generation of the frontier experience, which proved to be Populist bastions. The avidity with which farmers who were not tied to the crop lien and tenancy system accepted cotton culture and the region's remarkable kinship system provide additional sources for conflicting views. Since Hahn is very judicious in his conclusions, he has opened the way for a good deal of research.

24. Theodore Saloutos, *Pacific Historical Review* 47 (1978): 149–50.

25. Gilbert Fite, *Pacific Northwest Quarterly* 69 (1978): 137–38.

26. Robert W. Cherny, *Great Plains Quarterly* 1 (1981): 181–94. Many of the kinds of criticism that Cherny levels at Goodwyn were raised by R. Currie and R. M. Hartwell in their extended review of E. P. Thompson's *The Making of the English Working Class* in the *Economic History Review* 18 (1965): 633–43.

27. Stanley B. Parsons, Karen Toombs Parsons, Walter Killilae, and Beverly Borgers, "The Role of Cooperatives in the Development of the Movement Culture of Populism," *Journal of American History* 69 (1983): 866–85.

28. Lawrence Goodwyn, *Democratic Promise*, p. xviii.

29. Parsons et al., p. 884.

30. The above discussion of populism since Hicks, which has focused on only a few issues, is unfair to more than a score of scholars who have made valuable contributions to our understanding of the subject but whose works are not mentioned here. They represent paradigms as different as James M. Youngdale's *Populism: A Psychohistorical Perspective* (1975), which attempts a synthesis of Thomas Kuhn's views on revolution and Adlerian psychology, and Peter H. Argersinger's *Populism and Politics: William Alfred Peffer and the People's Party* (1974), which demonstrates how a literate biography of a politician can be enhanced by the skillful use of analytical and quantitative methods.

SCIENTIFIC MIND AND LEGAL MATTER: THE LONG SHADOW OF RICHARD B. MORRIS'S STUDIES IN THE HISTORY OF AMERICAN LAW

Stephen Botein

At the age of eighty, Richard B. Morris can take pride in an immense and varied bibliography that continues to grow appreciably. During the quarter century that followed his move from New York's City College to Columbia in 1949, he was an exceptionally prolific teacher of graduate students in the field of early American history. *The Peacemakers* won a Bancroft Prize in 1966; a decade later, amid the hoopla of the Bicentennial, Morris served as president of the American Historical Association. The tempo of his career, never leisurely, seems to have accelerated at mid-point.[1] Now, as the bicentennial of the U.S. Constitution approaches, he is prominent as co-chair of Project 87.

This latest role should be a reminder that Morris's solid professional reputation rests in large part on his earliest work, which contributed to the esoteric field of legal history. *Government and Labor in Early America*, published in 1946, drew upon some 20,000 court cases for evidence about colonial employment practices. It remains well regarded nearly four decades later. *Studies in the History of American Law, with Special Reference to the Seventeenth and Eighteenth Centuries* is even more noteworthy in these terms. This was Morris's doctoral dissertation at Columbia. It earned him the Ph.D. in 1930, appearing as Number 316 of Columbia University Press's Studies in History, Economics and Public Law. That same year Claude H. Van Tyne won a Pulitzer Prize for *The War of Independence*, Vernon L. Parrington produced the last volume of *Main Currents in American Thought*, and Samuel Eliot Morison did what he could to rehabilitate the Puritans with *Builders of the Bay Colony*. Morris's quaintly titled book did not make much of an impact at the time, nor did it subsequently come to occupy a ranking place in the mainstream literature of colonialists. But in certain select circles it has always had a following.

These days, as one "new" history rapidly supersedes another, connoisseurs of vintage historical scholarship will readily identify what is most remarkable about the book. More than half a century after it was written, *Studies in the History of American Law* speaks to the current research agenda of specialists. Few authors of history books half as old can make that claim. Indeed, the dissertation that Morris conceived during the presidency of Calvin Coolidge has stayed relevant enough to provoke sharp criticism in a recent review essay.[2] What accounts for the durability of this youthful academic performance?

The strengths of *Studies in the History of American Law* are conspicuous throughout. Despite his command of arcane legal matter, Morris worked in bold strokes for the benefit of lay readers. The stylistic vigor of the book is apparent from its very first paragraph, which presents an elaborate musical metaphor to announce such themes and counterthemes as natural law (strings), common-law precedents (woodwinds), and paternalism (brass). In format, too, *Studies* is striking. There are just four chapters, along with a bibliographical essay, running in all to fewer than 275 pages — this when complaints were beginning to be heard about the excessive length of American dissertations in history. Then, generalizing across different colonial jurisdictions, come three studies of "representative legal questions": distribution and alienation of land, women's rights, and doctrines of tortious liability. Unifying the book are repeated statements that argue for a progressive trend toward social democracy in seventeeth-century America. Such "advances" as relatively equal inheritance of real estate and an enhanced contract-making role for women are attributed to a combination of reformist social philosophy and frontier experience. In the eighteenth century, however, a "conservative reaction" occurred. Within a newly efficient system of imperial governance, professional lawyers representing the interests of "a propertied class" managed to reverse some tendencies of the earlier period.

As of 1930, *Studies in the History of American Law* looked *sui generis*. Here was legal history that rejected the orthodoxy of Roscoe Pound, the dean of Harvard Law School, who dismissed colonial justice as crude and untechnical for lack of strong guidance from the king's courts at Westminster. Here was legal history that focused on the relationship of law to the social and economic realities of colonial America, instead of seeking to trace the evolution of principles and institutions from medieval England. *Studies* has to be understood as the work of a precocious young scholar who uniquely blended the influences of his undergraduate years at C.C.N.Y. with the ideas of the major historiographical schools represented at Columbia in the 1920s.

For many of the intellectually ambitious young men who populated City College in its heyday, journalism, law, and scholarship formed a powerful cluster of competing vocational claims.[3] It was taken for granted that professionals would want to write effectively for the educated general public. At Townshend Harris Hall, the preparatory high school run by City College, Morris had already encountered teachers with expertise in law and early American history, and these two lines of interest appear to have converged in a special thematic concern of Morris's mid-teens. As a Jew, at a time when colonial America was considered the property of genteel Protestant antiquarians, he was intrigued to discover extensive reference to the Old Testament in New England's early statutory law. Contributing to a weekly called *The American Hebrew and Jewish Messenger* in 1920–21, he drew attention to the "Hebraic mortar" that cemented "the groundwork and substructure of American Government," as its premises were articulated by political leaders from Roger Williams to Alexander Hamilton.[4] On a much more sophisticated level, Morris pursued this theme through his later years at City College and in his master's paper at Columbia, which the *American Historical Review* published in 1926.[5] There was more of the same in chapter 1 of *Studies*, under the heading "Theologico-politico Concepts: the Law of Nature and the Law of God."

At City College Morris became a protégé of Morris Raphael Cohen, the liberal philosopher of law and science who for decades played Socrates to New York's intelligentsia. Uninhibited by the proprietary assertions of the new full-time professoriate in American law schools, Cohen had publicly rejected the idea that legal study was "a special field requiring technical knowledge" and therefore accessible only to lawyers. The bold speculative thrust of *Studies*, most pronounced in its first synthetic chapter, may have owed something to Cohen's theories of scientific method. In nothing was Cohen more consistent than his disdain for proponents of pure inductive reasoning. Again and again, he insisted that observation and discovery did not necessarily precede logic. "The notion that we can study facts apart from any assumption or working hypothesis," as he once put it, "has been repeatedly shown to be logically fantastic."[6]

Cohen found Morris "a very charming fellow personally," and soon provided him with entrée to a network of legal luminaries that included Harold Laski, Felix Frankfurter, and even the eminent Dean Pound, who responded magnanimously when Cohen sent him one of Morris's undergraduate papers criticizing *The Spirit of the Common Law*.[7] Moving on to the history department at Columbia, Morris was fortunate to have the run of the School of Law as well. He took courses there during an extraordinarily turbulent period. Traditionalists on the law faculty clashed bitterly with self-styled "realists" who championed a program of legal research modelled on the empirical social sciences.[8] Among the latter, Hessel E. Yntema supervised Morris's research on primogeniture and entailed estates, which first appeared as a *Columbia Law Review* article in 1927 and then was recycled as chapter 2 of *Studies*. Yntema, who taught English legal history at the Law School until his departure in 1928 for the Johns Hopkins Institute for the Study of Law, also had a hand in the development of Morris's fourth chapter — on tortious liability. Evidently, too, some of Morris's work on women's rights for chapter 3 figured in a seminar offered by Karl N. Llewellyn, the most intellectually flamboyant of the young legal turks at Columbia. Another newcomer to the Law School who had contact with Morris in this period was a specialist in American legal history named Julius Goebel, Jr.[9]

Meanwhile, at the history department, the scholarly heritage was usefully ambiguous. Under Herbert Levi Osgood's aegis, Columbia had been the center of "institutional" history at the turn of the century. By the time Morris arrived on the scene, however, James Harvey Robinson and Charles Beard had come and gone, for a while giving the department a reputation equal to Wisconsin's as a stronghold of Progressive history. Morris's dissertation advisor was Evarts B. Greene, an "institutionalist" who had come to Columbia in 1923 after nearly three decades at the University of Illinois. Apparently, this "gentle and somewhat absent-minded professor" who was the son of a missionary in Japan took a liking to the "short ebullient native of the Bronx" who knew his way around the local archives.[10] In 1929, a year before *Studies* appeared, they collaborated on a guide to New York City's sources for early American history, emphasizing in their introduction that the "richest mines of comparatively unworked material" were available to "students of economic and social history."[11] Greene, it seems, was himself in transition toward the more comprehensive definition of historical process implicit in some of his later work.

In short, Columbia was an educational setting that could be supportive of a purposeful young scholar like Morris who aspired to write legal history with a difference. What he ended up producing was a book that eludes easy classification. The overall perspective on seventeenth-century American law is recognizably "Turnerite," but *Studies* was unusual for its day in being so alert to the utopian content of Puritan ideology. If Morris showed his Progressive colors in describing briefly the growth of a reactionary propertied class in the eighteenth century, he gave no hint of being attuned to the kind of politics underlying Beard's analysis of the Constitution. Some of his later work, indeed, would reveal an unmistakable "Hamiltonian" bias, which may be said to have been anticipated here and there in *Studies*. At the end of chapter 2, for example, he expressed concern that subdivision of agricultural holdings could in the long run prevent experiments with large-scale farming to achieve economies of scale. More generally, *Studies* expressed admiration of seventeenth-century Americans for their innovative attempts at "social engineering" through law.[12]

It is a book, in other words, of the activist academic generation that came of age in New York during the governorship of Franklin Delano Roosevelt. Speaking in 1933 at the annual meeting of the Association of American Law

Schools, Morris made clear that he saw significant "parallels" between early American legislation and "the chief features of the present economic revolution."[13] Soon afterward, somewhat like a WPA operative, he began to range up and down the east coast ("from Wiscasset, Maine, and Woodsville, New Hampshire, to St. Augustine, Florida") in search of material for *Government and Labor*. That book was addressed frankly to "the student of contemporary social and governmental problems" as well as the professional historian.[14] Constantly in motion during the 1930s, inventorying legal records and organizing their publication as secretary of the American Historical Association's Committee on Legal History, the author of *Studies in the History of American Law* appeared to have a long-range vision of needs and opportunities in a promising new field of historical research.

How far the promise has been fulfilled is uncertain. The question calls for an assessment of what Morris's dissertation has meant to at least two succeeding generations of historians.

In the case of the second, which emerged in the mid-1960s, *Studies* benefited from the timing of the revisionist cycle. Never an out-and-out "progressive," Morris was still enough of a historian on the left to extend a welcome to neoprogressivism — even if the view of radical students from the top of Columbia's Fayerweather Hall persuaded him that their movement included elements of "self-centered nihilism" as well as "moral conviction."[15] *Government and Labor* gave Morris standing as a pioneer in the newly fashionable field of labor history; *Studies*, reexamined in the context of the latest interdisciplinary research into the conditions of early American communal and family life, suggested that all along his larger aim had been to make legal records the stuff of social history.

The interpretive paradigm structuring chapter 1 of *Studies* once again seemed meaningful, after a lengthy period when "consensus" historians held sway. Morris, it turned out, had been prescient enough to understand how social conflict intensified as provincial America experienced the process that historians in the 1970s took to calling "Anglicization." Just one year after *Studies* appeared, Morris published an article elaborating the theme in terms of the "significant paradox" that "the front rank in leadership in the cause of political independence should have been assumed by a group of men who were largely responsible for bringing America into subjection to the reactionary legal system of England prevailing in the eighteenth century."[16] There and in *Studies*, he failed to come to grips with a problem that continues to challenge students of the early American legal profession. What, besides a "strengthening of imperial discipline," sustained the remarkably regular development of professionalism in law from colony to colony during the middle decades of the eighteenth century? Morris pointed to the influence of large landholders. He also claimed that "the rapid growth of business necessitated the resort to the more technical legal system of England," although he had to acknowledge the habitual impatience of merchants with lawyers and their costly intricate proceedings.[17] The ambiguous relationship of the early American bar to commerical interests has yet to receive adequate treatment.

Morris's choice of "representative" topics for chapters 2 through 4 of *Studies* now looks to have been shrewdly foresighted too. On some matters regarding descent and distribution of land, such as the connection proposed between partible inheritance in New England and Kentish gavelkind, he has been proven flatly wrong. Even so, in this area as in others, *Studies* asked many of the same questions being asked today, except that now perhaps there is a tendency to pay more heed to the voluntary arrangements by which real property was transferred from generation to generation without any recourse to the courts.[18] Chapter 4 was Morris's most lawyerly performance, focusing as it did on the uniform and distinctive feature of colonial American law that imposed a duty on landowners to put up effective fences if they wished to be able to hold their neighbors accountable for any damages caused by trespassing cattle. Here, according to Morris, were "the foundations in America of the defense of contributory negligence." That does not sound like a social historian speaking. Nevertheless, there are grounds now to think that fencing policy — for what it reveals of how risks and costs were allocated in different social environments — deserves far more attention than it has been given since *Studies*.[19] As for chapter 3, its current critics do not deny that it has become what one specialist not so many years ago called "the standard essay on colonial women under the common law."[20]

For all such evidence of staying power, however, what is disquieting about the history of this long-lived book is the suspicion that it endures to some extent by virtue of neglect. If over five decades there had been anything like a serious professional response to Morris's imaginative conception of early American legal history, *Studies* by now should have come to be regarded as obsolete. However injurious to an author's ego, no other outcome is so convincing as testimony to academic influence.

Morris has himself been partly responsible for the curious remoteness of his early work in the eyes of colonialists who embarked on their careers immediately following World War II. After leaving C.C.N.Y., where for twenty years there had been no chance for him to teach graduate students, his interests and priorities began gradually to change. The revolutionary era and constitution-making period were designated his specialties in the history department at Columbia, and increasingly his scholarship was concerned with the "larger picture" perceived by "statesmen," instead of the "bread-and-butter question" that occupied the "average person."[21] Editing the papers of

John Jay kept him in touch with legal subject matter, but diplomacy and other affairs of state were involved in that project too. Not surprisingly, few of Morris's many able graduate students at Columbia carried on what he had started with *Studies*. Such protégés in the field of legal history as Milton M. Klein, Herbert A. Johnson, and David H. Flaherty have not formed a "school."

As time passed, their mentor began to look beyond the confines of specialized scholarship. It seems likely that the journalistic aspirations of Morris's undergraduate days at C.C.N.Y. had never quite subsided. Encouraged by Henry Steele Commager, a colleague who had done much to give postwar Columbia a reputation for semipopular history writing, Morris became a favorite of trade publishers in New York. As he has recalled this phase of his career, it was exhilarating to reach a substantial audience after laboring so long in an obscure scholarly corner. Besides, according to his own candid account, he needed the money.[22] Authoring and coauthoring, editing and coediting books like *The Treasury of Great Reporting*, *Fair Trial*, and *The Spirit of '76*, he soon enjoyed a gratifying measure of success — although there would be a certain unhappy irony in the Pulitzer Prize controversy of 1966, when a jury's recommendation of *The Peacemakers* was overruled by the advisory board in favor of a posthumous award to Perry Miller's *Life of the Mind in America*, an improbably esoteric opus to be so honored.[23]

There has also been talk that Morris declined whole-heartedly to pursue the implications of his earliest work because he could never forget having been taken aback by some of the original reviews. In particular, the legal professoriate had reacted with something less than enthusiasm. A mainstream historian like V. W. Crane could be cautiously appreciative, leaving aside evaluation of the book from a "technical standpoint."[24] And genial praise might be forthcoming from old John Henry Wigmore, the conservative former dean of Northwestern Law School. "This is the kind of historical writing which we like best," Wigmore proclaimed.[25] But a number of prominent legal scholars appeared determined to punish Morris for his audacity in invading their territory. J. H. Beale of Harvard Law School was prepared grudgingly to describe *Studies* as "a good piece of work" — "scholarly, painstaking, shrewd, and occasionally brilliant." Even while hailing Morris as "one of the most promising young historians of America," however, Beale dismissed his book as a self-evident failure. "It is so good," Beale observed rather disingenuously, "that it proves the impossibility of the author's aim and method."[26] This was the theme of more overtly hostile commentary by several younger law professors.

Obviously, Morris's legal critics were perturbed by his lack of suitable credentials. "He can not do his work," Beale said, "first of all, because he is not a lawyer. . . ."[27] In addition, there were systematic objections to Morris's research strategy and mode of historical argumentation. In a terse footnote to an article published a year after *Studies*, Columbia Law School's Julius Goebel, Jr., faulted Morris on various grounds, the last but by no means least regrettable of which was his treatment of seventeenth-century English law as a "relatively static corpus of dogma." [28] Goebel's lifework would stress the importance of local courts and local custom persisting alongside the common law administered by royal judges. Other features of Morris's book, including his fairly limited use of manuscript material, were the targets of random sniping; the author may well have invited rebuke by seeming to overstate the range of his archival research, which in fact concentrated heavily on a single volume of Massachusetts Superior Court records. [29] But this was not the heart of the argument advanced against *Studies* by the law professors.

Beale put it coolly enough. "The time has come to study the history of American law," he agreed; "but the first step is the study of the history of each colony." [30] Others were emphatic on this point. Theodore F. T. Plucknett, finishing an assistant professorship at Harvard Law School before going on to the University of London, noted that the results of "covering too much ground in a short work" had to be unfortunate. "In the present case," he complained, "the sense of chronological sequence has been obscured, and the feeling for local development within each jurisdiction has been sacrificed in an attempt to picture the whole panorama of American legal history." [31] And Karl Llewellyn weighed into the discussion, from the legal left, with one of the most intemperate reviews in the annals of American scholarship. Confessing in the *Columbia Law Review* that his low opinion of *Studies* reflected both admiration of a colleague (Goebel) and exasperation with a former student (Morris), Llewellyn pronounced the book "depressing and grotesque." Then followed a catalogue of the author's sins. Llewellyn could overlook Morris's insufficient certification for the task at hand, although a simple "cure" for the problem would have been to ask that "a careful professional go over the manuscript." What seemed truly inexcusable was Morris's pan-colonial approach. "No historian of law today," Llewellyn asserted, "has any business *presupposing, without demonstrating point for point*, that there was any one 'colonial' view on anything." The "grotesquerie" of *Studies* lay in its "overambition of scope, compared to achievement." [32]

Llewellyn explained that he offered such criticism not as a legal historian, which he was definitely not, but from "the common ground of general social science." [33] However sympathetic he might be to the basic political orientation of *Studies*, its synthetic presentation and speculative energy were at odds with the standards he espoused as a proponent of empirical inquiry. As he would write some years later, the discipline of history called for "detailed knowledge, for detailed background, and for discrimination even more detailed." History should be "scientific," and what that usually meant for Llewellyn was "sustained, insistent, cumulative digging after smaller bits of testible and tested knowledge about small things." At rare moments, he admitted, progress in the pursuit of science could be achieved by "going after Big Things," but that took genius.[34] Perhaps in "the fulness of time," as Plucknett had mused, an American Maitland would arise.[35]

Maitland was one of Morris's heroes. Did the young Ph.D. from Columbia presume to see himself in that role? Had he replied at once to his law school critics, it appears more probable that he would have modestly cited Morris Cohen on the value of hypothetical reasoning in science. In the early 1930s, as it happened, Cohen himself publicly broke rank with not only Llewellyn but Hessel Yntema, the two "realists" among Morris's teachers at Columbia Law School. The immediate issue was Cohen's unwillingness to disregard the force of "ethical ideals" in law. In the background was the same epistemological quarrel that had surfaced in the criticism of *Studies*. Eventually, as he watched the "growing annexation" of law schools by universities in America, Cohen grew pessimistic about what could be accomplished from interchange with academic lawyers. "Unfortunately," he would conclude, "relatively few teachers of law have had a scientific education, and so their conception of scientific method does not always rise above popular impressions."[36]

In the meantime, however, Llewellyn's conception of history tended to prevail within legal circles. In 1933, at the annual meeting of the Association of American Law Schools, Morris had to listen to the dean of Lamar School of Law at Emory University outline principles by which colonial law should be studied. "For the present," declared Charles J. Hilkey, "the history should be written from the particular to the general. . . . The present is the time for prospectors and miners. Artists may use the precious metals later."[37] Morris himself gave the appearance of slowly coming to concede the issue. The very massiveness of *Government and Labor*, drawn from "largely unpublished" court records, could be interpreted as an effort to ward off abuse of the sort to which *Studies* had been subjected. Indeed, one lawyer reviewing Morris's second book was moved to congratulate its author for having inspected so thoroughly "the trees which make up the forest of history."[38] In a foreword to the second edition of *Studies*, published in 1959, Morris was at pains to acknowledge the need for chronological and geographical specificity in investigating colonial law; some years afterward, providing a foreword to a collection of essays in the field, he anticipated still more "studies in depth" before a "definitive history" could be undertaken.[39]

Within law schools, where it had to be expected that the highly specialized field of early American law could at least count on a more sizeable constituency than anywhere else, the scholarship of Julius Goebel, Jr., proved exemplary in its meticulous rendering of detail. Joseph H. Smith, his protégé and successor at Columbia, was relentlessly preoccupied with the complexities of Anglo-American institutional development.[40] Pennsylvania's George Lee Haskins made it his mission to try to set early American law in a broader cultural context, but never so broad as to imply anything but full respect for the particularity of each colonial system. At the very outset of *Law and Authority in Early Massachusetts*, published in 1960, Haskins quoted Plucknett on the desirability of separate jurisdictional studies conducted with "minute accuracy and exhaustiveness."[41] Only astute readers could have realized that this was Plucknett reviewing Morris; *Studies*, despite its sensitivity to Puritan thought, was primly ignored throughout Haskins's book.

Little wonder that in 1965 Michael G. Kammen referred to Goebel, Smith, and Haskins as "the leading specialists" in early American legal history.[42] If frequency of citation may be relied on as evidence,[43] it is plain that the major scholars working within law schools have done more to shape the field than Morris from a history department outside the field. To most colonialists located on Morris's side of the disciplinary border, this is a state of affairs that must give pause. The "scientistic" history of academic lawyers has been impressive in its way, but so far the parts do not appear even to add up — much less to make a greater whole. Will it take yet another half century for a Maitland to come forth?

So, then, it is somewhat troubling to encounter the most recent criticism of *Studies in the History of American Law*. Doubtless Marylynn Salmon and others now rewriting the history of colonial American women are right to lament the shortcomings of chapter 3.[44] Morris's argument there that the rights of women expanded in seventeenth-century America is suspect because of his characteristic tendency toward overgeneralization in presenting the legal circumstances of both the mother country and the colonies. But in the light of what has resulted from earlier criticism along such lines, coming out of a very different quarter, the question is whether early American legal history might be better off in the near future with a less particularistic agenda of research. In practice, most early American historians are inclined to praise those who go after Big Things, while of course also honoring the small-scale prospectors and miners. A middle way has to be charted. To the extent that the history of early American law has evolved under the control or influence of law professors, the field has suffered from a failure to make room enough for scholarship on the model of Morris's first book.

In 1985, this should be a cause of concern to all colonial historians, for whose period legal records probably constitute the largest body of unexplored documentation. Who will do the exploring? "Lawyers are arrogant and think they can do anything," Stanley N. Katz remarked a couple of years back, "including write history." [45] Although few historians are paragons of humility, many or even most are apt to defer or at any rate grant a key role to academic lawyers when it comes to writing legal history. This may seem sensible enough, especially in a society with numerous professional institutions that support legal scholarship. On the other hand, the fate of *Studies in the History of American Law* raises certain doubts about the conventional academic wisdom. In the field of legal history, there may be reason to take a skeptical look at the cherished ideal of interdisciplinary inquiry. Let lawyers be their own legal historians, perhaps, and let historians be the same. Once in a while they may even have something to say to one another.

Stephen Botein, Department of History, Michigan State University, is the author of Early American Law and Society *(1983). This essay was written during the term of a National Endowment for the Humanities Research Fellowship at the American Antiquarian Society.*

1. Unless otherwise indicated, biographical information in what follows is drawn from Richard B. Morris, "History over Time," *William and Mary Quarterly* 3d ser., 41 (July 1984): 455–63; Michael Kraus, "Richard B. Morris: An Assessment," in Alden T. Vaughan and George Athan Billias, eds., *Perspectives on Early American History: Essays in Honor of Richard B. Morris* (1973), pp. 1–6; and from an interview with Professor Morris. For general historiographical trends, the basic source is John Higham et al., *History: The Development of Historical Studies in the United States* (1965). On colonial legal history as a field, see Herbert A. Johnson, "American Colonial Legal History: A Historiographical Interpretation," in Vaughan and Billias, eds., *Perspectives*, pp. 250–81; Stanley N. Katz, "The Problem of a Colonial Legal History," in Jack P. Greene and J. R. Pole, eds., *Colonial British America: Essays in the New History of the Early Modern Era* (1984), pp. 457–89. In the interest of further reducing the annotation of this essay, full citations will be omitted for books readily identifiable and referred to only in passing.

2. Marylynn Salmon, "The Legal Status of Women in Early America: A Reappraisal," *Law and History Review* 1 (Spring 1983): 129–51.

3. See generally S. Willis Rudy, *The College of the City of New York: A History* (1949), chs. 27–28.

4. Richard B. Morris, "Alexander Hamilton as a Hebraist," *The American Hebrew and Jewish Messenger*, May 7, 1920; "The Jewish Interests of Roger Williams," *ibid.*, Dec. 9, 1921. Morris collaborated on another article in this vein with a young rabbi named Louis J. Newman, "The Jewish Tradition at the Birth of America," *ibid.*, Sept. 30, 1921.

5. Richard B. Morris, "Massachusetts and the Common Law: The Declaration of 1646," *American Historical Review* 21 (April 1926): 443–53.

6. Morris Raphael Cohen, *Reason and Law: Studies in Juristic Philosophy* (1950), pp. 129, 178; and see David A. Hollinger, *Morris R. Cohen and the Scientific Ideal* (1975), ch. 6.

7. Leonora Cohen Rosenfeld, *Portrait of a Philosopher: Morris R. Cohen in Life and Letters* (1962), pp. 385, 96–97.

8. See generally Foundation for Research in Legal History, *A History of the School of Law, Columbia University* (1955); and William Twining, *Karl Llewellyn and the Realist Movement* (1973), ch. 3.

9. Richard B. Morris, "Primogeniture and Entailed Estates in America," *Columbia Law Review* 27 (Jan. 1927): 24–71. On Morris's association with members of the law faculty, see the

preface to *Studies* and the review by Llewellyn in the *Columbia Law Review* 31 (April 1931): 729–32.

10. For Greene's personality, see the obituary in *American Historical Review* 53 (Oct. 1947): 218–19; the description of Morris comes from Mary-Jo Kline, "The Writings of Richard B. Morris," in Vaughan and Billias, eds., *Perspectives*, p. 378.

11. Evarts B. Greene and Richard B. Morris, *A Guide to the Principal Sources for Early American History (1600–1800) in the City of New York* (1929), p. xvi.

12. *Studies*, pp. 124–25, 20, 69, 258.

13. Richard B. Morris, "The Sources of Early American Law: Colonial Period," *West Virginia Law Quarterly* 40 (April 1934): 212.

14. Richard B. Morris, *Government and Labor in Early America* (1946), pp. viii–ix.

15. Richard B. Morris, "The View from the Top of Fayerweather," in Harold M. Hyman and Leonard W. Levy, eds., *Freedom and Reform: Essays in Honor of Henry Steele Commager* (1967), p. 5.

16. Richard B. Morris, "Legalism versus Revolutionary Doctrine in New England," *New England Quarterly* 4 (April 1931): 418. This article might be compared with John M. Murrin, "The Legal Transformation: The Bench and Bar of Eighteenth-Century Massachusetts," in Stanley N. Katz, ed., *Colonial America: Essays in Politics and Social Development* (1971), pp. 415–49.

17. *Studies*, pp. 64–65, 48.

18. See George L. Haskins, "The Beginnings of Partible Inheritance in the American Colonies," in David H. Flaherty, ed., *Essays in the History of Early American Law* (1969), pp. 204–44; a good example of the literature stressing voluntary arrangements is Christopher M. Jedrey, *The World of John Cleaveland: Family and Community in Eighteenth-Century New England* (1979), ch. 3.

19. *Studies*, p. 210; and see generally David Thomas Konig, *Law and Society in Puritan Massachusetts: Essex County, 1629–1692* (1979), ch. 5.

20. Nancy F. Cott, *The Bonds of Womanhood* (1977), p. 21.

21. John A. Garraty, *Interpreting American History: Conversations with Historians* (1970), 1: 127; and see Richard B. Morris, "Current Statesmen's Papers Publication Programs: An Appraisal from the Point of View of the Legal Historian," *American Journal of Legal History* 11 (April 1967): 95–106.

22. Richard B. Morris, "Confessions of a Scholar Seeking a Wider Audience," *Wisconsin Magazine of History* 63 (Summer 1980): 301–02.

23. John Hohenberg, *The Pulitzer Prizes* (1974), p. 334.

24. V. W. Crane, Review, *Harvard Law Review* 44 (April 1931): 1157–58.

25. John Henry Wigmore, Review, *Iowa Law Review* 16 (April 1931): 452–54.

26. J. H. Beale, Review, *American Historical Review* 35 (July 1930): 921–22.

27. *Ibid.*

28. Julius Goebel, Jr., "King's Law and Local Custom in Seventeenth Century New England," *Columbia Law Review* 31 (March 1931): 417, n. 3.

29. *Studies*, p. 262, is perhaps slightly misleading; the volume in question covers the years 1721–25.

30. Beale, Review, pp. 921–22.

31. F. T. Plucknett, Review, *New England Quarterly* 3 (July 1930): 574.

32. Karl N. Llewellyn, Review, *Columbia Law Review* 31 (April 1931): 729–32.

33. *Ibid.*, p. 731.

34. Karl N. Llewellyn, "On Warranty of Quality, and Society," *Columbia Law Review* 36 (May 1936): 699n; Twining, *Karl Llewellyn*, pp. 188–96.

35. Plucknett, Review.

36. Hollinger, *Morris R. Cohen*, ch. 7; Cohen, *Reason and Law*, p. 1.

37. Charles J. Hilkey, "The Unpublished Sources for Early American Legal History," *West Virginia Law Quarterly* 40 (April 1934): 229.

38. The reviewer was Milton R. Konvitz, in the *Saturday Review of Literature*, June 8, 1946.

According to Konvitz's rhetoric, Maitland was also a historian of trees; Holdsworth saw the woods.

39. See p. viii of the second edition, which was published in Philadelphia and then later reissued from New York; George Athan Billias, ed., *Law and Authority in Colonial America* (1965), p. ix.

40. Smith's "Cases and Materials on Early American Law and Legal Institutions" (1969), for use at Columbia Law School, did include an excerpt from Morris's article on primogeniture and entailed estates in the *Columbia Law Review*.

41. George Lee Haskins, *Law and Authority in Early Massachusetts: A Study in Tradition and Design* (1960), p. viii.

42. Michael G. Kammen, "Colonial Court Records and the Study of Early American History: A Bibliographical Review," *American Historical Review* 70 (April 1965): 736.

43. Compare references to Morris's work in legal history with references to Goebel's and Haskins's, as recorded in the Social Sciences Citation Index.

44. See Salmon, "The Legal Status of Women in Early America," pp. 129–51.

45. Quoted in the *New York Times*, May 3, 1983.

RICHARD HOFSTADTER'S *THE AGE OF REFORM:* A RECONSIDERATION

Alan Brinkley

Even its detractors (and there are many) might be inclined to agree that Richard Hofstadter's *The Age of Reform: From Bryan to F.D.R.* is the most influential book ever published on the history of twentieth-century America. For more than a decade after its appearance in 1955, its interpretations shaped virtually every discussion of modern American reform. For longer than that, its methodological innovations helped recast the writing of history in many fields. Even those historians who have most vigorously and explicitly challenged its interpretations have usually been deeply, if at times unconsciously, in its debt. In this book, as in others, Hofstadter's signal achievement, the achievement that has most clearly marked him as one of the century's great American historians, lay less in creating durable interpretations than in raising new questions and establishing new modes of inquiry, in opening hitherto unperceived avenues of exploration. Robert Wiebe spoke for more than his own generation of scholars when he wrote in 1969: "To those of us who encountered *The Age of Reform* in graduate school, [Hofstadter] more than any other writer, framed the problems, explored the techniques, and established the model of literate inquiry that would condition our study of the American past."[1]

The book's most direct influence, of course, has been on the study of populism and progressivism. A remarkable number of the many important studies of both phenomena that have appeared since 1955 were augured, directly or indirectly, by Hofstadter's observations. His discussion of "the struggle over organization," for example, laid much of the groundwork for the important Weberian interpretations of progressivism by Wiebe, Samuel Hays, and others. His examination of the links between political machines and corporate power, and his description of popular resentment of both, foreshadowed some of the significant work of David Thelen on popular reform movements in Wisconsin. His controversial description of the

Populist mind opened the way for a series of subsequent studies (many of them explicitly critical of Hofstadter, yet nevertheless indebted to him for both interpretive and methodological inspiration) examining Populist ideology — an aspect of populism all but ignored in the work of Beard or Hicks and their disciples.

For historians of modern America, *The Age of Reform* has served a role comparable perhaps only to that of C. Vann Woodward's *Origins of the New South* in giving definition to a still undefined field. And yet unlike Woodward's monumental book, which remains the central work in modern southern history and whose interpretation many (if not most) scholars in the field continue to accept, *The Age of Reform* has begun in recent years to seem something of a relic. It is still widely read and widely cited. It continues to shape arguments and inspire debates. But it is now more often a target than an inspiration, a symbol of abandoned assumptions rather than a guide to further study. It has come, in short, to embody something of a scholarly paradox (to use one of Hofstadter's own favorite words): It is a book whose central interpretations few historians any longer accept, but one whose influence few historians can escape.

Woodward wrote *Origins of the New South* as part of a lifelong commitment to the field of southern history and after years of immersion in its sources. Hofstadter wrote *The Age of Reform*, by contrast, out of no longtime preoccupation with the subject (neither before nor after did he devote much attention to the Populists or Progressives) and after a strikingly thin acquaintance with the sources. It was not so much, then, a fascination with the reformers themselves that inspired Hofstadter to examine them, but rather the opportunity they gave him to test certain political, theoretical, and methodological concepts that by the 1950s had come to intrigue him. The self-consciously innovative tone of the study became its greatest strength; but its emphasis on innovation at the expense of evidence was also its most serious weakness.

Critics have most often cited the political concerns of intellectuals of the 1950s, and in particular their immersion in the highly charged atmosphere of the cold war, to explain the interpretations in *The Age of Reform*. Shaken by the memory of fascism and the reality of Stalinism, aghast at the success of Joseph McCarthy and other demagogues at home, deeply fearful of the intolerance and bigotry latent in unrestrained mass politics, intellectuals had committed themselves to the defense of what became known, in Arthur M. Schlesinger, Jr.'s felicitous phrase, as "the vital center." The task of intellectuals, some believed, was the defense of the pluralistic assumptions of American democracy and the delegitimation of the dangerous ideologies that challenged them from both the Left and the Right. In the hour of danger, all citizens were soldiers in the cause.[2]

As a member of the close-knit New York intellectual community, Hofstadter could not avoid absorbing, and indeed helping to formulate, many of these political concerns. "What started me off as an historian," he once said, "was a sense of engagement with contemporary problems. . . . I still write history out of my engagement with the present." Some of the ideas for *The Age of Reform* emerged from a celebrated 1954 conference at Columbia on the causes of McCarthyism (a conference that resulted in Daniel Bell's 1955 collection, *The New American Right*). And in the introduction to the book, Hofstadter admitted that he had focused his attention on "that side of Populism and Progressivism — particularly of Populism — which seems very strongly to foreshadow some aspects of the cranky pseudo-conservatism of our time" (p. 20).[3]

But it would be a mistake to attribute too large a role to political commitments in shaping *The Age of Reform*, or to see it — as many critics have — simply as an attempt to read McCarthyism back into the politics of the late nineteenth century. For Hofstadter, these political concerns coexisted with, and were often secondary to, a series of important theoretical and methodological innovations. Even the 1954 Columbia conference, for all its political urgency, influenced many of its participants (and particularly Hofstadter) less by its political agenda than by its illumination of new interdisciplinary approaches to the study of human motivation.

By the early 1950s, Hofstadter had been unhappy for some time with the central assumptions of the "Progressive historians," most notably Charles Beard, in whose shadow he and his contemporaries continued to work. He considered simplistic and excessively rigid the Progressive view that all political alignments derive from the economic interests of contending groups; he questioned its assumption that American history as a whole could be viewed as a persistent conflict between the "people" and the "interests." Historians, he came to believe, must find a place in the scheme of things for ideas. And they must recognize that ideas did not (and here he was challenging, among others, Vernon Parrington) always reflect material concerns.[4]

In searching for new ways to deal with the role of ideas in politics, Hofstadter drew heavily on the social sciences. Like most twentieth-century intellectuals, he was deeply affected by Freud (and by contemporary scholars employing Freudian concepts); he made use as well of the work of the German sociologist Karl Mannheim, who had redefined the concept of ideology to permit consideration of noneconomic interests. More immediately, he drew from the work of some of his own colleagues at Columbia: from the literary critic Lionel Trilling, who taught him to appreciate the importance of symbols in the human imagination (Hofstadter told friends that he had read everything Trilling had ever written); from C. Wright Mills, whose 1951 study *White Collar* defined the concept of "status" that would prove so crucial to *The Age of Reform;* and perhaps above all from Robert K. Merton, whose theory of the difference between "latent" and "manifest" functions furnished Hofstadter with a framework for incorporating the "irrational" into historical explanation. *The Age of Reform* became Hofstadter's first systematic effort to put these new approaches into practice.[5]

Hofstadter never claimed to offer a total picture of the reform movements he was examining: *The Age of Reform* was, rather, an effort to address an imbalance in historical understanding. Beard and his disciples had described populism and progressivism almost entirely in terms of clashing economic interests and had celebrated them as expressions of democracy and agents of social progress. Hofstadter did not deny the importance of economic factors, and he conceded that there was much of value in the reform tradition. But — and in this he made clear the central thrust of his argument — he pointed as well to an important strain of illusion and illiberalism in that tradition, which had made it sadly inadequate to the needs of a modern society. "I believe it will be clear," he wrote defensively in his introduction, "that what I am trying to establish is not that the Populist and Progressive movements were foolish and destructive but only that they had, like so many things in life, an ambiguous character" (p. 18). In time, however, as the ideas of the book traveled through the scholarly world, these careful qualifications ceased to be clear at all.

What primarily interested Hofstadter was what he considered a disjunction between the real and perceived interests of the men and women he was describing, a disjunction most clearly visible to him in the ideology of the Populists. American farmers, Hofstadter claimed, were by the late nineteenth century as much a part of the world of commerce and entrepreneurship as any other Americans. Yet they attempted to deny that reality and embraced instead an "agrarian myth," which encouraged them "to believe that they were not themselves an organic part of the whole order of business enterprise and speculation that flourished in the city . . . but rather the innocent pastoral victims of a conspiracy hatched in the distance" (p. 35). Populist politics, therefore, tended to express less the economic concerns of farmers than the essentially social and psychological anxieties that stemmed from the decline in their "rank in society." Instead of taking purposeful steps to adapt to the modern commercial world, of which they were already — economically — an integral part, they chose to rail defensively against it, taking refuge in a vision of an unrecapturable (and largely imagined) past.

Out of this tension between perception and reality emerged the central assumptions of Populist ideology: a dualistic view of social struggle, in which the great mass of the people stood pitted against powerful, selfish oligarchies; the "conspiracy theory of history," which attributed to these oligarchies an awesome and diabolical power; and a belief in the primacy of money, control of which had been the key to the ability of elites to subjugate the people, and control of which would be the key to a restoration of democracy. Out of that same tension came the characteristic features of Populist resentment: the preoccupation with scapegoats, the belief in ubiquitous plots, the apocalyptic vision of the future. Hence the semihysterical flailings at Wall Street, the Bank of England, cities, immigrants, and intellectuals. Hence the tinge of anti-Semitism that ran throughout the movement. ("It is not too much to say," Hofstadter wrote, "that the Greenback-Populist tradition activated most of what we have of modern popular anti-Semitism in the United States," although he was careful to add that such anti-Semitism was "entirely verbal," unaccompanied by any program of repression or violence) (pp. 61–62, 80).

Hofstadter's picture of the Populists found immediate favor among many social scientists; but within the historical profession, the interpretation was from the beginning the target of strenuous (and often vituperative) attacks. One of the first and most thoughtful critiques came in 1959 from Hofstadter's close friend C. Vann Woodward, in an influential essay, "The Populist Heritage and the Intellectual." Woodward did not single out *The Age of Reform* for criticism, but connected it with a much larger body of social science literature (among which Hofstadter's book, he claimed, stood out for its balance and sensitivity). Still, his reservations applied to *The Age of Reform* as clearly as they did to other works. The new view of populism was, he argued, fundamentally ahistorical — a deductive interpretation, based on contemporary concerns, that ignored the historical realities of the Populist insurgency, especially in the South. Other scholars made similar arguments: Walter T. K. Nugent, whose 1963 study, *The Tolerant Populists*, put Hofstadter's arguments to the test of evidence in Kansas and found little support for the allegations of nativism and xenophobia that were so central to *The Age of Reform;* Michael Rogin (a political scientist), whose 1967 book, *The Intellectuals and McCarthy*, challenged Hofstadter's implication that populism strongly foreshadowed McCarthyism.[6]

Meanwhile, other critics were offering more fundamental (and more explicitly ideological) critiques. Norman Pollack, who for a time made a virtual cottage industry out of his attacks on *The Age of Reform*, not only refuted Hofstadter's contention that the Populists were motivated by nostalgia, irrational fears, or prejudices. He also challenged the larger view of Populists as incipient capitalists working to reform but not fundamentally to alter the economic system. In fact, he argued, the Populists were forward-looking radicals who wanted not only a "democratized industrial system" but "a transformation of social values." Their critique "went beyond economic conditions to embrace the question of the individual's plight, his dehumanization, his loss of autonomy in a society which rapidly reduced him to a dependent state."[7]

Pollack was the first of a substantial group of historians whose own experiences with the Left in the 1960s led to a new appreciation for the Populist past and a new search for an authentic American radicalism within it. Foremost among them was Lawrence Goodwyn, whose *Democratic Promise: The Populist Moment in America,* published in 1976, was the first full-scale study of the movement since John D. Hicks's *The Populist Revolt* of 1931. A veteran of the civil rights movement and an admirer of the New Left, Goodwyn portrayed populism as a coherent, enlightened, and fundamentally democratic movement (indeed much of his book was devoted to his exploration of the Populists' "movement culture"), struggling to produce a cooperative, localistic alternative to the competitive, centralizing tendencies of industrial capitalism. The distinctive expressions of populism were not fevered resentments or apocalyptic warnings, but the hopeful, constructive efforts of thousands of communities to build institutions and establish values that would permit an alternative economy (and alternative value system) to survive. The failure of populism marked the end of America's best (and perhaps last) chance to construct a democratic alternative to modern, oligarchic capitalism.[8]

The post-Hofstadter studies of populism were of varying quality. Pollack's, in particular, suffered from a polemicism and an unsystematic use of sources that robbed it of any lasting credibility. But whatever their limitations, most of these works were far better rooted in the evidence than *The Age of Reform;* and their cumulative effect was, if not to demolish, at least substantially to diminish the persuasiveness of its interpretation. Critics were not, however, challenging Hofstadter on the basis of evidence alone. They were objecting, at least implicitly, to his apparent animus toward the provincialism he perceived running through the movement, his disdain for what he contemptuously called the "village mind." And they were objecting as well to what they considered his normative view of economic progress, the assumption (which lay at the heart of *The Age of Reform* and, indeed, at the heart of most of the historiography of the 1950s) that industrialization, commercialization, and centralization were at once inevitable and, on the whole, desirable; and that agrarian protest was, therefore, a futile, flailing effort to stand in the way of progress. (It is significant, perhaps, that the two groups from Hofstadter's own, urban world that he chose to equate with the Populists were the widely reviled musicians and building trades unions of New York, organizations popularly perceived to be fighting to preserve obsolete crafts regardless of the costs to society.)

Hofstadter's critics viewed populism from a fundamentally different perspective. To them, modernization was a far less happy phenomenon, a process that had exploited and degraded significant segments of the population. Industrialization did not, in this view, evolve naturally from the commercial society of the early nineteenth century; it was a revolution, which cut off large groups of Americans from the economic and emotional moorings that had given meaning to their lives. For the rural men and women who became the source of Populist strength, this transformation was particularly traumatic — not only psychologically, but economically, for what was at stake was not simply the psychic rewards of "rank in society," but the social and economic viability of a distinctive way of life. Steven Hahn's recent study of the Georgia upcountry in the late nineteenth century, for example, portrays a white yeomanry trapped in the jaws of a new commercial system of which they had never been and could never be a part. For them, populism would be not only an expression of symbolic, psychic anxieties, but also of real material interests, albeit interests in many ways antithetical to the prevailing order.[9]

The new accounts of populism, as successful as they have been in challenging Hofstadter, have also created problems of their own; and the larger debate over the nature of the agrarian revolt remains to a great degree unresolved. For one thing, none of the major studies has given sufficient attention to the significant regional differences within the movement. Hicks and Hofstadter concentrated primarily on the Midwest, Goodwyn largely on the South, Hahn on two counties in Georgia; virtually all other studies have been similarly provincial in focus. Nor have they dealt adequately with the ambivalence with which farmers appear to have responded to the new market system: the fearful hostility toward the costs of the new market economy combined with the ambitious grasping for its benefits, the simultaneous traditionalism and modernism. (Hofstadter may, in fact, have recognized this ambivalence more clearly than many of his critics, even if he distorted his picture of it by exaggerating the importance of its purely nostalgic elements.) And as James Turner has argued, one vital question has received virtually no serious attention: Why, in an economy where virtually all farmers were suffering economic difficulties, did some people become Populists while others did not? Turner suggests (on the basis of an analysis of Populist strength in Texas) that geographical isolation may have been an important factor in determining Populist tendencies — both because such isolation placed additional economic strains on struggling farmers, and because it left them bereft of the sorts of social and cultural reinforcements that might have helped reconcile them to the prevailing order. If Turner is correct, therefore, there may still be a place, even if a less central place than *The Age of Reform* suggests, for Hofstadter's emphasis on psychological anxieties, but less as the product of nostalgic mythologizing than as the result of objective conditions.[10]

Progressivism, Hofstadter argued, differed from populism in its location primarily urban), its constituency (largely middle-class professionals), and much of its program. But Hofstadter did not share the view of more recent scholars that progressivism was an impulse fundamentally different from, indeed antithetical to, populism. Instead, he portrayed the two movements as part of the same broad current of reform. The Progressives, he argued, shared with the Populists a suspicion of modern forms of economic organization, a fear of concentrated power, and perhaps above all an attachment to a vanished and unrecapturable past. And thus like the Populists, they were — despite their many important accomplishments — unable in the end to deal realistically with the problems of their age.

Hofstadter conceded that progressivism "had the adherence of a heterogeneous public whose various segments responded to various needs." But there was, he argued, a core group of Progressives "upon whose contributions the movement was politically and intellectually as well as financially dependent, and whose members did much to formulate its ideals" (p. 135). These were men (he gave scant attention to women) of the "mugwump type," located mostly in the Northeast. They enjoyed moderate wealth and longtime social standing. And they considered themselves the natural leaders of society. In the years following the Civil War, such men had looked with contempt on the corrupt and seamy world of politics and had largely withdrawn from it. But by the turn of the century they had become sufficiently alarmed by the rise to power of urban bosses and newly rich industrial titans, and sufficiently distressed at what they considered their own responsibility for having allowed it to happen, that they began to reenter the political arena and to reestablish what they believed was their rightful place as its leaders.[11]

On the surface, at least, progressivism was a phenomenon much better suited than populism to Hofstadter's mode of analysis. The Populists had mobilized in the face of genuine economic hardships; but the Progressives had operated in a climate of general prosperity, in which they themselves (as he identified them) were economically comfortable and secure. Thus the "paradox" that Hofstadter had seemed in some measure to invent for the Populists appeared real for the Progressives: the emergence of a popular reform movement unaccompanied by genuine economic grievances on the part of the reformers.

Hofstadter attempted to solve this paradox by introducing into historical studies the concept of "status," an idea he had extracted from recent work by C. Wright Mills, Seymour Martin Lipset, and other social scientists. This became, in the end, perhaps the most influential and certainly the most controversial of all his many scholarly innovations. The status model was an elaboration and refinement of ideas with which Hofstadter had been wrestling for years: the belief in "multivariate analysis" he had borrowed from Mannheim, the concern with the role of "latent" and "manifest" functions he had derived from Merton, the engagement with the psychological underpinnings of political beliefs he had taken from Freud, Lasswell, and Adorno. And while he had used the model implicitly in his discussion of the Populists, he applied it explicitly to the case of the Progressive leadership:

> It is my thesis that men of this sort . . . were Progressives not because of economic deprivations but primarily because they were victims of an upheaval in status that took place in the United States during the closing decades of the nineteenth and early years of the twentieth century. Progressivism, in short, was to a very considerable extent led by men who suffered from the events of their time not through a shrinkage in their means but through the changed pattern in the distribution of deference and power. (p. 135)

The Progressives, in short, were not engaged in "interest" or "class" politics, which Hofstadter elsewhere defined as "the clash of material aims and needs among various groups and blocs," but "status" politics, "the clash of various projective rationalizations arising from status aspirations and other personal motives."[12]

Those "projective rationalizations" did not often take such cranky or irrational forms among the Progressives as they had among the Populists (although Hofstadter did perceive a strong undercurrent of nativism and moral absolutism running through Progressive political thought). The Progressives did, however, develop a preoccupation with an imagined past no less central to their ideology than the "agrarian myth" was to the Populist mind. In a world coming to be dominated by large, impersonal organizations and bureaucracies, a world in which a few immensely wealthy men seemed to be seizing control of the economy and the society, Progressives harked back to an earlier America, one with "a rather broad diffusion of wealth, status, and power, in which the man of moderate means, especially in the many small communities, could command much deference and exert much influence" (p. 135).

It was to restore that world, to destroy the illegitimate concentrations of power that threatened it, that Progressives embarked on their various reform crusades. Muckraking journalists attacked powerful urban bosses and the great trusts. Intellectuals and professionals worked to recapture the "moral authority" to which they believed they were entitled and which they feared they had lost. Progressive politicians worked to limit the influence of party organizations and shift power to the people, who could — if properly instructed and led by an enlightened elite — be trusted to resist the destruction of liberty that the rise of organization threatened to produce:

> The American tradition had been one of unusually widespread participation of the citizen in the management of affairs, both political and economic. Now the growth of the large corporation, the labor union, and the big impenetrable political machine was clotting society into large aggregates and presenting to the unorganized citizen the prospect that all these aggregates and interests would be able to act in concert and shut out those men for whom organization was difficult or impossible. . . . The central theme of Progressivism was this revolt against the industrial discipline: the Progressive movement was the complaint of the unorganized against the consequences of organization. (pp. 215–16)

Hofstadter's picture of the Progressives was from the beginning more persuasive to historians than his picture of the Populists; and so it has remained. But it too soon became the target of important and effective critiques. Much of Hofstadter's interpretation rested on his answer to a single question: Who were the Progressives? And the most successful challenges to it, therefore, began by providing very different answers to that question. Critics did not often dispute the existence of the "displaced elites" Hofstadter described or question their credentials as Progressives.[13] They argued, rather, that such people did not constitute the whole, or even the most important segment, of the reform constituency.

David P. Thelen provided perhaps the boldest challenge by arguing that social tensions (whether the result of class or status conflicts) played almost no role in generating support for Progressive reform. Wisconsin Progressives, he argued, emerged from all classes and all social groups more or less equally; and thus the question of who the Progressives were was far less important than the question of what the Progressives wanted and what they did to achieve it. Most other studies, however, persisted in the attempt to identify a center of progressive strength and challenged Hofstadter by arguing that it lay in groups other than the "displaced elites" he described. Some located the Progressive core in groups "below" Hofstadter's old middle class; Herbert Gutman, J. Joseph Hutmacher, and John D. Buenker, for example, demonstrated how workers, immigrants, and urban machine politicians were central to some of the most important reform crusades of the era.[14] Others looked "above" Hofstadter's constituency: to the same corporate elites and agents of organization against whom Hofstadter had claimed the Progressives were reacting. Samuel P. Hays showed how upper-class business leaders dominated several municipal reform movements. Gabriel Kolko described Progressive regulatory reforms as an effort by corporate moguls to limit competition and strengthen their own economic hegemony. Robert Wiebe, the most influential of the challengers, viewed progressivism not as the nostalgic flailing of an "old" middle class, but as the purposeful efforts of members of a "new middle class," closely tied to the emerging national economy, "to fulfill its destiny through bureaucratic means." Progressivism was, in virtually all such accounts, not an effort to recapture the past, as Hofstadter had described it, but an adaptive, modernizing movement with its aim firmly fixed on the future.[15]

Ultimately, however, neither Hofstadter's "traditionalist" model of progressivism nor the "modernizing" view of some of his critics has satisfied scholars attempting to explain the enormous range and variety of early twentieth-century reform. No single class or interest group, most historians tend now to argue (accepting at least some of Thelen's contentions), can lay exclusive claim to the mantle of progressivism, just as no single ideology can account for the sweep of its concerns. Instead of identifying a single, dominant Progressive constituency or a clear, common Progressive program, scholars now tend to argue for a more pluralistic view that leaves room for many different groups and many different impulses. Some have gone so far as to challenge the existence of a Progressive movement at all; others have attempted to divide progressivism into two distinct impulses; still others have begun to look beyond the particular issues that dominated Progressive rhetoric and to place the phenomenon in the context of a much larger transformation of American political life.[16] As the debate continues, still without any sign of resolution, one thing does seem clear: that Hofstadter's impressively coherent picture of the Progressive mind is inadequate as a description of anything but a single segment of the Progressive constituency, a segment far less "strategic" in the larger scheme of reform than he claimed.

Like his picture of populism, Hofstadter's analysis of progressivism suffered from its excessive reliance on an explanatory theory — the idea of the dichotomy between "status" and "interest" politics — inadequately tested against the evidence. But it suffered as well from limitations in the theory itself. At the heart of Hofstadter's notion of status was the idea he had borrowed from Merton of "functional" as opposed to "nonfunctional" behavior. When people behaved functionally, they responded directly to their material interests. But there were, alas, times when they behaved nonfunctionally, when they responded not to economic but psychic needs, and when their behavior became symbolic and self-defeating. The dichotomy between "interest politics" and "status politics" accepted, in other words, the Progressive historians' assumption that all rational political behavior was rooted in economic concerns. What it rejected was the Progressives' belief that political behavior always *was* rational. The concept of "status," therefore, became a concept oddly similar to the orthodox Marxist idea of "false consciousness," attributing to politics not clearly rooted in class an aberrant, illegitimate quality.

Scholars who shared Hofstadter's dissatisfaction with the economic determinism of the Progressives and who absorbed his excitement over the ways in which psychological and sociological tools could deepen historical understanding faced a dilemma. Was it possible to accept the existence of noneconomic factors in history without accepting the rigid and pejorative picture of those factors that the "interests-status" dichotomy suggested? One solution to that dilemma was suggested by Joseph Gusfield, in his 1963 study of the American temperance movement, *Symbolic Crusade.* Gusfield shared Hofstadter's assumption that there was an identifiable difference between class and status politics; but he rejected the idea that status concerns were in any way less real or less rational than interest ones. David Thelen proposed another solution by contending that there was a realm of political concern that existed independent of either class or status tensions, that, in Wisconsin at least, "issues of corporate irresponsibility and tax evasion" touched virtually everyone, not only in terms of economic self interest but in terms of basic concepts of justice and fairness; such issues thus "transcended the social barriers that had divided individuals and groups" in the past.[17]

What Gusfield and Thelen suggested was perhaps the most fundamental question about the status model: Is it possible to distinguish clearly between economic and noneconomic behavior? Are battles over status and power really unrelated to economic interests? There are, of course, times when politics moves in patterns that do not reflect the economic concerns of the actors, even when people act in opposition to their own material interests. But there are also times in which battles over status and battles over class are the same battles. Workers fighting for control of the workplace, David Montgomery has shown, fought not only for the psychic rewards of greater autonomy and prestige, but for the ability to protect their economic interests. Agrarians battling the rise of corporate hegemony, many scholars of populism have argued, struggled not only against cultural obsolescence, but against the economic obsolescence that they perceived — correctly — would accompany it. Even Hofstadter's "displaced elites" were not, surely, unaware that their own economic standing was rapidly deteriorating, if not in absolute terms then certainly relative to the great new fortunes they could see springing up around them; and any definition of material interests that does not leave room for the sense of relative deprivation excludes a large portion of the economic concerns of twentieth-century Americans.[18]

In the last years of his life, when Hofstadter attempted on occasion to evaluate the most important achievements of his remarkable scholarly career, he expressed particular pride in having helped to introduce "complexity" to the study of history. It was a real and important contribution; in the wake of Hofstadter's work, few historians attempted to fit all historical causation into a neat pattern of clashing economic interests. But Hofstadter worried that this "keener sense of the structural complexity of our society in the past" might produce as well a paralysis of intellect and a "political immobility," that both historical study and political thought would descend into a crippling nominalism that would destroy the possibilities for coherent understanding or effective action.[19] Perhaps it had been that fear that led Hofstadter and others to fit their ideas of complexity into the restrictive terms of the "status-interest" model, to replace the simplistic determinism of the Progressive historians with a similarly rigid, if less one-dimensional framework of their own. For Hofstadter had identified a dilemma fundamental to historical studies, one that remains — and will perhaps forever remain — unresolved. Is it possible for scholars to take into account the enormous range of factors that affect human motivation and historical causation and still bring coherence to their picture of the past?

A "total history" of human experience will, clearly, remain forever beyond the grasp of scholars. But thanks in large part to Hofstadter's work — in *The Age of Reform* and elsewhere — it seems unlikely, as he once feared, that "the very idea of complexity will come under fire once again," or that historians will soon argue "that most things in life and in history are not complex but really quite simple." The repudiation by historians of many of the central ideas of Hofstadter's portrait of populism and progressivism is, therefore, to a large degree a measure of his success. For it is the inadequacy of the "status-interest" model's allowance for complexity, not the complexity itself, that has proved its most crippling feature.[20]

Hofstadter's analyses of populism and progressivism, controversial as they were, moved immediately to the center of scholarly debate and framed the discussion of both phenomena for decades. His brief analysis of the New Deal met resistance from the beginning and has never had much impact on subsequent interpretations. And yet while the central sections of *The Age of Reform* now seem less persuasive than they once did, the interpretation of the New Deal seems in certain ways more compelling than its earlier critics were willing to admit.

Populism and progressivism had, Hofstadter argued, been part of a long continuum of reform. The New Deal, he claimed, was a sharp break with that continuum, largely unaffected (and hence largely unmarred) by the backward-looking moralism of its predecessors, committed instead to the solution of immediate, debilitating economic problems. No grand strategies or philosophical visions there; Roosevelt and his circle were engaged in a "chaos of experimentation" (p. 307).

Although the New Dealers paid lip service to old Progressive verities, in practice they "bypassed, sidestepped" the old Progressive issues. The New Deal made no effort to combat the political machines; instead, Roosevelt attempted to conciliate and forge alliances with them. The New Deal "never developed a clear or consistent line on business consolidation"; the issue of monopoly became secondary to a "restless groping for a means to bring recovery." By the late 1930s, the New Deal, without ever expressing (or even recognizing) how sharply it was breaking with the reform past, had revolutionized American liberalism. It had stripped it of its old nostalgic moralism and had added to it "a social-democratic tinge that had never before been present in American reform movements." In the future, liberals would be less concerned with "entrepreneurial" reform and would be committed instead to social legislation: "social security, unemployment insurance, wages and hours, and housing." The New Deal, Hofstadter wrote, "represented the triumph of economic emergency and human needs over inherited notions and inhibitions" (pp. 307–16).

There are many problems with this portrait, as critics were quick to point out almost as soon as the book appeared. Hofstadter clearly underestimated the degree to which Progressive ideology had influenced New Deal policy-makers – in part, perhaps, because his view of Progressive ideology had been so narrow and incomplete.[21] At the same time, however, Hofstadter had touched on something important when he claimed that liberal ideology emerged from the 1930s fundamentally transformed. That it did so was not, perhaps, because the New Dealers themselves had openly repudiated the grip of the past in favor of pragmatic experimentation; it was because, in the course of more than a decade of political and ideological pulling and tugging, new ideas had slowly and haltingly emerged in response to the failure of old ones to deal with pressing realities. The antimonopoly impulse had ceased to play more than an occasional rhetorical role in reform ideology; the planning ideal had shifted its focus away from the structure of capitalism and toward Keynesian and social welfare goals. The language of liberalism, and the substantive direction of liberalism, had changed. Hofstadter's explanation of how and why was cursory and inadequate; but his identification of that change – and his challenge to the then prevailing view of a long, continuous stream of reform culminating in the New Deal and validating postwar liberal goals [22] — was an important and generally unappreciated accomplishment.

Critics of modern historiography have spent a large and perhaps inordinate amount of time and energy arguing over whether Hofstadter was truly a member of the "consensus school" that came to dominate historical writing in the 1950s. The answer, of course, depends on how that school is defined. [23] Hofstadter certainly shared, and indeed was among the first to state, the "consensus" assumption that economic conflict was not the dominant factor in American history, that beneath the disputes and controversies of the past (and, presumably, the present) lay a "common climate of American opinion," a "general framework" of shared ideas resting on "a belief in the rights of property, the philosophy of economic individualism, the value of competition," and a general acceptance of industrial capitalism. [24] Conflicts that seemed on the surface profound, among them the reform battles of the Populists and Progressives, had taken place within a relatively narrow ideological framework. Hence, even the most strenuous critics of the American political and economic structure could not (or would not) envision a genuinely radical alternative to it; and they vented their frustrations, therefore, not through attacks on bourgeois capitalism, but through attachment to "symbols" and "projective rationalizations."

At times in his work (although only passingly in *The Age of Reform*), Hofstadter attempted to qualify his attachment to these consensus assumptions. He pointed to those parts of the American past (the Revolution, the Civil War, racial and religious conflict) that could not be adequately explained in this way; and he conceded that "it is a valid comment on the limits of consensus history to insist that in one form or another conflict finally does remain, and ought to remain, somewhere near the center of our focus of attention." [25] Yet Hofstadter's purpose in most of his own work, and certainly in *The Age of Reform*, was not an effort to place conflict "near the center of our focus of attention." It was precisely the opposite: to refute "the almost obsessive concern with conflict as the central theme of historical writing" that his generation of scholars had inherited from their Progressive forebears. [26] Hofstadter was too sensitive and subtle a historian not to recognize the limitations of the approach. But in at least one sense, he stands firmly within, indeed very near the center of, the consensus school.

Hofstadter did not, however, always share, and at times strenuously opposed, another distinguishing assumption of many consensus scholars: the assumption that this "common climate of opinion," this lack of fundamental conflict, was a good and necessary thing that accounted for America's stability, freedom, and progress. This celebratory use of consensus is most commonly identified with the work of Daniel Boorstin,[27] but a similar (if usually more muted) tone can be found in the work of innumerable scholars of the 1950s and 1960s. Only rarely, however, can it be found in the work of Richard Hofstadter. It may be too much to say, as Arthur Schlesinger, Jr. did in a 1969 essay, that Hofstadter viewed consensus from a "radical perspective . . . and deplored it." But it is certainly true that he viewed it "from the outside," with considerable skepticism, and with occasional alarm.[28] He was not, of course, in any basic sense a critic of American capitalism or American democracy; he was fundamentally unsympathetic to the alternatives. He did, however, recognize that the narrow range of acceptable opinion in American politics, and the centrality within that range of the acquisitive values of competitive capitalism, exacted a significant price — both from the nation's public discourse and from the private lives of its people. The pragmatic opportunism that had played so central a role in shaping American institutions and American values had certain attractions; but it had failed, he believed, to provide a philosophically consistent or morally compelling basis for democratic politics.[29] A society whose greatest political triumph was the New Deal — that stumbling, chaotic exercise in political and economic self-preservation, unconnected to any coherent philosophy or moral vision — was not a society in which a sensitive humanist could take unambiguous pride.

Hofstadter was, in the end, a man caught between two competing, and perhaps incompatible, visions of society. As a scholar committed to the intellectual life and to the tolerant, cosmopolitan values he believed that life represented, he mistrusted the politics of unrestrained popular will and admired the conservative, pluralistic character of American life for providing protections against the far less attractive, far more menacing alternatives. Yet as a twentieth-century man sensitive to the unfulfilled yearnings of many of his world's and his nation's people, he could not help wishing, even if without real hope or definition, for something more. Perhaps that was why, in looking back upon America's past and ahead to its future, in one of his last published essays, he could summon up finally only grudging praise and tempered optimism:

When one considers American history as a whole, it is hard to think of any very long period in which it could be said that the country has been consistently well governed. And yet its political system is, on the whole, a resilient and well-seasoned one, and on the strength of its history one must assume that it can summon enough talent and good will to cope with its afflictions. To cope with them — but not, I think, to master them in any thoroughly decisive or admirable fashion. The nation seems to slouch onward into its uncertain future like some huge inarticulate beast, too much attainted by wounds and ailments to be robust, but too strong and resourceful to succumb.[30]

Alan Brinkley, Department of History, Harvard University, is the author of "Writing the History of Contemporary America: Dilemmas and Challenges," Daedalus 113 (1984): 121–42.

I am grateful to Daniel Aaron, Richard L. McCormick, and Daniel Singal for their perceptive comments on drafts of this article.

1. Robert Wiebe, "Views But No Vista," *The Progressive* 33 (1969): 47.

2. Arthur M. Schlesinger, Jr., *The Vital Center* (1949). For a thoughtful assessment of Hofstadter's political and intellectual assumptions, and of the role they played in shaping his scholarship, see Daniel Joseph Singal, "Beyond Consensus: Richard Hofstadter and American Historiography," *American Historical Review* 89 (1984): 976–81. Singal describes Hofstadter as a historical modernist, whose outlook reflected a set of values he, and others, have described as "cosmopolitanism" – an essentially urban cast of mind and one that attributed particular importance to such worldly values as tolerance of diversity and skepticism of inherited faiths. Hofstadter himself spoke frequently of his reverence for the skeptical, relativistic world of scholarship and – sometimes by implication, sometimes explicitly – of his mistrust of provincialism. For other discussions of the emergence of this "cosmopolitan ideal," see Terry A. Cooney, "Cosmopolitan Values and the Identification of Reaction: *Partisan Review* in the 1930s," *Journal of American History* 68 (1981): 580–98; and David A. Hollinger, "Ethnic Diversity, Cosmopolitanism and the Emergence of the American Liberal Intelligentsia," *American Quarterly* 27 (1975): 133–51. Richard Pells attempts to place Hofstadter (and *The Age of Reform* in particular) in the context of the intellectual history of the 1950s in *The Liberal Mind in a Conservative Age* (1985), pp. 150–55 and ch. 3 *passim*.

3. David Hawke, "Interview: Richard Hofstadter," *History* 3 (1960): 136; Daniel Bell, ed., *The New American Right* (1955).

4. See, e.g., Charles A. and Mary Beard, *The Rise of American Civilization* (1927); and Vernon L. Parrington, *Main Currents of American Thought*, 3 vols. (1927–1930).

5. Karl Mannheim, *Ideology and Utopia: An Introduction to the Sociology of Knowledge*, trans. Louis Wirth and Edward Shils (1957), esp. pp. 58–70; Lionel Trilling, "Reality in America," *The Liberal Imagination* (1950), pp. 3–21; C. Wright Mills, *White Collar* (1951), pp. 239–58 and *passim*; Robert K. Merton, *Social Theory and Social Structure*, enlarged ed. (1968), pp. 73–118. Hofstadter acknowledged his debts to these and other social scientists in his essay "History and the Social Sciences," in Fritz Stern, ed., *The Varieties of History: From Voltaire to the Present* (1956), pp. 359–70 and in the introduction to *The Age of Reform*, p. 13. Fuller discussions of the importance of Hofstadter's interdisciplinary interests can be found in Singal, "Beyond Consensus," pp. 986–88; Daniel Walker Howe and Peter Elliott Finn, "Richard Hofstadter: The Ironies of an American Historian," *Pacific Historical Review* 43 (1974): 7–11; Richard Gillam, "Richard Hofstadter, C. Wright Mills, and 'the Critical Ideal,'" *The American Scholar* 57 (1977–78): 72–73, 79–81; and Stanley Elkins and Eric McKitrick, "Richard Hofstadter: A Progress," in *The Hofstadter Aegis* (1974), pp. 309–10, 317–22.

6. C. Vann Woodward, "The Populist Heritage and the Intellectual," *The Burden of Southern History* (1968), pp. 141–66 (originally published in *The American Scholar* in 1959). Rogin's argument involved, as well, a much broader critique of the pluralistic assumptions that dominated American intellectual life and a charge that the work of Hofstadter and others represented an antidemocratic elitism.

7. Norman Pollack, *The Populist Response to Industrial America* (1962). See also the following essays by Pollack: "Hofstadter on Populism: A Critique of 'The Age of Reform,'" *Journal of Southern History* 26 (1960): 478–500; "The Myth of Populist Anti-Semitism," *American Historical Review* 68 (1962): 76–80; and "Fear of Man: Populism, Authoritarianism, and the Historian," *Agricultural History* 39 (1965): 59–67, from which the quoted passages are drawn (p. 59). Rejoinders include Oscar Handlin, "Reconsidering the Populists," *Agricultural History* 39 (1965): 68–74, and Irwin Unger, "Critique of Norman Pollack's 'Fear of Man,'" ibid.: 75–80. On the especially sensitive question of Populist anti-Semitism, see, in addition to the Pollack and Handlin essays above, Handlin, "American Views of the Jew at the Opening of the Twenti-

eth Century," *Publication of the American Jewish Historical Society* 40 (1951): 323–44; and John Higham, "Anti-Semitism in the Gilded Age: A Reinterpretation," *Mississippi Valley Historical Review* 43 (1957): 559–79.

8. Bruce Palmer, in *Man Over Money: The Southern Populist Critique of American Capitalism* (1980), offered an even starker statement of some of Goodwyn's assumptions, emphasizing the Populist critique of the acquisitive individualism of American society.

9. Steven Hahn, *The Roots of Southern Populism: Yeoman Farmers and the Transformation of the Georgia Upcountry, 1850–1890* (1983), esp. pp. 1–10, 137–69, 269–89.

10. James Turner, "Understanding the Populists," *Journal of American History* 67 (1980): 354–73. Martin Ridge, "Populism Redux: John D. Hicks and *The Populist Revolt*," *Reviews in American History* 13 (1983): 142–54, offers an overview of Populist historiography.

11. Hofstadter's portrait of the Progressives drew from (although it did not always fully coincide with) earlier studies by George Mowry and Alfred D. Chandler, both of whom had emphasized the relatively affluent, middle-class origins of reformers, hence raising a challenge to the prevailing stereotype of reformers as tribunes of the common man. See George Mowry, *The California Progressives* (1951) and Alfred D. Chandler, "The Origins of Progressive Leadership," in Elting Morison, ed., *The Letters of Theodore Roosevelt* vol. 8 (1954), pp. 1462–65.

12. Hofstadter, "The Pseudo-Conservative Revolt," in Daniel Bell, ed., *The Radical Right* (1964), p. 84. This is a revised edition of *The New American Right* (1955). Hofstadter's essay appears as well in his *The Paranoid Style in American Politics and Other Essays* (1965), where the quoted passage can be found on p. 53. See also Paula Fass, "Richard Hofstadter," *Dictionary of Literary Biography* 17 (1983), pp. 219–22.

13. Richard B. Sherman, however, did raise questions about the correlation between social standing and Progressive tendencies. In a study of political leaders in Massachusetts, he found that those who opposed the Progressives came from the same social background as the reformers. "If there was a status revolution," he asked, "how do we explain the difference in reaction to it?" See "The Status Revolution and Massachusetts Progressive Leadership," *Political Science Quarterly* 78 (1963): 59–65.

14. David P. Thelen, "Social Tensions and the Origins of Progressivism," *Journal of American History* 56 (1969): 323–41; Thelen, *The New Citizenship: Origins of Progressivism in Wisconsin, 1885–1900* (1972), *passim;* J. Joseph Huthmacher, "Urban Liberalism and the Age of Reform," *Mississippi Valley Historical Review* 59 (1962): 231–41, and *Senator Robert F. Wagner and the Rise of Urban Liberalism* (1968), chs. 2–3; Herbert G. Gutman, "Protestantism and the American Labor Movement: The Christian Spirit in the Gilded Age," in *Work, Culture, and Society in Industrializing America* (1976), pp. 79–117; John D. Buenker, "The Urban Political Machine and the Seventeenth Amendment," *Journal of American History* 56 (1969): 305–22. See also Richard Abrams, *Conservatism in a Progressive Era: Massachusetts Politics, 1900–1912* (1964), pp. 132–33, which identifies the working-class Irish as the truly reform-minded "insurgent" groups in Massachusetts.

15. Samuel P. Hays, "The Politics of Reform in Municipal Government in the Progressive Era," *Pacific Northwest Quarterly* 55 (1964): 159–69; Gabriel Kolko, *The Triumph of Conservatism* (1963); Robert Wiebe, *The Search for Order, 1877–1920* (1967), p. 166 and *passim.* In an earlier study, *Businessmen and Reform: A Study of the Progressive Movement* (1962), Wiebe argued, like Kolko, that business leaders had been at the forefront of Progressive reform efforts, although he was more careful than Kolko to distinguish among different segments of the business community.

16. See, e.g., Peter G. Filene, "An Obituary for the Progressive Movement," *American Quarterly* 22 (1970): 20–34; and John D. Buenker, "The Progressive Era: A Search for a Synthesis," *Mid-America* 51 (1969): 175–93, both of whom attack the notion of a Progressive "movement." The work of Richard L. McCormick on the rise of a politics of interest groups to replace the older politics of party is particularly important. See, especially, *From Realignment to Reform: Political Change in New York State, 1893–1910* (1981). A particularly valuable discussion of the many-sided debate over the nature of progressivism may be found in Daniel Rodgers, "In Search of Progressivism," *Reviews in American History* 10 (1982): 113–32.

17. Joseph R. Gusfield, *Symbolic Crusade: Status Politics and the American Temperance Movement* (1963), esp. pp. 1–24, 166–88; Thelen, *The New Citizenship*, pp. 2–3, 309–10; Thelen, "Social Tensions," pp. 323–30. See also Elkins and McKitrick, "Richard Hofstadter," pp. 338–42.

18. David Montgomery, *Workers' Control in America: Studies in the History of Work, Technology, and Labor Struggles* (1979); Hahn, *The Roots of Southern Populism*; Goodwyn, *Democratic Promise*. An early effort to express this objection, although one weakened by its stridency, is William Appleman Williams, "The Age of Re-Forming History," *The Nation* (June 30, 1956), pp. 552–54.

19. Hofstadter, *The Progressive Historians: Turner, Beard, Parrington* (1968), p. 466.

20. Ibid. For a provocative discussion of this and other dilemmas facing modern historians, see Bernard Bailyn, "The Challenge of Modern Historiography," *American Historical Review* 87 (1982): 1–24.

21. See, esp., Ellis Hawley, *The New Deal and the Problem of Monopoly: A Study in Economic Ambivalence* (1966). Otis Graham, *Encore for Reform: The Old Progressives and the New Deal* (1967) provides a different perspective on the role of Progressive ideology in the 1930s.

22. See Eric Goldman, *Rendezvous with Destiny: A History of Modern American Reform* (1952).

23. The most thoughtful efforts to define consensus historiography have come from John Higham, who first gave the school its name in his famous article "The Cult of the 'American Consensus': Homogenizing Our History," *Commentary* (February 1959), pp. 93–100. He has since revised and moderated this initial assessment in *History: Professional Scholarship in America* (1965), pp. 212–32.

24. Hofstadter first expressed what became the basic assumptions of "consensus history" in his brief preface to *The American Political Tradition* (1948), pp. v–xi.

25. Hofstadter, *The Progressive Historians*, p. 458.

26. Hofstadter, "History and Sociology in the United States," in Hofstadter and Seymour Martin Lipset, eds., *Sociology and History: Methods* (1968), p. 18.

27. See, e.g., Boorstin, *The Genius of American Politics* (1953) and *The Americans*, 3 vols. (1958–73).

28. Arthur M. Schlesinger, Jr., "Richard Hofstadter," in Marcus Cunliffe and Robin W. Winks, eds., *Pastmasters: Some Essays on American Historians* (1969), p. 289. Hofstadter offered a series of ambiguous assessments of his own of the consensus school, and of his place within it; see, e.g., "Communication," *Journal of the History of Ideas* 15 (1954): 328, and *The Progressive Historians* (1968), pp. 437–66.

29. In this, he shared many of the reservations expressed by Louis Hartz in *The Liberal Tradition in America: An Interpretation of American Political Thought Since the Revolution* (1955).

30. Hofstadter, "Reflections on Violence in the United States," in Hofstadter and Michael Wallace, eds., *American Violence: A Documentary History* (1970), p. 43.

THE AGE OF JACKSON: AFTER FORTY YEARS

Donald B. Cole

It is apropos in 1985 to be reconsidering Arthur M. Schlesinger, Jr.'s *The Age of Jackson,* for once again we have a popular older president in the White House – a horseback-riding, pugnacious president, loved by his friends, detested by his foes, who rode into the capital from the West determined to reform the government and return the nation to the ideals of a bygone era. Once again we have an underestimated president, written off by his opponents (even by some of his supporters) as an ignorant man with little chance of controlling the government or accomplishing much, who in his first five years won victory after victory – so many that he was able to change a number of the country's established institutions. Once again we have a president who wrapped himself in the flag and made his people proud to be Americans, who lashed out at the nation's foes and ushered in an era of nationalism, leading many to fear the likelihood of military adventures. The similarities even extend to each having been shot at by a would-be assassin. What better time to review the *Age of Jackson* than midway through the Age of Reagan.

But there are more fundamental reasons for taking another look at this book. When it was published in 1945, the political, economic, and social institutions that Schlesinger described emerging a century earlier during the Age of Jackson had reached the height of their power and prestige. Abroad, American democracy had triumphed over totalitarianism, American industrial capitalism was soon to dominate Europe through the Marshall Plan, and throughout the world scores of new nations were striving to emulate the American way, leading Henry Luce, the nationalistic publisher of *Time* and *Life,* to boast that the twentieth century would be known as the American century. At home, liberalism and the Democratic party were ascendant as the New Deal and World War II showed what democracy, industry, moderate reform, and restrained Keynesian economics could accomplish. American social groups had shown a remarkable willingness to suppress antagonisms and work cooperatively toward common goals as women, racial and ethnic minorities, and the economically deprived joined hands with those better off to end the depression and defeat the Nazis and the Japanese. It was an exciting time to be an American and a Democrat; for much of the next twenty years the United States would dominate the world, and Democrats would dominate the United States.

Forty years later the price of the hubris of those postwar years is being paid, and American institutions formed during the Age of Jackson and at their apogee in 1945 are under siege. Despite the cheer and optimism radiating from the White House no one is certain that American liberalism, our political system, industrialism, and society will ever be as strong again. With liberalism now more an epithet than a slogan, with national party organizations and state and city machines becoming anachronisms in an era of mass media, with the presidency often considered as much a menace as a benefit, with industrial America and its powerful labor unions giving way to a service economy with less union control, and with the social modus vivendi of the nineteenth and twentieth centuries no longer viable, the world of Andrew Jackson and Martin Van Buren, of Franklin Roosevelt and Harry Truman may be coming to an end – a sobering time to reread the *Age of Jackson*.

Americans in 1945 were quick to applaud this book describing the rise of American democracy. When the *Age of Jackson* was published in September of that year, a month after the Japanese surrender, it was an immediate success. It sold 90,000 copies (at five dollars apiece) the first year, including those distributed by the Book Find Club, was serialized in the *New Republic,* and twice became a successful paperback. This reviewer even received a copy while serving on an attack transport in the Pacific. Highly acclaimed by scholars as it was popular with the public, the *Age of Jackson* won the Pulitzer prize for history in 1946.

Arthur M. Schlesinger, Jr., was discharged from his duties overseas in the Office of Strategic Services near the end of 1945, too late to be on hand for the publication of his book, but in time to receive the Pulitzer. His background is well known. Son of the famed Harvard historian Arthur M. Schlesinger and descendant through his mother of the great nineteenth-century historian George Bancroft, "young Arthur" inherited his historical skills from both sides of the family. After graduating from Harvard in 1938, he studied at Cambridge University and published his first book, *Orestes A. Brownson: A Pilgrim's Progress* (1939), before returning to Harvard for three years as a Junior Fellow, during which time he wrote the *Age of Jackson*. When it appeared he was only twenty-seven years of age.

The comparison between Schlesinger and George Bancroft is striking. Born into families of learning, both were sent off to Phillips Exeter before matriculating at Harvard, and then continuing their studies abroad. Neither received the doctorate as we know it today, Bancroft because he predated such studies and Schlesinger because his three years as a Junior Fellow were in lieu of the ordinary Ph. D. program. Commencing their historical writing at an early age — Bancroft at thirty-three, Schlesinger at twenty-one — during the presidency of Andrew Jackson and the New Deal of Franklin Roosevelt, respectively, both became partisan, active Democrats, interpreting the events they chronicled from the perspective of their party. For Bancroft the American Revolution was a prelude to Jacksonian Democracy; for Schlesinger Jacksonian Democracy, including the contributions of Bancroft, was a prelude to the New Deal. Both rose to high office, Bancroft as Secretary of the Navy under James K. Polk, and Schlesinger as special assistant to John F. Kennedy. In their writing both covered great sweeps of history — Bancroft, the colonial period, the Revolution, and the Constitutional Convention, and Schlesinger, the national period from 1815 to 1860 in the *Age of Jackson* and the presidencies of Franklin Roosevelt and Kennedy in later works. They were both so well known for so many years as leading advocates of democracy and liberalism that their writing took on a comfortable nostalgic flavor.

The *Age of Jackson* commanded great attention because it presented a new interpretation of Jacksonian Democracy. Rejecting the standard Progressive view that Jacksonianism was a sectional movement led by western frontiersmen, Schlesinger argued that the movement should be "regarded as a problem not of sections but of classes," and that its ideas came from eastern workingmen and intellectuals (p. 263). Schlesinger later insisted that "*The Age of Jackson* [did] not argue that there was 'a class conflict between great capitalists on the one side, and a mass of propertyless wage-earners on the other,'" but he believed that Jacksonian Democracy was a "struggle of non-business groups against business domination of the government" on behalf of urban workers.[1] By giving a new twist to the old Progressive view, he provoked a fierce debate that dominated the study of the early national period for the next quarter-century.

The early reviewers appreciated the significance of this new interpretation. Allan Nevins, whose 1,850-word review appeared on page one of *The New York Times Book Review*, wrote that such an investigation of the ideas behind the "Jacksonian revolution" was long overdue.[2] While historians had carefully "sifted and examined" the ideas behind the American Revolution and the Constitution, they had ignored the Jacksonians, possibly because they had been distracted by the "rough and tumble" of the era. Instead of focusing on party battles and western agrarians Schlesinger had turned his attention to intellectual history and eastern radicals such as William M. Gouge,

Orestes Brownson, Theodore Sedgwick, and William Cullen Bryant. Perhaps anticipating his own study of the conflict in American society in the era of the Civil War, Nevins praised Schlesinger for treating the Jackson movement "as the outgrowth not of frontier development but of new economic strains and tensions" and for recognizing that the movement "brought up from the depths of American life a powerful set of new forces" that "revitalized our politics by the impact of profound impulses from below." Nevins's influential review helped establish the *Age of Jackson* as a historiographical breakthrough.

Other reviewers from the Progressive school were equally flattering. Bernard DeVoto, who had already examined the accomplishments of Young Hickory, James K. Polk, in *The Year of Decision: 1846* (1943), and who had been mentioned by Schlesinger in his acknowledgements, applauded the "richness, the brilliance," and "the pioneering novelty" of the book. Merle Curti in *Nation* was convinced that "class conflict figured more substantially in American development than Americans have been wont to think." George Fort Milton, who had written a defense of a later Jacksonian, Andrew Johnson, was as ready as Schlesinger to accept radical Jacksonian rhetoric at face value. The Jacksonians, said Milton in his review, "hammered home the deep-rooted conflict between the producing and the non-producing classes," and they demanded, in Van Buren's words, that labor receive the "full enjoyment of the fruits of its industry." [3]

Such approval by fellow Progressive historians was to be expected, but similar praise from Richard Hofstadter in the *New Republic* was a bit surprising. Hofstadter had recently published "William Leggett, Spokesman of Jacksonian Democracy," in which he argued that the Jacksonians were more interested in equality of economic opportunity than they were in class leveling, and his chapter on Jackson in *The American Political Tradition and the Men Who Made It* (1948) would soon become the standard criticism of Schlesinger's interpretation. In 1945, however, Hofstadter congratulated Schlesinger for his "intensive scholarship," "mature insight," and "analytical thinking," and said the book offered "relief from more partisan myth-making histories in the manner of Claude Bowers." In the review Hofstadter did show signs of departing from Schlesinger by insisting that the Jacksonians were not united against the property-owning class, but were divided into a variety of economic groups — inflationary westerners and hard-money easterners, middle-class southern planters and working-class eastern radicals. This emphasis on "significant cleavages" within the Democratic party led to the chapters in *The American Political Tradition* entitled "Andrew Jackson and Liberal Capitalism" and "John C. Calhoun, the Marx of the Master Class."

In actuality Schlesinger's work was not as original as his reviewers made it out to be. At about the same time that Charles Beard wrote his *Economic In-*

terpretation of the Constitution of the United States (1913) and J. R. Commons and others their *Documentary History of American Industrial Society* (1910), the Marxist writer Algie Simons published his *Social Forces in American History* (1911), in which he explained Jacksonian Democracy as an eastern labor movement. A decade later Arthur M. Schlesinger, Sr., called attention to the same movement in his influential book of essays, *New Viewpoints in American History* (1922), and gave credit to Willis Mason West, who had explored the subject in his *American History and Government* (1913). The similarity in viewpoint of Schlesinger and son can be seen in the following exuberant statement in *New Viewpoints*:

> The labor movement reached its floodtide while Andrew Jackson was in office. Indeed, he could not have been elected president if the votes of the laboring men of the Northeast had not been added to those of his followers in the Southeast and the West. Jackson capitalized this support when he waged battle against the great financial monopoly, the United States Bank, and gave express recognition to its demands when he established the ten-hour workday in the federal shipyards in 1836.

But the eastern labor thesis did not take hold, and during the twenties and the depression, historians, including even the Beards in *The Rise of American Civilization* (1927), continued to follow Frederick Jackson Turner in depicting Jacksonianism as a western movement and American history as a struggle between sections rather than classes. Young Schlesinger changed all that.

Reread in 1985, *The Age of Jackson* is almost as striking for what it is *not* as for what it *is*. Although the best-known book ever written about the era of Andrew Jackson, it is not a book about Jackson himself. Aside from an eight-page sketch of Jackson's early career, there is little direct treatment of the Old Hero, and the index carries more references to Martin Van Buren than to Jackson. In addition there is surprisingly little analysis of Jackson's eight years in office, for Schlesinger ignores the nullification crisis, the tariff bills, the Maysville veto, and Jackson's diplomacy. He, furthermore, gives almost no attention to women, blacks, and American Indians. In an index of some 1,100 citations only ten are to women, eight of which are brief references in which the woman is used to describe a male politician. Only the notorious Fanny Wright and Peggy Eaton receive more than passing attention. Although there is a lengthy discussion of the political issue of slavery, there is little concern for the social issue of race. Indians are omitted completely; even the Indian Removal Act fails to make it. The son of Arthur Schlesinger, Sr., who pioneered in the field of social history, did not show much interest in that field in *The Age of Jackson*.

The reason of course is that Arthur Schlesinger, Jr., is an intellectual historian not a social historian, and *The Age of Jackson* is a work of intellectual history. The book consists of six closely-tied essays, all devoted to developing the eastern labor interpretation. The author begins with a graceful essay sketching in the background of Jacksonian Democracy, with a great deal of attention to the Old Republicans John Randolph, John Taylor, and Nathaniel Macon. He follows with an extended description of the Bank War, interpreted in terms of class conflict, and with that he is done with the administration of Andrew Jackson. Next comes Jacksonian Democracy at the local level — the Loco Focos, the Albany Regency, and the Massachusetts Democratic Party — after which he returns to the struggle over banking, especially the independent treasury bill, during Van Buren's term in office. Schlesinger concludes with a lengthy analysis of Jacksonian Democracy as manifested in such nonpolitical areas as law, industry, religion, and literature, and a narrative account of the Jacksonians during the coming of the Civil War.

Instead of allowing Andrew Jackson to dominate the book, Schlesinger presents his age through scores of short biographical sketches — a technique that he used again with equal success in *The Age of Roosevelt*. In the first two hundred pages of *The Age of Jackson* there are at least fifty sketches of prominent figures, starting with Thomas Jefferson and concluding with Henry D. Gilpin. What is particularly striking is Schlesinger's fascination with Martin Van Buren. Long before the Little Magician would receive serious scholarly attention, Schlesinger describes him as "the first national leader really to take advantage of the growing demand of the people for more active participation in the decisions of government," and praises him for furnishing "the practical mechanisms which transferred Jackson's extraordinary popularity into the instruments of power" and without which "the gains of Jacksonian Democracy would have been impossible" (pp. 50, 52). Schlesinger makes Van Buren, not Jackson, the hero of *The Age of Jackson*, devoting more space to Van Buren's one term than he does to Jackson's two. The high point of the book and of Jacksonian Democracy comes on July 4, 1840, when Van Buren signed the independent treasury bill, which separated the government from the nation's banks and which Francis Preston Blair called the second Declaration of Independence. According to Schlesinger, Van Buren was a radical Loco Foco who won the support of "nearly all the radicals of the early thirties," and led the Democratic party and the nation to the left (p. 261). The hyperbole in this assessment is evident from the fact that these same radicals in 1836 backed Van Buren's running mate Richard M. Johnson but remained cool toward the Magician. Schlesinger's enthusiasm for Van Buren is similar to that shown by two other American men of letters: Ezra Pound, who featured Van Buren and the independent treasury in several of his *Cantos*, and Gore Vidal, who focused some of his *Burr* on Van Buren.[6]

The Age of Jackson was warmly received by both the public and the reviewers because it brought a half-century of Progressive synthesis of American history to a dramatic climax. Ever since the 1890s Progressive historians had followed James Madison's Federalist Number 10 by explaining American history as a rational struggle between rival interest groups — Turner's frontier versus the settled regions, Beard's realty interests versus personalty interests, Vernon Parrington's liberals versus conservatives. Although Schlesinger had revised Progressive history, he still assumed a rational struggle between conflicting interests. And by linking Jacksonian Democrats back to Jeffersonians and forward to antislavery Republicans, Populists, and even New Dealers, he offered the same broad synthesis of American history that Turner, Beard and Parrington favored. With its sweeping narrative synthesis, *The Age of Jackson* was history in the style if not always in the persuasion of Thomas B. Macaulay, George O. Trevelyan, Francis Parkman, and George Bancroft.

Several historians followed up on Schlesinger's interpretation. William G. Carleton in 1951 described the politics of the Van Buren era in terms of class conflict, and maintained that only in the 1790s and the 1930s had "the economic and social differences between the major parties been" as great as during the Van Buren presidency. Three years later Charles G. Sellers argued that similar class interests divided Democrats and Whigs in the Old South. The Southern Whigs, he said, were "controlled by urban commercial and banking interests, supported by a majority of the planters." The first volume of his biography of James K. Polk (1957) described Polk as an idealistic Jacksonian opposing those Whig interests.[7]

But *The Age of Jackson* also produced a critical response that directly created one school of historical interpretation and contributed to the rise of several more. The unanimity of praise for the book vanished as quickly as it had arisen, and a generation of historians was soon busy carving out careers attacking Schlesinger and establishing a new consensus view of American history. Led by Bray Hammond, former secretary of the Federal Reserve Board, and Columbia historians Joseph Dorfman, Richard B. Morris, Edward Pessen, and Richard Hofstadter, these detractors argued that workers were just as likely to vote Whig as Democratic and that Jacksonians were more interested in making money than in helping the underdog. Instead of being arrayed in two rival camps, Americans were united in a common selfish drive for the acquisition of property.[8] Hammond dubbed as "fiction" the notion that "the attack on the Bank was on behalf of agrarians against capitalists, of humanity against property, of the poor against the rich, and of 'the people' against 'the money power.'"[9] If Beard and Schlesinger had drawn on Madison, Hammond and Hofstadter looked back to Alexis de Tocqueville in describing an America controlled by liberal capitalism and innocent of class struggle. Hofstadter's *American Political Tradition* became the bible of this school, which controlled the writing of American history in the 1950s during the comfortable conservative years of Dwight D. Eisenhower.[10]

The consensus interpretation failed to bring about a complete change in the Progressive view because Hofstadter and his followers still based their studies on literary sources and still assumed that Americans were motivated by a rational drive for property. The new political history, on the other hand, which emerged at the start of the 1960s with the writing of Samuel P. Hays and Lee Benson, relied more on quantitative sources and assumed more pluralistic and less rational motivation.[11] In *The Concept of Jacksonian Democracy: New York as a Test Case* (1961) Benson reversed Schlesinger by arguing that Whigs rather than Democrats advocated the use of the state for reform purposes and that ethnic and religious background had more influence than economic class on voting. Further developed by Ronald P. Formisano and Robert Kelley, the ethnocultural interpretation used social science concepts such as negative reference groups, world view, lifestyle, and modernism and dealt with symbols to analyze American history in ways Schlesinger and the Progressives had not thought of.[12] The consensus and ethnocultural interpretations overturned most of Schlesinger's conclusions and damaged the concept of Jacksonian Democracy on which his work was based.

But they did not damage the prestige of *The Age of Jackson.* When historians were twice polled in the early 1970s to list the most influential books in American history since 1945, they chose *The Age of Jackson, The American Political Tradition,* and *The Concept of Jacksonian Democracy* as three of the top four books.[13] It was a tribute to Schlesinger that almost thirty years after his book was published historians ranked at the top of their lists both the book and the revisionist works that it had spawned.

The bitter confrontations that tore at American society and politics in the 1960s weakened the influence of consensus history and showed the necessity of widening the scope of historical studies to include a wide range of social groups — women, blacks, immigrants, and American Indians — and to explore all American culture rather than simply politics. At the same time the new political history began to reveal inadequacies that kept it from replacing the Progressive school. The new studies failed to explain why individuals or groups voted as they did, said little about how public policy decisions were made, and were unable to link political campaigns with those decisions. The historical studies of the so-called first and second political party systems were based upon a concept, modernism, that was rapidly losing favor among social scientists. And in the three decades since *The Age of Jackson* neither the consensus historians nor the new political historians had been able to produce a new synthesis to replace those of the Progressives.[14] As a result interest in political history waned, and the number of articles on Jacksonian Democracy, which had risen with the controversy over *The Age of Jackson*, declined rapidly in the 1970s.[15]

Amid the decline new schools continued to spring up more easily than syntheses. Spurred on by the civil rights movement in the 1950s and 1960s and the women's movement in the 1970s, the new social historians turned to social groups and classes to explain American history and sought to blend social with political history. Herbert Gutman's *Work, Culture and Society in Industrial America* (1975) studied the relationship between culture and class broadly in the nineteenth century; Paul E. Johnson's *A Shopkeeper's Millenium: Society and Revivals in Rochester, New York, 1815-1837* did it more narrowly in the Age of Jackson. By the middle of the 1980s, though, the new social history showed little sign of being able to link social and political history in a broad synthetic way.

Still another interpretation, the republican school of history, has made somewhat better progress in accomplishing those goals. With his *Ideological Origins of the American Revolution* (1967) Bernard Bailyn replaced the liberal Progressive self-interest interpretation of the Revolution with the idea that the founding fathers based the Revolution on certain classical ideals of virtuous republican government which they found lacking under British rule. Bailyn and Gordon Wood in his *Creation of the American Republic 1776-1789* (1969) argued that Americans fought the British and then shaped their new government with the goal of creating a republic of civic virtue. Other historians carried these concepts forward until republicanism was found all the way down to the Civil War. Most notable for the Age of Jackson was Robert V. Remini's *Andrew Jackson and the Course of American Freedom 1822-1832* (1981), in which Remini depicted the Old Hero as a statesman deeply motivated by republican ideals. With its tension between virtue and commerce the concept of republicanism provides a promising way to conceptualize Jacksonian Democracy. Instead of discussing whether class or ethnicity decided party affiliation during the era, historians can determine whether nineteenth-century politicians sought the virtue of the classical republic or the profits of the liberal capitalist economy.[16]

In the context of such concepts and such schools of interpretation the *Age of Jackson* remains remarkably relevant. Although Schlesinger's class conflict view of Jacksonian Democracy has not stood up, his concern for social classes, his skill in linking them with political history and his ability to deal with symbols give *The Age of Jackson* a modern flavor. And even though Schlesinger's vision of Jacksonian virtue is one-sided, it has the ring of the recent republican school. Note the modern tone of this passage from *The Age of Jackson*, in which Schlesinger discusses the significance of the independent treasury bill:

> Another century finds a strange disproportion between the uproar over the independent treasury and the plan itself, which, after all, simply proposed that the government take care of its own funds and require payment in legal tender. Why should the radical Democrats look on this innocent scheme as a second Declaration of Independence, and conservatives denounce it as wild, subversive and dangerous, deserving resistance almost to the barricades?
>
> The plan was certainly vulnerable on economic grounds. . . . But this was not the cause of the outcry against it. . . . Instead, the independent treasury was denounced for political and social reasons — as a movement toward despotism, and a conspiracy against private property. . . .
>
> For those who believed, with Hamilton, that the business class had a proprietary right to government favor, the bill thus seemed an assault on the very fabric of society. . . .
>
> For a Jeffersonian there could be but one answer. . . . In last analysis, said Martin Van Buren by his refusal to yield on the subtreasury, the democratically elected government *must* have control over the business community, for this may be the only way to safeguard the life, liberty and property of the humble members of society. (pp. 239–41)

Schlesinger does oversimplify history by making opponents of the independent treasury Hamiltonians and supporters of the bill Jeffersonians; and he is certainly romantic in his assessment of Van Buren as a defender of the "humble members of society." Nonetheless, the passage responds to many of the concerns of present-day historians. Not only does he relate social classes to political issues in a manner the new social historians could understand, but he also shows the symbolism inherent in economic issues in ways that the new political historians with their concepts of world view and lifestyle could accept. All he needs to do is to point out that both sides in the debate believed the opposition to be lacking in republican civic virtue. Historians of the Jacksonian era have always known that people then were emotionally and symbolically involved in the Bank war and the debate over the independent treasury, but they have found it difficult to make students and readers in the twentieth century understand the way that people felt at that time. With his ability to evoke the past in human terms through narrative synthesis and sharp vignettes Schlesinger comes closer than anyone else to conveying the feeling and emotion of the era. At a time when historians have lost ground to social scientists, novelists, and television writers in trying to explain the past, such skills are as modern and as needed now as they were then.

Donald B. Cole, History Department, Phillips Exeter Academy, is the author of Martin Van Buren and the American Political System *(1984).*

1. Arthur M. Schlesinger, Jr., to the Editor, *American Historical Review* 54 (April 1949): 785–86.

2. Allan Nevins, "At the Roots of Democracy," *The New York Times Book Review*, Sept. 16, 1945, pp. 1, 26.

3. Bernard DeVoto, *Weekly Book Review*, Sept. 16, 1945, p. 1; Merle Curti, "Jacksonian Democracy," *Nation* 161 (Oct. 20, 1945), p. 406; George Fort Milton, "A Straight Look at Old Hickory," *The Saturday Review of Literature* 28 (Sept. 29, 1945), pp. 10–11; and *The Age of Hate: Andrew Johnson and the Radicals* (1930).

4. Richard Hofstadter, "William Leggett, Spokesman of Jacksonian Democracy," *Political Science Quarterly* 57 (1943): 581–94; "Democracy in the Making," *The New Republic* 113 (Oct. 22, 1945): 541–42.

5. Arthur M. Schlesinger, *New Viewpoints in American History* (1922), p. 209. For a useful summary of the origin of *The Age of Jackson*, see Charles G. Sellers, "Andrew Jackson versus the Historians," *Mississippi Valley Historical Review* 44 (March 1958): 628–29.

6. Ezra Pound, *The Cantos of Ezra Pound* (1948), pp. 31–36; Gore Vidal, *Burr: A Novel* (1973).

7. William G. Carleton, "Political Aspects of the Van Buren Era," *South Atlantic Quarterly* 50 (April 1951): 167–85; Charles G. Sellers, *James K. Polk, Jacksonian, 1795–1843* (1957); "Who Were the Southern Whigs?" *American Historical Review* 59 (January 1954): 335–46.

8. Bray Hammond, "Review of *The Age of Jackson*," *Journal of Economic History* 9 (May 1946): 79–84; Joseph Dorfman, "The Jackson Wage-Earner Thesis," *American Historical Review* 54 (January 1947): 296–306; Richard B. Morris, "Andrew Jackson, Strikebreaker," *American Historical Review* 55 (October 1949): 54–68; Edward Pessen, "Did Labor Support Jackson? The Boston Story," *Political Science Quarterly* 64 (June 1949): 262–74.

9. Bray Hammond, *Banks and Politics in America from the Revolution to the Civil War* (1957), pp. 358–59.

10. Alexis de Tocqueville, *Democracy in America*, 2 vols. (1835).

11. Samuel P. Hays, "History as Human Behavior," *Iowa Journal of History* 58 (July 1960): 193–206.

12. Ronald P. Formisano, *The Birth of Mass Political Parties: Michigan, 1827–1861* (1971); Robert Kelley, *The Cultural Pattern in American Politics: The First Century* (1979); Richard L. McCormick, "Ethno-Cultural Interpretations of Nineteenth-Century American Voting Behavior," *Political Science Quarterly* 89 (June 1974): 351–77.

13. The other book was Richard Hofstadter, *The Age of Reform: From Bryan to FDR* (1955). Allan G. Bogue, "The New Political History in the 1970s," Michael Kammen, ed., *The Past Before Us. Contemporary Historical Writing in the United States* (1980), pp. 231–32.

14. For criticism of the new political history see McCormick, "Ethno-Cultural Interpretations," pp. 371–76; Sean Wilentz, "On Class and Politics in Jacksonian America," *Reviews in American History* 10 (December 1982), pp. 48–49. Formisano comments on the unlikelihood of a new synthesis in the near future in "Toward a Reorientation of Jacksonian Politics: A Review of the Literature, 1959–1975," *Journal of American History* 63 (June 1976): 42–46, 65. The best synthesis of the Jacksonian Era since *The Age of Jackson* is Edward Pessen's *Jacksonian America* (rev. ed., 1978), an indispensable work for historians, but one lacking in the narrative sweep that is appealing to the general reader.

15. Wilentz, "On Class and Politics," pp. 45–46.

16. *Ibid.*, pp. 54–57.

REVISITING FREDERICK LEWIS ALLEN'S
ONLY YESTERDAY

David M. Kennedy

"Every account of [the 1920s] begins with Frederick Lewis Allen, *Only Yesterday*," William E. Leuchtenburg declared in his own widely acclaimed book on the period, *The Perils of Prosperity*. Leuchtenburg magnanimously praised Allen's work as "a social history written in such a lively style that academicians often underrate its soundness."[1] They may have underrated it, but they nevertheless required their students to read it. Allen's several books, wrote Richard Hofstadter in 1952, had for more than two decades "been among the most popular books assigned for reading in American colleges."[2] *Only Yesterday* sold more than half a million copies from the time of its publication in 1931 to Allen's death in 1954, and it is still in print today.[3] More than any other single work, it has for longer than half a century shaped our understanding of American life in the 1920s.

Hofstadter agreed with Leuchtenburg that Allen's colorful, kinetic prose accounted for much of *Only Yesterday's* appeal. Allen wrote. according to Hofstadter, with a "feeling for the concrete and vivid" and a "firm sense for the relevance of the past."[4] This judgment echoed the comments of *Only Yesterday's* first reviewers. John Chamberlain applauded Allen for a "style that is verve itself."[5] Compared with William Preston Slosson's *The Great Crusade and After*, published one year earlier than *Only Yesterday*, Murray Godwin found Allen's volume "far fresher, more vivid, better organized, and more flowing in structure and style." No academic historian, Godwin gratuitously added, "could do so fine a job."[6] Stuart Chase demurred only slightly. "This may or may not be a great book," he wrote, "but it is a marvelously absorbing one."[7] Crowning this chorus of adulation, the *New York Times* later eulogized Allen as "the Herodotus of the Jazz Age."[8]

Allen appraised his own aspirations and accomplishments more modestly. "A contemporary history," he warned, "is bound to be anything but definitive."[9] He shied away from being identified as a historian, preferring instead to call himself a "retrospective journalist."[10] And he scrupulously described *Only Yesterday* in its subtitle as "an *informal* history of the nineteen-twenties."

In part, "informal" meant that Allen largely exempted himself from dealing with the usual historical topics of politics and diplomacy. It also meant that he was unconstrained by the respect for rules of evidence and argument that is beaten into graduate students. Years later, Allen acknowledged that his "best sources" for *Only Yesterday* had been "the daily magazines and news-papers of the period." Yet he conceded that these very sources "do not help much" in the effort "to observe clearly the life and institutions of one's own day," because "they record the unusual, not the usual."[11]

Allen had in fact relied on other than simply journalistic sources, including Robert S. and Helen Merrell Lynd's pioneering sociological work, *Middle-town*, Charles A. and Mary R. Beard's *Rise of American Civilization*, Stuart Chase's *Prosperity, Fact or Myth*, Silas Bent's *Ballyhoo*, Walter Lippmann's *A Preface to Morals*, and Joseph Wood Krutch's *The Modern Temper*. Indeed, so thoroughly did he digest the findings and opinions of these other authors that some reviewers complained that *Only Yesterday* amounted to little more than a survey of other surveys.

But if Allen stood on the shoulders of earlier students of the 1920s, he added his own distinctive contribution to the emerging image of the decade. That contribution derived from Allen's own keen observations of the lives of his contemporaries, and, as he acknowledged, from inventive reliance on journalism, especially "feature" articles, human interest stories, and, despite his disclaimers, the raucous sensationalism of the increasingly popular tabloids. His book focused on "the changing state of the public mind," and he plunged unhesitatingly into explorations of private sentiments and mass moods.[12] No supply-side analyst of how or why popular literary works were crafted, he instead conjectured fearlessly about what readers were thinking and feeling as they turned the pages of *The Education of Henry Adams* or *Main Street*. In a similar vein, he imaginatively projected himself into the brain of a flapper, from which vantage he explained the allegedly self-conscious semiotics of her dress and demeanor. Elsewhere he sweepingly summed up his countrymen's emotional state as "weary" or "unhappy" or, most famously, as "disillusioned." Citing some overheard conversations and a handful of Broadway plays, he proclaimed that in the realm of sexual behavior and attitudes "an upheaval in values was taking place."[13] While few professionally trained historians would have dared to erect such lofty generalizations on such a flimsy evidentiary foundation, Allen's towering thematic structures, somewhat miraculously, have continued to stand for more than fifty years.

For all the license that his posture of "retrospective journalist" afforded him, Allen still shared some of the objectives of the traditional historian. He sought, his preface explained, not only to "tell" but also to "interpret" the 1920s. More important, he strove to find "some sort of logical and coherent order" in his subject — to present the events of the decade "woven into a pattern which at least masquerades as history."[14]

Readers might be forgiven for not immediately discerning that pattern. So richly ornamented was the fabric Allen wove that it might seem at first to be merely a fanciful arabesque, wildly eclectic and devoid of any consistently informing logic. What possible interpretive scheme might hold in balance such prodigiously diverse items as the tragedy of Woodrow Wilson's failure to secure ratification of the Treaty of Versailles and the triumph of Jack Dempsey over Georges Carpentier? The execution of Sacco and Vanzetti and the founding of Simon and Schuster? The Red Scare and Mah Jong? The Ku Klux Klan and Emil Coué? Flappers and Tut-Ankh-Amen? The Model A and the Pig Woman? Flag-pole sitters and H. L. Mencken? Prohibition and the Teapot Dome scandals? The Big Bull Market and Charles Lindbergh? Dion O'Bannion and Calvin Coolidge? The rise of radio and the collapse of the Florida land boom? To add to the confusion, Allen portrayed everything in the 1920s as in constant and simultaneous motion, ascending and falling on a roiling sea of change. Stocks, hemlines, and Al Capone's income went up; automobile prices, necklines, and the public's interest in politics went down.

Yet like an opulent oriental carpet, on close inspection Allen's elaborately crafted portrait of the 1920s did reveal a controlling design. The very organization of the book provided a clue to what was predominantly on Allen's mind. After a breezy evocation of the texture of everyday life in 1919, touching on fashions, food, sports, music, movies, and drinking habits, Allen began in earnest with a moving account of Wilson's doomed struggle to shepherd the United States into the League of Nations. This was immediately followed by a description of postwar labor disorders, race riots, and the Big Red Scare — a frantic series of episodes at last terminated when the country began "to regain its sense of humor" as the American people gratifyingly "were coming to their senses."[15]

Allen then punctuated his story with two chapters containing the sort of social history for which he is justly renowned. Here he described in fetching detail the emergence of the radio industry after the pioneering broadcast by station KDKA in East Pittsburgh on November 2, 1920, the rise of mass spectator sports, the waves of fads in games and popular entertainments, and, most notoriously, the "revolution in manners and morals," especially as it affected women.

There followed a carefully researched narrative (according to Allen, the first comprehensive account) of the Harding scandals, a history of the early advertising industry, and then another descent into what Allen called "a series of tremendous trifles — a heavyweight boxing-match, a murder trial, a new automobile model, a transatlantic flight." The "striking" thing about these events, Allen noted, "was the unparalleled rapidity and unanimity with which millions of men and women turned their attention, their talk, and their emotional interest" to them.[16]

The phrase "mass culture" would later be invented to describe the phenomena that struck Allen as so unprecedented. Allen, of course, could not be expected to employ that term, but it powerfully testifies to his skill as a social observer that he identified the emergence in the 1920s of frenetic, fickle, media-induced consumerism on a colossal scale. A novelty to him, this kind of behavior seemed in the post–World War II era to have become a permanent feature of affluent democratic culture. Unfamiliar with such behavior, and not much given to analytical explanations in any event, Allen blamed this "carnival of commercialized degradation" on hyperaggressive advertising ("ballyhoo"), and on the contemptible tabloids, which "presented American life not as a political and economic struggle, but as a three-ring circus of sport, crime, and sex."[17] Yet he believed that the carousel of ballyhoo and the bizarre eventually lost its momentum as the decade proceeded. It was slowed most notably by the genuine heroism of Charles A. Lindbergh, whose unadorned simplicity reminded jaded Americans what the right stuff really looked like. Once again, a distracted public showed signs of returning to its senses — though Allen ominously concluded this section of his book by anticipating the levitation of the Big Bull Market into its "sensational phase" less than a year after Lindbergh's flight.[18]

Allen next turned his attention to "The Revolt of the Highbrows," concentrating especially on the scoffing cultural criticism of H. L. Mencken and the social satires of Sinclair Lewis. (Conspicuously absent was any mention of some of the highest brows of all, T. S. Eliot and Ezra Pound. And like many of his contemporaries in the 1920s, Allen took no notice of William Faulkner). This chapter, though attenuated and curiously selective, is in a sense the spiritual heart of *Only Yesterday*, for here Allen could summon onto his pages his intellectual brethren — those writers who shared his sense of disillusionment that Americans in the postwar decade were obsessed with business and monkey-business, to the neglect of serious public affairs. Allen's master motif for the decade was the common lament of these authors for the transient vanity of wartime idealism. "Disillusionment," he concluded simply, "was the keynote of the nineteen-twenties."[19]

Like virtually everything else that materialized in the turbulent twenties, even the "offensive against Babbittry spent itself, if only because the novelty of rebellion wore off."[20] Allen therefore moved on, in his concluding hundred pages, to describe the accelerating whirligig of distractions and delusions that beset the republic as the decade approached its climax — including prohibition and crime, the Florida real estate craze, and, most conspicuously, the Big Bull Market and the Crash of 1929.

So frequently foreshadowed, now finally at center stage, the story of the steep rise and spectacular fall of the stock market was the denouement toward which *Only Yesterday* built not only chronologically but also thematically. Coming conveniently in the last year of the 1920s, the Crash tidily wrapped up Allen's history of the decade. But the catastrophe of Black Tuesday also neatly clinched the moral judgment that informed Allen's entire work — "that nobody during the Twenties really had a good time and that we deserved the Crash," as one reviewer put it.[21]

By the time the reader reaches Allen's conclusion, the "pattern" of *Only Yesterday* — the "logical and coherent order" that Allen sought to bring to his narrative — is clear. Fugue-like, the storyline has mounted to the crescendo of the Crash by alternating discussions of serious public issues (the fate of the League, Sacco and Vanzetti, the lack of probity in the Harding administration) with descriptions of the incessantly diverting ephemera of mass culture (the Hall-Mills murder trial, Red Grange, and Rudolph Valentino). Between the covers of *Only Yesterday* Allen conducted a running debate with himself about the sobriety and rationality of the American people. Faced with the grave necessity of managing a modern state, they proved distressingly susceptible to all kinds of frivolous distractions — some of them insidious, like the Red Scare, but most of them harmless, like Mah Jong and crossword puzzles. Repeatedly, as they began to tire of trivia and get serious again about life, Americans were once more diverted, like kittens in a catnip shop, by a new fad, by speculative mania, or by "hysterial preoccupation with sex."[22] Unable to knuckle down for long to the task of running the republic, they did in a sense bring the Crash — and the ensuing Great Depression, the full scale of which Allen could not clearly see in 1931 — upon themselves.

And yet if Allen was critical of his countrymen, he was also tolerant, generous, and at bottom an optimist. He had more in common with the sympathetic satirizing of Sinclair Lewis than he did with the rasping mockery of H. L. Mencken, though he clearly shared both men's disappointment at the failure of Americans to be finer chaps. *Only Yesterday* was in the end a gentle Jeremiad, delivered not stridently, but in the voice of Increase Mather reborn as a reform-minded Unitarian (Allen was, in fact, an Episcopalian). The book's humane warmth has probably been among the major determinants of its durability.

Much of the book's warmth was kindled by the sense of intimacy with his readers that Allen skillfully cultivated. In the opening sentence of his first chapter he beckoned his readers to join personally in his journey back into time by addressing them in the second person. He employed this device frequently in subsequent pages, particularly on those occasions when he was compelled to deal with the kind of numeric data that deadens so many conventional histories. "Pick up one of those graphs with which statisticians measure the economic ups and downs of the Post-war Decade," he suggested at the introduction of his discussion of Coolidge prosperity, and then proceeded charmingly and succinctly to summarize the history of business activity from 1920 to 1931.[23]

This sort of artful writing came naturally to Allen, a journalist of considerable accomplishment. A tall and tweedy Bostonian, the son of an Episcopal minister, he had prepared at Groton and graduated from Harvard in 1912. Like his eminent contemporary, Franklin Roosevelt, he felt that this education obligated him to a life of public service (though where Roosevelt had edited the *Crimson*, Allen, perhaps significantly, wrote for the *Lampoon.*) He worked for a time at the *Atlantic Monthly* and at *Century Magazine*, served in Woodrow Wilson's war administration (at the Council of National Defense), and then in 1923 began his long association with *Harper's Magazine*, rising in 1941 to the editorship, a position he held until the year before his death in 1954.

Allen's field of vision, for all its comprehensiveness, was severely bounded by the view from the New York editorial offices of *Harper's*. The limitations of that perspective are evident when one considers what's left out of *Only Yesterday*. Allen's gaze penetrated scarcely at all into what one of his favorite authors, F. Scott Fitzgerald, called "that vast obscurity beyond the city." Out there where the dark fields of the republic rolled on under the night, some 31 million farmers — almost one in three Americans — toiled and dwelled in 1920. Few of them appeared in Allen's account, except as quaint spectators at the Scopes trial. Allen noticed black victims of race riots in Chicago and Tulsa, but the great majority of blacks who lived in the Old South were as invisible to him as was Faulkner. Perhaps even more surprising, the immigrants who teemed through lower Manahattan were somehow shielded from Allen's eyes; the historic ending of unrestricted immigration in 1924 scarcely warranted a mention.

What Allen did see with vivid clarity were the lifestyles of *Harper's* readers. He could write about them so deftly, and speak to them so intimately, because they were so familiar to him. They were both his audience and his subject matter. Knowing their tastes and habits, he could make easy reference to places like "Sauk Center" (sic) without further explanation, confident that the encoded meaning of the name would be easily decrypted by his readers. He could illustrate the erosion of mannerly behavior by describing the "flappers and their wide-trousered swains [who] took the porch cushions out in the boats and left them there to be rained on, without apology."[24] For those unacquainted with the details of Sinclair Lewis's upbringing, or without access to the waterside pleasure pavilions of the summering rich, Allen's book must have seemed like a report from a distant country.

If Allen's upscale provincialism was confining, it was not smug. He did not simply chronicle, and he certainly did not uncritically celebrate, the manners and morals of his subject-readers, and his history did more than cater to their presumed prejudices. He repeatedly donned the mantle of the objective scholar, setting the record straight, for example, about the conditions that underlay the Boston police strike, or the laughably small size of the Communist party that had inspired the Big Red Scare. Here Allen exceeded the usual mission of the journalist, even a retrospective one. He assumed instead the role of the historian, who seeks not merely to record the novel and trumpet the sensational, but to discover the subtextual and to explain the ordinary.

Yet even as an analytic historian, Allen stayed safely within the limits of the conventionally liberal, urban outlook of his day. He displayed a magnanimous sympathy for labor and for the victims of the Red Scare, but he showed little interest in understanding religious fundamentalism, which he dismissed as an archaic vestige scorned by "civilized opinion." [25] The Ku Klux Klan rightly merited his vigorous condemnation, but the forces that produced it did not merit much of an explanation. This omission was especially unfortunate, because the cultural tide that washed up the Klan ran sharply counter to the flood of modernity that Allen found so fascinating and so apparently irresistible. "We are a movement of the plain people, very weak in the matter of culture, intellectual support, and trained leadership," Klan Imperial Wizard Hiram Wesley Evans lamented in 1926. "One by one all our traditional moral standards went by the boards, or were so disregarded that they ceased to be binding. The sacredness of our Sabbath, of our homes, of chastity, and finally even of our right to teach our own children in our own schools fundamental facts and truths were torn away from us. Those who maintained the old standards did so only in the face of constant ridicule." [26]

This was no less an authentic voice of the 1920s than Sinclair Lewis's, but Allen did not hear it. Had he attended to it, and discussed both the ebb and flow of the clashing currents that Lewis and Evans represented, he would have made his narrative less one-dimensional, given it more texture and dramatic interest — and rendered it more complete and more accurate. He would also have robbed future historians of the chance to discover what *Only Yesterday* masterfully obscured: that the 1920s did not witness the utter triumph of urbane "modernism." Fundamentalists, traditionalists, "dries," and all varieties of "hicks" still lived, and they clung tenaciously to values and mores utterly different from those whose seemingly unimpeded ascension Allen recorded.

Delimited geographically by the Hudson and East Rivers — or perhaps by

Cape Cod and the Hamptons — and restricted sociologically to his eastern urban and suburban subscribers, Allen's vision had temporal limits as well. He
contributed to an artificial chronological isolation of the decade that has
proved perversely persistent. Like a magus summoning Excalibur from the
depths, Allen commanded the 1920s to arise unanchored and unbridged out
of the lake of time. Bounded by the latitudes of the Great War and the Great
Crash, the decade formed what Allen called "a distinct era" — a little island in
history, unlapped by waves from the past.[27] Virtually everything that happened in the 1920s, therefore, had only proximate causes. Rarely did Allen
forge an explanatory chain whose links ran back more deeply into the past
than 1917. Nowhere was this radically abbreviated historical perspective
more apparent than in Allen's discussion of the alleged "revolution in manners and morals," a concept that he almost single-handedly planted in the
popular as well as the scholarly literature about the 1920s. "A number of
forces," Allen wrote, "were working together and interacting upon one
another to make this revolution inevitable." Yet in his account none of those
forces had been in motion for very long: the war and its "eat-drink-and-be-
merry-for tomorrow-we-die spirit"; the Nineteenth Amendment and the con-
comitant liberation of women from housework and for wage labor; the popu-
larization of Freud's works; and finally "prohibition, the automobiles, the
confession and sex magazines, and the movies."[28]

Few historians today would take this as even a minimally adequate explanation for the history of manners and morals in the 1920s, and few would be
comfortable with confining the discussion of women to a treatment of their
dress and sexual habits. Allen had little appreciation of what is by now a
richly elaborated understanding of the deep roots of modern sexual practices
in the nineteenth century and even earlier. He had even less inclination to
view women's history as anything other than sexual history. What's more, as
he did in so many realms, he vastly exaggerated the role of the war in precipi-
tating sexual change. And by speaking of a "revolution" in manners and
morals, he almost certainly exaggerated the extent of the behavioral transformations he described.

What *had* assuredly changed was the volume and pitch of public discussion
of sexual topics. A new candor about sexuality had burst into the sources
upon which Allen primarily relied — the mass-circulation magazines, best-
selling books, and popular plays that he imaginatively mined and mistakenly
took for sure guides to actual behavior. In so doing, he created a monument
of historical hyperbole that it has taken several generations of subsequent
scholars to scale down to its proper dimensions.

Allen's freewheeling, inventive style of historical argumentation in *Only
Yesterday* contrasted vividly with that of William Preston Slosson in *The*

Great Crusade and After, which Slosson had the great misfortune to publish at almost the same time that Allen's book appeared. A volume in the respected History of American Life series edited by Arthur M. Schlesinger and Dixon Ryan Fox, *The Great Crusade* was the work of an academic historian then an associate professor at the University of Michigan. Where Allen was selective, anecdotal, judgmental, and unfailingly interesting, Slosson was comprehensive, scientific, objective, and a trifle boring. If Allen's prose lilted musically along, Slosson's soldiered stolidly forward.

Yet for serious students of the 1920s, Slosson's book still repays the effort of reading it, probably more handsomely than does *Only Yesterday*. Despite his title, Slosson did not resemble Allen in making the European war the ultimate cause of the events of the postwar decade. He had a far keener sense than Allen of the deeper historical context of the 1920s. He consequently did not elevate the specifically postwar theme of "disillusionment" into his controlling explanation for the ills of the age. Nor did he neglect, as Allen did, life beyond the Hudson. *The Great Crusade* offered sensitive chapters on "The Changing Countryside" and "The South in Black and White." Its chapter on "The American Woman Wins Equality" passed quickly over the colorful trivia of feminine fashions and changing tastes in cosmetics, unlike *Only Yesterday*, and instead probed the political implications of the Nineteenth Amendment and recounted the debate among feminists about the wisdom of the Equal Rights Amendment. Like Allen, Slosson paid a great deal of attention to prohibition, automobiles, spectator sports, and the efflorescence of advertising. But he also included cogent discussions of immigration, education, and the truly revolutionary mechanization of agriculture (its dimensions suggested by the ten-fold increase in the use of tractors in the decade) — subjects that Allen, much more interested in middle-class urban lifestyles and a supposed revolution in sexual habits, had ignored altogether.

For all its considerable virtues, *The Great Crusade and After* has long since passed out of print, and probably goes unread today even by specialists. Consigned to even deeper oblivion is a massive compendium of information about the 1920s, *Recent Social Trends*, the report of a special presidential research committee published in 1933. With its attendant monographs, it contains a small treasury of data, compiled by more than two dozen eminent social scientists, about every conceivable aspect of American life in the postwar decade.

That *Only Yesterday* survives in print while these two impressive works have languished not only constitutes an imposing compliment to the power of Frederick Lewis Allen's pen. It also sadly suggests that the reading public prefers style to substance in its historians, and doesn't mind if they are a bit blinkered, a little preachy, and good-naturedly given to the spinning of myths. All this can be overlooked if they are colorful writers and stick to popular subjects. Frederick Lewis Allen was, and he did. Therein lies much of the explanation for *Only Yesterday*'s enormous readership, and for its longevity.

David M. Kennedy teaches American history at Stanford University. He is currently working on a volume covering the period from 1932 to 1945 in the Oxford History of the United States.

1. William E. Leuchtenburg, *The Perils of Prosperity* (1985), p. 277.

2. Richard Hofstadter, Foreword to Frederick Lewis Allen, *The Big Change* (1952), p. vii.

3. *The New York Times*, February 14, 1954, p. 1. *Only Yesterday*'s 1931 price of $3.00 has escalated to $30.00 for the hardcover edition. But in a striking demonstration of the economics of the "paperback revolution," the softcover edition sells for only eighty cents more than the 1931 original.

4. Hofstadter, Foreword, p. vii.

5. John Chamberlain, *The New York Times Book Review*, December 6, 1931, p. 1.

6. Murray Godwin, *The New Republic*, December 9, 1931, p. 106.

7. Stuart Chase, *Books* (the *New York Herald Tribune* book review), December 6, 1931, p. 3.

8. *The New York Times*, December 14, 1954, p. 1.

9. Frederick Lewis Allen, *Only Yesterday* (1931), p. xiii.

10. "F.L.A.," *Harper's*, April, 1954, pp. 74–75.

11. *The Big Change*, pp. 156, 234.

12. *Only Yesterday*, p. xiv.

13. Ibid., pp. 112–13.

14. Ibid., pp. xiii–xiv.

15. Ibid., pp. 70, 75.

16. Ibid., p. 186.

17. Ibid., pp. 216, 81.

18. Ibid., p. 225.

19. Ibid., p. 238.

20. Ibid., p. 243.

21. D. O. Stewart, *The Yale Review* 21 (Spring 1932), p. 605.

22. *Only Yesterday*, p. 348.

23. Ibid., p. 159.

24. Ibid., p. 120.

25. Ibid., p. 206.

26. Hiram Wesley Evans, "The Klan's Fight for Americanism," *North American Review* 223 (March 1926): 33–63.

27. *Only Yesterday*, p. xiii.

28. Ibid., pp. 94–99.

THE GROWTH OF AMERICAN THOUGHT:
A RECONSIDERATION

Robert Dawidoff

The Growth of American Thought is no longer standard classroom fare. It was once regarded as American historians' "most favored" book (out of those published between 1936 and 1950), and is still referred to as a founding text of American intellectual history. The successor to Parrington, Merle Curti's 1943 volume appears not so much to have been replaced as superannuated, although the book is canonized and its author venerated. An admired and, indeed, ideologically characteristic book in its day, *The Growth of American Thought* seems today to suffer from the irritating blandness of old pieties and to impose the burden of masses of information within an unexciting framework of explanation. I say *seems* because Curti's book, in my view, has not really been replaced; but the kind of thinking it represents and the ground it pioneers have been abandoned by a profession that lost its bearings in specialization and has sought to recover them on too small, too high, and too undemocratic an intellectual plane. Professor Curti's social history of ideas certainly cannot be taken for the whole of his distinguished writing and teaching career; what follows reconsiders *The Growth of American Thought*, but a single instance of this preeminent professional historian's work.

There is something old-fashioned about the very scale of *The Growth of American Thought*. This 800-page book, with a high degree of scholarship but little scholarly apparatus, makes an awkward presence in the university classroom. "Curti says" or "according to Curti" are seldom heard or read now, although his pervasive influence is clear. It was Curti who wrote the intellectual history on which most of American history of the last forty years has been based. In addition, *The Growth of American Thought* has had great influence outside the particular precincts of intellectual history, although even within the field Curti is a force, a contrary influence to Perry Miller and American Studies.

Miller and Curti represented alternative possibilities for their field in their time. Miller's directions were social critical without being significantly social. He used the Puritans to view and criticize the history of American democracy, which he regarded as materialistic, spiritually limiting, and as showing the baleful effects of the Enlightenment on the depth of human understanding. This did not make him illiberal, although it created some of the same internal tensions in his work that bedeviled American mid-century liberalism. Thus the sources and nature of the figures Miller preferred were often at odds with his own modern beliefs. Many of Miller's heroes — think of his Jonathan Edwards, for instance — antagonized the American present in some deep, disowning way.

Curti lacked Miller's need to search for a way around his own intellectual legacy in the interstices of argument. He apparently believed in the progress of enlightened ideas, and in reform, and in the kinds of democratic developments he described. The calm tone of Curti's book, so different from the wrought complexity of Miller's, stems from an unusually happy blend of methodology, subject, history, ideology, and temperament. He was not writing out of turbulence, but out of a kind of optimistic content, working with a good theory and arriving at congenial and hopeful, if not necessarily convenient or complacent, conclusions. Curti's intellectual history does not seem so very different from good old American history.

Curti expected ideas to serve social purposes, and he was not scandalized when they turned out to do just that. Just because ideas had functions did not mean to Curti that they could not be ideas. Nor was Curti prey to the Progressive *noire* mode. That ideas represented and argued interests did not necessarily implicate their holders in a corrupt conspiracy. Curti was also free from the (Boorstinian) notion that grip and grasp are all and that the way people hold views obviates the consideration of the views themselves as ideas.

Scholarship since 1943 has pretty much developed Curti's ground. What use is his book, once the agenda is completed? Beyond its introductory or gazetteer utility, is there any further need for it? One answer derives from the continuing value of the general to the specialist. It is in fact important that the student of English-American colonial culture be reminded of the ethnic diversity of the colonial population, if only to moderate an emphasis on the dominant culture and its hegemony. The general is one of the historian's best controls for forays into the particular. The general survey such as Curti's reminds the historian that there is a larger picture into which the special foreground must sooner or later fit.

There is also the value of Deweyite functionalism in Curti. Dewey is due for rediscovery by historians. Most historians think like Dewey anyhow. Their metaphors and their unspoken assumptions about the way ideas are held and used indicate that they tend to the Deweyite path. Among historians of ideas theorizing flourishes, but a reading of even Marxist historians will reveal among the tall trees of theory and the dialectic, the ecological system that Curti's book makes explicit and to some extent justifies. Curti grasped that intellectual life takes place, with or without connections, on all levels of social life at all times. Although he dwells on the literate and the scientific and the philosophical, the practical really interests him. He collects specimens of thought, sorts and identifies them, but leaves them in recognizable form.

Curti's organizing principle is two-fold. First, he employs a metaphor of growth to guide the story of American thought, and then he emphasizes within that story certain themes that turn out to be his own view of what was best and most characteristic in American thought. Although he uses many metaphors to express how thought worked in a culture, that of "growth" occurs most frequently. In the course of one paragraph on the legacy of English social ideas to the new nation, Curti has the "English ideal of the gentleman" and "remnants of English economic ideas" *taking root* in America and characteristically concludes the paragraph: "Above all, the growing idea of free economic enterprise figured in the British-derived legacy" (p. 5). One reads such passages with a certain sinking of the heart; the metaphor, even if one is dulled to its use, seems obligatory and timid. Like it or not, however, the usage is recurring. It may even be the best we have.

Curti's own metaphor "took root" in a Turnerian soil. Land, environment, growth, and climate provided the strong figures for the transformation of European into American that remained for Curti the important event of American history. In his chapter "The Old World Heritage Modified" Curti sums up the book's theory:

> Intellectual life in colonial America was much like that of the Old World from which in so large a measure it was derived; on both sides of the Atlantic there were always the fundamental postulates and categories of civilized western thought. But one cannot understand the intellectual equipment of the rising American nation without taking into account how the American physical environment and the new social environment modified the Old World intellectual agencies. . . . New Problems beget new thoughts. . . . (p. 26)

At first, it is almost impossible to read this, so familiar, so encasing, and so general is its point. But on second look, it appears sound and roomy and, after all, true. Curti sets boundaries to the study and interpretation of our intellectual history that still describe the territory. Written from the point of view of the white European settler, Curti's statement does not favor that point of view, let alone magnify it into something divinely or historically ordained. Curti includes the critique of that point of view and often suggests it.

Curti's notions of environmentalism, enforced gently by the metaphor of growth, serve all his purposes. They also tend to answer certain large questions by omission. For example, what about the thoughts and ideas that, in Curti's view, did not grow? Curti's book is essentially about thoughts that *did* grow in America as well as the thoughts that *should*. In the mild and unfocussed yet genuine tension between these two hangs the book's meaning and its interest.

> The interrelationship between the growth of thought and the whole social milieu seem to be so close and have been so frequently neglected that this study of American life has tried consistently to relate that growth to the whole complex environment. It is thus not a history of American thought but a social history of American thought and to some extent a socio-economic history of American thought. (p. x)

The Progressives advanced their points deliberately in the re-creation of divisive struggle. Merle Curti presented the struggle as between kinds of thinking and suggested the interests that lay behind thoughts, although he was careful not to dwell on the relation of interest to idea. He sees uses and functions as often as interests, and grants the ideas their own lives as well as livelihoods. Curti does not propound the same view of American history that his acknowledged masters did. When you boil down Curti, you don't get Beard.

What you do get is ideas about that which persists and is to be valued in human life. The largest idea in Curti is democracy. The notion of democracy as a principle of historiography is increasingly foreign to us. Who celebrates the expansion of the suffrage? Who lauds abundance? Who writes lovingly of "the People?" Who without flattery, foolishness, or low guile praises democracy and sees it as the ruling idea of the rise of our historical situation?

Merle Curti is such a historian. He resisted the Tocquevillian urge to locate his criticism of democracy outside the culture. His social history of American ideas bears down on those ideas. Curti is no Ralph Henry Gabriel; he neither reduces nor enlarges the subject of American thinking to democratic ideas. He explores how, at the outset, the environment and situation of America necessitated or fostered a free, pluralistic democratic tradition. The Curti environment is democratic in that its primary receptivities are to those things that validate democracy as a way of thinking about life in English North America and the United States. The democratic in Curti emerges as a complex idea of right that is posited, not narrow, and not especially critical.

Curti doesn't play the "American mind" game. He refrains from constructing a mind. Rather, he assembles thinkers under the categories of successive themes of thought. The social history of ideas becomes a second voice to history proper. The relation between event and thought is not as important as the reasonably consistent, albeit uninsistently held view that both events and thoughts are history, responsive to other things, that a nation's view of the world is a response in some elephantine way to that world. Curti's interest in democracy is therefore, in part, his conviction that America was democratic. And since, America was democratic, it came to pass that it should be.

Everybody who writes about America chooses moments when America becomes American. Not satisfied with watersheds or turning points, we expect such moments to show us where things became, if not inevitable in the real world of action, decided in the inward imagination. Perry Miller's studies of the New England Mind, for instance, chart the establishment of that *mind*, and then its repudiation, and, substantively, the interesting but changed *mind* that succeeded it. There is a tone of urgent regret in Miller's body of work. At the same time that Miller didn't like what America had become, he knew that it had become itself. This recognition, passionate in Miller, was a great theme of 1930s interpretations. Unwilling to be apart from the achievements of American civilization and yet seeming to know better than them, subsequent American studies interpretation came to look for a place from which to judge democratic culture. This Tocquevillian mode varies in the critical ends it serves, but Tocqueville remains the patron saint of the insider's attempt to look at America as if from the outside, which is what some people mean by social science.

Curti, who was Progressive to the core, refused outright the Tocquevillian catbird seat. He would not transform himself into the observer of a massive and irrefutable historical force when talking democracy. Where Tocqueville sees American movement as democracy's movement, Curti identifies certain things within America as democratic or not, as the case strikes him. Curti prefers Whitman and Bryce to Tocqueville. He does not accept the Tocquevillian critique of democracy, the claim that democracy replaced the Enlightenment, or the vision of the tyrannical majority. One reason for Curti's eclipse among students of American civilization has been his dry reserve about Tocqueville, whom he cites but briefly and appraises cooly. Curti joins Tocqueville to Francis Lieber, Cooper, and Melville as conservative critics of democracy, not conservatives within the workings of democracy. Here one must note Curti's difficulty with granting to conservatives a place within democracy.

For Curti, democracy is a ground. He does not like to attribute democracy to the enjoying, imperial, capitalist, consuming, modern American nation. Unembittered by the fault lines he sees in the democratic process, he looks for democratic values within a democratic regime. The process of democracy seems to him, as it does not to Tocqueville, multiple and pluralist. Discussing

Calhoun and the political thought the Old South required, Curti makes a characteristic analysis. He sees the South as attempting to substitute a static moment in historical development for the process by which nations and their thinking evolve. Calhoun's antidemocratic statics proceeded, Curti saw, from a concern for minority rights. One of the strengths of Curti's way is his capacity to respect Calhoun's synthesis by showing how its instrumentality is worth regarding, even if its interests be abhorrent and its tendency unacceptable:

> If democracy be regarded as multiple leadership, multiple participation, and the sharing of values deemed good, Calhoun's conception was indeed limited. But this limitation should not obscure the fact that he did make a bold and original effort to come to grips with one of the great problems of democracy — the protection of minorities. (p. 444)

Later on, discussing George Fitzhugh, Curti presents democracy in the same curious way, as that which southerners wanted to reform. The southern conservative ruling class was a model of how to prevent the excess of democracy:

> Thus the South, Fitzhugh argued, was free from that turbulence which marked the North and indeed, all other societies. In the South, unlike the North, the interest of the governing class was conservative. This prevented those violent fluctuations between conservatism and radicalism, fluctuations inherent in the fact that no society had ever existed or could exist, in which the immediate interests of the majority of its constituents did not conflict with all existing institutions, including the family, property rights and established order. In slavery, northern property owners and capitalists would find a shared ally against the subversive radicalisms — feminism, abolitionism, socialism, communism. (p. 444)

Curti was not disenchanted with America or democracy. Experiencing as he was writing his book the wrenching change from pacifist idealism to high democratic realism brought on by the Second World War, he made hopeful sacrifices for democracy and takes it and its values seriously. No wonder he finds in Whitman that expressive figure he does not in Melville or Tocqueville:

> Walt Whitman, dismissed from a minor federal office for the alleged immorality of his poems, expressed in *Democratic Vistas* in movingly beautiful language the powerful conviction that the war, by melding together the nation and lifting it to new spiritual heights, had set the stage for the long hoped for glories in American art, letters, and thought. But Whitman's realistic insight also enabled him to detect signs that it had heightened materialism and corruption, that democracy was on trial, that the promise of American life was yet to be fought for and won. (p. 477)

The Tocquevillian finds the nation's arts and letters imperiled in the perfecting of democracy, and sees democratic corruption and materialism as all too characteristic. Curti, with Whitman, sees instead a fight for democracy. No wonder Whitman claimed Lincoln and no wonder Curti claims Whitman. If his antebellum story feeds democracy with likelihood, principle, luck and possibility, his postwar story documents its struggle in the realm of thought to be of, by, and for the people.

Curti's survey of the ground of American intellectual history is comprehensive, emphasizing several large themes. He reads the colonial period broadly. He treats the English experience as first among equals, and his emphasis comports well with the recent historiographical tendency to stress the heightened receptivity of colonial English North America to the traditions of English political thinking. Curti pictures a colonial society in which several transplanted European cultures forced the dominant English culture to the edges of its own inherent capacity for tolerance and liberation. Although attentive to the Puritans, Curti was less impressed by them than by the rise of the Enlightenment.

The Enlightenment deism that succeeded Calvinism among many intellectuals was Curti's darling. What is remarkable about his survey is his sympathy for even the orthodox belief he dislikes. His sense of his own errand, writing the unwritten history of American thought, makes him careful to show how the clergy aided education, how the cosmology and theology of the Puritans contained a character, not only a belief. What Curti also does is add to the list of legitimate American religious forbears issues and figures who expand the notion of legitimacy far beyond the orthodox. The very scope of Curti's assignment means one can choose John Woolman, Anne Hutchinson, or Jonathan Edwards. In addition, his interest in the beliefs of ordinary people broaden his judgments. The Great Awakening prompts him to remark:

> Here it is important to emphasize the fact that the Awakening counteracted the growing secularism, rationalism, and skepticism of the eighteenth century on the one hand and on the other challenged the traditionally dominant intellectualistic and authoritarian expositions of Christianity. In kindling the religion of the heart in the great mass of plain peoples the revivals gave a broader base to the Christian heritage. (p. 57)

The best compass Americans have ever followed, he suggests, was one magnetized by the Enlightenment:

> It was a protest against traditional reliance on authority in religious and secular life. It asserted man's ability to understand the universe without supernatural

revelation and without the authoritative guidance of earthly superiors. It assumed
the original worth and dignity of all men, and challenged the comfortable to
alleviate the harsh lot of the poverty-stricken and ignorant masses and the victims
of irrational and inhumane social conditions. (p. 103)

Curti believed both in the Enlightenment and in its rootedness in the custom
of its day. He understood and made clear that the figures who articulated the
rationalist dream of liberty were no more democratically selected than their
scientific ideas were universally available to popular understanding. His
"militant common man" is like Jefferson's yeoman farmer, a pastoral more
necessary than real.

Curti wanted to make clear what people thought and to establish the
legitimacy of some thoughts he especially valued. Because Curti sought a
history of American thought growing not only organically but morally, his
normative standard was carefully taken from the rationalist liberal Enlightenment as expressed by the Founding Fathers. Curti differs from others who
have celebrated this tradition in that he declines to hold it up as a piety. He
does not confuse our national institutions with the intellectual climate that
may have produced them. No constitutionalist Curti. What he loves about
American democracy is not its institutions, which he appears to regard as always worth reforming. What Curti loves about democracy is the future its
history suggests it might bring *and* the variety and interest it gives to human
lives. Nor does he flinch from the undemocratic implications of the Enlightenment by dressing down Jefferson or denying Franklin his hard won upward
mobility.

Having found the American Enlightenment where he could, Curti defined
it pointedly as a reform tradition — rationalist, but, for a religious people, it
will represent the bold spirit of reform. The Enlightenment stamped the
Founding, and dominated a certain portion of American intellectual life. This
is his explicit story. But Curti also tells another story. He first chronicles the
special participation of the literate American classes in the international Enlightenment and tells of how they viewed, shaped, and expressed those
thoughts in their efforts to control their new world and make it their own.
The other story begins in Curti's value for the implications of those views and
involves their inaccessibility to the common folk and yet their peculiar
necessity to ordinary people if democracy was to work. The bridge for Curti
from Enlightenment to democracy is reform. And it is in reform and its role in
democracy and in the cyclical patterns of its influence, as opposed to the apparent environmental growth of American thought, that we discover the
book's passion and its beauty.

Curti summons the Great Chain of Being, Calvinism, and conservative
classicism as high culture habits of thought especially resistant to the idea of

Progress. He implies that the people need to be educated to see that what they are *really* talking about in their own lives is that kind of Progress the Enlightenment sponsored. One of the bounties of Curti's realism is that he can suggest how the popular interest may be well served by an appropriate ideology. In this case, the Enlightenment does advance the colonial interest. The conservative classes will have to be, one supposes, re-educated. Curti claims that the Enlightenment, properly and popularly understood, will not serve their interests. A member of that class must end as a Jefferson following an intellectual leading to change his interest or a Fitzhugh following his interest to an explicity antidemocratic philosophy.

The inner life of Curti's book, so often slighted, manifests itself in his treatment of reform. He admires and values the humanitarians. He understands that the middle class bore responsibility for many of the evils they deplored. He understands how short of social change ameliorative reform may fall. He is not prepared to go beyond his instrumental realism to a view of history in which motive and thought are subsumed by structural interests. He defends the middle-class reform impulse by positing a modern version of the moral sense, that of a conscience-heeding person "being sensitive in the way that all human beings are more or less sensitive" (p. 120). Skirting the attribution to a religious motive, he allows that the Christian doctrine of the brotherhood of man will serve. This common sense intervention says: look here, we do have consciences, or most of us do, after all, and the sincerity of the reformers counts for something. Curti despairs of analyzing motive. What he will say is that the reformers meant what they said, even if they were middle class, and that what they said and did deserves our respect.

The middle class is in Curti's view the principal American class. It is hewn out of the people and not isolated from them. This class is implicated in the inescapable evils of capitalism unless active in the reform of escapable evils. Reform becomes an exculpating test: you can be absolved of the responsibility of opposing a regime you have learned to condemn if you try to reform it. You can be absolved if you reform what is susceptible of reform because you value what may not survive a revolution. In Curti, we see most clearly the moment when Progressive becomes liberal. Curti must give up a part of his critique of America for the sake of what he believes America has achieved.

Curti's treatment of humanitarianism is a quiet *tour de force* of intellectual history in which influence, *Zeitgeist*, politics, religion, and literature are blended into a brief and intense account of how even a compromised class might select from its intellectual inheritance a higher interest than the national or material. When we examine the blend of ideas that Curti identifies with the humanitarian impulse, we find that it depends mostly on "Christian ethics and piety, especially as exemplified by Quakers and the evangelical sects. The

Quaker doctrine that the golden rule should be put into practice led to concern for the unfortunate classes. Evangelicism also took account of the poor
and miserable" (p. 121). Their spiritual errand to the less fortunate brought
them to reform. This view of Christianity, of which John Woolman and
Granville Sharp are representative, also suggests that kind of religion the
deists bargained for. Some might say that the religious legacy of the Enlightenment (and perhaps its failure to become a view of life the mass of people
might avow) was one that tried to limit and situate religion. Franklin's caution, Jefferson's improvement, Paine's denunciations, the First Amendment's
delimiting of a public role for religion have been regarded as attempts to
make for religion a free, private space but to deny it public legitimacy. Curti
suggests that deism paralleled Christian humanitarianism in its effort to improve this world and that in some way they were partners, not adversaries.

Curti's treatment of Enlightenment suggests a connection between the few
and the many. It defends intellectual history as the province of the elite by
suggesting the crucial connection between an Enlightened elite and the social
good of the many and between rationalism and popular humanitarian convictions. This view has fallen on evil days. The best and brightest are spoken
of with irony and the privileged are once again encouraged in private interests. But the Progressives and their liberal successors, like the reformers and
their Enlightenment and religious forbears, were more ashamed not to do
what they thought they could than embarrassed by the difficulty of the attempt.

If the purpose of *The Growth of American Thought* was to facilitate the
establishment of intellectual history as a respected and solid special subject
within American history, Curti accomplished his end. He wrote a book that
should have discouraged his colleague William Hesseltine's claim that writing
"intellectual history is like trying to nail jelly to the wall." Indeed, Curti's
awareness of the historical profession's resistance to his subject gives his book
its shape. He had to prove to the mandarin academics that there was a history
of American ideas, and to professional historians like Hesseltine that it had
anything to teach a "real" historian. Curti addressed the first doubt by writing
a chronological history of American thought, oriented toward European intellectual development. Curti writes modestly but firmly, playing up Franklin and Jefferson and American inventors and heroes but refusing the defensive boasting or exceptionalism of the anxious booster. The book stakes an
American historical claim to be considered from its start a busy province of
European culture and from its independence an intellectual seat of its own.

Unlike contemporaries who were refurbishing the Puritan mind, Curti did
not interest himself in the detailed history of ideas but in the history that ideas

affected. Historians could not only follow Curti's reconstruction of thought but imagine thinking that way themselves; this was never the case with Perry Miller. Curti's important treatment of the institutions of intellectual transmission: the church, the school, the newspaper, the store, the circuit, the lyceum, mediated the flow of ideas so one could see how people encountered them and came to understand them. The terms of common understanding did not distress Curti or rouse him to contempt. Whatever kind of tragedy America might be, it was not for Curti an intellectual tragedy. In part, he reserved his scorn for those whose conservative views he disliked — although his scorn was mildly expressed — and in part, he had not that attachment to the pure enunciation of ideas or literature that would make him champion their unvulgarized, unadulterated state. Use delighted him.

The Growth of American Thought boasts a surprising cast of characters. Curti has big eyes for the variety of American thinkers. The quotations are good ones, juicy with the flavor of the writer, as well as apt to Curti's purposes. They exhibit a wide variety of moods. Students who pay Curti's book mind will come away with their own favorite pieces of lore or odd types. The wonderful section on colonial American contributions to classical scholarship typifies Curti at his best. Without claiming for American classical scholarship a distinction it did not gain, he lists the translations, mentioning Ezekiel Cheever's Latin grammar (Accidence, A Short Introduction to the Latin Tongue) quoting Cotton Mather's tribute: "Do but name Cheever, and the Echo straight/Upon that Name, Good Latin, will repeat." Curti answers a minor question well without magnifying its significance. He gives his account, satisfying a civilized curiosity. He relies upon all the instances to create the atmosphere of American thought, and they do.

Curti's unvarnished interest in what people knew, his admiration for intellectual achievement and curiosity, for its welter of forms, complements his own themes. Despite his sense of audience, Curti never surrenders his interest in the unpredictable issue of intellect, freed by democracy, nourished by tradition, confused by the lack of uniformity, tried by newness and uncongenial, unestablished conditions, buoyed by democratic hopes, sometime companion to a great notion, sometime laggard. The impelling internal and external narrative necessities do not blur one's impression of Americans thinking, reflecting, teaching, studying, cogitating, arguing, orating, praying, dissecting, translating, figuring, reading, scheming, reforming, preaching, painting, calling to arms, composing, printing, lamenting, rhapsodizing, prosing and poetasting, enlarging, drawing, mapmaking, classifying, founding, obstructing, disbelieving, doubting, copying, mistaking, foretelling. . . . We the people teem in Whitman-like fashion, albeit sobered and muted, in Curti's crowded pages.

Characteristic of Curti is his portrait of "contributions to knowledge" in the early (middle) west. Ranging from natural history to the practice of medicine and philosophical and historical societies, Curti takes the intellectual and cultural life of Cincinnati and Louisville seriously. He does not interpret their interests. Curti understands how the life of that country grew up in stores, printers' shops, church halls, around cracker barrels, and also relied on the recognition of individual talent by a people anxious to improve. There is nothing bitter, sentimental, or ironic in his picture, Curti's America is not Winseburg, Zenith, or Lake Wobegon, although you see how those places got imagined. He can write J. Daniel Drake of Cincinnati, "the Franklin of the West," with genuine appreciation, born of an uncondescending sympathy with the interest and possibilities of the American heartland — and a politics and a view of intellectual life and of scholarship that supports such sympathy (pp. 277–78).

Curti not only prefers what he calls cultural democracy, he does not blanch at terms that would now be hard to use: "On a higher political and moral level and yet partaking of many of the features of the new journalism was Horace Greeley's *New York Tribune.* Its advocacy of reforms promising to elevate the common man to vast heights appealed to the self-interest and idealism of the plain people who subscribed to it in mounting numbers" (p. 348). History gives Curti an estimating distance on Greeley but does not appear to have rendered their vocabularies discontinuous. Common man, plain people, have real meanings for Merle Curti, probably not all that different from Greeley's.

The theoretical sophistication and the terms that haunt our own writing of history are largely unnecessary to Curti's plain song instrumentalism. He could write "idealism" and make a point about motive and ideologies. Straight talk about the reception of conservative ideas, fonder talk about the intellectual life of the common man — and woman too, for Curti is respectful of women's thought and work — tolerant enthusiasm for the creative effusions of Americans as they went about their personal and democratic business, these characterize Curti, whose instrumentalism does not undermine the middle class or, even before the Civil War, claim it too eagerly for the standing order. Curti could criticize the American Christian middle class without excoriating it. He himself writes with the happy ease of one sharing its nonpolitical values.

Reading *The Growth of American Thought,* then, remains worthwhile — not just for the information, but because of Curti's multilayered and consistent advocacy of certain traditions and values and the respect he shows his subjects. It may be that his advocacy of the Enlightened reform liberal tradition is unavailable to us, although for many the battleground of values he discerned remains one of serious engagement. Curti wrote intellectual history as if it was supposed to influence the values and traditions Americans would choose. His view of democracy made him respectful of popular choices but not determinist with regard to the voice of the people as heard through the din of material civilization. Curti's tone is mild and his almanac of American thought sometimes too clearly revised by subsequent work or made obvious by subsequent shifts of tone or style. It remains uniquely useful for scholar and general reader alike, however, because Curti's is still a fighting creed, an American intellectual history that really stands for something and stands up for the subject in the process. *The Growth of American Thought* is the real McCoy.

Robert Dawidoff, Claremont Graduate School, is presently writing a study of the modern interpretation of American civilization.

THE CHALLENGE OF ALFRED D. CHANDLER, JR.: RETROSPECT AND PROSPECT

Thomas K. McCraw

In 1988, Harvard University Press will publish *Scale and Scope*, a book that will represent the crowning achievement of one of the most productive careers of any twentieth-century American historian.[1] *Scale and Scope* is a comparative analysis of the rise of big business in three industrial economies: the United States, Great Britain, and Germany. Because of the depth of its research, it is certain to become one of the classic studies of American historical scholarship. For its author, Alfred D. Chandler, Jr., it will comprise a third such landmark study, the other two being *Strategy and Structure* (1962) and *The Visible Hand* (1977). Both of these earlier works won the Thomas Newcomen Award, given for the best book on the history of business published during the preceding three years. In addition, *The Visible Hand* received the Pulitzer Prize and the Bancroft Prize. But more important than any prizes, Chandler has influenced a generation of scholars in many countries, including Britain, France, Germany, Japan, Italy, Spain, and Belgium; and in several disciplines, among them history, economics, sociology, and business administration. For all these reasons, and as an overture to the appearance of *Scale and Scope*, it is timely to review Chandler's career and to trace the roots of his achievement.

Taking the bare facts first, Chandler came from a patrician but not extremely wealthy family which, during his youth, moved about in the United States and Latin America. He was educated at Phillips Exeter Academy, Harvard College, the University of North Carolina (where he took an M.A. after his five years of Navy duty during World War II), and Harvard University (where he completed his Ph.D. in history in 1952). His career as a working historian has been spent primarily in three institutions: the Massachusetts Institute of Technology (1950–1963), the Johns Hopkins University (1963–1971), and the Harvard Business School (1971–present).

Since 1946, when his first published article appeared, Chandler has written four major books, coauthored a fifth, edited and compiled nine other books, written thirty-two articles and twenty-six chapters plus scores of book reviews, and has been assistant editor or editor-in-chief of ten volumes of presidential papers—four on Theodore Roosevelt, six on Dwight D.

Eisenhower. He has directed numerous dissertations and has served in a variety of administrative posts: as a department chairman, head of an institute, president of professional associations, editor of the series Harvard Studies in Business History, and member of the editorial boards of academic journals. He has also devoted a substantial part of his energies to other time-consuming tasks, not the least of which has been a rich family life with his wife Fay (an accomplished painter and sculptor) and their four children.

One of the most noteworthy aspects of such a broad career has been Chandler's maintenance of a sharp focus in his work. For any scholar or artist, this is a difficult task, as the English poet Stephen Spender recently remarked, reflecting from the vantage point of his seventy-fifth birthday:

> You wonder exactly when something clicked, at what point a person became a Reputation. . . . . But what you realize most of all — it's what Edmund Wilson was always pointing out to me — is that people can be enormously talented and gifted, but that the essential thing is that they should really want to use their gifts and not become distracted by the various other attractions that life has to offer. It's a fearfully difficult problem, though. I think Auden is the only person I've known who really had a clear idea of what he wanted to do when he was 20 and just sat down and wrote and didn't allow himself to be diverted. I'm an example myself of the opposite, of someone who is always getting distracted.[2]

While most other scholars have followed the pattern of Spender (how aptly named!), Chandler has taken the opposite course. He has become the Auden of postwar American scholars. Perhaps more than any other major historian of his generation, he has not allowed himself to be diverted. With resolute singlemindedness, he has kept his focus clear for more than four decades. In exploring how this focus developed, it will be useful to consider a number of episodes in Chandler's career. Some of these occurred before he became "a Reputation," some afterward. But all are of one piece.

Chandler did his first extensive historical research at Harvard College during the academic year 1939/40. The result was a 186-page undergraduate honors thesis entitled "The [Gubernatorial] Campaign of 1876 in South Carolina." This document is hardly the work of a mature scholar, yet in several ways it foreshadows the characteristic Chandler method.

First, the focus of the thesis is on change — in this case, the dramatic end of Reconstruction in South Carolina. The incumbent governor, Daniel Henry Chamberlain, was a brilliant, well-educated man, extremely popular with a variety of voters despite being a carpetbagger from Massachusetts and a Republican. As Chandler tells the story, Chamberlain seemed certain of re-election as late as June 1876. Yet in November he lost to the Democratic nominee, Wade Hampton, a prominent native South Carolinian and a Confederate war hero. Chandler tried to pinpoint exactly what happened between June and November to produce this surprising outcome.

Second, Chandler's method was initially to immerse himself in a sea of facts. He did extensive research at Harvard's Widener Library, then traveled to South Carolina for additional study. This included not only archival work but also interviews with persons still living who were knowledgeable about the upheavals in the state during the late nineteenth century. The young Chandler then read, day by day, the *Charleston News and Courier,* in order to get a sense of the society he was studying. This newspaper constituted his most important single source; and his ability to absorb, retain, and organize vast quantities of information provided an early example of a trait that came to underlie the entire body of his historical work.

Third, Chandler's undergraduate thesis exhibits signs of the sociological preoccupations that animate his later scholarship. It is symptomatic that the first page of this first work is not even a page of prose. Instead, it is a map. The map depicts the counties of the State, each one shaded to indicate percentages of black and white voters. The differences from one county to the next are so dramatic that it immediately becomes evident that South Carolina was not a single homogeneous society, but several different ones existing in uneasy symbiosis: the newly-enfranchised Blacks, concentrated in a few areas of the state devoted to plantation agriculture; the old planter class of whites, gathered around the city of Charleston and comfortable with Republican rule; and the much larger number of upland poor whites, who responded to the white supremacist rhetoric of the newly-organized Democratic "Redeemers" of 1876. Through careful attention to chronology, Chandler managed to show how the surprising result of the election ensued from a series of complex events and cultural shifts. Overall, considering that his work was done as an undergraduate thesis, the research seems remarkably painstaking.

After Chandler's graduation in 1940, he, like his classmate John F. Kennedy (a fellow member of the Harvard sailing team), became an officer in the United States Navy. Some of Chandler's experiences during his five years of service during World War II reinforced his interest in change, especially within large organizations. One of his first jobs as an officer of the Atlantic Fleet Camera Party was to set up a new and more accurate system for analyzing naval gunnery exercises — surface and antiaircraft — by means of photo triangulation. Meanwhile, the Japanese attack on Pearl Harbor had plunged the United States itself into the war, and the American government began to construct an enormous new navy, of which nearly every ship in the Atlantic fleet was serviced by Chandler's unit. Thus, he found himself in the midst of one of the greatest national mobilizations in history. The whole undertaking produced feats of organizational innovation unprecedented in human experience — and, for Chandler himself, an unforgettable example of the anatomy of change within giant organizations — the subject that later became his consuming preoccupation as a scholar.

In view of this later focus of his scholarship, the most significant of his military assignments proved to be his work toward the end of the war when he became an interpreter of aerial reconnaissance photographs of German and Japanese territory — photos taken before, during, and after bombing runs. For Chandler, two major points emerged from this experience. First, during his training at the photo interpreters' school, it became clear to him that strategic bombing often failed to achieve its goals of crippling the enemy's industrial capacity. Factories would appear to be destroyed; but they might simply have been moved underground, where they could keep producing so long as they could be provided with raw materials and power. Only if supply lines were severed or sources of energy knocked out would production capability be destroyed. From these lessons came some of the later emphasis in Chandler's work on logistics, industrial production, and key sectors of national economies. Second, the whole experience reinforced his interest in the study of change. Toward the end of the war, for example, he pored over hundreds of aerial photographs, taken over several months' time, of a large beach in Kyushu which was a potential site for the expected American invasion of Japan. Assessing the strengths of the defensive emplacements, he pondered the subtle changes going on as the Japanese worked to improve logistical support for the site. Years later, in his books and articles, he asked again and again a series of questions about industrial change: how were things done at a certain time, how were they done later, and what had happened to cause the change. During World War II, he had confronted each of these questions daily, as a twenty-six-year-old naval officer equipped with a stereoscopic magnifying glass.

After V-J Day and his release from the Navy, Chandler returned to school. He had known, "for as long as I can remember," that he wanted to become a professional historian.[3] In 1945, intending to continue his study of southern history, he enrolled at the University of North Carolina. Paul Buck, who had been Chandler's adviser on his undergraduate thesis, suggested that this would be the best place to study his chosen topic, especially if he could work under Fletcher Green, America's leading trainer of graduate students in the field. As it turned out, Chandler enjoyed his year in Chapel Hill, but the most important influences on him came neither from Green nor any other historian. Instead, they came from the university's two great sociologists and southern regionalists, Rupert Vance and Howard Odum. Here began for Chandler what would become a fateful marriage with formal sociology. Concurrently, he decided to abandon southern history in favor of some other field (still not clearly defined), and to return to Harvard for a new beginning, a second start in graduate school.

At Harvard, he first encountered as a supervisor the formidable Samuel Eliot Morison, who, at their initial meeting, showed up resplendent in his Navy uniform, heavy with gold braid and rows of ribbons. When Chandler tentatively broached his own wish to take sociology as a minor field, Morison pronounced this option "unacceptable," advising instead that Greek would be a more appropriate field — not Greek history, but the Greek language. After working a few years with Morison, from whom he did learn valuable lessons about clear writing, Chandler switched advisers. He came under the more sympathetic tutelage of Frederick Merk, and he also assisted in the classes of Robert G. Albion, who shared Chandler's emerging interest in economic history.

Yet, at Harvard as at North Carolina, Chandler's most important teachers came from neither economics nor history, but sociology. The greatest single influence was Talcott Parsons, who introduced Chandler to the work of Max Weber, Emile Durkheim, and the entire tradition of historical sociology. Now, for the first time, Chandler became truly excited intellectually.[4] Parsons's emphasis on role theory and structural-functionalism profoundly affected him, coming as it did against the background of his first-hand experience in the ways of the giant Navy organization. In one way or other, for the next forty years, Parsonian and especially Weberian sociology informed the corpus of nearly all of Chandler's organizational studies.[5]

Before considering this work, I want to mention three other aspects of Chandler's graduate training at Harvard. The first was his "cell," or study group, in the History Department's Henry Adams Club. Other members included John Morton Blum, whose self-confidence and superb prose style convinced the modest and self-effacing Chandler that he was now in very fast company and had better work as hard as he could to survive the competition; the late Sydney Ahlstrom, whose pioneering studies in the history of American religion and romanticism, together with his great synthesis, *A Religious History of the American People* (which won the National Book Award in 1973) made him the leading historian of American religion of his generation; and Bernard Bailyn, whose eminent achievements in his own field of colonial history parallel Chandler's.

The second distinctive aspect of Chandler's Harvard experience proved to be his participation in the Center for the Study of Entrepreneurship. This undertaking had a precarious but productive existence between 1948 and 1958. Financed by the Rockefeller Foundation, it was started by Joseph Schumpeter (shortly before his death in 1950), and by Arthur Cole, an economic historian who had come to the Harvard Business School and had built its Baker Library into the world's leading repository for the study of business. Cole, though not a great scholar himself, was a superb organizer of scholarship, particularly of the cross-disciplinary variety. He shaped and directed the Center, bringing in such established historians, sociologists, and economists as Thomas Cochran, Leland Jenks, William Miller, and Fritz Redlich. He also attracted a number of younger scholars whose names now read like a Who's Who of economic historians from the 1950s to the 1980s: Hugh Aitken, Bernard Bailyn, David Landes, Douglass North, Henry Rosovsky, and John Sawyer, as well as Chandler himself.[6]

A third aspect of Chandler's graduate-school years was the fortuitous way in which he came by his dissertation topic. Chandler's friend Bailyn has written that the selection of a topic is perhaps the hardest and most important step in historical research.[7] Through a remarkable combination of good luck and good judgment, Chandler chose a subject that would affect his whole approach to the writing of history. The selection came about in the following way. During his early years in graduate school, when he was looking for a place to live in crowded postwar Cambridge, Chandler's elderly great aunt Lucy Poor, who lived in a two-family house in nearby Brookline, suddenly died. Chandler and his growing family then moved into Lucy's half of this house. In a storeroom, they discovered a large volume of papers belonging to Henry Varnum Poor, Lucy's father and Chandler's own great-grandfather.

Henry Varnum Poor had been famous in his time as an analyst of railroads. For more than a decade, starting in 1849, he had edited the *American Railroad Journal*. Afterward, from 1868 to 1887, Poor published the *Manual of Railroads of the United States*. Thus, from the time of the early construction of railroads in the 1840s all the way to the creation of the Interstate Commerce Commission in 1887, Poor was perhaps the best-informed person in the country about the state of American railroads. For the graduate student Alfred Chandler, now equipped with Poor's personal papers and with the immense backfiles of Poor's newspapers and other publications housed in Baker Library, the prospect of a dissertation centering on Poor represented a bonanza on the order of the Comstock Lode. But the ore had to be dug out and refined with care, lest, owing to its very immensity, Chandler lose control over his material. The result was a series of articles, then a dissertation, and finally a book entitled *Henry Varnum Poor: Business Editor, Analyst and Reformer*.[8]

As it turned out, Chandler was not only lucky in choosing his ancestor, he also showed superb judgment in knowing what to do with the treasures he found in Lucy Poor's storeroom. On the surface, this first book appeared to be a straightforward biography of Henry Varnum Poor. Beneath, it was a "life and times" in the best sense, with the emphasis on times. The book represented nothing less than a comparative history of the great American railroad corporations during their formative years. Still another level beneath that, it comprised a history of the early evolution of American corporate finance and management, which happened to have started with the railroads.

Because Poor lived such a long life (1812–1905), because he was so prolific a writer, and because he himself pioneered in the comparative analysis of corporations, Chandler had to find and absorb a prodigious amount of data. In so doing, he took an approach that would serve him and his students well over the years to come; for, in addition to coping with a huge base of information, he was compelled to work within the comparative method—because that is how Poor worked. Putting these two circumstances together, Chandler developed what became his characteristic way of extracting clear historical patterns that in turn became inductively-derived theory. From his ancestor Poor, Chandler thus inherited not only a collection of papers but also a proclivity to make empirical comparisons that would yield useful theoretical generalizations.

Poor's own name lives on, of course, as one-half of Standard and Poor's Corporation, the house that provides comprehensive business information and comparative bond ratings. Henry Varnum Poor started this practice by advising investors on which railroads were better bets than others, and this obviously required that he know a great deal about railroad finance, management, future plans, and organizational structures. Poor's writings, like Chandler's a hundred years later, are full of comparative analyses of a wide range of information about a large number of companies.

Eventually, Poor compiled running histories of no fewer than 120 different railroad companies—plus a great mass of statistical and organizational data on other firms. A century later, his great-grandson Alfred Chandler plowed relentlessly through all of this material. In the process, Chandler acquired a great deal of knowledge about the early development of big business in the United States. He also recapitulated, in uncanny detail, the explanatory and interpretive functions of his ancestor. For the generation of the 1950s through the 1980s, Chandler did just what Poor had done for his own generation of exactly a century before. The only difference was that Chandler wrote as a historian, Poor as a journalist and reformer. Otherwise, the parallel holds. Here, for example, is Poor writing to his wife in 1860, trying to explain the nature of his work:

> To tell you what I am doing would be to show you columns of figures to be added, divided, or subtracted, or the memoir of some rr. or canal, which is little else than a record of names, & dates, & distances—all this is the most

prosaic business possible. It may lay the foundation, by the by, for something better. First comes the form — then the soul, the natural sequence must be respected . . . I am getting along well though slowly. The work I am doing will never be done over again. So I am making it as valuable and complete as possible. It will be the record of a great achievement — of the greatest material development the world has yet seen.[9]

Chandler himself might have written the same lines one hundred years later.

Even before completing his biography of Poor, Chandler had begun to move beyond an interest in railroads alone to a concern with the history of large enterprises in general. This was a natural evolution, because the railroads — with their multiple functions of tying the nation together, creating a vast internal market, and pioneering in organizational innovations — laid the essential groundwork for the development of the modern industrial state. The story of this evolution, as Chandler saw it, with his continuing emphasis on the role of big business, became explicit in both of his major books, *Strategy and Structure* and, especially, *The Visible Hand.*

Chandler first worked out his ideas through a series of important articles published in the *Business History Review* during the middle and late 1950s.[10] Collectively, the articles proved to be a prologue to *Strategy and Structure,* which appeared in 1962. This book, as a work of business history, represented so unorthodox an approach that some reviewers either did not know what to make of it or simply missed its enormous significance. In their defense, the book is not easy to read. Essentially, *Strategy and Structure* is made up of an introduction adapted from Chandler's influential article of 1959, "The Beginnings of 'Big Business' in American Industry," followed by long case histories of organizational upheaval and innovation in four giant companies: Du Pont, General Motors, Standard Oil, and Sears, Roebuck. Originally, Chandler had begun the book with two additional case studies of railroads, but the referee for MIT Press had suggested that these be deleted lest an already long and complex manuscript become unmanageable.

In his final version of *Strategy and Structure,* Chandler recounted the crises and opportunities that led to the adoption of a "multi-divisional structure" by each of the four pioneering companies. He then proceeded to survey the seventy largest industrial corporations in America, and to generalize about the reasons for and against organizational change. The entire effort represented a monumental historiographical achievement: a *tour de force* of comparative research and conceptualization, and a matchless example of a business historian's willingness to generalize.

Before Chandler's comparative studies began to appear, most histories of business consisted of monographs on individual firms or industries. Though much of this work tended toward apologetics, a good deal of it attained a high degree of accuracy, perceptiveness, and even excellence. Nor were all historians of business before Chandler reluctant to generalize. Far too often, however, their generalizations were couched in a mode of attack or defense — of muckraking or shilling. Endlessly, they debated whether Rockefeller, Gould, Carnegie et al. were "Robber Barons" or "Industrial Statesmen." The overwhelming majority of all writing about the history of American business fell into this pattern. [11]

Chandler's own response to the timeworn debate was simple: he sidestepped it. To this day, one can read any of his books without knowing (except by an occasional passing reference) that such a debate ever took place, let alone that it dominated historical writing about business. In taking such a stance, Chandler was implicitly saying, in his unassuming way, that neither the pro nor the antibusiness polemicists knew what they were talking about. He was faulting both sides for failing to make the requisite effort to understand the managerial revolution in American business; for not doing even a fraction of the primary research necessary to support sweeping characterizations of business executives as either robber barons or industrial statesmen; and, more important, for accepting such terms of debate as legitimate in the first place. Chandler himself insisted on asking a very different set of questions, and in so doing he transformed the nature of the field.

Here he took a role reminiscent of that marked out by Willard Hurst in the study of legal institutions; or, previously, by Roy F. Nichols in political history. As David Potter once described Nichols's contribution, "Most of all, I think the narrowness and conceptual poverty of American political history at the time when he embarked on his professional career virtually compelled a man of high talents either to abandon political history or to attempt to rehabilitate it as a scholarly study." [12] For Chandler, there was not much to rehabilitate beyond the promising beginnings made by his predecessors at the Harvard Business School (N.S.B. Gras, Henrietta Larson, Arthur Cole, and Ralph Hidy), plus the superb work done by Thomas Cochran, Edward C. Kirkland, and Allan Nevins (at least the nonpolemical portions of Nevins's studies). What Chandler did, then, was not so much rehabilitate a field gone to seed, but instead *establish* business history as an independent and important area for study.

His initial vehicle was an article published in 1959, entitled "The Beginnings of 'Big Business' in American Industry." [13] This piece, in addition to its breadth of learning and boldness of generalization, has the additional virtue — absent from some of Chandler's other writings — of being entirely accessible to nonspecialists. His purpose and method seem clear from the outset, and his first sentences have a disarming appeal:

> The historian, by the very nature of his task, must be concerned with change. What made for change? Why did it come when it did, and in the way it did? These are characteristically historians' questions. For the student of American business history, these basic questions can be put a little more precisely. What in the American past has given businessmen the opportunity or created the need for them to change what they were doing or the way they were doing it?[14]

Overall, Chandler appears to be asking the question, "What were the dynamic factors in the growth of the American economy and its business system during the late nineteenth and early twentieth centuries?" His answers are, in chronological sequence, the rise of the railroad, the development of concentrated urban markets for industrial and consumer goods, the emergence of mass-production technology, the coming of electrification and the internal-combustion engine, and the emergence of organized research and development. None of this would have surprised any well-informed reader.

But the real heart of the article lies in its extremely subtle subversion of the conventional wisdom. Its actual topic is not the items listed above, but instead the process of bureaucratic change inside giant corporations. Nearly every important comment in the piece is concerned with the evolution of vertically-integrated companies. Chandler's base of information here was his own intimate knowledge of the behavior of the largest industrial corporations in the United States; and his central concern was the galaxy of forces that led to the formation of these firms, specifically the combination of mass production with mass marketing. He gives brief but memorable case studies in the evolution of modern management (Swift & Company, American Tobacco, Singer Sewing Machine, International Harvester, National Biscuit, U.S. Rubber, Standard Oil, U.S. Steel, Ford Motor, General Electric, Westinghouse). By the time the reader has finished the article, he or she has enjoyed a primer in American business history, together with a powerful thesis about the imperatives for vertical integration. In addition, the whole piece is capped off, as it was introduced, by a disarming and, considering the prodigious research that underlay Chandler's argument, perhaps disingenuous disclaimer: "There must be an emphasis here on the words 'seem' and 'appear.' The framework used is a preliminary one and the data itself, based on readily available printed material rather than on business records are hardly as detailed or accurate as could be desired."[15] However "preliminary" it might have been, the article stands as a landmark in the evolution of business history as a field. It has been anthologized in many different collections, and, one suspects, has formed the staple for lecture notes on the history of business for a great many instructors in survey courses.

Chandler incorporated parts of the article in the introductory chapter of *Strategy and Structure*. Whereas the article was a primer, the book represented an advanced course in the ways of business decision-making at the highest levels. Even for experienced historians, the assignment of reading *Strategy and Structure* constituted a formidable task. Chandler's minute concerns about precisely what happened when, his apparent preoccupations with details that appear at first blush unimportant or even trivial, seemed off-putting. Furthermore, the very title of the book expressed an impersonal sociological model of business behavior that smacked of the kinds of determinisms historians dislike.[16] And Chandler was, in fact, arguing an explicit behavioral model: that businesses, like other organizations, are governed by inertia; that they change their overall direction (which Chandler calls their "strategy") only when forced by competitive pressures to do so; and that a change in strategy is likely to be successful only if accompanied by a decisive change in organizational structure.

In making this argument Chandler took his readers deep into the recesses of the four companies that comprised his case studies. For most scholars, this was uncharted territory. Many historians had an *a priori* distaste for business, and particularly for the big companies that so fascinated Chandler. (Consider, for example, that the influence of Gabriel Kolko's *Triumph of Conservatism*, which appeared one year later, in 1963, was much more widely felt among historians.) As for *Strategy and Structure*, it may actually have had less effect on the historical profession than did Chandler's 1959 article on the rise of big business.

Meanwhile, however, *Strategy and Structure* had an immediate and profound impact on other disciplines. Students of business administration at once recognized it as a conceptual breakthrough, and heaped praise on it. Entire courses in major business schools were built around the concept of corporate strategy as defined primarily by Chandler. Consulting firms such as McKinsey & Company used his case studies on corporate diversification to teach their clients about the need for and timing of strategic change and the accompanying mandate to adjust their organizational structures. As the years passed, the book was cited again and again in the literatures of sociology, economics, history, and especially business administration.[17] The maxim "strategy precedes structure" became a byword of corporate management during the 1960s and 1970s, not only in the United States but all over the world, perhaps most notably in Japan. The notions of upper, middle, and lower management — crucial constructs in Chandler's argument —

became clearly delineated in the minds of executives in all capitalist economies. Translated into several languages, *Strategy and Structure* found its
way onto the shelves of thousands of business managers, who intuitively
understood and appreciated its message. For them, it seemed a book of
parables demonstrating how they had arrived at whatever current dilemma
they found themselves in: a book that explained the sea to the fish who
swam within it. To this day, a quarter-century after its first publication,
MIT Press still sells about two thousand copies of *Strategy and Structure*
every year. Within business schools, and for corporate executives, it remains the most widely read history of business enterprise ever written.

Meanwhile, certain developments within the historical profession created
a more fertile ground for the seeds sown by Chandler's work. Elements of
an emerging "new institutionalism" and an "organizational school" of historiography began to appear and to be duly noted.[18] Chandler's name began to
be associated with those of political and intellectual historians such as
George Mowry, Robert Wiebe, and Samuel Hays—as well as with other
prominent students of business enterprise such as Louis Galambos. In fact,
Galambos himself, more than anyone else, has diligently identified and
charted the growth of this historiographical movement.[19]

No member of the organizational school would dispute the proposition
that to the extent that the school has an individual founder, it can be no
other than Chandler. By his own leadership, his direction of graduate students who in turn became productive (William Becker, Charles Cheape,
Harold Livesay, Edwin Perkins, Glenn Porter, Mary Yeager), his impact on
scholars in Europe (Franco Amatori, Herman Daems, Patrick Friedenson,
Wilfried Feldenkirchen, Leslie Hannah, Maurice Levy-Leboyer, Franz
Mathis, Barry Supple) and Japan (Kesaji Kobayashi, Hidemasa Morikawa,
Koichi Shimokawa, Yoshitaka Suzuki, Moriaki Tsuchiya, Shin-ichi Yone-
kawa), and, most of all, through his example of devoted and sustained
scholarship, Chandler has probably done more to promote the systematic
study of modern bureaucratic administration than has any other scholar
since his own mentor, Talcott Parsons.

When Chandler moved in 1963 from MIT to Johns Hopkins, he himself
acquired a host of administrative duties: the editorship of the Eisenhower
Papers (a doubly sensitive task given that the general was still alive and that
Hopkins's president at the time was Milton Eisenhower); the directorship of
the Center for the Study of Recent American History; and the chairmanship
of the History Department. Even though Hopkins proved, with its famous
historical seminars, to be an exciting intellectual milieu, Chandler inevitably
felt pressed by administrative tasks. Now, his publications tended to become ad hoc pieces for this or that collection—all interesting in themselves,

but lacking the sustained Auden-like pattern of his work during the 1950s. He did manage to coauthor with Stephen Salsbury a long biography of Pierre du Pont (published in 1971, and again more a study in the building and administering of great corporations — Du Pont and General Motors — than a conventional biography); to bring out in 1970 the first five volumes of the Eisenhower papers; and to supervise, as noted above, a number of important dissertations. In turn, the research of his students became useful sources for Chandler's own future work.

At this time, Chandler knew precisely what that work should be: a synthesis of the evolution of big business in America — starting with the railroads, proceeding through the rise of mass production and its integration with mass marketing, and the simultaneous development of a "new class" of professional salaried managers. Yet, given the administrative burdens represented by his multiple duties at Hopkins, he found it increasingly difficult to pursue that work. At one point, as he passed the age of fifty, he actually considered retiring from academia and devoting all of his energies to the writing of his grand synthesis. Such a step, and the financial sacrifice it would have meant for both Chandler and his wife, may be taken as a measure of their sense of mission and of Chandler's determination to pursue his work to its logical conclusion.

Again, almost as with the fortuitous discovery of the Henry Varnum Poor papers twenty-five years earlier, a solution appeared: Chandler was offered the Straus Professorship of Business History at Harvard. This was then the world's only endowed chair in the field. In addition, the offer provided an opportunity to return to the Harvard Business School and to the unparalleled riches of Baker Library, where Chandler had done nearly all of his important early research. After thinking the matter over at length (wondering in particular whether he might be leaping from the frying pan into the fire by joining an institution where intensive attention to the teaching of large classes was taken for granted), Chandler decided to accept.

He was drawn to the Harvard Business School for other reasons than those mentioned. For one thing, the School offered generous research support, and it was committed to the comparative cross-disciplinary research that Chandler had always enjoyed. He would be exposed daily to professors of finance, business policy, and organizational behavior; to economists, sociologists, and social psychologists. Furthermore, he would not by any means be the only historian in the Business School. Fritz Redlich, Chandler's old friend and mentor from the days of the Center for the Study of Entrepreneurship would be there, as would James P. Baughman, a talented and versatile historian and editor. Then, too, the Harvard Business School sponsored in conjunction with the Newcomen Society an annual postdoctoral fellowship, and it published the *Business History Review,* the journal in which most of Chandler's important articles had first appeared. The *Review* had just come under the editorship of Glenn Porter, one of his own best students from Hopkins. Finally, Chandler's work was universally known among the Business School's 180 faculty members. Most of them had read *Strategy and Structure*, and a significant body of doctoral work based on his ideas was going on, involving a series of dissertations on the strategy and structure of corporations in advanced economies.[20]

In this new setting, freed from administrative duties, assisted in the classroom by the other historians, and with copious archival and monographic sources immediately available, Chandler set to work on *The Visible Hand*. This book appeared in 1977, to universal acclaim, and Chandler made a point of saying that he could not have written it in any milieu other than the Harvard Business School. Even so, to a much greater degree than *Strategy and Structure*, it was read by large numbers of historians.

Among other things, *The Visible Hand* exemplifies Chandler's instinct for memorable titles. Like *Strategy and Structure*, this second book presents in its title a vivid metaphor that captures its thesis in only three words. In *The Visible Hand*, Chandler argues that the internal workings of modern corporations (i.e., the overt hand of management) have replaced Adam Smith's impersonal marketplace (the invisible hand) as the principal allocator of resources within modern industrial economies. As always, the argument is systematically organized, grounded in extraordinarily deep research, and presented in copious detail. The book totals 500 pages of text, 608 pages altogether, as Chandler rejected the advice of one of his editors to limit his exposition to 300 pages, correctly saying that merely to assert a thesis is one thing, but to demonstrate it conclusively is something entirely different. As with *Strategy and Structure*, the argument contains a fair amount of subtle economic determinism; and it is not accidental that Chandler, though hardly a man of the Left, has provided some useful grist for the Marxian mill.

To convey the full range of information and interpretation contained in *The Visible Hand* would require an inordinate amount of space. Suffice it to say that it is encyclopedic in nature, that it contains several powerful sub-themes (concisely presented in ten "propositions" contained in the opening chapter), and that altogether it represents the fullest and best-researched synthesis ever written on the history of American business enterprise. Even its critics concede its great virtues. As one knowledgeable and un-Chandlerian economic historian recently commented, it stands as "perhaps the most influential book in American business and economic history [written] during the past decade."[21]

Part of Chandler's mission over the last twenty years has been to affect the thinking of cliometricians and, more broadly, of economists in general.

Chandler believes that economists' fixation with static equilibrium theory, their propensity to write in ever more abstract and less accessible mathematical language, and above all their reluctance to respect irrefutable empirical evidence that may fly in the face of their models, dooms them to growing irrelevance at the very moment when their insights are most needed. This becomes the more regrettable because, of all the social sciences, economics has developed easily the most powerful paradigms — some of which have proved extremely useful to Chandler himself. In hewing to the institutionalist, sociologically-oriented approach he learned long ago from Parsons and Schumpeter, Chandler has swum against the tide of modern developments in economics (and even economic history, considering the growing dominance of that field by economists). Chandler himself, like most of his students, respects and has used the results of quantitative research, but he has not employed mathematical notation as a favored method in his own work. He remains a bit skeptical of highly theoretical mathematical manipulations, which, though elegant in themselves, seem to lead researchers away from the historian's distinctive task of intelligible generalization about the past. In his rare saturnine moments, Chandler refers to such computer-based historical work as "a dream that dimmed" — but this judgment has as much to do with the overselling of the method in the early 1960s as with the achievements and failures of the new economic history.

Yet it remains true that if Chandler is correct in his depiction of the workings of modern industrial economies, the models of mainstream academic economics need to be modified significantly. This process of conversion is now underway, and it will likely continue. Chandler's insights have already affected the work of eminent economists such as Oliver Williamson and Richard Caves, and they in turn have begun to reshape the entire subfield of industrial organization, including especially the theory of oligopoly.[22] They and other economists influenced by Chandler have warned explicitly that historical findings grounded in such deep empirical research simply cannot be ignored — that models of oligopolistic behavior need to be thoroughly reconsidered in view of what Chandler and his students have produced. And when Chandler's own new comparative work entitled *Scale and Scope* appears, demonstrating the similarities and differences among national industrial economies, the power of his thinking may well punch a large hole in the dike of economic orthodoxy.

As economics, Chandler's "story" of the development of big business organizations will likely remain beyond significant challenge for many years to come. To the extent that his work as a whole is vulnerable to criticism, the points of effective attack lie elsewhere. They lie in his relative deemphasis on the human impact of industrialization, his neglect of the role of labor, and his implicit (and sometimes explicit) argument that the political state has played only a minor role in the rise of industrial capitalism.[23] Chandler realizes these relative weaknesses, probably better than any critic. Although some of his assumptions are grounded in his own generation's idea of value-free social science (best articulated in Daniel Bell's book, *The End of Ideology*), Chandler understands that his portrayals of large corporations as centers of innovation and productivity in effect justify their existence, despite the ills they have wrought. Above all, he knows, as William Appleman Williams once remarked, that the best reviewer of a body of work is the author himself or herself, who comprehends more fully than anyone else what has been overemphasized, underplayed, or left out altogether. For Chandler, the choice of focus has been deliberately "narrow but deep," as he puts it. Yet, in view of his achievement, it is difficult to argue that he made the wrong choice — especially considering that these other topics, crucially important in themselves, have been addressed by dozens of first-rate historians. The simple fact is that nobody can do everything: if Auden had tried to be novelist, short-story writer, playwright, and newspaper columnist as well as poet, the world would be much the poorer.

When we concentrate on Chandler the person, the whole issue of scholarly controversy seems somehow ironic. Throughout his career, he has managed to avoid overt disagreements, and it is difficult to believe that this is all mere coincidence. It is not that he has ever retreated from controversy, but rather that he has chosen to make his influence felt through quiet example rather than strident self-promotion.[24] In fact, Chandler's salient characteristic, in all his personal relations, remains a pronounced lack of pretentiousness. From the beginning of his career, his primary motivation has been an abiding and sometimes obsessive intellectual curiosity. Even now, after forty years as a working historian, he retains a youthful intellectual excitability, an infectious enthusiasm about the latest item he has read or piece of evidence he has uncovered. The fires of research have never been banked in Alfred Chandler; and in *Scale and Scope,* as in *Strategy and Structure* and *The Visible Hand,* they will light up a landscape that had been only dimly perceived, if at all.

Thomas K. McCraw, Harvard University Graduate School of Business Administration, is author of Prophets of Regulation, *which won the 1985 Pulitzer Prize in History and the 1986 Thomas Newcomen Award.*

1. Because I have worked alongside Alfred Chandler for more than a decade, I cannot claim complete objectivity here. Portions of this essay will appear in a collection of Chandler's articles which I am editing, to be published in 1988 by the Harvard Business School Press.

2. Quoted in John Gross, "The Inner Age of Stephen Spender: 'I'm Probably an Adolescent,'" *The New York Times Book Review*, February 26, 1984, p. 40.

3. Here and throughout this essay, quotations and other comments not otherwise attributed come from my conversations with Chandler, members of his family, and his colleagues.

4. Although Chandler took no formal courses in economics during his graduate years, it is significant that both Parsons and Max Weber had been trained originally not as sociologists but as economic historians.

5. See Chandler, "Business History as Institutional History," in George Rogers Taylor and Lucius F. Ellsworth, eds., *Approaches to American Economic History* (1971), pp. 17–24. For a fuller survey, see Louis Galambos, "Parsonian Sociology and Post-Progressive History," *Social Science Quarterly* 50 (June 1969): 25–45.

6. The story of the Center is well recounted in Steven Arthur Sass, "Entrepreneurial Historians and History: An Essay in Organized Intellect" (Ph.D. diss., Johns Hopkins University, 1978); pp. 199–205 and 209–215 treat Chandler in particular.

7. Bernard Bailyn, "The Problems of the Working Historian: A Comment," in Sidney Hook, ed., *Philosophy and History: A Symposium* (1961), pp. 92–101.

8. Alfred D. Chandler, Jr., "Henry Varnum Poor: Business Analyst," *Explorations in Entrepreneurial History* 2 (May 1950): 180–202; "Henry Varnum Poor: Philosopher of Management," Ch. 10 of William Miller, ed., *Men in Business: Essays on the Historical Role of the Entrepreneur* (1952); and *Henry Varnum Poor, Business Editor, Analyst and Reformer* (1956).

9. Chandler, "Henry Varnum Poor: Business Analyst," pp. 184–85.

10. Alfred D. Chandler, Jr., "Patterns of American Railroad Finance, 1830–1850," *Business History Review* 27 (September 1954): 248–63; "Management Decentralization: An Historical Analysis," ibid. 30 (June 1956): 111–74; and "The Beginnings of 'Big Business' in American Industry," ibid. 33 (Spring 1959): 1–31.

11. The classic statement of the Robber Baron thesis is Matthew Josephson, *The Robber Barons: The Great American Capitalists 1861–1901* (1934). Perhaps the leading defender of "Industrial Statesmen" was Allan Nevins. Useful collections of essays exemplifying both approaches include Earl Latham, ed., *John D. Rockefeller: Robber Baron or Industrial Statesman?* (1949); and Peter d'A. Jones, ed., *The Robber Barons Revisited* (1968), which contains an essay by Chandler himself. See also Gabriel Kolko, "The Premises of Business Revisionism," *Business History Review* 32 (Autumn 1959): 330–44.

12. David Potter, "Roy F. Nichols and the Rehabilitation of American Political History," in Don E. Fehrenbacher, ed., *History and American Society: Essays of David M. Potter* (1973), pp. 206–207; the essay was originally published in *Pennsylvania History* 37 (1971).

13. Alfred D. Chandler, Jr., "The Beginnings of 'Big Business' in American History," *Business History Review* 33 (Spring 1959): 1–31.

14. Ibid., pp. 1–2.

15. Ibid., p. 31.

16. In an otherwise favorable notice, for example, Edward C. Kirkland wrote: "Many features of the book may put off the general historian. The early spate of necessary definitions, the inclusion of organization charts, as complicated as the models physicists have made for molecules, may convince him that here is just another book on business organization, best assigned to students in management courses to give them historical depth and perspective." Kirkland went on to add, "Such a conclusion would be a great mistake. No other book that I know of brings the specialty of business history so much into the stream of economic and general history." *American Historical Review* 67 (October 1962), p. 159.

17. A computerized search of journal citations done through the *Social Sciences Citation Index* for the years 1969–1984 shows 684 articles citing Chandler's work appearing in journals published in thirteen different countries. Of the total citations, 34 percent came in journals of business administration, 19 percent in history (including 4 percent in economic history), 11 percent in economics (including the same 4 percent in economic history), 13 percent in sociology, 6 percent in organization theory, and at least one citation in twenty–eight other fields. Fifty–seven percent of all citation were to *Strategy and Structure*, 22 percent to *The Visible*

Hand, which at the time of the search had been in print only seven years, in comparison to twenty–two for *Strategy and Structure.*

18. As John Higham wrote in a book published in 1965, "Deriving partly from studies in entrepreneurial and business history and partly from contemporary American sociology, this kind of history is less concerned with motives than with structure and process. It shows men managing and being managed through rational systems of control and communication. Perhaps we may call this the new institutionalism; for it is bringing back to life a morphological study of organizations, now freed from the formalistic, evolutionary emphasis of nineteenth century scholarship. Although institutionalists thus far have not gone much beyond the monographic level, the breadth and importance of their contribution seem sure to grow." See Higham, Leonard Kriger, and Felix Gilbert, *History: The Development of Historical Studies in the United States* (1965), pp. 230–31.

19. Louis Galambos, "The Emerging Organizational Synthesis in Modern American History," *Business History Review* 64 (Autumn 1970): 279–90; "Technology, Political Economy, and Professionalization: Central Themes of the Organizational Synthesis," *Business History Review* 57 (Winter 1983): 471–493. See also James H. Soltow, "American Institutional Studies: Present Knowledge and Past Trends," *Journal of Economic History* 31 (March 1971): 87–105; Robert D. Cuff, "American Historians and the 'Organizational Factor,'" *Canadian Review of American Studies* 4 (Spring 1973): 19–31; and Robert F. Berkhofer, Jr., "The Organizational Interpretation of American History: A New Synthesis," *Prospects* 4 (1979): 611–29.

20. See the following D.B.A. dissertations, all from the Harvard Business School: Derek F. Channon, "The Strategy and Structure of British Enterprise" (1971); Gareth P. Dyas, "The Strategy and Structure of French Industrial Enterprise" (1972); Robert D. J. Pavan, "The Strategy and Structure of Italian Enterprise" (1972); Richard P. Rumelt, "Strategy, Structure, and Economic Performance" (1972); and Hans T. Thanheiser, "Strategy and Structure of German Industrial Enterprise" (1972). The dissertations of Channon, Dyas, Rumelt and Thanheiser were later published as books.

These studies were done principally under the supervision of Professor Bruce R. Scott, who later applied the strategy-structure paradigm to the analysis of entire national economies, thereby instituting a second major effect on the curriculum of the Harvard Business School influenced by Chandler's work.

21. Gavin Wright, "Regulation in American History: The Human Touch," *Reviews in American History* 14 (June 1986), p. 166.

22. See, for example, Richard Caves, "Industrial Organization, Corporate Strategy and Structure," *Journal of Economic Literature* 18 (March 1980): 64–92; Oliver Williamson, "Emergence of the Visible Hand," in Alfred D. Chandler, Jr. and Herman Daems, eds., *Managerial Hierarchies: Comparative Perspectives on the Rise of the Modern Industrial Enterprise* (1980), pp. 182–202; and especially Williamson, *The Economic Institutions of Capitalism: Firms, Markets, Relational Contracting* (1985), a book which is dedicated to Chandler and three other pioneering scholars, all three of whom are economists.

In addition to Caves and Williamson, a third economist deeply influenced by (and influential upon) Chandler is William H. Lazonick. See, in particular, Lazonick, "Industrial Organization and Technological Change: The Decline of the British Cotton Industry," *Business History Review* 57 (Summer 1983): 195–236; and Bernard Elbaum and Lazonick, eds., *The Decline of the British Economy* (1986).

23. For a thoughtful critique of Chandler's avoidance of the issue of power in the modern industrial state, see Richard B. Duboff and Edward S. Herman, "Alfred Chandler's New Business History: A Review," *Politics and Society* 10 (1980): 87–110. Although the heart of his work has always been the history of large industrial enterprises, Chandler has done a surprising amount of writing and editing on public-sector subjects. Here the most important experiences were his editing of the letters of Theodore Roosevelt in the early 1950s (along with his MIT colleagues Elting Morison and John Blum), and his role as editor-in-chief of the Dwight D. Eisenhower Papers at Johns Hopkins during the 1960s. Even here, though, as in his earlier work on Henry Varnum Poor, his real subject was not biography but administration. For

example, Chandler published an article in 1951 entitled "Theodore Roosevelt and the Panama Canal: A Study in Administration," *Explorations in Entrepreneurial History* 4 (December 1951): 103–111. Then, too, his widely-read piece "The Origins of Progressive Leadership," published as part of his annotations in appendix 3, vol. 8 of Elting E. Morison, ed., *The Letters of Theodore Roosevelt* (1954), is concerned primarily with the organization of a new political party. And his interest in Eisenhower always focused on the general's genius in decisionmaking, in knowing at what time and especially at what level of an organization—whether it be the Army, Allied Headquarters in Europe, or the U.S. government—a given decision should or should not be made.

For other examples of Chandler's comments on public policy, see his essays entitled "Jacksonian Democracy: The Bank War" in Merrill D. Peterson and Leonard W. Levy, eds., *Major Crises in American History: Documentary Problems*, vol. 1 (1962), pp. 334–42; "The Depression and the Emergence of the Welfare State," in ibid., vol. 2, pp. 330–38; and "Government Versus Business: An American Phenomenon," in John T. Dunlop, ed., *Business and Public Policy* (1980), pp. 1–11.

24. Chandler's work is only beginning to affect the received knowledge of American history as reflected in textbooks. Most existing general texts take little account of the managerial revolution. Yet this situation seems certain to change, if only slowly given the usual lead times involved in historical writing. For an explicit example of his influence in a recent text, see James A. Henretta, W. Elliot Brownlee, David Brody, and Susan Ware, *America's History* (1987), p. 528 ff. In addition to the works cited in notes 19–22 above, Chandler's influence is examined in Richard R. John, Jr., "Recent Developments in American Business History," *Trends in History*, forthcoming.

CENTURY OF STRUGGLE, DECADES OF REVISION: A RETROSPECTIVE ON ELEANOR FLEXNER'S SUFFRAGE HISTORY

Carol Lasser

In 1963, before the slightest ripple even hinted at the possibility for a "second wave" of feminism, Betty Friedan declared that American women lost themselves in the "feminine mystique" at least in part because of their ignorance of their past. To remedy this defect, she recommended Eleanor Flexnor's *Century of Struggle*, calling it the "definitive history of the woman's rights movement in the United States." "In my opinion," she continued, "it should be required reading for every girl admitted to a U.S. college."[1] Today, a scholarly and linguistic generation later, *Century of Struggle is* required reading for students in women's history and women's studies classes throughout North America and abroad. Academics and activists who cut their feminist teeth on this landmark volume now offer it for the nourishment of their intellectual progeny. Proof of its ongoing popularity can be found in its publishing history: a paperback of the original 1959 edition appeared in 1968, and a slightly revised edition was issued in 1975. It has become the classic and essential text on the "first wave" of American feminism, the nineteenth-century woman's rights movement.

The enduring popularity of *Century of Struggle* derives from both its simple elegance and its scholarly reliability. In form it is a straightforward, well-crafted, brisk narrative. After a summary chapter on women's lives, work, and legal rights in the colonial period, the first major section of the book details the emergence of a self-defined woman's rights movement in the years before the Civil War. Flexner stressed the emergence of gender consciousness from efforts made by women to organize themselves. Acutely aware of the significance of race, class, and place of residence in the lives and attitudes of antebellum American women, she carefully noted not only the efforts of women reformers, particularly within the antislavery movement, to claim for themselves the rights to speak and act but also the achievements of women workers fighting for better conditions of employment in the textile factories of early New England, and of black women seeking to elevate both their race and their sex. The middle third of the volume illuminates the late nineteenth century, charting the ebb and flow of efforts to broaden women's opportunities in education, trade unions, clubs, and, of course politics. Flexner details the causes and consequences of the division of the woman suffrage movement into two rival organizations, the National Woman Suffrage Association and the American Woman Suffrage Association, noting both animosity and achievement. Her work on the significance of women's organization in labor and social reform points to the crucial connections of each to the suffrage movement in these difficult years. The final third of the book carefully details the last twenty years of the fight for woman suffrage, closely following national and state politics, analyzing the tactics and methods of leaders and their supporters, and ending with a triumphant celebration of the passage of the nineteenth amendment.

Throughout, Flexner skillfully interweaves short biographies of women who contributed to the legal, educational, professional, and industrial progress of women, thus giving a rich texture to her comprehensive volume. She zestfully portrays the pioneers of the woman suffrage movement, including Lucy Stone, "its most gifted orator," Elizabeth Cady Stanton, "its outstanding philosopher," and Susan B. Anthony "its incomparable organizer" (1959, p. 84). Yet she also introduces less well-known figures whose contributions broadened and strengthened the movement: Augusta Lewis, president of the Women's Typographical Union No. 1, a post Civil War leader in women's labor militancy; Ida Wells-Barnett, an outspoken journalist and activist against lynching, and a crucial force in the emergence of the black women's club movement; Caroline V. Still, among the first black women to become a doctor in nineteenth-century America. Moreover, she never fails to report the actions of black and working-class women both in conjunction with and in opposition to the work of white middle-class women who dominated the movement. Flexner reports unflinchingly on attempts to deny delegate status to Josephine St. Pierre Ruffin, a founder of the black New Era Club, at the 1900 convention of the General Federation of Women's Clubs; and she notes as well the inability of the suffrage movement to enlist the participation of turn-of-the-century working women for whom employment issues, including safety, overwork, sexual harassment, and the double day were preeminent material concerns, while suffrage and education were distant and remote.

Above all, Flexner demonstrated that the history of the woman's rights movement could be an area for serious scholarly endeavor. Her careful citations and ample footnotes present an enduring model of professional documentation in the field, and still serve today as guides to major manuscript collections in women's history. The handful of earlier writers who referred even in passing to the nineteenth-century woman's rights movement generally relied upon either their own partisan reminiscences or turned to the six-volume *History of Woman Suffrage* collected over the years by Elizabeth Cady Stanton, Susan B. Anthony, and their followers.

Flexner sought out additional published materials and uncovered previously unnoticed manuscripts. She found these documents in unusual locations, including in the home of Edna Stantial, an activist in the National American Woman Suffrage Association, who acquired the papers of several important leaders which she stored unsorted in her attic in Melrose, Massachusetts. And she traveled to what Gerda Lerner has since described as "that treasure trove in the brownstone" in New York City where Miriam Holden kept her superb private collection of rare books and journals by and about women. Scholars today with easy access to microfilms, reprints, and neat catalogues of the manuscript collections shelved at libraries can only wonder at the shoe leather, inventiveness, and perseverance required to conduct research in the "prehistory" of women's history.[2]

What motivated Eleanor Flexner to undertake this prodigious project at a point in the mid-twentieth century which has subsequently been called the nadir of American feminism? In the preceding decades, a small but significant generation of women historians, including Julia Cherry Spruill, Mary Sumner Benson, Elisabeth Dexter, and Mary Beard, published the pioneering work that served as the foundation for subsequent scholars in the field. Most of them held academic credentials and wrote professional, carefully footnoted history, although their interests lay primarily in the eighteenth and early nineteenth centuries. Suffrage history itself was still identified with the memoirs of a few outspoken partisans. When Flexner began her project, there were few recognized scholars doing similar work.[3] As Anne F. Scott has reminisced, "In 1958 all the historians of women in the United States could have met in the tiny hotel room, which was all any one of the three could afford at historical meetings."[4]

In her original preface to *Century of Struggle*, Flexner explained matter-of-factly that she undertook her study because the work needed to be done. "The story," she wrote, "deserves telling." And recognizing the then current aversion to feminism, she modestly admitted to what she called a "point of view": "This book has been written in the belief that opportunity for complete human development could not, and should not, have been withheld from one-half of the nation because such opportunity inevitably brought with it new problems" (1959, p. vii). She then explicitly linked her work to the Progressive tradition in American history by citing Arthur M. Schlesinger, Sr.'s pathbreaking essay on women's role in American history in his classic work *New Viewpoints in American History* (1922).

Before she began the project, she had visited Schlesinger to receive the assurance that, even without graduate training in history, she could write a much needed volume on the history of the suffrage movement. From him she took not only encouragement, but also Schlesinger's perspective of "the protracted struggle of the sex for larger rights and opportunities" as "one of the noblest chapters in the history of American democracy."[5] Thus, for Flexner, suffrage became "a solid historical milestone" (1959, p. x). Her understanding of the necessity for struggle in order to expand the electorate, and her appreciation of conflicts between opposing interests in a democratic society, reflected the concerns of Schlesinger and his generation.

Yet, where Progressive historians chronicled battles between labor and capital, North and South, farmers and businessmen, Flexner portrayed battles between women and men for their public and political rights; between women workers and their capitalist employers for their wages and rights to organize; between black women and the racist establishment for full citizenship and participation. Flexner's understanding of the connections between issues of race, class, and gender led her to interpret the parameters of women's struggles broadly. As she pointedly remarked in her discussion of organizational efforts of women mill workers in antebellum Lowell: ". . . unless the movement for woman's rights is to exclude the issues of equal pay and shorter hours, which alone would enable working women to enjoy the benefits of education or full citizenship, the Lowell mill girls must be considered pioneers in the same cause as the Grimkes and Emma Willard" (1959, p. 61).

While Flexner approached her subject from a Progressive viewpoint, her work nonetheless can be read as an affirmation of the consensus perspective championed by many scholars at the time her volume was published. Flexner's assertion that "political citizenship was, for women as for any other group arbitrarily deprived of it, a vital step toward achieving human dignity," had a particular resonance for her audience (1959, p. ix). In the more conservative context of the 1950s, women's admission to political participation appeared as belated recognition of their essential agreement with men on the fundamentals of a democratic society, not as the victory of the dispossessed.[6]

The very title of Flexner's volume suggests conflict and heroic effort, but readers could infer instead from the narrative the inexorable march of women toward the realization of their goals of full citizenship, greater freedom, and more pure democracy. And whatever her intentions, Flexner presented a profoundly "whiggish" image of women's history. Moving forward in time seemed to mean for women, as for the American people as a whole, moving forward toward greater freedom and equality. In this account, women strove to become part of the political world. Rarely did they quarrel with the values it projected. In the end, women did not seek to challenge the consensus, they simply wanted to join it.

When Eleanor Flexner took her unfinished manuscript to commercial publishers, the field of women's history still lay sufficiently distant from the interest of most middle-class readers that all the presses rejected it, many apparently without reading it. One publisher did, however, suggest that the text would be reconsidered if Flexner would excise the material on blacks, a change she refused to make. Flexner then determined to complete the project without a contract, and she retired to Northampton to pursue her work.

There she struck up a friendship with Arthur Mann, then teaching American History at Smith College. A Harvard-trained historian who had worked on reform in Gilded Age Boston, Mann encouraged Flexner, read the manuscript and commended it to his friend, Harvard Professor Oscar Handlin, at that time a member of the Board of Publication of the Harvard University Press. It was a fortuitous match, for Handlin's interest in immigration history gave him a perspective on Flexner's account of women's history. And through Handlin, the volume found a prestigious academic publisher.

Like Flexner, who wrote about women struggling to enter the mainstream of American society, Handlin analyzed immigrants and their adaptation. At the same time, Flexner valued gender identity, and Handlin prized ethnicity. So too both also assumed that the basic elements of national identity transcended group differences. Cultural diversity was for them balanced by ideological assimilation. In terms of the struggle for woman's rights, this meant that by working to enlarge democratic participation, women proved their fitness to enter the political community. The irony was that in doing so, they eventually submerged the particular political concerns in which gender made a difference. To be fair, Flexner insisted that the enfranchisement of women "did not overcome the remaining obstacles to equality of opportunity," but she noted, "Never since [the achievement of woman suffrage] has there been the same measure of agreement among women as to the further goals they desire, or how these goals can be achieved" (1959, p. x). Once women had won for themselves the vote, the single sex-specific end for which they had been united, they lost sight of their common political issues; the momentum to push for full gender equity in American society was gone. Flexner's account thus presses the limits of a pluralist analysis, recognizing the need for women to achieve access to political institutions, while, at the same time, making clear the limits of such change.

Despite the recognition of a few reviewers that *Century of Struggle* should be seen in the context of a "broad struggle for human rights and dignity, the culmination of which may characterize our era," the book's reception more generally underscored the marginality of the study of women's history in 1959.[7] While some reviewers acclaimed it as "a godsend" for its comprehensive treatment of the woman's rights movement, others demonstrated their ignorance of the subject by, for example, unwittingly referring to "suffragettes" when they meant "suffragists." Moreover, many commentators seemed more concerned with ideological, not substantive or scholarly criticisms. The New York *Times* reviewer sought more on "the bright and shining army of business and professional women in America." A supporter of the National Woman's Party who wrote for *Saturday Review* took Flexner to task for preferring low-key Carrie Chapman Catt to militant Alice Paul. And *Science and Society* called for "something more [on] the relationship of the socialist movement to the women's rights movement."[8]

At least one commentator understood and appreciated the tension between Flexner's Progressive principles and her consensus context, musing, "Appearing in a day indifferent to causes, *Century of Struggle* may serve as a timely reminder of the idealism of the great American reform movements."[9] The attempt to link *Century of Struggle* to an activist perspective was understandably tentative. The book awaited the audience which emerged with the rebirth of the women's movement; it was an audience that would first embrace, then criticize, and then attempt to incorporate it in a new synthesis.

The years since *Century of Struggle* was written have demonstrated both the strengths and the limits of Flexner's interpretation. Like Friedan, other activists within the twentieth-century women's movement were captivated by *Century of Struggle*'s lively and optimistic narrative of women's strengths, and the early intellectuals and theorists of the Second Wave recognized and rightfully praised the volume for its scholarly achievement.[10]

But subsequent years have witnessed a marked shift in the emphasis of studies in women's history; more recent scholarship has drawn upon Flexner's classic text, but moved away from suffrage history as its central focus. A new generation of scholar-activists came of age in a period of political disillusionments which began with the Civil Rights Movement, included the Vietnam War, and concluded with Watergate. They had little faith in electoral politics. Convinced from their experiences in the first stirrings of the second wave of American feminism that "the personal is political," these new historians of women reasoned that changing consciousness must precede social change. They viewed with distrust and dissatisfaction an institutional analysis of the suffrage movement, both because it assumed that "organization . . . initiates social change," and because such history "reflects the implicit assumption that it is only when women are behaving in ways usually attributed to men — that is, politically — that they deserve mention."[11]

Thus, in the name of a new politics, women historians in the 1970s insisted that Flexner's volume was no longer sufficient. Feminist principles combined with the rise of the new social history to impel women's history away from the study of the ballot box toward investigations of women's lived experiences and the meaning of gender in everyday life. While such concerns were not absent from *Century of Struggle*, they had served as counterpoints to the main focus of Flexner's analysis of the centrality of political advance.

Ironically, 1975, the year in which Harvard University Press issued its revised edition of *Century of Struggle*, saw the ascendence of a new paradigm with the publication of Carroll Smith-Rosenberg's transformative essay, "The Female World of Love and Ritual" as the first article in the first issue of *Signs*, the germinal publication on the new scholarship on women. Smith-Rosenberg demonstrated the importance of studying women's private lives and especially the cultural realm in which women lived apart from men. She brought to light hidden domestic voices — the whispers of women to other women — in "a female world of varied and yet highly structured relationships."[12] Her work opened the way for a flowering of scholarship on the history of women's culture, most notably Nancy Cott's *Bonds of Womanhood* (1977). In these accounts, the private and domestic worlds which women created for themselves were viewed as keys to comprehending the power they held in their daily lives. Evidence of female autonomy became a question investigated in terms of women's control of marital sexuality and not simply suffrage; the empowerment of women was discovered in sororial affection, not just union organization. Crucial was the idea that women had created and defined for themselves worlds unrecognized by traditional historical accounts.[13]

From this new perspective evolved a new critique of suffrage history, perhaps best summarized by a review of the 1975 revision of *Century of Struggle* which charged that "Ms. Flexner does not question whether it is valid to measure achievement in a framework of accomplishment defined by men; whether women who gained recognition by succeeding in overcoming institutional obstacles are the only women whose lives are worth recording."[14]

These developments have made many historians aware of the need to study further the "private" areas of women's lives, particularly sexuality and affective relations. But more recently, others have expressed concern that the trend toward exploration of women's culture has gone too far, depoliticizing and devaluing explicitly feminist struggles, while romanticizing women's achievements under conditions of fundamental repression.[15]

The political history of suffrage has, in fact, developed along lines laid out by Eleanor Flexner. More than a quarter-century later, there is still no volume to rival *Century of Struggle* for its comprehensive analysis of who marshalled which forces and how in the woman suffrage campaign, particularly in its last dozen years. Aileen Kraditor's *Ideas of the Woman Suffrage Movement, 1890–1920* (1965; 1981), which appeared soon after Flexner's volume, provided an intellectual history complementary to its predecessor, dealing, as its author explained, with "ideological questions" necessarily excluded from *Century of Struggle* because of "its very breadth." More recently, neither Ellen

DuBois's *Feminism and Suffrage* (1978), a fine, though more chronologically limited volume, nor Mari Jo and Paul Buhle's *Concise History of Woman Suffrage* (1978), a one-volume compendium drawn from the multivolume record, supplants the classic in the political history of women. Both instead complement Flexner's work, reinforcing Flexner's assertion of the significance of the fight for woman suffrage as a social movement and her view that the enfranchisement of women represented a real advance. These authors also share with their predecessor an appreciation for the importance of self-organization among women in general, and especially for women in particularly oppressed groups, most notably working women. In addition, all would agree that the achievement of suffrage could not have solved all of the difficulties confronting women. For these reasons, *Century of Struggle* remains the classic political history of women precisely because it places the political activities of women in perspective, and combines this sensitivity to context with unsurpassed broad chronological coverage and detailed narrative precision. The handful of useful and important monographs on state campaigns that have appeared have relied heavily on Flexner's framework and have, on the whole, underscored her conclusions. They reinforce the broader sketch she first proposed.

New biographies of suffrage and woman's rights leaders further illuminate the cast of characters Flexner introduced. Even the publication of *Notable American Women, 1607–1950* (1971) and *Notable American Women: The Modern Period* (1980) which filled out the pantheon of suffrage heroines fit well with Flexner's scholarship. In fact, Flexner served on the Advisory Board for the project and contributed twelve entries. In addition, Flexner's suggestive analysis of the links between women organizing for temperance, socialism, labor, and women's education on the one hand, and for woman's rights on the other have been developed in the works of a new generation of scholars. Today, volumes have been written exploring topics suggested by a chapter or even a paragraph of *Century of Struggle,* and women's struggles to better themselves at work, in the marketplace, at the bar, or at the altar have received much scholarly attention.[16]

Yet the most successful and innovative current work in women's history has attempted a new synthesis between public and private, personal and political. Drawing upon Flexner's scholarship as a starting point, the current studies of female political experiences seek to integrate an understanding of the relationship of the culture of woman's sphere to feminist consciousness and public activities. For example, Nancy Hewitt's *Women's Activism and Social Change: Rochester, 1822–1872* (1984) returns to themes of self-organization, abolitionism, and feminism, yet treats such matters with careful attention to the private "bonds of womanhood." Mari Jo Buhle's *Women and American Socialism* (1983) reevaluates the relationship between feminist consciousness and socialist consciousness. Barbara Epstein's very title, *The Politics of Domesticity* (1981) points toward her incorporation of Flexner's interest in popular movements and political activism on the one hand, and women's experiences within their sphere on the other.

Scholars working on women's history in the postsuffrage years have perhaps most successfully integrated the old and the new, scholarship on feminism and women's culture. Susan Ware's *Beyond Suffrage* (1981) follows the role of a network of women in the politics of the New Deal era, much as Flexner charted women in politics in an earlier period; yet Ware does so with an understanding that it is women's shared gender identity as well as their party experience and political commitments which sustained their activism. Similarly, Paula Giddings in *When and Where I Enter* (1984) has developed themes in the history of black women first suggested in *Century of Struggle*, and brought them into the twentieth century, developing a stimulating, new perspective on the interaction of race and sex, lived experiences and consciousness, culture and politics.

In 1984, the Eighth Berkshire Conference on the History of Women held a reception to honor Eleanor Flexner twenty-five years after the publication of *Century of Struggle*. The occasion was a success, a long overdue celebration of the significance of a landmark volume in the subsequent development of our history. Where Anne Scott had counted only three historians of women a quarter-century before, by 1984, there were hundreds. Most of us would not have been there without Eleanor Flexner. Even as we seek to build upon her achievement, *Century of Struggle* stands as a monument to the difficulties overcome in earlier eras. It challenges historians today to live up to the highest scholarly standards as we reconceptualize how public, political history fits with the private dimensions more recently uncovered; how to comprehend and interpret the interactions of both the personal and the political realms of women's lives and women's experiences.

Carol Lasser, Department of History, Oberlin College, is coeditor, with Marlene Merrill of Friends and Sisters: Letters between Lucy Stone and Antoinette Brown Blackwell, 1846–93 *(1987), editor of* Educating Men and Women Together: Coeducation in a Changing World *(1987), and the author of several articles on domestic service, including "The Domestic Balance of Power: Relations between Mistress and Maid in Nineteenth-Century New England,* Labor History *(Winter 1987).*

I thank Eleanor Flexner, Janet Wilson James, Arthur Mann, and Barbara Miller Solomon for talking with me about *Century of Struggle*. They bear no responsibility, however, for the interpretation presented here which is entirely my own.
1. Betty Friedan, *The Feminine Mystique* (1963; Dell reprint, 1977), p. 382. Flexner returned

the compliment in the preface to the revised edition of *Century of Struggle* (1975, p. ix), noting that *The Feminine Mystique* was a "powerful weapon" in the reemergence of a struggle for woman's rights.

2. Conversation with Eleanor Flexner, Northampton, Mass., May 23, 1985; Gerda Lerner, "Miriam Holden – In Remembrance and Friendship," *Princeton University Library Chronicle* 41 (Winter 1980): 164.

The Library of Congress and the Schlesinger Library have acquired Stantial's materials, and Holden's superb collections became a part of the Princeton University Library, making accessible to a wide variety of users sources Flexner struggled to locate.

3. Julia Cherry Spruill, *Women's Life and Work in the Southern Colonies* (1938; Norton reprint, 1972); Mary Sumner Benson, *Women in Eighteenth-Century America: A Study of Opinion and Social Usage* (1935); Elisabeth Anthony Dexter, *Colonial Women of Affairs: A Study of Women in Business and the Profession Before 1776* (1924) and *Career Women of America, 1776–1840* (1950); Mary Beard, *Woman as a Force in History* (1946). In addition, a small but intrepid group gathered around the Radcliffe Women's Archives for scholarly study in women's history, 1951–1958; their manuscript records are in the collections of the Schlesinger Library.

4. Anne Firor Scott, "Woman's Place Is in the History Books," in Scott, ed., *Making the Invisible Woman Visible* (1984), p. 364. Eleanor Flexner was probably one of the assembled trio to which Scott referred.

5. Arthur Meier Schlesinger, "The Role of Women in American History," *New Viewpoints in American History* (1922), p. 127.

6. In conversation with the author, Eleanor Flexner said she was unfamiliar with the term, "consensus history"; that she did not employ the concept intentionally is quite likely.

7. Marion Galbraith Merrill, review of *Century of Struggle*, *Pacific Northwest Quarterly* 51 (April 1960): 90.

8. Carl Degler, review of *Century of Struggle*, *Mississippi Valley Historical Review* 46 (1959–60): 733–34. Ishbel Ross, review of *Century of Struggle*, "The Suffragette Parade and Where it Led," New York *Times Book Review*, August 9, 1959, p. 3+; Alma Lutz, review of *Century of Struggle*, *Saturday Review* 42 (August 15, 1959): 35; Dorothy Rose Blumberg, review of *Century of Struggle*, *Science and Society* 25 (1961): 92.

9. Janet Wilson James, review of *Century of Struggle*, *New England Quarterly* 33 (1960): 119.

10. Robin Morgan, ed., *Sisterhood is Powerful* (1970); Alice Rossi, *The Feminist Papers: From Adams to de Beauvoir* (1973); Gerda Lerner, ed., *Black Women in White America: A Documentary History* (1972).

11. Mari Jo Buhle, Ann D. Gordon, and Nancy Schrom, "Women in American Society: An Historical Contribution," *Radical America* 5 (July-August 1971): 12.

12. Carroll Smith-Rosenberg, "The Female World of Love and Ritual: Relations between Women in Nineteenth-Century America," *Signs* 1 (Autumn 1975): 1–30, p. 1. (Smith-Rosenberg has incorporated this essay into her volume *Disorderly Conduct: Visions of Gender in Victorian America*, 1985, pp. 53–76.)

13. Julie Roy Jeffrey, *Frontier Women: The Trans-Mississippi West, 1840–1880* (1979); Catherine Clinton, *The Plantation Mistress: Woman's World in the Old South* (1982); and Lillian Faderman, *Surpassing the Love of Men: Romantic Friendship and Love Between Women from the Renaissance to the Present* (1981).

Daniel Scott Smith, "Family Limitation, Sexual Control, and Domestic Feminism in Victorian America," *Feminist Studies* 1 (Winter-Spring 1973): 40–57; Nancy Cott, "Passionlessness: An Interpretation of Victorian Sexual Ideology, 1790–1850," *Signs* 4 (Winter 1978): 219–36; Blanche Wiesen Cook, "Female Support Networks and Political Activism: Lillian Wald, Crystal Eastman and Emma Goldman," in Nancy Cott and Elizabeth Pleck, eds., *A Heritage of Her Own: Toward a New Social History of American Women* (1979), pp. 412–44.

14. *Vassar College Miscellany News*, October 10, 1975; I thank Harvard University Press for providing this review.

15. The clearest opposition to the trend away from the history of the woman suffrage move-

ment was voiced by Ellen DuBois, in "Politics and Culture in Women's History: A Symposium" *Feminist Studies* 6 (Spring 1980): 28–36.

16. A few examples from this voluminous literature: Ruth Bordin, *Woman and Temperance: The Quest for Power and Liberty, 1873–1900* (1981); Mari Jo Buhle, *Women and American Socialism* (1983); Nancy Schrom Dye, *As Equals and As Sisters: Feminism, The Labor Movement, and the Women's Trade Union League of New York* (1980); Barbara Miller Solomon, *In the Company of Educated Women: A History of Women and Higher Education in America* (1985); Barbara Harris, *Beyond Her Sphere: Women and the Professions in American History* (1978); Alice Kessler-Harris, *Out to Work: A History of Wage-Earning Women in the United States* (1982). For a fuller review of relevant literature, see Elaine Tyler May, "Expanding the Past: Recent Scholarship on Women in Politics and Work," *Reviews in American History* 10 (December 1982); 216–33.

MORTON WHITE'S *SOCIAL THOUGHT IN AMERICA*

James T. Kloppenberg

Morton White ranks among the most distinguished and prolific students of American thought. The range of his work has been extraordinary. Since his first book, *The Origins of Dewey's Instrumentalism*, appeared in 1943, White has written or edited twelve volumes. From analytic philosophy, (*Toward Reunion in Philosophy*, 1956) and cultural history (*The Intellectual Versus the City*, 1962), he has moved through the philosophy of history (*Foundations of Historical Knowledge*, 1965) and the history of philosophy (*Science and Sentiment in America*, 1972) to the history of political ideas (*The Philosophy of the American Revolution*, 1978) and the study of ethics and epistemology (*What Is and What Ought to Be Done*, 1981). Among American historians, though, White is doubtless best known for *Social Thought in America: The Revolt Against Formalism*, published in 1949 and in print now for nearly four decades. *Social Thought in America (STA)* belongs to a select group of books that not only live but breathe. White has twice added spirited arguments connecting the book to contemporary scholarly debates, in 1957 challenging the neo-orthodoxy of Reinhold Niebuhr and Walter Lippmann, and in 1976 defending his approach to the study of ideas against the techniques of social historians and psycho-biographers.

White claimed in his 1976 foreword that he had tried "to write not only a historical work but also a philosophical work" (p. xxvii). In this essay I will assess his success in both spheres. It is worth noting at the outset how influential White's argument has been. A partial list of historians and philosophers whose work reflects the impact of *STA*, which would include at the very least Richard Hofstadter, Christopher Lasch, Robert Wiebe, Thomas Haskell, David Hollinger, Dorothy Ross, Richard Pells, Edward Purcell, James Gouinlock, and H. S. Thayer, suggests the force exerted by White's conception of the revolt against formalism. But as those names suggest, reactions to White's work have been negative as well as positive.

Critiques of White's work have often shown the odd congruence typical of responses to those who step outside conventional disciplinary boundaries. As a philosopher, this argument runs, White is a good historian; as a historian, a good philosopher. This pattern is apparent in the first reviews of *STA*.

Writing in *Ethics*, T. V. Smith termed it "an earnest but light book"; John Hallowell complained in *The South Atlantic Quarterly* that White's "probing does not go far below the surface"; and Richard Hofstadter charged in the *New York Times Book Review* that White failed to deal successfully with "the inner urgency, the personal dimension, of ideas, or with their historical context." Others disagreed. J. H. Hexter, for example, proclaimed enthusiastically in *The American Historical Review* that White "has achieved a work with so many facets of excellence that a brief review can scarcely do it justice."[1]

So it has continued to go, as historians and philosophers establish their own substantive and methodological positions by aligning themselves with, or distancing themselves from, White's argument. In "The Problem of Pragmatism in American History," an essay published in *The Journal of American History* in 1980, David Hollinger contended that White's *STA* "remains after more than thirty years the best book" in its genre (p. 92); while Robert Crunden, writing in *Progressivism* (1977, p. 145) a volume he coauthored with John Buenker and John Burnham, insisted that White's book "does not really succeed in unifying the men discussed, is poorly written, and retains its vogue only among students who specialized in areas other than intellectual history" (p. 145) Whatever private discomfort such dissensus may have caused White, in the revised editions of *STA* he has projected a tone of Olympian serenity. Comparing oneself to John Stuart Mill, as White did in his preface to the 1957 edition, or to Kant, as he did in the foreword for 1976, requires a certain self-confidence. Noting Kant's retrospective judgment that the *Critique of Pure Reason*, "taken in its unity, [was] not in the least endangered" by his critics' quibbles, White concluded, boldly shouldering Kant's mantle, that "although my youthful venture may be open to objections in this or that respect, "taken in its unity" its fundamental argument has not been endangered; and I now leave it to another generation of readers to see whether my confidence is justified" (p. xxvii).

Before accepting White's challenge to evaluate his argument, I will offer a brief description of the book for those who know it only by its reputation as one of the classics of American intellectual history. *STA* is a study of some — and that is worth stressing — of the writings of five thinkers who reformulated liberalism for the twentieth century — John Dewey, Thorstein Veblen, Oliver Wendell Holmes, Jr., Charles A. Beard, and James Harvey Robinson. A common orientation united these five. They all opposed the "formalism" of abstract and deductive approaches to the study of philosophy, economics, law, politics, and history. They preferred to approach such questions by attempting "to explain facts by reference to earlier facts" and by attempting "to find explanations and relevant material in social sciences other than the one which is primarily under investigation" (p. 12). White's focus on "historicism" and "cultural organicism," as he labels these approaches, leads him to emphasize the similarities among these thinkers' methodologies rather than the substantive differences that he acknowledges occasionally but does not explore. Thus there is, as his critics have noted repeatedly, something curiously abstract, even formalistic, about White's treatment of these antiformalists. His analysis, and his critique, of their ideas remain perched at a lofty level. Directing his attention to the logic of their method, White brilliantly illuminates the difficulties of their approach without discussing in detail the strengths or weaknesses — or the inconsistencies among — the discoveries that approach could yield.

After introducing his cast of characters and his concepts of historicism and cultural organicism, White convincingly uses these ideas to tie together these thinkers' challenges to prevailing orthodoxies. Having outlined the revolt against formalism, he sketches "The American Scene" by presenting a straightforward, and surprisingly uncritical, account taken directly from Beard's 1914 textbook *Contemporary American History*. He examines the centrality of historical analysis for the arguments presented in the early work of Robinson, Beard, Dewey, Holmes, and Veblen, implying along the way that these ideas powerfully influenced progressive reform. At the beginning of chapter 8, he summarizes his argument to that point:

> By 1912 the outline of what I have called "the liberal ideology" had been drawn. It was anti-formalist, evolutionary, historically oriented; it was deeply concerned with the economic aspects of society. Veblen had dissected the leisure class and had set up his war between business and industry; Dewey gave philosophical support to the distinction between formal and effective freedom; Holmes had defined the law in practical terms and had lent a hand to the reformers; Robinson had started his propagandizing for the new history; and his younger colleague Beard was beginning his study of the economic basis of politics. Pragmatism was already a national password. [p. 107]

As White develops his critical analysis of these ideas in the second half of the book, the tension between these thinkers' common method of inquiry and their quite different political commitments becomes increasingly apparent, despite White's efforts to minimize its significance. He notes Holmes's bitter criticism of Beard, for example, and admits that Holmes's celebration of danger and violence as breeders of leadership could hardly have been further from the convictions of Veblen and Dewey.

Much of the remainder of *STA* concerns Dewey's ideas. White's discussion of Dewey's conception of experience, one of the most important ideas examined in the book and one that might have engaged White's philosophical talents, dissolves into a half-hearted defense of Dewey's ideas from some of the most wrong-headed criticism directed toward James's pragmatism. Examining Dewey's support for American participation in World War I, White shows little appreciation of Dewey's reasons for defending America's entry as a way to secure international arbitration. From White's perspective as from Randolph Bourne's, Wilson's failure at Versailles becomes somehow the consequence of Dewey's instrumentalism rather than its betrayal. White contends that Dewey's writings in the 1920s, like those of Veblen and Robinson, remained too vague to be useful. But he fails to discuss much of what Dewey wrote during the decade, notably *The Public and Its Problems* (1927), which contains some of his most important ideas about democratic reform. Finally, White contends that whereas Holmes was obscure and Veblen silent about the relation between the empirical and the normative in the scientific method, Dewey tried but failed to solve this problem in his naturalistic ethics.

In his concluding chapters, White explains why the ideas that fueled the antiformalists' revolt appear untenable from the perspective of 1949. First, whereas Beard believed that historians' values should infuse their scholarship, White insists that the "ideal purpose of history . . . is to tell the *whole* truth" (p. 227), and that neo-Rankean standard rules out the subjectivity encouraged by the new history. White notes that Beard "was the only member of the group I have examined who has given a full account of the methods and aims of the social sciences," but he contends that of "all the philosophical positions examined in this book, Beard's later philosophy of history seems most implausible" (pp. 233f.). Second, White's rebels not only broke down artificial barriers between different social sciences, they also shattered the standards of logical analysis, leaving only the alternatives of despair, cynicism, and reaction. "It is not exaggerating to say that the revolt was speedily followed by a reign of terror in which precision and logic and analytic methods became suspect" (p. 241). Third, these thinkers' ethical writings obscured the proper relation between fact and value. Finally, their abstract injunction to use social intelligence and historical analysis offered policy makers insufficiently clear guidelines for constructing political programs. As a result, the techniques of social engineering were employed aimlessly and pointlessly. Fearing dogmatism, White's rebels backed into an indefensible relativism.

Despite the severity of White's criticism, he concludes that his rebels were "a force for the good in American intellectual life" (p. 243). They respected freedom and endorsed social responsibility, and they brought to the difficult questions of social analysis "a good and humane temper; it was honest, courageous, rational, and enlightened" (p. 245). But if they were also wrong about logic, wrong about ethics, and wrong about politics, White's closing endorsement seems faint praise indeed. They meant well, he seems to conclude, but they did not think well. However humane their temper, they left

their followers wandering in a fog, unclear about the philosophical foundations — and confused about the political implications — of their beliefs.

Many American intellectuals shared White's ambivalence about the legacy
of liberalism after World War II, but others extended arguments similar to
those White advanced in *STA* as part of a broader assault on the liberal position. White responded to those challenges in the preface and epilogue he
added to the paperback edition of *STA* published in 1957. There he made
clear that, unlike apostates such as Niebuhr and Lippmann, he remained
faithful to liberalism. Notwithstanding his criticism of the antiformalists' failings, which he explicitly refused to withdraw, he wanted to align himself
"spiritually with Dewey and Holmes on the new battlefield that has emerged
in the fifties" (pp. xxxif.). He dismissed Niebuhr's concept of original sin and
Lippmann's concept of natural law. The first rested on an incoherent account
of the relations between choice and inevitability, White claimed, while the
latter assumed the self-evidence of arguments that, as Locke showed, cannot
be established without recourse to religious faith. White's scornful tone
throughout this discussion implies that no thinking individual could entertain
ideas shown to be grounded on faith rather than reason. But precisely because
neo-orthodoxy appealed to metaphysics rather than experience, it stood
beyond the reach of White's critique. Locke, after all, could maintain
simultaneously an empiricist epistemology based on science and a natural
rights political theory based on faith. So chastened American thinkers such as
Niebuhr could plausibly claim to preserve their credentials as pragmatists
while substituting for the relativism White found distressing a religious faith
that supplied a solid foundation for their convictions. If White remained convinced in 1957 that his criticism of the weakness of antiformalist liberalism
was on target, he remained equally incapable of advancing arguments that
would enable later liberals to escape that earlier crisis of judgment. Perhaps
because Niebuhr's psychology derived from Augustine rather than Dewey, he
was able to confront directly the problem of standards in ethics, and the
problem of power in politics, that White's antiformalists consistently
avoided.

Must one then choose between Niebuhr's faith and the fuzziness of White's
liberals? White may have been content to align himself with the spirit of the
thinkers whose shortcomings he had catalogued, but readers taking his
analysis seriously might question the adequacy of those ideas. The search for
an alternative, paradoxically, might profitably begin by reconsidering the
thinkers White examined in *STA*. White traced the antiformalists' achievement to their historicism and their cultural organicism. They acknowledged
the historical dimension of ideas and the broadly cultural approach necessary
to understand the process by which ideas emerge from the interaction be-

tween creative minds and shifting socioeconomic conditions. To paraphrase Justice Holmes's familiar dictum, these thinkers realized that the life of the mind has not been logic but experience. As a result, they appreciated that thinking inevitably involves evaluating, willing, and acting to shape a culture's perception of itself rather than attempting to frame ideas according to presumably abstract and unchanging logical rules. Their work seemed unsuccessful to White in part because he judged it by standards unlike the antiformalists' own. When viewed from the perspective of hermeneutics rather than the perspective of analytic logic, however, their ideas appear considerably more sturdy. A reconsideration of White's arguments concerning history, science, ethics, and politics should clarify this different perception.

White criticized the relativism of the new history, arguing that neutrality remains the historian's goal just as it remains the physicist's or the logician's. By 1965, when he completed *Foundations of Historical Knowledge*, he had evidently changed his mind. There he argued that historians' value judgments inevitably enter into the process of selecting topics, choosing which facts to include in a true narrative, and explaining why things happened as they did. Moreover, value judgments likewise color readers' responses to historical narratives, making both the creation and the criticism of history inevitably value-laden. *Foundations of Historical Knowledge* concludes with the argument that such an enterprise should not be confused with science, as Beard and Robinson did; but historians persuaded by Heisenberg's or Kuhn's account of scientific knowledge may be no more convinced by this distinction than were the antiformalists themselves. As White points out in *STA*, Holmes, Dewey, and Veblen believed, together with Beard and Robinson, that knowledge always emerges from a complicated process of cultural development, and that all judgments, including those of social scientists and philosophers, reflect the twists and turns of meanings as they shift historically. All ideas, including our own, develop historically, and that knowledge makes the analytic philosopher's attempt to escape from culture, although it springs from a persistent impulse, only a dream. Doing history well requires the self-conscious examination of one's own values as well as the values of those one studies. Although White conceded the value-laden quality of historical writing in *Foundations of Historical Knowledge*, he did not acknowledge either that his argument there contradicts his argument in *STA*, or that it validates the approach of the antiformalists whose new history he had previously considered overly subjectivist.

White claims in *STA* that the liberals' revolt culminated in dangerous excesses. Not only did its partisans turn against the unnecessary rigidities imposed by formalism, they also rejected the necessary discipline imposed by logic. But what White dismisses as imprecision might seem from a different perspective only a justifiable sensitivity to the meaningfulness of all cultural inquiry. From his earliest until his most recent work, White has remained committed to a foundationalist epistemology that roots knowledge in sense experience. Not surprisingly, he has shown far less sensitivity to the part of Dewey's philosophy, recently emphasized by Richard Bernstein and Richard Rorty, that challenged the dominant tradition in Anglo-American philosophy and advanced instead a version of pragmatism perhaps closer to the hermeneutics of Dilthey than to the logic of Peirce.[2]

Seen in this light, Dewey's "persistent failure to see the virtues of logical analysis in philosophy," for which White takes him to task in the concluding pages of STA, simply suggests the acuity of Dewey's pragmatic vision. White quotes a long passage from Reconstruction in Philosophy (1920) in which Dewey argued forcefully that philosophy must turn away from logic and concentrate on social and moral issues, but White uses this passage only to make a comparison with Holmes's dispassionate account of how law develops according to social desires rather than logic (pp. 191–93). The striking contrast between Holmes's stoic resignation, and his darkly pessimistic, even nihilistic assessment of the consequences of such social struggles, on the one hand, and Dewey's commitment to the active intervention by intelligence to shape such struggles in order to broaden the range of effective freedoms available to all citizens, on the other, escapes White's attention, apparently because he is interested in the similarities between the logical form of the two arguments.

Concerning the question of ethics, White likewise criticizes Dewey on the basis of categories whose legitimacy Dewey set out to deny. Dewey insisted that all valuings, which occur within an ongoing social project reflecting individual, social, and historical choices and consequences, must be examined critically and weighed against developing personal and community standards rather than against general logical principles.[3] By contrast, White's own ethical arguments, as his recent What Is and What Ought to Be Done illustrates, rely on a quite different conception of moral feelings as noncognitive, a conception alien to Dewey's understanding of experience as culturally mediated at its most fundamental level.

Finally, White considers his antiformalists' political ideas either too vague or, when specific, too utopian to be useful. While his argument properly skewers much of the wishful thinking that has passed for liberal social analysis, his failure to examine carefully Dewey's writings about democracy vitiates the force of his critique. For it was precisely Dewey's emphasis on popular participation as the political corollary of scientific reasoning that prevented him from pronouncing ex cathedra the proper course for reformers.[4]

White's failure to explore the connection between Dewey's conception of democracy and his understanding of experience and ethics is puzzling, especially since he quotes one of Dewey's many explicit statements of the link between his philosophy and his politics. In *Creative Intelligence* (1917), Dewey pointed out that philosophy as he conceived of it "becomes not a contemplative survey of existence nor an analysis of what is past and done with, but an outlook upon future possibilities with reference to attaining the better and averting worse" (*STA*, p. 141). The standard for evaluating better and worse must be generated from the critical analysis of history; in Dewey's case at least, the commitment to historical inquiry was more than methodological. From Dewey's perspective, history serves also as the source of values and the basis for judgment, as critical intelligence reflects on and evaluates the concrete consequences of the individual and collective choices that shape a culture over time.

Dewey wrote at length about specific political issues, although White does not discuss those writings in *STA*. Yet Dewey always insisted that the process of democratic decision making mattered more than any specific reforms, and in that sense White is correct to stress method as the heart of Dewey's politics. If that commitment was vague, as White contends, it was vague for good reasons. Dewey's conception of democracy reflected his understanding of experience, ethics, and politics as inextricably connected parts of an ongoing and open-ended cultural project, which could have no foundation in certain knowledge and could have no predetermined goal beyond the continuing quest to attain the better and avoid the worse. Dewey's enthusiasm for the prospects of democracy was certainly problematical. But when Dewey's political arguments are placed in the context of his writings about epistemology and ethics, his idea of democracy continues to represent an intriguing alternative to the pessimism of Niebuhr, on the one hand, and to the good-hearted, humane temper of White's liberalism on the other.[5]

Thus far I have tried to engage White's arguments on their own terms, discussing their persuasiveness at the level of analysis White prefers: the interpretation of the meaning of the ideas themselves. If I have challenged some of his arguments, it should be apparent that the difference reflects not only a different conception of the ideas being discussed, but also a different conception of how one should pursue the historical study of ideas. For the remainder of the essay, I will discuss White's approach to intellectual history, indicate what I consider to be its strengths and weaknesses, and then suggest an alternative.

Much of the criticism that has been directed toward *STA* has resulted from White's own contradictory remarks about what he set out to accomplish in the book. In his introduction to the original edition, he claimed his method extended beyond "mere textual analysis" and that he "tried to treat the subject historically." White assumed throughout *STA* that his antiformalists exerted a broad and deep influence, although the only evidence he presented concerned their influence on each other. This was one of the principal complaints of his critics, notably David W. Noble, who argued in *The Mississippi Valley Historical Review* in 1950 that White failed to connect his thinkers to the "basic social forces" shaping the society from which they emerged, and that he also failed "to establish the influence and role of those men in the social scene" (p. 155). As his 1976 foreword makes clear, White considered such criticism unfair. He quoted from some of the favorable reviews the book received. He recounted the praise of a deceased historian who told White he had "illuminated the ideas of the thinkers discussed — both philosophical and otherwise — by viewing them as part of a larger intellectual movement in a clearly delineated social setting." The book, White claimed, contains "discussions that link Dewey's philosophical beliefs with his educational and political beliefs, and with his impact on the political world; it also tries to situate the intellectual activity of figures like Holmes, Veblen, Beard, and Robinson in the society in which they lived" (p. x).

Yet *STA* contains no discussion of Dewey's activities as an educational or political reformer, there is almost no biographical information in the book, and the only references to "the society in which they lived" derive either from Beard's and Robinson's own texts or from a paragraph in Frederick Lewis Allen's *Only Yesterday* (1931). To be generous, White's portrait of the individuals whose ideas he examines, and their social setting, is painted with fairly broad strokes. Although he claimed that *STA* is "an example of intellectual history which moves from level to level," and that he considered it "misleading" to contend that the book "deals only with what Marx somewhere calls the celestial sphere" (p. xxiii), it seems clear, at least from the perspective of a generation raised on history from the bottom up — the later generation White invited to assess his achievement — that his account descends little lower than society's penthouse.

At least for a moment, White himself seems to have realized what he did and did not accomplish in *STA*. In the opening paragraphs of his final chapter, "Yes and No," he conceded, "I have not gone into great detail about [these thinkers'] contributions to law, history, economics, and political science, nor have I concentrated on the social scene. My main purpose has been to consider the philosophical ideas which underlay their work. . . . I am aware of the monumental work I have not written. But monuments need bricks, and I have tried to fashion a few with which future historians, critics, and philosophers may build further, or with which they may destroy a few shiny, opaque windows" (p. 237). Those remarks capture precisely White's notable achievement in *STA*; the later controversy surrounding his grander claims for the book should not distract us from his initially more modest, and more accurate, assessment of its value.

White has been a consistent and articulate spokesman for a very important idea: intellectual historians must understand the writings of those they study before they can presume either to criticize the ideas or to estimate their influence — or lack of it — in society. As White argued vigorously in his 1976 foreword, it is impossible to talk about the connection between intellectuals and society unless one is willing to pay close attention to difficult ideas. Too many cultural historians, he points out, are fighting above their weight when they presume to discuss the broader significance of ideas as they "trickle down" from the realm of philosophical discourse to the realm of *mentalité*. In White's pet formulation, *Annalistes* of ideas should first be analysts of ideas. "Even the historian who is primarily concerned to trace the social causal consequences of believing must be prepared to analyze the content of the belief. And that is the long and the short of the matter" (p. xviii). White is surely right that one cannot "assert and establish the causal connections between beliefs and society without knowing much about the insides, so to speak, of the beliefs" (p. xix), yet one wonders whether establishing such connections is possible without also knowing much about the "outside" of the beliefs as well.

The Philosophy of the American Revolution, White's brilliant study of Jefferson's Declaration of Independence, illustrates this difficulty and demonstrates at once the strength and the weakness of his approach to intellectual history. Despite the bravado of the book's title, White does not attempt to explain the ideas that motivated those who fought the War for Independence. But if it does not tell us all we would like to know about the world in which that struggle occurred, or even all we might like to know about what the colonists thought they were doing when they declared their independence, the book does tell us more than anyone else has about what Jefferson himself meant. Illuminating some of the more shadowy corners of his mind, and unpacking the meaning of some of the more familiar but most unclear passages in the Declaration, is in itself a remarkable achievement. Examining the ideas of less articulate revolutionaries, who were innocent of Burlamaqui and unclear about the distinction between primitive and adventitious rights, is an enterprise White leaves to other historians concerned, if you will, with the "outside" of Jefferson's beliefs.

The value of White's careful analysis is undeniable, and it should be apparent that I share his conviction that the detailed examination of complex ideas is a necessary, if perhaps not sufficient, condition for doing certain sorts of intellectual history. But if he is correct to insist that historians writing about the history of philosophy should study philosophy, he should also concede that philosophers writing about the same subject should study history. The ability to follow arguments and write about them with clarity and precision is essential, but so too is the ability to locate those ideas in their historical context with equal clarity and precision. Exaggerating the importance of either element in that equation can lead one down either of the blind alleys described in the introduction to *Philosophy in History* (1984), a recent collection of essays edited by Richard Rorty, Jerome Schneewind, and Quentin Skinner. One can assume, as White at his most imperious sometimes seems to do, that philosophers, because they know what philosophy is and understand where their predecessors went wrong, must instruct their readers about the inadequacy of earlier arguments from the privileged position they inhabit as possessors of Truth. Or one can assume, as Rorty, Schneewind, and Skinner's archetypal intellectual historian does, that since we cannot know which arguments are better than any others, we must only present the arguments of earlier thinkers on their own terms without presuming to have any views whatsoever concerning their adequacy. Between those poles, obviously, lies a middle ground occupied more or less consciously by everyone who actually writes about history, a rocky terrain in which present beliefs and knowledge bump awkwardly against the quite different, and sometimes incomprehensible, ideas of thinkers inhabiting another world. In short, the practice of intellectual history always involves a more or less serious conflict between the analysts's convictions about what he knows and the *Annaliste's* sensitivity to what others have experienced and what they have believed. Resolving that conflict is a challenge that requires hermeneutical understanding. The historian must consciously acknowledge his own values without allowing his interpretation of the past to become an exercise in self-gratification.

If one were to study the revolt against formalism from the perspective of 1986, and attempt to take its context as seriously as White took the texts he examined in *STA*, several additional dimensions might be added to the story as a result of the work done by historians in the last four decades. First, it would be necessary to consult the biographies of these thinkers, not in order to construct the psychoanalytical readings that, as White points out, can reduce ideas to symptoms of various pathologies, but in order to understand as clearly as possible the contours of their lives and the factors that helped shape their characters and beliefs. White's aversion to this sort of inquiry has gone so far that he expressed his regret, in his 1976 foreword, for even the few scattered comments concerning personal motivation that appeared in *STA*. But most intellectual historians, even those suspicious of psychohistory, would find the portrait of Beard in Hofstadter's *Progressive Historians* (1968), for example, or of Dewey in George Dykhuizen's comprehensive biography, indispensable to a well-rounded understanding of their ideas.

Second, a great deal of work has been done on the history of these thinkers' academic disciplines and on the process of professionalization. While these phenomena appear to have interested White not at all, one need not now be a card-carrying sociologist of knowledge to appreciate the importance of the connection between these intellectuals and their institutional settings.

Third, social and political historians have put considerable meat on the skeletons of industrialization and progressivism to which White referred, and connecting the antiformalists' ideas to a more fully fleshed out portrait of their world would enrich the analysis of their ideas. White concerned himself with the adequacy of Dewey's ethical arguments but took for granted the adequacy of Beard's and Robinson's historical accounts. It would be instructive now to test their arguments against the accumulating evidence.

Fourth, a more comprehensive consideration of all of the writings of these thinkers would help to place their more familiar texts in perspective. Dorothy Ross reported in the *Intellectual History Newsletter* in 1986 that White's humane, liberal Justice Holmes was not very much in evidence at a conference sponsored by Stanford Law School and attended by scholars who have examined his less celebrated writings. Likewise, as I have suggested, Dewey's philosophical work appears somewhat different when viewed in the context of the political writings that are now conveniently available in his *Early* and *Middle Works*. More thorough examination of everything these prolific writers produced would reveal the relation between the texts White explored in *STA* and those he ignored. Finally, these thinkers might be placed in the transatlantic context in which they worked. That comparative framework might reveal the similarities and differences between America's revolt against formalism and the revolt against positivism examined by historians following the lead of H. Stuart Hughes's *Consciousness and Society* (1958).

Such a study, attractive as it is in the abstract, might unfortunately be impossible to complete in a single lifetime. Having attempted myself to analyze the philosophy and politics of this period by examining various thinkers, texts, and contexts, I can understand why White chose to write what he did in *STA*. Life is short, and our books are often already too long. But the difficulty of writing such a fully hermeneutical and contextualist study of ideas is a separate question from its desirability. I would insist here only on the attractiveness of this ideal for intellectual history, an ideal distinct from both the austere history of philosophy that White practices and from the facile social history of ideas that he quite properly criticizes. Taking ideas and their contexts equally seriously, uniting what John Higham in 1954 termed the internal and external approaches, should be our model for studying ideas historically.[6]

If White's writing does not measure up to that standard, neither does this retrospective assessment of his book. A fully adequate interpretation of *STA* would require all the preliminary sorts of analysis I have described as relevant to the reexamination of the antiformalists' revolt. Biographical information about White himself, a discussion of professional philosophy after World War II and White's place in it, a more thorough examination of all of White's writings than I have been able to provide here – all of that would be necessary before any interpretation of *STA* could approach the standard I have suggested White's own book failed to reach. I too am aware of the monumental essay I have not written. But it is a measure of the significance of White's work, and of my sense of the lasting significance of his contributions to the life of the mind in America during the last four decades, that I expect such a full-scale study of his ideas will be written someday. If that future historian treats White's ideas as carefully as he has treated the ideas of those he has studied, he will be fortunate indeed. If that future historian can be both analyst and *Annaliste* of the ideas of White and his generation, however, the results will be even richer.

James T. Kloppenberg, Department of History, Brandeis University, is the author of "Deconstruction and Hermeneutics as Strategies for Intellectual History," Intellectual History Newsletter *9 (April 1987) and "The Virtues of Liberalism: Christianity, Republicanism, and Ethics in Early American Political Discourse,"* Journal of American History *74 (June 1987).*

1. T. V. Smith, *Ethics* 60 (1950): 148–49; John H. Hallowell, *The South Atlantic Quarterly* 50 (1951): 122–24; Richard Hofstadter, *New York Times Book Review*, Dec. 18, 1949, p. 3; J. H. Hexter, *American Historical Review* 56 (1950): 152–54.

2. Richard Rorty, "Dewey's Metaphysics," in Steven M. Cahn, ed., *New Studies in the Philosophy of John Dewey* (1977); *Philosophy and the Mirror of Nature* (1979); and *Consequences of Pragmatism* (1982); Richard J. Bernstein, *John Dewey* (1966); *Praxis and Action* (1971); *The Restructuring of Social and Political Theory* (1976); and *Beyond Objectivism and Relativism* (1983).

3. The best brief discussion of Dewey's ethics from this perspective is Elizabeth Flower and Murray Murphey, *A History of Philosophy in America* (1977) 2: 859–74; for a more elaborate analysis, see James Gouinlock, *John Dewey's Philosophy of Value* (1972).

4. Bruce Kuklick, *Churchmen and Philosophers* (1985), pp. 230–33, provides an especially good analysis of the foundation Dewey's early religious faith provided for his later democratic convictions.

5. I discuss my conception of the connection among Dewey's ideas about epistemology, ethics, and politics in greater detail in *Uncertain Victory: Social Democracy and Progressivism in European and American Thought, 1870–1920* (1986).

6. John Higham, "Intellectual History and Its Neighbors," *Journal of the History of Ideas* 15 (1954): 339–47, reprinted in Higham, *Writing American History* (1970).

MERRILL JENSEN AND THE REVOLUTION OF 1787

Thomas P. Slaughter

Merrill Jensen never romanticized America's Revolutionary Era or the task of those who write its history. His founding fathers manipulated, prevaricated, and even urinated as they went about their daily routines of wheeling, dealing, and propagandizing for independence from Great Britain. They plotted, schemed, and sometimes responded to such unheroic motives as lust, greed, or fear in the course of their labors to fulfill their own political and economic ambitions while creating stable governments for the new nation.[1]

How unlike the ponderous marble images that adorn and encumber traditional portrayals. And yet, paradoxically, it is Jensen, not the more worshipful legions, who elevates our eighteenth-century forebears by rendering them credible, raising our estimations of men who had foibles and thus accomplished their herculean tasks despite the usual array of human frailties. How much more heroic their achievements in light of the profound divisions among them; how much more real is Jensen's world in which politicians represented a variety of regional and economic interests, conflicting prejudices, and disparate ideological convictions. "They were strong-minded men," Jensen contended, "and it was natural that they should differ with one another as to what political goals were best for the new nation they founded. It is in those differences and the great debates and party warfare that followed upon them that lies the greatness and significance of the American Revolution in America."[2]

Jensen believes that his analysis would be more recognizable to participants in the upheaval than accounts that homogenize the various cultures, classes, and perspectives that provoked America's first civil war. He denigrates the work of scholars who argue that "agreements among Americans of the Revolutionary generation were more important than their disagreements"; and he frequently quotes John Adams as a counterpoint to consensus historians, whom Jensen criticizes for intellectualizing, simplifying, and abstracting reality. "The principles of the American Revolution," according to Adams, "may be said to have been as various as the thirteen states that went through it, and in some sense almost as diversified as the individuals who acted in it."[3]

In Adams's observation is the wellspring of Jensen's understanding of the period and one key to comprehending his life's work. In Jensen's eyes, as in Adams's, the Revolutionary movement was one of "vast complexity"; the War for Independence included an "internal revolution" that brought about dramatic "political and social change." This transformation of the socio-political scene was not accomplished without meaningful dissent. Indeed, according to Jensen, "the stride was not taken without vigorous and sometimes violent political battles among Americans." These "violent political battles" were not caused by the Revolutionary upheaval, nor did they end with the surrender at Yorktown. The internal revolution merely intensified existing conflicts and shifted the emphases of controversy. Jensen argues that "the old social cleavages which had produced political battles in the states long before 1776 became even more marked when the restraining, if often clumsy, hand of the British Empire was removed."[4]

Complexity, conflict, and change are the central themes that Jensen attempts to document in books on the Revolutionary and Confederation periods. To these three interrelated theses might be added Jensen's notion of class struggle, although he vigorously denies that "internal revolution," as he uses the phrase, and "class struggle," as Marx or Marxists use it, are synonymous terms. He does insist that eighteenth-century Americans "took for granted the existence of social classes in history and in their own society. Furthermore, many of them saw in the revolutionary movement either a potential or an actual 'class struggle' — as they understood and defined classes *at that time*."[5]

One way of thinking about the historiographic war in which Jensen was (and remains) a partisan is to conceptualize the battle lines as drawn between historians more interested in external perspectives of time and space versus those more concerned about understanding the past on its own terms. Jensen castigates those who have less regard than he for the way eighteenth-century Americans experienced events. He has no appreciation for interpretations that rely on comparisons to the French or Russian Revolutions, for example, or to subsequent episodes in American history, which were obviously outside the purview of American Revolutionaries and thus, in Jensen's mind, beside the point for understanding the War for Independence as it was endured by those who lived through it. "Americans in 1776," Jensen observes, "were not concerned with 'comparative history' but with political and economic realities within America." Only if we try to see history "as the men who lived it saw it and to write of it in their terms . . . may [we] achieve some semblance of reality." The future is irrelevant, indeed counterproductive, to interpreting the 1760s, 1770s, and 1780s. Like J. H. Hexter, in his essay on "The Historian and His Day," Jensen stamps his colleagues as either "present-minded" or "history-minded," and he has no use for those misguided souls whom he brands with the first label. To Jensen, the clinching argument against consensus interpretations is that "the last to agree with such an approach would be the leaders of the Revolution themselves." And again, John Adams is the exemplary source: "This country, like all others, has been a theater of parties and feuds for near two hundred years." [6]

This commitment to studying the past as nearly as possible on its own terms is one factor that limits the influence of Jensen's work. He does not provide the sort of usable past that appeals to civic clubs, ancestor-worshiping cults, amateur history buffs, or conventions of high school principals. Jensen's is not the vision of our past that seems meaningful to institutional supporters and patriotic celebrants of the Constitution's bicentennial. This is not history that mainstream politicians of whichever party, regional, or special-interest persuasion can easily grind for the rhetorical hash fed to sated constituencies.

Jensen's history is the United States sans mythology, heroes, flag-waving, or anachronistic visions of national consensus. His books will never inspire a musical-comedy sequel to "1776" or to the mini-series portraits of George Washington and Benjamin Franklin. Jensen's characterizations of Adams, Madison, Hamilton et al. would not readily lend themselves to synchronized choreography, harmonious song, or stilted acting. It is easier to imagine adapting his scholarship for a Greek tragedy with choruses of wailing, clashing, off-key voices than as a musical sit-com peopled by selfless demigods casually joking about America's future.

Nor do Jensen's books make for entertaining reading. Braver souls than I may assign his tomes to undergraduates, but graduate students sometimes find them "boring," "tedious," "excruciatingly dull." Partly, such reactions reflect current fashions for a kind of social history with power and politics left out, a taste that some of us hope will soon pass from center stage in the profession. It is also true, however, that reading Jensen is about as much fun as slogging one's way through a Valley Forge winter in bare feet. The writing is clear, the organization is logical, and the language refreshingly precise, but the method can be ponderous to the point of exhaustion.

Jensen piles fact upon fact, nuance upon nuance, variation upon variation, exception upon exception. His focus on complexity, variety, conflict, and the interrelationships among different categories of evidence can bewilder, and sometimes verges on cataloguing or listing "facts." By the same token, this wealth of information is one of the values of Jensen's books for those of us (myself and the graduate students) who have much to learn about details of the period.

Rarely do glimmers of humor shine through Jensen's gray, business-like prose. And where such welcome rays do appear it is always for the cold, calculated purpose of carrying forward an argument, never just to warm a beleaguered reader. When Jensen tells us the story of Judge Aedenus Burke of South Carolina, who wrote an essay in 1783 attacking the Society of Cincinnati on moral grounds, it is to ridicule yet another example of an *apparently* principled American Revolutionary. "Enemies at once charged," according to Jensen, "that the judge had written the pamphlet because he had not served in the army long enough to become a member. The man who said that was a liar, replied the judge: he had been opposed to the order even before he had been turned down for membership."[7]

In an introspective moment Jensen almost acknowledged that his books tended toward the ponderous and apparently recognized that he surrendered more fully to facticity over the course of his career. "Conceivably," Jensen mused, "one could write a book on the Revolution with one line of generalization at the top of each page, with the rest of the page consisting of footnotes pointing to the exceptions, qualifications, and contradictions. It might be history, but I doubt it." Clearly, he was not apologizing for the evolution in his approach, but rather criticizing his first book, *The Articles of Confederation*, for being too simplistic and its argument insufficiently documented. Each book was longer than the last — 245, 432, 704 pages; each one strayed farther from the main path of argument and deeper into the thicket of details. It is fitting that he ended his career embarked on a massive editorial project designed to gather all the "facts" surrounding the revolution of 1787 and the overthrow of the document he considered "the constitutional expression of the philosophy of the Declaration of Independence." He never travelled far from his initial interest and ultimately came back, with the editorial project, to documenting the transition from the Articles to the Constitution. The editorial project was an extension of his attempt to recover the Articles from "one of the most inglorious roles in American history." He sought to restore the Articles to their rightful place, a position denied them by Federalist party propaganda and historians who have naively adopted the nationalist perspective as their own.[8]

The argument, the themes, the method are all there in *The Articles of Confederation*; and Jensen's prefaces to subsequent printings of that marvelous and still unsurpassed study of our first national constitution are useful maps to the development of his thought. Writing before the Second World War, Jensen was attempting, in this his most accessible book, a synthesis of social and political history. He found such integration lacking even in the work of J. Franklin Jameson, who saw the Revolution as a social movement. Jensen presents a vision of the Revolutionary Era stretching back before the adminis-

trative reforms attempted by British politicians in the 1760s through the ratification of the Constitution, and incorporating social-structural stresses within
America that neither began in 1763 nor ended in 1789. Context, continuity,
and conflict are the keys he offers for unlocking the Revolution's meaning.[9]

Jensen hoped to overcome the problem of patriotic hindsight that blinds
other historians to the propaganda content of such nationalist tracts as the
Federalist papers. To him the debate over the Constitution was a political war
with social dimensions. "The Federalist party, as none knew better than John
Adams, was the party of the 'education, the talents, the virtues, and the property of the country.' As such it had no faith in the democracy made possible
by the Articles of Confederation." Delegates to the Constitutional Convention agreed that democracy was the fundamental evil of the times. The
revolution had been in part a series of battles, Jensen tells us, between "those
who enjoyed political privileges and those who did not." The internal conflict,
indeed chaos, of combat among Americans is the essential background to
Jensen's understanding of the Articles; his measure of their success is how
much order they helped restore during the 1780s and how much they
broadened the base of political participation, not how much further
American politics had to go before stabilization during the early nineteenth
century or the realization of "Jacksonian democracy."[10]

The defeat of the "radicals" by "conservatives" who favored a stronger central government speaks neither to the success nor failure of the Articles. The
lesser ambitions and comparative lack of political experience among the
"radicals" provides a partial explanation for the "conservative" victory in
1787. "When the radicals had won their war, most of them were well con-
tented to go home," believing they had secured their goals of local autonomy
and an expanded demographic base for political power. What the "radicals"
failed to see was that their essentially democratic victory could be reversed,
"that the conservative elements in American society had learned a bitter
lesson at the hands of the radicals. They too could call conventions." (In turn,
the "conservatives" failed to anticipate the "radicals'" ability to recapture
power on a national scale as happened in the Revolution of 1800.) Jensen
finds nothing in the social-economic-political history of the states during the
1780s to justify John Fiske's label "critical period." Recovery was apparent by
1787, and, in any event, the "conservatives'" quest for centralization predated
the short-term economic dislocations that followed the war.[11]

Jensen thus exposes some fundamental tensions in consensus interpretations of the Confederation Era. The 1780s were not so "critical" in Fiske's
sense of the word. Economic recovery was proceeding apace, which means
that the consensus understanding of social causation which denies the validity
of Charles Beard's *Economic Interpretation* is itself built upon false economic

analysis. Jensen concludes, therefore, that consensus historians have adopted a partisan vision of the period as historical reality and grafted onto it an analysis imbued with anachronism failing to comprehend the 1780s on its own terms. Consensus historians ignore, or dismiss as "exceptions" or "anomalies," alternative evidence that abounds in the documents of the age. And Jensen produces scores of "facts" to illustrate profound and unresolved divisions among eighteenth-century Americans.[12]

Nonetheless, Jensen's interpretation is no less immune to the ills of uncooperative evidence than those of his historiographic foes. For example, if the period, understood on its own terms (and Jensen's), was not so "critical" economically, why were debtor-farmers up-in-arms in New England and elsewhere on the nation's rural periphery? Jensen does not deny the seriousness and scope of agrarian discontent under the new order, but he shuffles his interpretive feet a bit and concludes that evidence of economic conflict "should not blind us to the fact that the period was one of extraordinary economic growth." Thus, in a pinch, Jensen abandons his analysis of the period "on its own terms" and embraces the sort of anachronistic cop-out that he blasts consensus historians for sharing.[13]

The difference is that Fiske's "critical period" was economically painful for the "conservatives," while, according to Jensen, supporters of what he terms the "radical" cause suffered most in the immediate aftermath of the war. The paradox is that the 1780s were most "critical," in an economic sense, for those who opposed the Constitution, while the period was perhaps most critical politically for the nationalists who feared the potential consequences of social discontent run amok. (Remember that many "radicals" did not participate in drafting the Constitution or the ratification procedures.) Jensen is correct that social conflict was a crucial dimension of political warfare over the Constitution, although quantifiable economic evidence, which suggests to him that agrarian-debtors *should* have been less concerned, confuses him on this score. The problem, as Jensen ought to have recognized, is one of alternative perceptions rather than stark economic or political "realities" as understood two hundred years after the fact. Jensen is closer than Fiske to the economic truths of the age, but he, too, oversimplifies and overgeneralizes. Gordon Wood's *Creation of the American Republic, 1776–1787* (1969) is a brilliant reconciliation of the two perspectives, although Jensen, among others, has not understood it that way; and Wood's book is much more of an intellectual history and far less of a social history of the Constitution's birth than Jensen advocated.[14]

Jensen's analysis of the Confederation Era also suffers from an unfortunate focus on the "democratic" components of the "radical" agenda. It actually seems that the "conservative" position on representation, for example, which favored voting weighted by state population in the Continental Congress, was more democratic than that of the "radicals," who insisted on one state, one vote. Perhaps Jensen should have dwelt on issues of regional and local autonomy, which are certainly related to questions of "liberty," representation, and thus to "democracy." Jackson Turner Main's concept of "localist" is an important advance over Jensen's notions of radical democrats populating the ranks of mainstream "radical" politics. Jensen might have made a better case for radical democracy by looking at independent statehood movements where his "radicals" favored better representation (indeed overrepresentation, at least based on population) of agrarian and frontier interests in the central government as a counterweight to the influence of cosmopolitan eastern "conservatives."[15] Although even for the frontier the case is significantly more complex than Jensen's categories allow.

This mountain of uncooperative sociopolitical facts is one of the challenges bequeathed by Jensen's books and editorial project. Much of his evidence does not fit at all well with the "critical period" or consensus visions of the era, and to dismiss it as a list of exceptions or not terribly significant details seems less than intellectually candid. Nor does Jensen's own analytical framework accommodate all the bits of information that he unearthed, as he acknowledged on numerous occasions.

Some advocates of the consensus model have chosen to ignore the problem and continue to write, for example, internalist political histories of the Continental Congress as if social contexts were irrelevant. Some still offer "political" analyses of the Confederation Era with inconvenient evidence of ideological, social, and economic conflict left out, or "intellectual" history with both real politics and real people nowhere to be found. Celebrating the founding fathers as American embodiments of Roman heroes may present challenging intellectual exercises and result in elegant literary exegesis, but it is not credible history. Another alternative adopted by some of Jensen's self-proclaimed followers, but never in print by Jensen himself, is to deny the validity of ideological justifications for political actions that appear in such printed sources as the pamphlet literature of the Revolutionary decades. Jensen often cautioned against depending on pamphlets exclusively, and provided examples of traps awaiting those who take the Revolutionaries' principled rationales for their political ambitions at face value. But he also berated himself for failing to integrate "a detailed discussion of the political thought of the times" into *The Articles of Confederation*, noting in retrospect that this was "the most important addition" to the book that he could imagine twenty years after its publication.[16]

When Jensen delivered the Anson Phelps Lectures at NYU, over thirty years after *The Articles of Confederation* first appeared, he still found few examples of the sort of social/political history that he advocated. The social historians of the 1960s and early 1970s were discovering social science models, modernization theory, and comparative studies of revolution. They were rediscovering Jensen's favorite topics of social tension, conflict, and violence in American history. And yet, this new generation of social/political historians was not learning the lessons of many of the best histories of early America, which lay unread on library shelves since the 1950s. Jensen recommended four books as lost classics: William B. Weeden's *Economic and Social History of New England, 1620–1789*, 2 vols. (1890); Thomas J. Wertenbaker's *Patrician and Plebeian in Virginia* (1910); Charles A. Beard's *The Economic Basis of Politics* (1922); and Robert A. East's *Business Enterprise in the American Revolutionary Era* (1938).

What these four books have in common is not a shared interpretation of the 1780s or any obvious validation of Jensen's interpretation. Indeed, East's *Business Enterprise* is the sort of nationalist apologia that often riled Jensen. Wertenbaker's *Patrician and Plebeian*, despite its title, eschews class-based analysis while Beard's *Economic Basis* utilizes class as an organizing principle. Weeden's *Economic and Social History* endorses Fiske's "critical period" interpretation while East's *Business Enterprise* rejects it. Nor is it the authors' collective "politics" that recommends these books. Jensen was always suspicious of attempts to glean a historian's personal politics from his scholarship and noted that naive readers often got Charles Beard, a lifelong Republican, all wrong. In any event, Wertenbaker and Beard would have made very uncomfortable intellectual bedfellows.

The lessons that Jensen must have taken from these authors was their method and, not surprisingly, the often forgotten details or "facts" they uncover. Each argues for the integration of social and political perspectives. According to Beard, "the science of any subject is not at its center but at its periphery where it impinges on all other sciences." The historian should begin his enquiries wondering "whether there has been in fact a close relation between the structure of the state and the economic composition of society." Since an examination of our first state constitutions and the notes on debates during the Constitutional Convention reveal that Americans had not abandoned the Old World belief that government rests upon property, then the political historian must proceed to a study of the distribution of wealth upon which such governments were built. "If the first American constitutions were more democratic than those of Europe," Beard concludes, "the fact is not to be attributed to radical changes in human nature induced by a voyage across the Atlantic, but . . . by a wide distribution of property, due mainly to cheap land." Economics and social structure, not disembodied ideals and ideas, were the critical factors in Beard's, and Jensen's, understanding of the Revolution of 1787.[17]

Weeden also contends that there is a fundamental relationship between the great events of the time and the routines of day-to-day living. "The life of man," he writes, "his daily action — closely allied to his thought and to his affections — must yield up its fact, its daily doing, before we can comprehend the whole action, the whole story of man in his relation to history. Little things are becoming great in that they reveal the sources of greater principles which occasion the movements and currents of humanity." The historian must know a carpenter's tools to comprehend his politics; he needs to understand the farmer's relations with his family before judging the origins of his commitment to a political cause. In New England, Weeden believes, "the popular form of church . . . fostered the same civic development which the home lot, the common right, and the freeman's ballot carried into the direct political action of the town." Land tenure is an "absolute factor" in the forming of citizens and their relationship to the state. Like Beard and Jensen, Weeden contends that "politics are the essence of the main current of history, but history is not mere politics." The social condition of a people, they all argue, shapes the great political and economic activities of an age. Weeden, like the others, "would not make overmuch of economics, yet it is the basis of life; it moulds peoples, it builds or it destroys states." Jensen certainly agreed.[18]

To East, "politics and business are closely related," and he could not imagine writing the history of one without exploring its relation to the other. The Revolution seems to East primarily economic in origin and responsible for fundamental economic change within the business community. Like Jensen, he maintains that "the country was not left in the deplorable economic state frequently attributed to it," and that the Revolution of 1787 found "a minority with powerful economic interests" successfully overriding the majority which opposed its interests and ideas. Unlike Jensen, whose sympathies lie with the masses, East thinks that this very undemocratic victory was an unmixed blessing, at least from a purely mercantile perspective.[19]

Even Wertenbaker, whose patrician mien seems so alien to the styles and perspectives of Beard and Jensen, offers lessons that Jensen thinks we would forget to the peril of our understanding of the past. Although Wertenbaker's method is much more simplistic, anecdotal rather than analytical, and takes literary evidence much more at face value than Jensen ever would, he does emphasize the influence of economic, political, and social causes on the "character" of a community. Like Weeden and Jensen, Wertenbaker argues that "in man's existence it is the ceaseless grind of the commonplace events of every day life that shapes the character. The most violent passions or the most stirring events leave but a fleeting impression in comparison with the effect of one's daily occupation." Wertenbaker, too, finds selfishness, ambition, and greed among the primary causal factors in the political world. He, too, directs us to examine the economic self-interests of historical actors in order to understand their political behavior, and he also takes for granted that power and politics are the most important business of the historian. In this he is of a mind with Jensen and Beard.[20]

We have yet to fulfill the ambitious agenda set for us by Jensen and his historiographical forebearers. We are still writing partial and hence flawed accounts of American cultures, ideologies, economies, and politics. Jensen was not content with his own attempts to synthesize social and political history, and recognized his almost total failure to incorporate the political thought of the times into his books. His legacy is, nonetheless, one of heroic accomplishment and even greater ambition. His biggest disappointment with the rest of us would probably not be that we have yet to succeed in reintegrating subfields of study, but that so many of us have given up or never tried, and contentedly write intellectual *or* social *or* political history. May his ghost haunt us all until we do a better job.

Thomas P. Slaughter, Department of History, Rutgers University, is the author of "The Historian's Quest for Early American Culture(s), c. 1750-1825," American Studies International 24 (1986): 29-59.

1. Jensen's reference to a "call of nature" actually refers to a very reluctant Revolutionary who used this excuse to escape from a session of the Massachusetts legislature (*The Founding of a Nation: A History of the American Revolution, 1763-1776,* 1966, p. 469).

2. Merrill Jensen, *The Articles of Confederation: An Interpretation of the Social-Constitutional History of the American Revolution 1774-1781* (1940), p. xxvi.

3. Ibid., p. xxv; *Founding of a Nation,* p. xii.

4. *Founding of a Nation,* pp. xiv, xxv, xxiii; Jensen, "The Articles of Confederation: A Re-Interpretation," *Pacific Historical Review* 6 (1937): 120-42.

5. *Articles of Confederation,* p. xxii.

6. J. H. Hexter, "The Historian and His Day," in *Reappraisals In History* (London: Longmans, Green and Co., 1961); Jensen, *The American Revolution Within America* (1974), p. 70; Jensen, *The New Nation: A History of the United States During the Confederation, 1781-1789* (1950), p. xiii; *Articles of Confederation,* pp. xxv-xxvi.

7. *New Nation,* p. 262.

8. *Articles of Confederation,* pp. xxix, 3.

9. Ibid., p. 5; J. Franklin Jameson, *The American Revolution Considered as a Social Movement* (1926).

10. *Articles of Confederation,* pp. 3, 6-7; Jensen, "The American People and the American Revolution," *Journal of American History* 57 (1970): 5-35.

11. *Articles of Confederation,* pp. 245, 246; John Fiske, *The Critical Period of American History* (1888). Jensen labels Fiske's *Critical Period,* "a book of vast influence but of no value as either history or example" (*New Nation,* p. xii).

12. *Articles of Confederation*, pp. 6–7, and passim.

13. *New Nation*, p. 423.

14. Jensen found *Creation* confusing and thus did not fully appreciate it as the sort of "detailed discussion of the political thought of the times" that he advocated in the 1959 preface to the third printing of *Articles of Confederation*. Undoubtedly, Jensen did not approve of Wood's characterization of John Adams as having "missed the intellectual significance of the most important event since the Revolution," (*Creation*, p. 567), since this estimation of Adams's "irrelevance" represents perhaps the most serious challenge to Jensen's interpretation in print. See Wood, *Creation*, ch. 14, "The Relevance and Irrelevance of John Adams." Jensen makes no reference to the book in his 1973 Phelps Lectures. See Jensen, "A Long and Complex Book," *Virginia Quarterly Review* 45 (1969): 682–86; "Forum: *The Creation of the American Republic, 1776–1787*: A Symposium of Views and Reviews," *The William and Mary Quarterly* 3d ser., 44 (1987): 549–640.

15. Jackson Turner Main, *Political Parties Before the Constitution* (1973).

16. *Articles of Confederation*, pp. xxvii–xxviii.

17. Beard, *Economic Basis*, p. 5. Here Beard is paraphrasing Henry Thomas Buckle, the Scottish historian. *Articles of Confederation*, pp. 29, 41, 46–47.

18. Weeden, *Economic and Social History*, 1: iii–iv, 68; 2: 728, 875.

19. East, *Business Enterprise*, pp. 7, 238, 286. It is from East that Jensen borrows the labels "radical" and "conservative" to describe the two political factions that battled over the Constitution (ibid., p. 195). Jensen later regretted his use of these terms, since they were so often misunderstood, and wished that he had substituted "popular leaders" for "radicals." He was, however, prepared to defend "conservative" as entirely appropriate (*Articles of Confederation*, pp. xxvi–xxvii).

20. Wertenbaker, *Patrician and Plebeian*, pp. 1, 3, 214.

DAVID POTTER'S *PEOPLE OF PLENTY* AND THE RECYCLING OF CONSENSUS HISTORY

Robert M. Collins

The perception that the United States has been blessed with an exceptional physical endowment is as old as the nation itself. Alexis de Tocqueville long ago wrote that "the physical causes . . . which can lead to prosperity are more numerous in America than in any other country at any other time in history," and other commentators reiterated the observation during the century of America's industrialization.[1] The appreciation of abundance easily crossed political lines and often transcended the immediate vicissitudes of the business cycle. At the very end of the Great Depression, Leo Huberman wrote a socialist tract which began with a portrait of an earlier American Promised Land "flowing with steel and oil as well as with milk and honey" and concluded with the assertion that socialism could again make the United States "a going concern, for America has everything. Rich and fertile land in abundance; coal, iron, oil, beyond the dreams of avarice."[2] A few years thereafter, in the middle of World War II, the president of the Chamber of Commerce of the United States, in a capitalist manifesto entitled *America Unlimited*, attributed the nation's "civilization of abundance" to the workings of a reinvigorated private enterprise system.[3]

In the postwar era, American prosperity amidst worldwide devastation made the nation's abundance all the more striking—in the minds of many at home and abroad the one unmistakable characteristic of life in the United States. At the dawn of the American Century, *Life* rhapsodized about shoppers whose market carts "became cornucopias filled with an abundance that no other country in the world has ever known."[4] The modern supermarket quickly became a metaphor for American culture writ large. John Updike wrote of the new American Superman who drove to the supermarket along superhighways to buy his Super Suds.[5] Norman Mailer heralded the political triumph of John F. Kennedy in an essay entitled "Superman Comes to the Supermart."[6] The poet Randall Jarrell observed "The slacked or shorted, basketed, identical food-gathering flocks"; and Allen Ginsberg marveled at "Whole families shopping at night! Aisles full of husbands! Wives in the avocados, babies in the tomatoes!"[7]

Even later, after stagflation and a host of other ills had seized the economy and wrenched the national psyche, the supermarket image retained its usefulness and evocative power. Recently the novelist Don DeLillo portrayed America in its climacteric as a supermarket where all the shelves have been rearranged without warning. Confusion reigns; carts collide; shoppers grow sullen as they confront "the plain and heartless fact of their decline." "And this is where we wait together, regardless of age, our carts stocked with brightly colored goods. A slowly moving line, satisfying, giving us time to glance at the tabloids in the racks."[8] Abundance has been viewed as the hallmark of American life, in both our ascent and our decline. It is hardly surprising, therefore, that at the precise midpoint of the twentieth century a historian elevated this insight into a full-fledged interpretation of the American experience.

In 1950, David M. Potter of Yale University delivered the Walgreen Lectures—six in all—on the influence of economic abundance on American life and the American national character. Four years later, the University of Chicago Press published Potter's revised and polished thoughts under the title *People of Plenty: Economic Abundance and the American Character*. Now, at a time when many scholars are earnestly echoing the fictional historian Moses Herzog's plaintive cry that "What this country needs is a good five-cent synthesis," it behooves us to recall what Potter wrote, to examine the influences that shaped his thought and its reception, and to wrestle with the implications and unexploited possibilities of his work.[9]

In his lectures, Potter undertook two basic tasks: the first theoretical, to establish a valid concept of national character; the second historical, to examine closely the impact of economic abundance on that character and on American life in general. Both assignments were daunting. The concept of national character had fallen into disrepute, and Potter readily admitted that historians had been imprecise and careless in their use of the idea. Yet, although some historians disavowed the concept, others continued to apply it in practice: "Art requires it," Potter wrote, "even if the data do not impose it, and the need for such a concept in historical synthesis is so great that, if it did not exist, it would, like Voltaire's God, have to be invented."[10]

What art required, the relatively young behavioral sciences of psychology, sociology, and anthropology promised to provide in a new, more acceptable formulation. Specifically, Potter contended that the emergent behavioral disciplines offered a more searching and illuminating definition of national character: i.e., that which resulted from "culture" (a society's way of life) acting upon and shaping "personality" (the totality of an individual's behavioral and emotional tendencies).

The work of Margaret Mead, David Riesman, and Karen Horney seemed to Potter to exemplify the promise of the social science approach. In *And Keep Your Powder Dry* (1942), Mead affirmed the concept of national character and underscored the American preference for success over status. Riesman's exercise in social psychology, *The Lonely Crowd: A Study of the Changing American Character* (1950), portrayed Americans as increasingly adaptable team players who constantly sought the approbation of the group. The psychoanalyst Karen Horney argued in *The Neurotic Personality of Our Time* (1937) that much of our society's psychological pathology was culturally induced, the result of competitive pressures that afflicted the individual from cradle to grave. Indeed, the work of all three scholars converged on the matter of competitiveness. The typical American, they seemed to say, strove ceaselessly for mobility, flirted with conformity when not openly embracing it, and suffered as a result debilitating anxieties from which there was no earthly release.

The behavioralists failed to agree, however, on the causes of the competitive character they observed from their various disciplinary perspectives. It was here, Potter argued, that history reentered the picture. If culture molded national character, it was history that shaped culture and determined the pace and direction of cultural change. And the single most powerful force in America's history, he concluded, had been the nation's economic abundance.

The "land of plenty" had molded a "people of plenty." Abundance made possible the social equality and mobility that gave life in America much of its fundamental decency. Potter recognized that the equality was not absolute, the opportunity not universal—he noted explicitly that blacks had not shared in the bounty of American life—but he emphasized that the United States had provided "a condition of mobility far more widespread and pervasive than any previous society or previous era of history."[11] At the same time, the resultant social flux of an open society had stripped Americans of the psychic comfort of simply "having a place" in an organic social order that bound together the individual and the community. Thus abundance had both conferred benefits and exacted costs.

Among the benefits that flowed from abundance, the foremost in Potter's judgment was American democracy. Unfortunately, he never defined democracy clearly; sometimes he seemed to equate it with personal freedom and equalitarianism, at other times with free-enterprise capitalism, and often he simply contraposed it to socialism, thereby rather hopelessly confusing the political with the economic. In any event, American plenitude had yielded a unique politics of abundance. Encouraged by the perception that life is a positive-sum game from which all the players can emerge winners, Americans cultivated a reformist politics that pursued social justice by constantly increasing national and individual wealth rather than redistributing it.

Potter found considerably less cause for celebration in the characteristic institution of modern abundance, advertising, which he argued had become an increasingly powerful and ominous instrument of social control. "Certainly it marks a profound social change," he observed, "that this new institution for shaping human standards should be directed, not, as are the school and the church, to the inculcation of beliefs or attitudes that are held to be of social value, but rather to the stimulation or even the exploitation of materialistic drives and emulative anxieties and then to the validation, the sanctioning, the standardization of these drives and anxieties as accepted criteria of social value."[12]

Working through advertising and other means, abundance had an impact on the individual of the most intimate sort. It created a national life-style, Potter asserted, in which the experiences of childhood and adolescence all reflected a base of material well-being. In such developments Potter saw "a bridge between the general historical force of economic abundance and the specific behavioral pattern of people's lives."[13] In other words, plenty shaped personality in identifiable ways, and in this fashion were cemented the enduring links between history, culture, and personality.

In retrospect, it is easy to see the influence of the times on *People of Plenty*. The postwar economic boom had made for flush times. The ascendancy of the social sciences was in the air. The burgeoning American Studies movement gave new impetus to the search for that which was characteristically American. In essential ways, Potter's analysis shared and reflected both the strengths and weaknesses of the best scholarship of the day. It was replete with what Daniel Bell approvingly identified as the hallmarks of contemporary intellectual discourse: irony, paradox, ambiguity, and complexity.[14] When Potter addressed cultural matters, he was hardly the smug, uncritical 1950s intellectual of popular mythology. His concerns were important ones — the absence of community, the threat of mass culture, and the dangers of unbridled materialism — and he shared them with the finest intellectuals of his generation; their misgivings remain our own, but their articulation of these apprehensions stands unsurpassed. On matters political, however, Potter's inability to admit even the possibility of a democratic socialism bespoke the mind-numbing political conservatism that afflicted many mainstream intellectuals during America's Ike Age. Thus, for both good and ill, Potter was in touch with the dominant intellectual currents of his day.

On another level, Potter was self-consciously reacting *against* a kind of ethnocentrism that seemed to pervade Cold War America. Cautioning that "one can never be certain how one gets hold of a thesis," he subsequently recalled:

> But I think I was influenced partly by a reaction to what seemed to me the pre-vailing attitude that there was a certain superior virtue in American ideas. . . . I felt that nations generally, like people, have the kind of ideals which they can afford, and that we had had the good fortune to be able to afford some rather expensive ideals.[15]

If, in the end, Potter was an approving social critic, even a loving one, he was not one who offered easy comfort or cheap self-congratulation.

Finally, Potter was responding as well to history's "internal dialogue." In an important sense, historians write messages to one another which are fully comprehensible only in the context of previous correspondence. For several generations, American historiography had been dominated by the Progressive historians, who emphasized conflict as the dynamic, defining element in the nation's past. The publication of Richard Hofstadter's *The American Political Tradition* in 1948 ushered in a competing "consensus" school of interpretation. Potter later explained the rise of the consensus view as chiefly "a reaction to what I would call the excesses of the conflict school . . . and [the fact] . . . that the emphasis upon issues had been exaggerated to a point where it was pretty inevitable because of tendencies of revisionism which are always at work in history, to revise this conflict interpretation by emphasizing the other side of the coin, and that was their shared values."[16] In his search for the American national character and his consequent emphasis on shared values and common experiences, Potter came to be identified as one of the most prominent of the new school. He himself neither rejected nor embraced the label—in truth it fit.

Reviewers responded warmly but unevenly to Potter's overarching interpretation. The *New York Times Book Review* applauded *People of Plenty* as "comparable in scope and implication" to Frederick Jackson Turner's frontier thesis, and Karl Deutsch compared the book favorably with David Riesman's *The Lonely Crowd*.[17] But others thought that Potter had been overawed by the claims and achievements of the behavioral sciences.[18] The harshest critique appeared in the *Mississippi Valley Historical Review*, where Fred Shannon savaged the volume as an example of the sort of "cosmic interpretation" that allowed some historians to escape the rigors of research. Shannon's review was by turns wrong-headed, perceptive, and crotchety. Astoundingly, he accused Potter of "glorifying" national advertising, as complete a misreading as one can imagine. More to the point were the objections that Potter had exaggerated the scope and embrace of American abundance and that in any event there quite probably existed 162,000,000 different American characters.

If this be history, Shannon concluded, "then a great number of us old codgers have lived entirely too long."[19] The success of Potter's study soon outran both the praise and the reservations of reviewers, however.

Over the years, *People of Plenty* came to be considered a major work in American historiography. It was translated into Spanish, French, Japanese, and Korean; and parts of Potter's analysis were reprinted in at least seven different volumes.[20] A paperback edition appeared in 1958, and a decade later the book remained among the ten most widely used supplemental works in undergraduate and graduate United States history courses.[21] The importance of the study was clearly established, and the foremost critic of consensus history called Potter "one of the most persuasive general historians of the 1950s."[22]

One senses, however, that *People of Plenty* had already, at some indeterminate point in the late 1960s or early 1970s, moved into a very special historiographical category: the dazzling but fundamentally flawed classic. As such, it became something of a curiosity, undeniably brilliant but unmistakably wrongheaded, in much the fashion of Stanley Elkins's controversial study, *Slavery: A Problem in American Institutional and Intellectual Life* (1959).[23] In the midst of the intellectual, political, and cultural turmoil of the 1960s, the underpinnings of Potter's analysis seemed to crumble and the specifics of his argument appeared increasingly at odds with both contemporary reality and the latest scholarly styles and findings.

By the late 1960s, the concept of national character was once again in disrepute. David Riesman explained that he and his coworkers had advanced their hypotheses about inner- and other-direction to describe not all Americans but only the metropolitan upper middle class.[24] Students of American Studies shared the doubts about national character. In 1971 David Stannard subjected the idea, and Potter's use of it in particular, to withering scrutiny. Calling *People of Plenty* "an important historical work" and praising its discussion of American abundance *per se*, Stannard observed that "in trying to connect abundance to that devilishly elusive concept, national character, Potter attempted more than could be handled."[25]

Attacking the idea of national character on broad intellectual and ideological grounds, Robert Sklar of the University of Michigan declared that the discipline of American Studies was in crisis and had to face changing realities, including the fact that an increasing number of students were learning to call their nation Amerika. The social concerns of the 1960s had produced a host of new areas of scholarly interest—the experiences of blacks, American Indians, hispanics, women, workers, and the poor—all of which called for attention. In light of such ferment, Sklar argued, the search for *one* uniquely American pattern of anything was chimerical.[26]

Most important for the reputation of Potter's study, a similar tide was running in the discipline of history at the same time, as historians moved from consensus history with its emphasis on shared values and common experience toward what Thomas Bender has subsequently labeled "centrifugal scholarship."[27] A number of developments contributed to this sea change. One was a longrunning trend noted by Richard Hofstadter in 1968: "If there is a single way of characterizing what happened in our historical writing since the 1950s, it must be . . . the rediscovery of complexity in American history: an engaging and moving simplicity, accessible to the casual reader of history, has given way to a new awareness of the multiplicity of forces."[28] The rise in the 1960s of a highly variegated New Left revisionism also struck sharply at the foundations of both Progressive and consensus history, as many New Left critics called for a new diversity, an American history seen "from the bottom up." The emergence of a "new" social history in the years following was in no small way a response to this summons, one that focused attention on the private lives of those who had all too often been denied access to political and economic power and hence denied historical visibility. The convergence of these developments—reinforced by the relentless drive to specialization within American academe—resulted in a flood of studies defined and informed by the particularities of place, family, race, gender, ethnicity, and class. Taken together, the studies seemed to John Higham to represent a new pluralist paradigm, "a celebration of group autonomy and diversity."[29] As an inchoate alternative to the earlier interpretive frameworks, pluralism appeared to many commentators to threaten the fragmentation of history, the substitution of group and subculture singularities for a common national history.[30]

In the new intellectual environment, *People of Plenty* stood as an anachronism. Potter once observed that historians reminded him of zoologists, who as a matter of course in their discipline give both a generic and a specific name to all forms of life. Some, known in professional circles as "lumpers," emphasize similarities and place closely related forms into one genus; others, called "splitters," emphasize differences and place closely related forms into separate generic categories. Historians, he said, often worked in a similar fashion.[31] By 1970 it was clear that lumpers such as Potter were being eclipsed by a new generation of historical splitters.

Developments outside academe also undercut the appeal of Potter's analysis. When *People of Plenty* first appeared, America stood as "the only rich nation in a poor world," and this exaggerated and inevitably transitory dominance made an emphasis on American abundance natural if not inevitable.[32] Plenty seemed less compelling as a unifying theme in the face of the rediscovery of poverty in the 1960s. The powerful movements against racism and sexism that gave the 1960s their distinctive coloration compounded the challenge by reminding Americans of those systematically *excluded* from so much of American life for so long. The stagflation of the 1970s brought with it still another crisis of confidence, which Seymour Martin Lipset has labeled "neo-Malthusianism."[33] Driven by fears of exploding populations and shrinking resources, the new ecopolitics viewed economic growth in a negative light quite alien to the spirit of Potter's analysis. *People of Plenty* appeared inanely sanguine compared to the apocalyptic vision of the new pessimism.

Potter was himself mindful of the criticisms of his work. On the matter of overgeneralization he seemed prepared to give ground. In a lecture at Stetson University in 1959, he observed that a truly comprehensive study of national character required a new attention to the historical experiences of women, especially in light of "the formidable truth that the transformations of modern life have impinged upon men and women in different ways."[34] Later he admitted that *People of Plenty* had failed to take poverty sufficiently into account; but he adhered to his basic premise regarding the signal importance of abundance, adding "I would not qualify my argument very much. Problems of poverty in American life have been the problems of disadvantaged minorities in an affluent society." And on the large issue of conflict and consensus, he remained convinced that "for a large part of American history . . . the points of agreement have been underestimated by historians."[35] In short, Potter retreated on matters of emphasis and balance, but held firm to his central insights. The question remains, however, to what degree those insights will continue to inform the work of other scholars.

Potter's lasting contribution is his perception of the centrality of abundance in American history. The idea of a culture of abundance can and should be salvaged and elaborated upon, but without the national character apparatus to which Potter tied it. The concept of a national character has been shattered by the historical pluralism of the past two decades; like Humpty Dumpty it is beyond saving. The most historians can aim for now is to reconstruct the content and contours of a national culture which has, after all, distinguished America's historical experience from that of other societies.

The elaboration of Potter's theme of plenty will require the modification of his analysis in at least three important regards. First, historians will need to recognize that plenty, and especially its handmaidens economic growth and development, have generated division and conflict as well as consensus. On the one hand, many groups and individuals have not shared fully in the nation's opulence. On the other hand, there has emerged formidable evidence that the unbridled pursuit of plenty has elicited strong counterpressures. David Shi's *The Simple Life: Plain Living and High Thinking in American Culture* (1985) illuminates an undercurrent of antimaterialist thought and behavior that waxes and wanes but never disappears entirely from the American scene.

Herbert Gutman's *Work, Culture, and Society in Industrializing America* (1976) lays bare the difficulty of socializing successive generations of workers to the regime of industrial progress. Lee Clark Mitchell's *Witnesses to a Vanishing America: The Nineteenth-Century Response* (1981) finds a "broad intellectual movement" which articulated and acted upon a deep apprehension about the costs of destroying a wilderness in the course of exploiting a continent.[36] Other scholars have observed widespread, multifaceted, popular resistance to the encroachments of marketplace capitalism and industrialization on community values and traditions in the same period.[37] My own research on attitudes regarding economic growth in the years since the appearance of Henry George's *Progress and Poverty* in 1879 finds a fundamental ambivalence in American ideas and behavior. Clearly the pursuit of plenty has excited people in very different ways, and has created division as well as agreement.

As a second matter, historians must recognize also that abundance and scarcity have coexisted in America, and that they have often been linked together in important, if paradoxical, ways. America has been a land of plenty which has experienced at various times important scarcities of labor, capital, manufactured goods, land in older sections of the nation, water in the West, and most recently energy.[38] Abundance and scarcity both have derived a part of their meaning and significance from the existence of the other. For example, in Robert Gross's *The Minutemen and Their World* (1976), the "World of Scarcity" that was Concord abutted a bountiful continent, and it was the coexistence of these conditions that produced the social reality of the minutemen. In other cases, the arresting feature is not the coexistence of plenty and scarcity but rather their alternation. August Giebelhaus argues that in both the nineteenth-century Age of Illumination and the twentieth-century Age of Energy, the oil industry developed in response to a rhythm imparted by successive periods of glut and scarcity.[39]

Finally, Potter's analysis needs to be made more dynamic. *People of Plenty* has a certain timelessness about it, imposed in part by the essentially static concept of national character, and the study is the weaker for this quality. The overall result is a kind of freeze-frame history, stripped of movement, change, and development over time. Yet Potter himself suggests several lines of development or evolution; the shift from an individualistic, agrarian society to a highly organized, urban, industrial order seems implicit throughout the study. The problem is that no such schema is fully or rigorously developed, or systematically imposed upon the analysis. However, Potter does introduce in passing a theme of development which anticipates some of the most exciting scholarship of our own day and which deserves elaboration.

All too briefly, Potter tantalizes the reader with a discussion of the "vital" transformation wherein "the most critical point in the functioning of society shifts from production to consumption . . . and . . . the culture must be reoriented to convert the producer's culture into a consumer's culture." "In a society of abundance," Potter writes:

> the productive capacity can supply new kinds of goods faster than society in the mass learns to crave these goods or to regard them as necessities. If this new capacity is to be used, the imperative must fall upon consumption, and the society must be adjusted to a new set of drives and values in which consumption is paramount.[40]

It is here, in his sketch of a fundamental reorientation of our culture, that Potter speaks most instructively to a generation of historians attempting to find large patterns of meaning in the nation's past.

A substantial body of scholarship has emerged that harkens back to the concepts of abundance, growth, and a consumer culture limned by Potter a generation ago.[41] There exists some uncertainty about the precise timing of the cultural reorientation involved in a shift of emphasis from production to consumption, but it seems clear nonetheless that the shift was underway during the crucial period from 1880–1920, that its distinctive features came clearly into view in the 1920s, and that the transformation blossomed unmistakably in the years after World War II. The shift was a process, not an event, and it unfolded on a variety of fronts, often in an untidy fashion. It entailed: (1) the attainment of a high level of production, especially of durable and sophisticated consumers' goods; (2) a distribution of wealth beyond the upper class, and notably the expansion of middle-class purchasing power; (3) the relentless commodification of life, the making of an ever-increasing portion of human experience into salable commodities; (4) the development of characteristic institutions and practices in the crucial areas of product design, advertising, mass merchandising, and credit; (5) the emergence of exemplars of consumption, models for imitation and emulation provided increasingly by the media of mass communication; (6) a change in the culture's modal personality type; (7) changes in behavior involving patterns of consumption, saving, and investment; and (8) the development of a "consumer ethic," that is, values and expectations that validate and legitimate consumption, leisure, indulgence, self-fulfillment, and self-absorption. Of course, such a listing does no more than sketch the bare outlines of what has become the dominant way of life in American society—in the words of its chroniclers, a culture of abundance or a culture of consumption, whose emergence represents a historical watershed.[42]

Scholars are presently exploring the nature and extent of the consumer culture from a variety of angles. The pioneering studies of the political, institutional, and cultural dimensions of the consumer culture are particularly illustrative of the promise and the challenges of the new approach. The consumer culture is, we are reminded, at once "an ethic, a standard of living, and a power structure," and it is precisely this multifariousness that makes its political dimension both compelling and elusive.[43] David Thelen finds in the emergence of a consumer consciousness the basis for a new mass, conflict-centered politics and an era of progressive reform.[44] Alan Wolfe traces the development after World War II of a political consensus on the primacy of economic growth that both unified policy and obscured the need for basic changes in the political economy.[45] Richard Wightman Fox and T. J. Jackson Lears argue more broadly that consumption became "a cultural ideal, a hegemonic 'way of seeing' in twentieth-century America."[46] It is indeed striking that all three findings—conflict, consensus, and hegemony—have thus far been fitted into left-of-center critiques of modern America. The conservative promise of Daniel Boorstin's treatment of consumption communities and democratic materialism in *The Americans: The Democratic Experience* (1973) remains unfulfilled.

The institutional outlines of the consumer culture seem clear, but here too complexity appears a dominant note. As befits its central role, advertising has received the greatest attention from scholars. In the most sophisticated study thus far, Roland Marchand posits an active yet subtle role for advertising, viewing it as both an influential apostle of modernity and a mediating buffer which cushioned the impact of the impersonality, overwhelming scale, and sheer inexplicability of modern life.[47] Susan Porter Benson finds a similar complexity in another hallmark institution, the department store, where the cultures of women, workers, managers, and the urban bourgeoise all converged and interacted to make consumption one of our society's most richly textured cultural rituals.[48]

The social and cultural character and consequences of the consumer culture and its rituals have yet to be fully plumbed by either historians or anthropologists. But a start has been made. William Leach's essay on the impact of the consumer culture and especially department stores finds that these developments stimulated women to imagine new worlds of possibility, of experience, action, and satisfaction, as well as of commerce and ownership.[49] Neil Harris discovers a similar pattern—for both women and men—in American fiction of the same transitional period. In their finely nuanced treatment of things and possession, authors such as F. Scott Fitzgerald and Sinclair Lewis were in actuality describing a new ideology of consumption which sought "to individualize rather than standardize, by grafting onto mass production the alluring, psychological qualities that answered private dreams."[50] Thus have historians returned to the ground where history, culture, and personality converge and interact, a nexus that Potter sought to survey some thirty years ago.

It is not at all clear where a Potteresque emphasis on the consumer culture fits in the profession's search for new interpretive frameworks. The literature on consumption is already too vast, rich, and coherent to be overlooked; it will have to be taken into account, but just how this should be done is uncertain. One possibility is for this scholarship to be subsumed under one or another of the synthetic schemas presently vying for acceptance. It is doubtful, however, that the Marxist concepts of "social structures of accumulation" or "modes of production" can be made sufficiently elastic to capture the ethereal subtleties of the consumer culture.[51] The organizational synthesis, a second alternative, illuminates related phenomena but reserves its primary attention for organizational variables that appear relatively tangential to the matters which have thus far most concerned the historians of the culture of abundance.[52] Although the organizational and consumptionist approaches are so essentially different that they cannot be telescoped together, they are complementary and together they shed much light on the nature of modern America. This being the case, the consumer culture can be viewed as an ideological construct and combined with the modern bureaucratic ideology to fit into Daniel J. Singal's synthetic vision of cyclical ideological development, a third aspirant in the synthesis sweepstakes.[53] Finally, the consumer culture could conceivably become the modern centerpiece of an even broader conception, Thomas Bender's idea of a public culture, the making of which provides yet another alternative synthesizing theme.[54]

It is also possible that Potter's approach will stand on its own, either as a grand synthesis covering all of American history or as a middle-level generalization particularly applicable to the history of the last hundred years. The concept of abundance has been used as an overarching interpretive theme in both economic and urban history.[55] More particularly, the concept of a consumer culture offers a new and unique way of periodizing and analyzing the history of modern America. In *Class Conflict and Cultural Consensus: The Making of a Mass Consumer Society in Flint, Michigan* (1987), Ronald Edsforth examines progressive reform, normalcy, the creation of the New Deal welfare state, the triumph of organized labor in the 1930s, and the emergence of a Cold War culture as historical phenomena which revolve around "the central development of twentieth-century social history"—"the creation of, and ongoing attempt to sustain, a true mass consumer-oriented society."[56] The result is a sophisticated view of a society where conflict occurs within parameters established by a cultural consensus based on highly organized mass production and mass consumption. The approach is clearly consensus history, recycled with some new twists. It recognizes the ethnic, political, and class conflicts that occurred within the boundaries of the dominant consensus, the achievements and consequences of such struggles, and the ultimately hegemonic nature of the consensus. It is a brand of consensus history that speaks with a special immediacy to the political Left. Its moral message is sobering rather than celebratory. Most important, the new consensus history makes excellent sense of America's recent past. If in 1960 Norman Mailer captured the spirit of the age in an essay entitled "Superman Comes to the Supermart," it is likely that in the future historians will view the 1980s as the time when Clio went to the shopping mall.

Robert M. Collins, Department of History, University of Missouri-Columbia, is presently at work on a study of American attitudes regarding economic growth.

1. Alexis de Tocqueville, *Democracy in America,* J. P. Mayer, ed. (1969), P. 280; Josiah Strong, *Our Country* (1891), pp. 7–29; and Ray Stannard Baker, *Our New Prosperity* (1900), p. 254.

2. Leo Huberman, *America Incorporated: Recent Economic History of the United States* (1940), pp. vii, 233.

3. Eric Johnston, *America Unlimited* (1944), pp. 40–48.

4. Quoted in William Leuchtenburg, *A Troubled Feast: American Society Since 1945,* rev. ed. (1979), p. 55.

5. John Updike, "Superman," in *Verse* (1965), p. 55.

6. Norman Mailer, "Superman Comes to the Supermart," *Esquire,* November, 1960, pp. 119–27.

7. Randall Jarrell, "Next Day," in *The Complete Poems* (1969), p. 279; Allen Ginsberg, "A Supermarket in California," in *Howl and Other Poems* (1956), p. 23.

8. Don DeLillo, *White Noise* (1985), pp. 325–26.

9. Saul Bellow, *Herzog* (1964), p. 207.

10. David M. Potter, *People of Plenty: Economic Abundance and the American Character* (1954), p. 30.

11. Ibid., p. 94.

12. Ibid., p. 188.

13. Ibid., p. 208.

14. Daniel Bell, *The End of Ideology* (1960), p. 300. A judicious assessment of the social criticism of the 1950s is found in Richard Pells, *The Liberal Mind in a Conservative Age: American Intellectuals in the 1940s and 1950s* (1985).

15. David Potter Interview in John Garraty, ed., *Interpreting American History* (1970), 2:316.

16. David Potter Memoir, Oral History Collection, Columbia University. The bulk of this interview appears in Garraty, ed. *Interpreting American History;* this particular exchange, however, is not found in the published version.

17. Reviews by Gerald Carson, *New York Times Book Review,* 14 November 1954, p. 41; and Karl W. Deutsch, *The Yale Review* 44 (December 1954): 292–95.

18. Reviews by Irvin G. Wyllie, *Journal of Economic History* 15 (1955): 189–90; and George Caspar Homans, *The New England Quarterly* 27 (December 1954): 553–54.

19. Review by Fred Shannon, *Mississippi Valley Historical Review* 41 (March 1955): 733–34.

20. See George Harmon Knoles, comp., "Bibliography of the Published Works of David M. Potter," in Potter, *Freedom and Its Limitations in American Life,* Don E. Fehrenbacher, ed. (1976), pp. 73–75.

21. The list of best-selling history books is found in Robert Fenyo [history editor at Prentice-Hall] to Richard Hofstadter, February 29, 1968, Box 5, Correspondence, Richard Hofstadter MSS, Columbia University.

22. John Higham *et al., History: The Development of Historical Studies in the United States* (1965), p. 223.

23. For the complicated and fascinating story of the response to Elkins's study, see August Meier and Elliott Rudwick, *Black History and the Historical Profession, 1915–1980* (1986), pp. 140–42, 247–60.

24. David Riesman, "Some Questions about the Study of American Character in the Twentieth Century," *Annals of the American Academy of Political and Social Sciences* 370 (March 1967): 37–38.

25. David E. Stannard, "American Historians and the Idea of National Character: Some Problems and Prospects," *American Quarterly* 23 (May 1971): 212–13.

26. Robert Sklar, "American Studies and the Realities of America," *American Quarterly* 22 (Summer 1970), p. 601.

27. Thomas Bender, "The New History—Then and Now," *Reviews in American History* 12 (December 1984), p. 620.

28. Richard Hofstadter, *The Progressive Historians: Turner, Beard, Parrington* (1968), p. 442.

29. John Higham, *History: Professional Scholarship in America* (1983), p. 240.

30. See, for example, Carl Degler, "Remaking American History," *Journal of American History* 67 (June 1980): 16–17; Herbert G. Gutman, "The Missing Synthesis: Whatever Happened to History?" *Nation*, 21 November 1981, pp. 521, 553–54; Eric Foner, "History in Crisis," *Commonweal*, 18 December 1981, pp. 723–26; Jonathan Yardley, "The Narrowing World of the Historian," *AHA Perspectives* 20 (September 1982): 21–22; Thomas Bender, "The New History—Then and Now," pp. 612–22; Thomas Bender, "Making History Whole Again," *New York Times Book Review*, 6 October 1985, pp. 1, 42–43; Thomas Bender, "Wholes and Parts: The Need for Synthesis in American History," *Journal of American History* 73 (June 1986): 120–36. The call for synthesis has also produced a backlash of sorts. See Eric H. Monkkonen, "The Dangers of Synthesis," *American Historical Review* 91 (December 1986): 1146–57. The discussion is continued in the contributions of David Thelen, Nell Irvin Painter, Richard Wightman Fox, Roy Rosenzweig, and Thomas Bender to "A Round Table: Synthesis in American History," *Journal of American History* 74 (June 1987): 107–130.

31. David Potter Interview in Garraty, ed., *Interpreting American History*, 2:318–19.

32. The phrase is from William O'Neill, *American High: The Years of Confidence, 1945–1960* (1986), p. 204.

33. Seymour Martin Lipset, "Growth, Affluence, and the Limits of Futurology," in Kenneth Boulding *et al.*, *From Abundance to Scarcity: Implications for the American Tradition* (1978), pp. 65–66.

34. David M. Potter, "American Women and the American Character," in *American Character and Culture: Some Twentieth-Century Perspectives*, John A. Hague, ed. (1964), pp. 83–84. It is likely that we will learn more about Potter's response to his critics when the Potter papers deposited at Stanford University are opened to researchers in 1991.

35. David Potter Interview in Garraty, ed., *Interpreting American History*, 2:316, 327.

36. See also Donald J. Pisani, "Forests and Conservation, 1865–1890," *Journal of American History* 72 (September 1985): 340–59.

37. David Thelen, *Paths of Resistance: Tradition and Dignity in Industrializing Missouri* (1986); Steven L. Piott, *The Anti-Monopoly Persuasion: Popular Resistance to the Rise of Big Business in the Midwest* (1985); and Steven Hahn and Jonathan Prude, eds., *The Countryside in the Age of Capitalist Transformation: Essays in the Social History of Rural America* (1985). For a subtle discussion of the issue of resistance, see George M. Fredrickson, "Down on the Farm," *New York Review of Books*, 23 April 1987, pp. 37–39.

38. The list of shortages is taken from Michael Kammen, "From Scarcity to Abundance—to Scarcity? Some Implications for the American Tradition from the Perspective of a Cultural Historian," in Boulding *et al.*, *From Abundance to Scarcity*.

39. August W. Giebelhaus, "Petroleum's Age of Energy and the Thesis of American Abundance," *Materials and Society* 7 (1983): 279–93.

40. Potter, *People of Plenty*, p. 173.

41. A superb bibliographic essay on the consumer culture is found in Daniel Horowitz's perceptive monograph, *The Morality of Spending: Attitudes toward the Consumer Society in America, 1875–1940* (1985), pp. 187–201. Three pioneering historical efforts, sometimes over-

looked, are Daniel M. Fox, *The Discovery of Abundance: Simon N. Patten and the Transformation of Social Theory* (1967); Daniel Boorstin, *The Americans: The Democratic Experience* (1973); and William Leuchtenburg, *A Troubled Feast: American Society Since 1945* (1973).

42. A general introduction to the topic of a consumer culture is found in Richard Wightman Fox and T. J. Jackson Lears, eds., *The Culture of Consumption: Critical Essays in American History* (1983); and Warren I. Susman, *Culture as History: The Transformation of American Society in the Twentieth Century* (1984).

43. Fox and Lears, eds., *Culture of Consumption*, p. xii.

44. David P. Thelen, *The New Citizenship: Origins of Progressivism in Wisconsin, 1885–1900* (1972); and Thelen, "Patterns of Consumer Consciousness in the Progressive Movement: Robert M. LaFollette, the Antitrust Persuasion, and Labor Legislation," in Ralph M. Aderman, ed., *The Quest for Social Justice: The Morris Fromkin Memorial Lectures, 1970–1980* (1983), pp. 19–47.

45. Alan Wolfe, *America's Impasse: The Rise and Fall of the Politics of Growth* (1981)

46. Fox and Lears, eds., *Culture of Consumption*, p. x.

47. Roland Marchand, *Advertising the American Dream: Making Way for Modernity, 1920–1940* (1985). An excellent bibliographic essay on advertising and the consumer culture is found on pp. 419–26.

48. Susan Porter Benson, *Counter Cultures: Saleswomen, Managers, and Customers in American Department Stores, 1890–1940* (1986). See also Gunther Barth, *City People: The Rise of Modern City Culture in Nineteenth-Century America* (1980), pp. 110–47; and Alan Trachtenberg, *The Incorporation of America: Culture and Society in the Gilded Age* (1982) 130–35.

49. William R. Leach, "Transformations in a Culture of Consumption: Women and Department Stores, 1890–1925," *Journal of American History* 71 (September 1984): 319–42.

50. Neil Harris, "The Drama of Consumer Desire," in Otto Mayr and Robert C. Post, eds., *Yankee Enterprise: The Rise of the American System of Manufactures* (1981), p. 212. In this regard, see also Mary Douglas, *The World of Goods* (1979).

51. This is not to deny the importance of the work on mass culture and the culture industry that we associate with Critical Theory and the Frankfurt School. One cannot help but observe, however, the degree to which such work strayed from the central concerns of classical Marxism: the mode of production, the labor process, structural contradictions, class conflict and proletarian revolution, political power and the role of the state. See Martin Jay, *The Dialectical Imagination: A History of the Frankfurt School and the Institute for Social Research* (1973), pp. 57–75, 79; Eugene Lunn, *Marx and Modernism: An Historical Study of Lukacs, Brecht, Benjamin, and Adorno* (1982), pp. 149–241; and Tom Bottomore, *The Frankfurt School* (1984), *passim*.

52. See the exemplary reports by Louis P. Galambos in "The Emerging Organizational Synthesis in Modern American History," *Business History Review* 44 (Autumn 1970): 279–90; and "Technology, Political Economy, and Professionalization: Central Themes of the Organizational Synthesis," *Business History Review* 57 (Winter 1983): 471–93.

53. Daniel Joseph Singal, "Beyond Consensus: Richard Hofstadter and American Historiography," *American Historical Review* 89 (October 1984): 976–1004.

54. Bender's ideas regarding the public culture are found in the essays cited in footnotes 27 and 30 above.

55. Edwin J. Perkins and Gary Walton, *A Prosperous People: The Growth of the American Economy* (1985); Martin V. Melosi, *Coping with Abundance: Energy and Environment in Industrial America* (1985); Zane L. Miller, "Scarcity, Abundance, and American Urban History," *Journal of Urban History* 4 (February 1978): 131–55.

56. The quotations are from p. 221.

READING MARY BEARD

Suzanne Lebsock

Woman As Force in History is an exasperating book. It rails at the founders of American feminism. It misconstrues the history of women's legal rights. Its organization is unconventional at best, and at worst, perverse; it is partly for this reason that the book is virtually unusable in undergraduate courses. It is true that *Woman As Force* has been the subject of a number of perceptive essays. Still, except for a handful of specialists in the legal history of women, or in the history of women's history, no one is compelled to read it. Among the younger generation of scholars, hardly anyone does.

Tributes to the author, however, are commonplace and increasing all the time. With the explosive growth of women's history, Mary Beard is honored as a founder of the field, a position she earned not only by the publication of *Woman As Force in History* in 1946, but by her extraordinary persistence in promoting the study of women.[1] Beard wrote or edited a total of six books about women; she made sure that women were included in the *Rise of American Civilization*, which she coauthored with Charles A. Beard; she designed courses in the history of women and pressed them upon professors; she tried valiantly to get the *Encyclopaedia Britannica* to make its categories more inclusive of women; she struggled for years to establish an international women's archive. All this she attempted with no institutional backing, and in a period when the women's movement was divided and weak. Several of her efforts met with hostility, indifference, or defeat—which in retrospect renders her leadership the more remarkable. That she persisted with such conviction, for so long, with so little support, and in the face of such resistance is cause for deep admiration.

Does it make sense to revere the author and ignore the book? Mary Beard, if she had to choose, would probably have preferred we studied the book and bypassed the author. The book does have power—else it could not be exasperating. It also has many peculiarities, which go a considerable way in explaining its relative neglect. There are questions, too, of readership and timing. *Woman As Force in History* received little fanfare when it was first published. Twenty-five years later, women's history took off and at last gave the book an appreciable readership. In several ways, however, the new women's history was out of sympathy with Mary Beard's interests and style, and *Woman As Force* thus looked all the stranger by contrast. This essay, to risk overdoing the alliteration, is about a book's peculiar power, its powerful peculiarities, and the reception of an antiprofessional author by an audience just finding its professional feet.

The central proposition of *Woman As Force in History* was that women had not always been the victims of total subjugation. According to Beard, the idea that women had ever been a subject sex was a myth—"one of the most fantastic myths ever created by the human mind" (p. 144)—and about half of her book was devoted to an exploration of how in her view this myth had come to be. The other half described an impressive line of forceful women, mystics and politicians, the occasional warrior, artisans and scholars. Ranging over the centuries and across Europe and America, Beard demonstrated decisively that from antiquity forward, some women had made history.

Much of the time, she cast her argument in negative terms: women had not been totally, thoroughly, or universally victimized by men. The advantage of this phrasing was that it made the point easy to prove: a queen here and a saint there—or even a law code that gave women some form of control over property—and the case was made. This approach also gave a coherence to the book that was otherwise lacking. Whether in a section on women and bolshevism (where the book begins) or a discussion of the salons of eighteenth-century France (where the book ends), all the evidence contributed to the central message.

On the face of it, this theme would not seem capable of generating much controversy. So women were not totally victimized at all times and in all places. "Would anyone seriously maintain the contrary?" asked Berenice Carroll in an essay of 1972. "Unfortunately, yes," Carroll answered. Carroll's essay, which is the starting point for any Beard enthusiast, went on to point out that the concept of total victimization was alive and well within a reputable strain of feminist theory.[2] The best known of the theorists in question was Simone de Beauvoir, whose renowned *The Second Sex* portrayed women as utterly passive: "They have gained only what men have been willing to grant; they have taken nothing, they have only received." From thence Beauvoir proceeded to commit such travesties as "in the past all history has been made by men."[3] Had Beauvoir taken Mary Beard seriously, she would have known better.

Beauvoir, of course, was only giving the stature of theory to the assumptions implicit in the vast bulk of work by professional historians. It scarcely needs restating here that historians of Beard's day hardly ever wrote about women, that when inclusion of an individual woman seemed inescapable it was often done in such a way as to either downplay her achievements or to emphasize her exceptional qualities in ways that degraded women as a group. In its insistence that women, too, had helped to make history, *Woman As Force* was a fundamental challenge to history as it was typically written. And here the book's extraordinary range was significant. Beard's work made it clear that all historians of the western tradition—be they students of the ancients or students of the fascists—might vastly enrich their histories, if only they would pay attention to women.

In 1946 few historians were prepared to be thus enriched. For fifteen years or more *Woman As Force in History* had no appreciable impact on the way history was written. In part this can be attributed to Beard's casting of the problem. It was one thing to show that some women had been active agents throughout history; this Beard did. It was quite another to demonstrate that history could not be understood without reference to women.[4] This much larger task Beard only hinted at. And even had Beard and a pack of like-minded researchers been able to make the case, it is doubtful that the profession at large would have listened. The discovery of *Woman As Force in History* awaited the rebirth of feminism and the coming of age of a new generation of historians.

Woman As Force had its greatest direct impact on those who pioneered the history of women in the 1960s. "Traditional history," Gerda Lerner writes, "fixed women into marginality; I knew and now found confirmation in Mary Beard's writing that this was not the truth. . . . In a very real sense I consider Mary Beard, whom I never met, my principal mentor as a historian."[5] Yet *Woman As Force* was never treated to a full-blown revival. Instead, at the very moment when women's history found a sizable and eager audience, Beard's book was rendered obsolete.

Or perhaps it is more accurate to say that as the history of women came into its own, part of Mary Beard's message was swiftly incorporated and granted the status of conventional wisdom, while other parts seemed passé. About two thousand people attended the Second Berkshire Conference on the History of Women in 1974. There several hundred of them heard Gerda Lerner proclaim, with due credit to Beard, that we should not view women in the past primarily as victims. Lerner conveyed in ten sentences what it had taken Beard an entire book to say, and subsequent trends showed that Lerner spoke for the majority of historians of women. It is theoretically possible to write the history of women solely as a story of victimization (from, say, seclusion in ancient Athens to the burning of witches to the Dalkon Shield); the point would be to comprehend the changing forms of oppression. But oppression never caught on as the central preoccupation of professional historians of women. To that extent, Mary Beard prevailed. At the same time, her insight, one that in 1946—or 1966—was luminous, by 1974 had come to seem obvious.

Once it did seem obvious, once it became a given that women in the past were resourceful people and not mere victims, it became less needful to make the resurrection of great women a primary task of women's history. Common to all three of the keynote addresses of the Second Berkshire Conference was a critique of the women-worthy approach to the past. Gerda Lerner, Natalie Zemon Davis, and Carroll Smith-Rosenberg in turn granted that the study of the greats was all right in its place, but that it needed to be moved aside in favor of scholarship that asked more interesting questions, that explored sex roles and the experiences of women as a group (and women in different groups), that gave full play to the private sphere and to relations between the sexes, that challenged conventional notions of what mattered in history, and that ultimately would make history itself look different.[6] *Woman As Force in History*, with its parade of women worthies, was left in the analytical dust.

Mary Beard's major themes, in other words, did not provide adequate conceptual frameworks for the scores of historians who in the 1970s took up the study of women. Granted, this was due to the state of the field as well as to Beard's argument. Narrative was in low repute in the middle seventies. Historians of women, much in debt to social history, frequently adopted social history's highly analytical approaches, a tendency that was probably reinforced by the knowledge that many historians regarded women's history as faddish or polemical. *Woman As Force* was also out of place in a profession given over to specialization. A book that moves from Seneca Falls to the Levellers (with stops in between at the French Revolution and Marcus Aurelius) in four pages is not a book that most professors would risk assigning in a course, and while Beard's lickety-split tour through European history provided dozens of research leads, few topics were covered in sufficient depth to be mined for lectures or otherwise put to immediate use. (The major exception was Beard's treatment of the Anglo-American law of married women's property, which occupies 130 pages of the book's middle.) *Woman As Force* did not appear to be a teachable book, nor was it in any simple way a model for the scholarship of the 1970s. As the study of women's history mushroomed, the existence of *Woman As Force* became widely known, but it did not become required reading, even in a specialty so new that there was relatively little to read. The paperback edition, first issued by Collier in 1962, slipped quietly out of print in 1978.

Those who picked up the book anyway were likely to be repulsed by still another set of difficulties. One was Beard's attack on the nineteenth-century feminists, delivered in the course of her chapters on the changing law of married women's property. No one would ask that the founders of the women's rights movement be placed above criticism; indeed, many of the major works on American feminism have been critical more or less. But Beard was so cranky as to be embarrassing—and to render suspect her entire treatment of the law.

A second problem was Beard's denial that there had ever been any such thing as gender oppression. For Beard oppression was a matter of class. According to *Woman As Force*, women who were treated badly were treated badly along with men, and just like men, as members of particular classes.[7]

Third, for all its extraordinary range, *Woman As Force* ignored vast reaches of female experience. Although some of Beard's other writings suggested that she placed great historical value on the personal and domestic side of life— she proposed, for example, that archivists collect grocery lists[8]—this did not inform her major statement on the significance of women in history. In itself this was hardly a fatal flaw; there was, and is, plenty of room for studies that concentrate on women's public lives. Given Beard's argument about oppression, however, her neglect of the personal, especially of the body, seems more like a blind spot than a choice. Had Beard taken up sexuality, reproduction, and a fuller range of relationships between the sexes, it is difficult to see how she could have sidestepped wife-beating and rape—the practices that demonstrate with greatest clarity that some women were victimized as women, and often by men of their own class.[9]

For all these reasons, *Woman As Force in History* was not a book for the 1970s. Might it be a book for the nineties? One sign is that it is in print once again, brought out recently by Persea Books. Since about 1980, women's history has in some respects moved in Beard's direction. There have been repeated calls for greater attention to women in public life, and there is growing support— realized occasionally in research and more often in the classroom—for approaches that cross the Atlantic and more generally transcend national boundaries. Meanwhile, the establishment of graduate courses in women's history may be creating a new market for the historiography of women, in which Mary Beard surely deserves a prominent place. Finally, as time goes on, we try to ask tougher questions about the meaning and purposes of feminism. The fate of *Woman As Force* in the last years of the twentieth century may ultimately hinge on its power to help us think through those questions— questions Beard raised primarily in her chapters about the law. As it happens, that is also the one part of the book dedicated to American history, and it is to the law we now turn.

It is least arguable that the central theme of Beard's treatment of the law was a critique of liberal individualism. Beard herself did not phrase it that way. Her stated target, among grand principles, was equality—or more specifically, the use of equality as the guiding principle for women's escape from legal subjection. First, Beard argued, women had never really been in a state of legal subjection, restrictive as the common law may at first appear. Second, when in the course of the nineteenth century the states reformed the common law, the main result was confusion, much of it a consequence of the misguided attempt to make women equal. On both counts, for getting both the problem and the solution wrong, Beard blamed the nineteenth-century feminists.

The feminists' first sin, according to Beard, was their persistent portrayal of the American woman as the legal slave of her husband. This the feminists did by presenting the common law as the only system of jurisprudence available to women, and in this the feminists were neither the only nor the original sinners. The first perpetrator was Sir William Blackstone, whose eighteenth-century *Commentaries on the Laws of England* exalted the common law and slighted equity, a second system of jurisprudence which offered women an escape from their common-law disabilities. Then came the lawyers of nineteenth-century America, many of whom adopted Blackstone as the sole authority on the law of husband and wife, or as one of Beard's subheadings put it, "Lawyers in America Bow Down to Blackstone" (p. 108). Then, finally, came the advocates of women's rights: "American Feminists Bow Down with the Blackstone Lawyers" (p. 113).

It seems unfair to criticize feminists for taking their legal advice from the legal authorities. But Beard believed the feminists should have known better (treatises other than Blackstone's were available), and she suggested that the feminists concentrated on the common law because it made for such effective propaganda.[10] Anyone who has taught married women's property law knows this to be true; undergraduates are stunned by women's common law disabilities, and on exams fire them back with uncommon accuracy and passion. Under the common law, a married woman could not own personal property and she could not control real estate. She had no right to her own labor or wages. She could make no contracts, nor could she make a will. She had no standing in court. She could not serve as the legal guardian of her own (or anyone else's) children, nor could she fill any other position of financial trust. If all went well, the wife was merely passive. If either her marriage or her family's fortunes failed, then she was extremely vulnerable. It was legal, for example, for her husband to collect her wages directly from her employer and then spend the money on another woman. For the injured wife, the common law offered no remedy.

Equity, however, offered a way out. Equity had developed alongside the common law, largely to provide relief from the rigidity of the common law. In equity the judges (called chancellors) were to rule according to the inherent justice of the particular case, and as Mary Beard hastened to point out, this often meant something quite different from the wifely subjection dictated by common law. In equity the property of a married woman could be exempted from the control of her husband and the depredations of the husband's creditors. Some married women acquired the right to own and dispose of property and to appear in court. Some were able to run businesses. By the early nineteenth century, Beard claimed, equity had emancipated "millions" of women from their common law subjection (p. 158).

Could it have been so? Subsequent research says no. Whether they focus on treatises, on appellate cases, or on the legal instruments that created separate estates, scholars have consistently found Beard's claims to be exaggerated and off-center.[11] On close inspection, it turns out that relatively few women were able to take advantage of equity. The first obstacle to obtaining a separate estate under equity was the ideology of male dominance; to acquire or bestow a separate estate was to imply incompetence or ill will on the part of the husband. For those who overcame that barrier, there were a host of concrete problems. Equitable settlements were often expensive. They frequently required the services of lawyers and trustees. Some of them occasioned numerous actions in court. In short, equity worked best for the wealthy. And there is some question as to how well equity worked for anyone. Equity was intended to provide flexibility where the common law did not. But this very flexibility could itself be a problem, replacing the all-powerful husband with a powerful—and unpredictable—chancellor. In one category of cases, for example, the validity of a married woman's contract hinged on whether a particular contract did or did not endanger the woman's livelihood at a particular level of comfort. How was anyone to know in advance whether such a transaction would hold up in court?

The problem here was that equity was not as different from the common law as Beard suggested. Beard portrayed the enlightened forces of equity locked in a titanic struggle with the barbarous forces of common law, and in truth there were significant numbers of women who did assume substantial powers under equity. But on the whole, equity in practice reinforced common-law theory: both assumed that married women should have little or no legal responsibility for economic decisions, and that women should have manly protection. The fundamental difference between the two systems was that equity provided an alternate set of protectors in cases where the husband botched the job. As nineteenth-century critics of the common law pointed out, equity helped perpetuate the common law by providing an escape route for the well-to-do.

Enter the married women's property acts. In the 1830s various states began to reform the common law, enacting new statutes that gave married women the right to own property in their own names. These statutes were then revised, usually over a period of years, to stipulate what property counted as separate property and what powers wives could exercise. To Beard's mind, this was both unnecessary and misguided, unnecessary because equity had already liberated so many women from the common law, and misguided because the married women's property acts represented an attempt to impose an impossibly simple principle—equality—on a complex set of interests and problems that required more flexible and nuanced treatment. The second half of the century saw the law splinter into a "positive riot of variations" and, according to Beard, the campaign for equality was to blame (p. 166).

Married women's property law was indeed a mess, as any bleary-eyed student of the subject will readily testify. The search for equality, however, was not the problem: it had not been the driving force behind the married women's property acts, nor was it the reigning principle behind judicial interpretations of the new statutes. The reforms were pushed through for a variety of purposes, many of which had nothing to do with the status of women, and some of which were incompatible with one another. Legislators wanted to protect debtors without stripping creditors; they wanted to protect inheritances while still promoting the flow of capital; they had to give women some active powers over their property (else how could a deserted wife manage?) but wanted to protect those same women from endangering their property; under normal circumstances they wanted to maintain male authority in families; and after all that, they wanted to streamline the law, too. Judges were mindful of all these interests, and they added to the confusion with rulings that generally preserved as much of the common law as possible. Equality would have been far simpler. Instead, issues that for decades had been litigated in equity now surfaced in complex dialogues between legislatures and the courts, dialogues that proceeded differently in every state.[12]

That a feminist historian should feel compelled to write an extended polemic against equality (and it *was* extended—characteristically, Beard took the discussion all the way back to Seneca) was in large part a manifestation of the war within American feminism in the post-suffrage era. When Beard looked at the legal reforms of the nineteenth century, she saw the shadow of Alice Paul and the National Woman's Party. Decades before the writing of *Woman As Force*, Beard had worked closely with Paul in the militant wing of the woman suffrage movement. They broke before 1920, however, and Beard's opposition intensified after Paul and her supporters introduced the Equal Rights Amendment in 1923. Paul had many critics, of course, the majority of whom believed that Paul's campaign for full and formal legal equality was an assault on the real interests of women, especially of working women who needed the hard-won benefits of protective legislation. Beard was an activist as well as a scholar, and her location in all this was complex. She tried to mark out a "third path" for feminism; she maintained friendships across ideological lines; and she criticized the ideas of both major camps. Her harshest judgments, however, were reserved for Paul and Paul's supporters. *Woman As Force in History* reverberates with these struggles and implicitly documents their bitterness and longevity. Published when Beard was 70, it may also reflect her personal frustration and fatigue.[13]

If Beard's experience of post-suffrage feminism caused her to misread the role of equality in the property law reforms of the nineteenth century, it may nevertheless have given her a salutary appreciation of the complexities inherent in certain kinds of feminist claims. The problem with the nineteenth-century feminists, Beard charged in a single titillating sentence, was that they "steadily fixed their attention on legal and political equality rather than on women's force, potentialities, and obligations" (p. 147). Another teaser appeared four pages later, where Beard found "positive aspirations" in the "doctrine of equality": "For women it often meant, simply, taking the stature of man as the measure of excellence and endowing woman with his qualities, aims, and chances in the world for personal advantages" (p. 151).

In those two sentences lie the materials for pages of exegesis. It is probably not overinterpreting to say that Beard saw the strategic advantages of claims to equality (just as she saw the propagandistic value of women's common-law disabilities), while she also feared the consequences of striving for honor and power on terms defined by and for men. To take a none-too-subtle example, Joan of Arc has often been cited (though not by Mary Beard, who cited obscurer women warriors) as someone who shows that a woman can be courageous, successful in battle, and a patriot. But how far can this take us? For one thing, there were not many Joans; women as a group will always come up short when men are the measure. More important, what have we done if we accept nationalism and bloodshed as virtuous? It is time, as Beard proposed, for a more serious look at *women's* "force, potentialities, and obligations."

Beard never spelled out what she meant by those words, but it seems worth suggesting that in the context of married women's property law, the key word was "obligations." Underlying Beard's critique of the changing law was a concern for the survival of collectivity in America. Nineteenth-century individualism, as Beard described it, "was atomistic in its social effects. It split families, communities, and society at large into units, into individuals. . . . The individual was exalted and the competitive urge among individuals was regarded as a natural and socially wholesome human attribute. . . . In the struggle of individuals for a foothold and survival, the family and even society in the large would in some mysterious way take care of themselves . . ." (pp. 154–55).

Today most historians of women would rephrase that: The family and society "in the large" would be taken care of by women. The early nineteenth century's ideology of individualism needed women, in ways both abstract and concrete. Abstractly, the idea of individualism depended upon a belief that women as a group would keep the country's social and moral fabric from unraveling. More concretely, it was control of the reproductive and productive labor of wives (and among the propertied, control of wives' capital as well) that allowed actual men to approximate the ideal of the untrammeled individual competing in the marketplace. In neither case, of course, could women aspire to be individuals. Individualism, like most concepts with claims to universality, was gendered.

This was especially the case while the common law of married women's property remained in force, concentrating in the husband the capacity to make all economic decisions for the family. While the common law thus gave strong legal backing to male individualism, it also reinforced the family's integrity. In its legal character, the family was a unit, bound not only by the husband's sole control of the property, labor, and persons of his wife and minor children, but also by his sole obligation to support them. For those who liked to eat their cake as well as have it, the common law insisted on a theory of family unity even while it accommodated the rise of individualism.

Mary Beard was no fan of the common law. But Beard herself tended to portray the interests of the husbands and wives as one,[14] and she seems to have been most troubled by those aspects of the married women's property acts that threatened to make women into atomistic individuals, exposing families thereby to the ravages of competitive individualism. This was only suggested, as Beard wrote no conclusion and instead bailed out of her treatment of American law by presenting a long list of issues (thirty-one, to be exact) that had been litigated in the wake of the married women's property acts. The questions she selected, however, are instructive; the largest clusters had to do in one way or another with whether and how the law would force husbands and wives respectively to take financial responsibility for one another and for their children. Once the wife was allowed to own property, was she then obligated to support the family? Was the bankrupt husband of a wage-earning woman still obligated to support the family? Was anyone obligated to anyone?

In other words, Mary Beard's attacks on the married women's property

reforms and on nineteenth-century feminism work better as a critique of individualism than of equality. Not that individualism and equality were mutually exclusive. For Beard, the problem with equality in the modern world
was that it foisted individualism, already rampant among men, on women.
"Forward to the individualistic struggle among struggling men!" (p. 32), she
wrote, in this instance in parody of the attitudes of business and professional
women in the 1930s. To Beard's mind, the perils of individualism were self-
evident, but *Woman As Force* also provided some specific if scattered indict-
ments. Individualism reinforced the privileges of the privileged classes. Individualism distorted history, making history a chronicle of the deeds of particular men, when all along the history of politics and the State prior to the
nineteenth century should have been written as family history.[15] Most of all,
individualism was hostile to the building of civilization, for "the civilization
of men and women occurs in society, and all the agencies used in the process
. . . are social products, the work of men and women indissolubly united by
the very nature of life . . ." (p. 331).

Would Beard accept this focus on individualism as a friendly amendment?
"No," she might say, "I said the problem was equality and I meant it." "In
that case," I imagine myself replying, "with all due respect, you should have
argued it better." *Woman As Force* is the kind of book that inspires such fan-
tasies, for it grabs its readers, jerks us across centuries, asserts the outrageous,
slides away from its own conclusions, and in some places—as in the case of
the thirty-one questions—invites us to formulate ideas of our own. It is, to
say the least, an engaging and highly contentious book.

We could wish that Beard had contended more—and had had more help—
so that she herself might have come to terms with more of her book's problems. For an author devoted to demonstrating women's agency in history,
the law was a curious choice of subject. Women might be treated well (in
equity), or badly (under the common law), or haphazardly (after the married
women's property acts), but in all cases male justices and legislators were the
actors. Except for her critique of the feminists' use of Blackstone, Beard's legal
history was a study in female passivity.

Beard seems not to have been troubled by this (she was even slightly smug
in mentioning that some legislatures reformed the law without the help, or
even the knowledge, of feminists). After listing the perplexities that followed
in the wake of the American married women's property acts, Beard added
yet another chapter on law, this one on "long legal history." Here were more
nails for the common law's coffin. Beard argued that the common law as
Blackstone constructed it had a relatively short life: not only was the common
law under significant revision by the 1840s, but the provisions cited by Black-

stone in the eighteenth century were of relatively recent origin, having os-
sified at some point after the high middle ages. As late as the thirteenth century, women still had considerable legal dignity, and before that, in the sixth
century, women had it even better.

Whatever the merits of this case (and in general outline, they appear to be
considerable), Beard's exploration of medieval law led to one of the book's
richest insights. "It would appear that under the feudal law, which formed
the basis of the common law, married women possessed less freedom than
was accorded to them in times deemed more primitive and unenlightened"
(p. 184). There was, in other words, no positive correlation between the rise
of civilization, as it has conventionally been defined, and rising status for
women. We might in fact have better luck if we look for an inverse relation
between the two. Beard went on to surmise that the long process of disin-
heriting medieval women began with the rise of powerful centralized states.
Could it be that in "long history" civilization has generally done its rising at
the expense of women?[16]

If this was so, even some large fraction of the time, then the implications
for the history of the West are potentially stupendous. To the degree that the
rise and decline of civilization still stands (or lurks) as a concept in our broad
understanding of history, we face a whole new recognition of that history's
inadequacy. It is not just that traditional history left out half the population.
It is that for half the population traditional history was dead wrong.

Beard did not take the case so far, and indeed, would have had a good deal
of trouble doing so without undermining her central purpose of demonstrating the nonsubjection of women throughout history. Still, the idea that civilization and the status of women do not rise and fall together, and that the
process of civilization-building has often been detrimental to women, was at
least suggested in *Woman As Force*, and it remains useful now—in western civ
courses, for example—at least as a working hypothesis.

Beard had her own ideas about the meaning of "civilization," a term which
she ultimately connected to the core purpose of studying the female past. At
the very end of her book, Beard defined the idea of civilization: "In its com-
posite formulation it embraces a conception of history as the struggle of human beings for individual and social perfection—for the good, the true, and
the beautiful—against ignorance, disease, the harshness of physical nature,
the forces of barbarism in individuals and in society" (p. 331). And how did
women figure in this struggle? "Despite the barbaric and power-hungry pro-
pensities and activities in long history, to which their sex was by no means
immune, women were engaged in the main in promotion of civilian interests.
Hence they were in the main on the side of *civil*-ization in the struggle with
barbarism" (p. 331). The history of women, then, "must be regarded as in-

dispensable to the maintenance and promotion of civilization in the present age" (p. 332).

This was a ringing challenge to historians. The trouble is, Beard's vision of woman-as-civilizer does not appear until the final chapter, and little that has come before has prepared us for it. Indeed, in most respects *Woman As Force* accumulated evidence of commonality and likeness between the sexes. First, in her determination to show women's agency in history, Beard was prone to choose examples that demonstrated that women could be just as mean and rotten as the meanest and rottenest men. Second, Beard's class analysis led her at many critical points to stress what men and women—as long as they were members of the same class—had in common. Third, Beard's emphasis on public life kept her from discussing obvious possible sources of civilizing activity—motherhood, for one. Beard was hardly the first to want it both ways—to portray women at once as equal and as special. From the beginning, this has been a central tension in American feminism, within individuals as well as in the larger movement. But we could ask that Beard recognize the potential problem and try to make some headway with it.

So *Woman As Force* ends on a note of whopping contradiction.[17] In a 1984 essay called "Seeing Mary Beard," Bonnie G. Smith argued that to focus on such contradictions is to miss the point. Concentrating on Beard's earlier works, Smith suggests that we drop the search for pure reason and instead appreciate Beard's "breakthrough" in terms "historiographical and herme-neutical." Smith's intriguing essay does not submit easily to summary, but central to her argument is that in Beard's "weirdness"—the term was Beard's own—lie many of the keys to her significance. Beard's work challenged "the masters" (another term of Beard's) not only by insisting that women mattered in history, but by disrupting the conventional forms of historical writing. When Beard circled and zigzagged through time, she "problematized the nar-rative linearity of history."[18] This was one way in which Beard went about subverting the pretensions of positivism. Another form of sabotage was Beard's recognition that history was essentially interpretive, and that a great deal depended on point of view; the pages of Beard's books contained mul-tiple voices—women's, men's, and several of Beard's own. The invocation of voice is also important for understanding the organization of *Woman As Force*, which Smith suggests was contrapuntal. (Perhaps Smith's essay could equally have been titled "Hearing Mary Beard?") In any case, hearing Beard also involves listening to jokes. Beard was often funny, and she coedited a whole collection of women's humor. According to Smith, Beard used humor and sarcasm in ways that once again exposed the pretensions of male au-thority while simultaneously establishing an independent base on which she could take her own authoritative stance.

That Beard was out to rattle some cages, there can be no doubt. Further evidence comes from the dustjacket of the original hardcover of *Woman As Force*, where her biography begins: "Mary Ritter Beard belongs to no professional guild and permits no designation of herself other than that of student and writer." It would take a better-than-average power forward to do as good a job of projecting innocence while throwing an elbow. The title of the book, too, has its jogging and jostling qualities. *Woman As Force in History* is in itself a challenging title; it claims a great deal while remaining poetic and mysterious. Not surprisingly, it is sometimes misquoted as *Women As a Force in History*, which is far more pedestrian, which bears much greater resemblance to the titles of typical scholarly monographs, and which has the effect of cutting Beard and her messages down to size.[19] Beard, in other words, used all the parts of her book to question the authority of the masters. If there were such a thing as subversive binding, Beard's book would be the place to look for it.

Still it is difficult to know how much of this was intentional and to what degree Beard herself would have claimed her book's eccentricities as meaningful. It can be a thin line between the transgressive and the confused. Beard herself, at least in one of her voices, faulted her own historical subjects (among them, the nineteenth-century feminists) for failures of reasoning and consistency. It is hardly picky, nor is it siding with the masters, to want from Beard greater clarity and resolution than *Woman As Force* usually provides.

To conclude an essay on Mary Beard is a tough assignment, given her own inconclusiveness—and elusiveness, which is Ann Lane's word for the woman and Bonnie Smith's word for the work.[20] But here is an attempt at a Beardian conclusion. Remember grade-school book reports? They depended on suspense, and they almost always concluded with the ritual sentence: "Read the book and find out." This seems like appropriate advice in the case of Mary Beard, who often threw the task of concluding to her readers. And it seems doubly appropriate for *Woman As Force*, a book that never really had its day, that was never sufficiently read.

Woman As Force in History is above all a book that occasions intellectual struggle. Granted, a good part of this struggle goes into trying to figure out exactly what Beard was saying. But what makes this sort of effort worthwhile is that Beard took on questions of enormous importance. What is the purpose of history, and what is its central subject matter? What is the meaning of equality? How does it work in concrete cases? How do we foster individuality *and* community? How important is the law, and to what ends should the state exercise its power? What does the inclusion of women mean for our perspective on all these questions? To study Beard is to grapple with fundamental issues, for history, for feminism, for the future of us all.

Suzanne Lebsock, Department of History, Rutgers University, is the author of The Free Women of Petersburg: Status and Culture in a Southern Town, 1784– 1860 *(1984), which won the Bancroft Prize and the Berkshire Conference Prize in 1985.*

1. Quotations are from the original edition by MacMillan. On Beard's life, see Nancy F. Cott, "Mary Ritter Beard," in Barbara Sicherman and Carol Hurd Green, eds., *Notable American Women: The Modern Period* (1980), pp. 71–73; Ann J. Lane, *Mary Ritter Beard: A Sourcebook* (1977); Barbara K. Turoff, *Mary Beard As Force in History* (1979).

2. Berenice A. Carroll, "Mary Beard's *Woman As Force in History*: A Critique," in Carroll, ed., *Liberating Women's History: Theoretical and Critical Essays* (1976), pp. 29–30. Carroll's essay originally appeared in the *Massachusetts Review* in 1972.

3. Quoted in ibid. On p. 41, however, Carroll points out contrary evidence in Beauvoir's book.

4. On this problem, see Carl N. Degler, "*Woman As Force in History* by Mary Beard," *Daedalus* 103 (1974): 71–72.

5. Gerda Lerner, *The Majority Finds Its Past: Placing Women in History* (1979), pp. xxii–xxiii.

6. Gerda Lerner, "Placing Women in History: Definitions and Challenges," *Feminist Studies* 3 (Fall 1975): 5–14; Carroll Smith-Rosenberg, "The New Woman and the New History," ibid., pp. 185–98; Natalie Zemon Davis, " 'Women's History' in Transition: The European Case," *Feminist Studies* 3 (Spring-Summer 1976): 83–103.

7. Beard's most succinct statements on the relative importance of gender and class are on pp. 178–79, 191, and 194–95. It should be noted, however, that these statements are all about the premodern era. On pp. 308–9, Beard suggested that one specific form of gender oppression—the removal of women from politics—did develop in the course of the "commercial and political revolutions" of the eighteenth century. Lane, *Mary Ritter Beard*, pp. 66–67 and 173, makes much of this suggestion, but I think it is unclear how firm or important it was in Beard's thinking. On p. 309 Beard immediately undercut her own suggestion about the rise of gender oppression in the modern era by minimizing the significance of women's disfranchisement. This is, in any case, one more area in which we are thrown back on extrapolation. *Woman As Force* does not attempt an explicit analysis of the relative significance of gender and class oppression for the modern period. Beard's focus in the modern period narrows to the law and the family, and here again she makes a case against gender oppression, first by minimizing the impact of common law, and second by portraying the interests of husband and wife as identical. See especially pp. 131–32.

8. Lane, *Mary Ritter Beard*, p. 35.

9. On p. 243 Beard did mention wife-beating in the Middle Ages; it was typical of her approach that she emphasized that men were often punished for it, priests tried to stop it, and women were themselves "free with their fists."

10. On the propagandistic uses of the law, see Norma Basch, *In the Eyes of the Law: Women, Marriage, and Property in Nineteenth-Century New York* (1982), pp. 168–70, 198–99.

11. Basch, *In the Eyes of the Law*, pp. 26, 30–36, 64–66, 70–112, 229–30; Richard H. Chused, "Married Women's Property and Inheritance by Widows in Massachusetts: A Study of Wills Probated Between 1800 and 1850," *Berkeley Women's Law Journal* 2 (1986): 48–58; Carol Elizabeth Jenson, "The Equity Jurisdiction and Married Women's Property in Ante-Bellum America: A Revisionist View," *International Journal of Women's Studies* 2 (1979): 144–54; Linda K. Kerber, *Women of the Republic: Intellect and Ideology in Revolutionary America* (1980), pp. 139–55; Suzanne Lebsock, *The Free Women of Petersburg: Status and Culture in a Southern Town, 1784–1860* (1984), pp. 54–86; Marylynn Salmon, "Equality or Submission? Feme Covert Status in Early Pennsylvania," in Carol R. Berkin and Mary Beth Norton, eds., *Women of America: A History* (1979), pp. 92–113.

12. Basch, *In the Eyes of the Law*, pp. 200–223; Richard H. Chused, "Late Nineteenth Century Married Women's Property Law: Reception of the Early Married Women's Property Acts by Courts and Legislatures," *American Journal of Legal History* 29 (1985): 3–35; Suzanne

D. Lebsock, "Radical Reconstruction and the Property Rights of Southern Women," *Journal of Southern History* 43 (1977): 195–216.

13. The fatigue factor was suggested by Anne Firor Scott. The third path idea is Nancy F. Cott's, elaborated in her insightful paper "How Weird Was Beard? Mary Ritter Beard and American Feminism" (unpublished paper presented at the Seventh Berkshire Conference on the History of Women, 1987). Cott suggests that I have given one of Beard's central ideas—the refusal to take men as the measure—too little credit for its influence on historians of women in the 1970s. This may well be true. It may also be that Cott's more positive assessment springs in part from the fact that she is considering Beard's entire opus. While *Woman As Force* has been regarded as Beard's most important book on women, it is arguably not her best; many of the themes present in *Woman As Force* were articulated more crisply in Beard's earlier published work or in her private correspondence. Perhaps as a consequence, Beard gets more positive readings from scholars who assess her life and her larger body of work than from those who concentrate on *Woman As Force*. In any case, I am grateful to Nancy Cott for sharing her paper with me and for her comments on an earlier version of this review.

14. Basch, *In the Eyes of the Law*, pp. 34–35.

15. Beard, *Woman As Force*, pp. 286–87. On this point see also Degler, "*Woman As Force in History*," p. 72.

16. An early statement about this problem may be found in Hilda Smith, "Feminism and the Methodology of Women's History" in Carroll, ed., *Liberating Women's History*, pp. 382–83.

17. Carroll, "Mary Beard's *Woman As Force in History*," pp. 35–39; Lane, *Mary Ritter Beard*, p. 65. I am not arguing that the portrayal of women as both equal and special is necessarily contradictory. On the contrary, it is possible to have it both ways, as American feminists did for many decades. The inability of feminism to accommodate both similarity and difference in the sexes appears to be a relatively recent development (largely of the 1920s?) It was Beard's lack of clarity on these issues—not any inherent contradiction—that gives *Woman As Force* its contradictory cast.

18. "Seeing Mary Beard," *Feminist Studies* 10 (Fall 1984): 407, 413. On p. 399, Smith quotes Beard's opening line in *On Understanding Women* (1931): "This book may appear weird and unsymmetrical to the masters with a profounder sense of system." *Woman As Force* opens with a similar disclaimer: "This volume, as its subtitle distinctly states, is a *study*. In no part of it is any claim made to an all-embracing fullness or to philosophic completeness." This latter disclaimer lacks the transgressive edge of the earlier one; perhaps after Hitler it was harder to tease masters.

19. See, for example, Thomas Bender, "The New History—Then and Now," *Reviews in American History* 12 (December 1984): 621.

20. Lane, *Mary Ritter Beard*, p. 7; Smith, "Seeing Mary Beard," p. 414.

BERNARD DEVOTO AND THE MAKING OF
THE YEAR OF DECISION: 1846

Louis P. Masur

On May 19, 1940, Bernard DeVoto stepped into his '39 Buick and rode West. Exhausted from what was, even for him, a remarkably diverse and productive year, he took to the road with "a young historian for a companion," family friend and former student, Arthur Schlesinger, Jr. DeVoto intended to write a book on the pre–Civil War frontier and he wanted to visualize the landscape before trying to contextualize it, "to recapture the sights and smells and feel of my native country, in part to revisit the sources of my thinking."[1]

It was a dreadful and lyrical time for such a "pilgrimage." As DeVoto and Schlesinger made their way over the old Santa Fe Trail, they followed on the car radio reports of a different Westward movement, the Nazi march across Europe into Paris. On May 26, at Trinidad, Colorado they pulled over to listen to Roosevelt's war message on national defense. Later, from Santa Fe, DeVoto observed: "We were the war generation and then some called us the lost generation and then we were the depression generation and now we regress to our first estate." With war on his mind, he returned home to Massachusetts in mid-July and began to write.[2]

Eighteen months later, DeVoto sent *The Year of Decision: 1846* to his publisher, Little, Brown. Serialized in the *Atlantic* and chosen as a Book-of-the-Month-Club main selection, *The Year of Decision* became one of the most widely-acclaimed books of 1943 and has remained a familiar title to American historians since. And yet, as with so many other "classics" of American history, the book is seldom read, studied, or enjoyed. Some historians have maintained their reputations despite the relegation of their books to the shelf of frequently invoked and mostly unread masterpieces, but DeVoto has not been so fortunate. Always the outsider, he cut his own path across the 1930s and 1940s, slashing or cultivating as he saw fit. He was a westerner in the

East, a nonacademic with a foot inside academic heaven's door, and a liberal at a time when radicals grabbed most of the attention. As a result, his place in American intellectual life, as composed largely by easterners, academics, and radicals, has been almost completely ignored.

Viewed retrospectively, DeVoto's career offers instruction on the life of a book, on the way in which an intellectual and his work became marginalized and superannuated, and on the significance of historical writing and even history itself. These issues are touched on here, but do not constitute the central focus of this essay. Rather, my aim is to use the occasion of the republication of *The Year of Decision*, by Houghton Mifflin as a volume in the American Heritage library, to evaluate the making and meaning of a classic work of American historical literature.

When DeVoto began his study of the frontier, he was a widely-known and influential essayist, editor, and critic. He wrote a monthly column for *Harper's* under the title "The Easy Chair," had served for two years as the editor of the *Saturday Review of Literature*, and had recently accepted the editorship of the Mark Twain Papers. In addition to scores of articles and reviews, his major works included *Mark Twain's America* (1932), two volumes of collected essays (*Forays and Rebuttals* in 1936 and *Minority Report* in 1940), and several novels, some of which he published under the pen-name John August. He resisted all attempts at categorization and described himself as a professional writer and journalist; at one self-deprecating moment he told his close friend, Garrett Mattingly, that he considered himself nothing more than a "good journeyman hack."[3]

DeVoto's interest in history cannot be separated from his birthplace or his literary endeavors. The son of "an apostate Mormon and an apostate Catholic," he left Ogden, Utah in 1915 for an undergraduate education at Harvard, and afterwards spent several years teaching English at Northwestern before settling in Massachusetts in 1927. Through the early 1930s he occasionally offered courses in composition and literature at Harvard. His belief in the "interdependence" of literature and history, and his friendship with Kenneth Murdock, Perry Miller, Arthur Schlesinger, Sr., Frederick Merk, and Samuel Eliot Morison, led him to play a role in planning the Ph.D. Program in American Civilization that was established in 1937.[4]

His earliest work, particularly a scathing essay about Utah and Mormonism published in Mencken's *American Mercury*, reveals his struggle to understand the meaning of the West in personal, literary, and historical terms. During the 1930s, DeVoto's criticism of Van Wyck Brooks, Sinclair Lewis, Lewis Mumford, Malcolm Cowley, and Edmund Wilson had as much to do with his belief that these authors did not have a rigorous historical understanding of the American experience as it did with his ideological opposition to literary

Marxists. (DeVoto's politics ranged between cranky conservatism and maverick radicalism, depending on the issue. He once described himself as being "a half Mugwump, 60 per cent New Dealer, 90 per cent Populist dirt-roads historian.") In *Mark Twain's America*, DeVoto attacked the reigning literary opinion of Twain (primarily Brooks's psychoanalytic portrait) by developing the social context of Twain's life. A year after its publication, he informed his friend Franklin Meine, a Chicago bookseller and folklorist, that "my book appears on the reading list of Arthur Schlesinger's [Social and Intellectual History] and Fred Merk's [Western Movement] courses at Harvard. . . . It seems we were historians all along and didn't know it."[5]

DeVoto cherished history, and he participated in the discussion of the quality and nature of historical writing that flared in the 1930s. The discussion revolved around several related issues: popular versus scholarly history, history as a literary craft, and the problem of historical truth. One can enter the debate at any of several points, including Carl Becker's address "Everyman His Own Historian," delivered to the American Historical Association in 1931, Charles Beard's address "Written History As An Act of Faith" given in 1933, Arthur Schlesinger's critique of "Amateur History" in 1936, and Maurice Mandelbaum's *The Problem of Historical Knowledge*, which appeared in 1938.[6]

In 1939, Allan Nevins published an especially searing indictment of the historical profession. In an article titled "What's the Matter with History," Nevins lamented "the comparatively barren patches in our historical writing." He blamed the drought on "the pedantic school of historians," those "dryasdust monographers" who gathered facts, accumulated footnotes, and stalked the universities where they had professionalized themselves into obscurity. The touch of the pedant, Nevins warned, was "death. . . . [H]e is responsible for the fact that today a host of intelligent and highly literate Americans will open a book of history only with reluctant dread." Although Nevins also viewed the amateur popularizer as a threat to history, he heralded the best work as "a fusion of facts, ideas, and literary grace in a single work," and he proposed the establishment of a nonprofessional historical magazine for "those who believe in history as literature."[7]

DeVoto agreed with Nevins's diagnosis but differed as to the cure. He derided as a "beautiful illusion" the idea that the reading public would flock to a popular history magazine. Compared to the "sub-zero cave of literary scholarship," DeVoto found some value in the labors of the purely academic historian. For his purposes, "even the dreary monographs by fifth-rate professionals" proved useful to someone seeking to synthesize and analyze research. The problem with both professional and amateur historians, DeVoto argued, was that they wrote poorly, held a simplistic view of history, and were afraid to render judgments. Taken together, these beliefs formed the foundation of DeVoto's approach to history.[8]

DeVoto had always been appalled by the awkward style of scholarly writing. In a line that is an indication of his own literary talents, he once observed that "most historians and most scholars appear to write with something between a bath sponge and an axe." He reiterated this complaint in his response to Nevins, but admitted it was unfair to ask that all historians also train as journalists, a background he shared with Nevins. Still, DeVoto hoped for the elimination of the "caste division" between scholar and writer, arguing that the historian should aspire to be both.[9]

Related to the problem of poor writing was the historians' lack of appreciation for literary technique and the "literary problems of history." Historians needed to learn more from novelists, DeVoto thought. What made Parkman great was that "the art of history," as he practiced it, "closely resembles the art of fiction." Time and again DeVoto preached the importance of using narrative form to express meaning: "The men and events that history deals with are real whereas those that fiction deals with are imaginary; the historian reveals realities whereas the novelist simulates them. But the integrity of both is to deal justly with experience and they have a common aim, to make a reader understand what happened, why it happened, and what came of it. This requires them to measure and to impart significances—and there is no way of imparting them except by artistic form."[10]

In *The Year of Decision*, as well as in the two works of history that followed, *Across the Wide Missouri* (1947) and *The Course of Empire* (1952), DeVoto labored to realize the objective of history as literature. Writing to a friend in Utah he proclaimed that "very few historians of our time, practically no academic historians, realize that history is not only knowledge, not only knowledge and wisdom even, but is also art. I do. My books employ the methods and techniques of literature and especially they have structure as literature. They have form . . . [and] that form is used to reveal meaning."[11]

While the best writing offered literary design, the best history offered dynamic complexity. Between the two was a tension with which all historians struggle, the tension between telling a captivating story and capturing the complexity of experience. The problem with the amateur historian, DeVoto warned, was the tendency toward "over-simplification." In an essay called "How Not to Write History," DeVoto argued that "the past of America is immensely complex and immensely at war with itself. No unity exists in it. Its discords and contradictions cannot be harmonized. It cannot be made simple. No one can form it into a system and any formulation that explains it is an hallucination." The work he most admired was the Beards' *Rise of American Civilization* because it "reveals the tremendously complex interrelationships of the forces in our past," relationships that inform an understanding of the present. Nowhere was the problem of historical writing as evident as in the treatment of the Civil War, where "you can find a ton of monographs . . . and several first-rate general histories of it but none that studies it as a pattern somewhat like our own, as a pattern of energies still to some extent operating among us."[12]

Forces and energies. DeVoto used these words regularly, and they tell us something further about one of the influences on his approach to history. Though he repeatedly cast doubt on theoretical understandings of history and literature ("no abstract analysis is worth much"), for a time in the 1930s he was enamored of Vilfredo Pareto's approach to the study of society. Pareto, an engineer and economist who left Italy in 1894 for Switzerland where he died in 1923, wrote the multivolume work *The Mind and Society* (translated in 1935).[13]

Pareto sought to create a science of society, but what appealed to DeVoto was not the idea that the study of society could be made scientific, if by that one meant the identification of invariant laws and objective facts, but the recognition that "all results are partly arbitrary, all relationships are relative." In this sense, Pareto's science was a scientific inquiry into the nonscientific. Unlike Comte, Hegel, Marx, and Spencer, argued DeVoto, Pareto did not try to transform "the overwhelming preponderance of humanity's non-logical actions" into logical and reasoned ones. Instead, Pareto sought to create a method for capturing the complexities of social events, to account for the role of irrationality in society, and to trace the continuities of social experiences. It was for these reasons, the emphasis on complexity and irrationality, on social systems and equilibriums, that DeVoto acclaimed Pareto's work as "the most important single instrument I have ever used for the analysis of the field of knowledge in which I have some authority, American social history."[14]

In DeVoto's estimation, the best historians not only offered work that was literary and multidimensional, they also rendered evaluations and judgments. Too many scholars were cowed by a love of facts: "the reverence for fact that is the necessary condition of research has too often become a screen for timidity." Though DeVoto sometimes affected hostility to factual knowledge ("I am quite incapable of determining facts, recognizing facts, appraising facts, putting facts in relation to another, confining myself to facts, guiding myself by facts, or even recording facts"), he believed that a mastery of the facts of the past was an essential first step in writing history. When one reader wrote DeVoto to express appreciation for his "historical novel" *The Year of Decision*, DeVoto shot back that if the book "contains any fiction whatever by anyone, then it escaped the most rigorous factual analysis I am capable of making."[15]

Yet too many scholars stopped with the facts. "The public," DeVoto insisted, "sincerely wants those facts appraised, judged, interpreted, and converted to an explanation of the present." DeVoto repeatedly emphasized the importance of finding "the past in the present, which is a radically different thing from finding the present in the past." He also held little sympathy for the idea of recovering the past as it actually was. In a broadcast on historical fiction that he gave in 1937 he warned that "we must not delude ourselves with an idea that the past is recoverable. We are chained and pinioned in our moment. . . . What we recover from the past is an image of ourselves, and very likely our search sets out to find nothing other than just that." The depth and density of ideas often leads us to create false dichotomies and isolate individuals on one side or the other: in DeVoto's case positivism and presentism, empiricism and relativism, realism and romanticism, scholarship and craftsmanship, science and art came together in his assumptions about history and historical writing.[16]

Of all historical subjects, it was the Civil War that DeVoto thought the most central: it is "the best single lens through which to look at American history." To be sure, his earliest writings discussed westward expansion and the frontier experience, but in certain ways these subjects posed less pressing problems than the origins of the Civil War. Besides, as of 1933, he had just written a book that revealed "the complexity of the frontier," and he had in mind doing the same for the Civil War. In an essay on the cycles of historical fiction about the War, spurred on by the success of Margaret Mitchell's *Gone With the Wind* (1936), he commented that "the Civil War was the greatest strain that has ever been put on the structure of our national life. . . . It was the most important event in the history of the United States." Through the 1930s and 1940s, DeVoto passionately opposed revisionist historians such as Avery Craven and J. G. Randall, who seemed to argue that the war could have been avoided and that the South, if anything, was a victim of northern fanaticism and aggression. Symbolic of a new interpretive emphasis that sought to exculpate the South was the reference to the Civil War, or the War of the Rebellion, as the War between the States. One reviewer who used the more neutral term heard from DeVoto: "THEY LOST THE WAR, AND GODDAMN IT, WE ARE NOT GOING TO LET THEM WIN THE TERMINOLOGY."[17]

Despite his desire to write about the Civil War directly, DeVoto backed away from the idea when Schlesinger and Merk advised him that "everything worth doing had been done with the war," and that he should not "waste his packed years of study about the frontier." In the summer of 1933, DeVoto decided to write the book that would become *The Year of Decision*. He wanted to "isolate the frontier bacillus by selecting a year when it was most in evidence and describing that year as completely as possible, following all the lines of force back to their origin," and he asked Mattingly to inform him "whenever you think or hear of anything that happened in 1846." DeVoto

had discovered one of the heroes in his book, the mountain man James Clyman, whose career ("it's history, not my invention") intersected with the central events of the period including the Oregon migration, the Bear Flag Revolt,
the Donner Party, the Mormon trek, and the sighting of first gold. "I'm plung-
ing into my frontier book—" DeVoto proclaimed, "and I mean frontier."[18]

In the introduction to *The Year of Decision*, DeVoto said that he sought to tell
"the story of some people who went West in 1846," to "realize the pre–Civil
War, Far Western frontier as personal experience." He wrote to provide a synthesis because the historical profession had not tried to pull all the monographic pieces together, and he wrote as well "for the nonexistent person
called the general reader" (pp. xix; 4).[19] In order to realize his objective from
a creative standpoint he devised a narrative strategy that relied on synec-
doche, allowing the part to stand for the whole, and simultaneity, switching
focus between simultaneously occurring events. A "dynamic narrative" he
called it.[20]

The "invocation" to the volume was from Thoreau: "Eastward I go only by
force; but westward I go free." Of those depicted on DeVoto's pointillist can-
vas, some appear as dangerous fools, others as romantic heroes. DeVoto
thought it the duty of the historian to judge, and judge he did. Bronson Alcott
is called the "Great Inane" (p. 33); Polk's mind is described as "rigid, narrow,
obstinate, far from first-rate," and Calhoun's is labeled "a maze of metaphysical subtleties" (pp. 7; 214); Taylor had "no nerves and nothing recognizable as intelligence" (p. 193); Frémont "was worse than a fool, he was an
opportunist, an adventurer, and a blunderer on a truly dangerous scale" (p.
471); Joseph Smith was a "psychotic boy who took his puberty walking in the
woods" (p. 82). Even his beloved Parkman is chastised for those "Brahmin
snobberies" which kept him from comprehending what was taking place on
the frontier before his failing eyes (p. 175). The figures in the book whom
DeVoto admired for their skill, competence, and courage included, in addition to Clyman, Brigham Young, Alexander Doniphan, Stephen Kearney,
and William Eddy.

The engaging literary and narrative qualities of the book cannot be separated from the equally forceful interpretive line that DeVoto presented. Part
of that interpretation is embedded in the form of the book which uses individuals to stand for movements and a single year to stand for the destiny of
the American republic. DeVoto viewed history as interactive and complex,
contingent and yet inexorable, and the stories he told by introducing the central actors in the drama in the first chapter and then moving them ahead piece
by piece, detail by detail, was intended to capture the texture of history as
experience and process. He wanted the reader to bear in mind simultaneously
the relationships between all the larger themes—westward expansion, mili-

tary conflict, religious enthusiasm, political maneuvering, technological advancement, utopian dreams—while considering each through a representative part. In developing individual characters, shifting between scenes, eschewing strict chronology, and offering a narrative voice that commented on the events taking place, the book was, as DeVoto later remarked about all of his histories, "constructed and written" like a novel, "to exactly the same end" as a novel, and with the hope that historians would recognize that the telling of a story and the meaning of a story were inseparable.[21]

Although for a time he thought of calling the book "Empire" or "American Empire," he titled it *The Year of Decision*. As a way of approaching DeVoto's overarching themes, it is worth asking what decision was made and who made it? At one level, DeVoto meant the variety of individual decisions that shaped lives, decisions that seemingly could have gone in many directions but went the way they did and, in so doing, shaped history: Frémont's decision to seize California; Young's decision to allow a Mormon Battalion to participate in the U.S. occupation of California; Taylor's decision to use artillery at the battle of Palo Alto and to attack it at Resaca de la Palma; Donner's decision to follow the Hastings cutoff instead of the Fort Hall Road; Susan Magoffin's decision to join her husband in the push West across the Santa Fe Trail.

These choices are the drama of the book, but by *The Year of Decision*, DeVoto meant more than the endless individual decisions of inconsequence and consequence that mold personal experience and national history. In 1846, DeVoto argued, three issues were "decided," issues so momentous that the year 1846 allows us to fathom nothing less than the meaning of the nineteenth century. First, during 1846 the yearning for continental expansion to the Pacific was satisfied, thus relieving Americans of their deepest fears that a foreign government would permanently occupy any territory between the two oceans. Manifest destiny, they called it, meaning "the continent was there, they felt that destiny bade them occupy it, and they did." Though DeVoto emphasized the inexorable power of expansion, he thought it best to regard manifest destiny less as a deterministic ideology than as a social movement: "the truth is that the destiny of the U.S. has never been manifest, but only manifested." "The West," he concluded in *The Year of Decision*, "had made the United States a continental nation" (p. 494). This was a central point of Lincoln's inaugural address ("physically speaking we cannot separate . . ."), upon which DeVoto claimed to have "calculated every participle and semi-colon [in the book] to land with a great bang." The President "was telling his countrymen that the achieved West had given the United States something that no people had ever had before, an internal, domestic empire" (pp. 495–96).[22]

External threats had been neutralized, but it remained to be seen whether the new empire would be "balkanized" by internal divisions, and this constituted the second issue decided in 1846—the Civil War. As it turns out, DeVoto had written a book about the Civil War after all. (He privately told the editor of the *Atlantic*, "In my mind, the book is about the Civil War, and about the justice of the Northern cause.")[23] The creation of a continental nation had made the war "inevitable," he thought. The issue was not so much whether to allow slavery into the territories, though this was the way the problem of slavery entered into the "nation's consciousness," but the struggle between the past, in the form of the "low-energy economy and the chattel slavery" of the South, and the future, in the form of "the railroads, the telegraph lines, the turbines" and the efforts of those who "made the nation a continent" (pp. 495–98). The Civil War is conspicuous throughout *The Year of Decision* in a dramatic and deterministic formulation: "David Wilmot . . . had made A. Lincoln President of the United States" (p. 299); "a great part of the defeat of the Confederate States of America was inflicted in the muggy Mexican sun on May 8, 1846" at the Battle of Palo Alto (p. 194); "some people went west in '46, and so sentenced Edmund Ruffin to death" (p. 498); "at some time between August and December, 1846, the Civil War had begun" (p. 496).

The third issue decided in 1846 followed from the first two: America would become a technological, industrial power and the West would play a key role in the economic development of the nation. He called it the theme of "industrial revolution."[24] It is a theme that is implicit in DeVoto's depiction of the North and West as the dynamic future triumphing over the stagnant, backward South. It is explicit from his discussion in the opening chapter of Thoreau's belief that "the factory could not be fled from and that it could not be beautified by refining the passions" (pp. 34–35), through an "Interlude" titled "World of Tomorrow" that focuses on the Washington National Fair and examines the patents issued in 1846 (pp. 215–21), to the final sentences of the book that describe Jim Clyman sitting by the Truckee River in August 1848 and hearing for the first time about the discovery of gold.

In *The Year of Decision*, DeVoto had found his voice as a writer. By allowing him to tell stories that were both narrative and analytical without forcing him to take cover behind his characters, history liberated DeVoto in ways that fiction could not. The reviewers responded enthusiastically. At *Time*, the editors recounted the contents of the book in five columns. John Chamberlain, in the daily *New York Times*, called it "wholly magnificent," especially for its "mixture of narrative and social analysis." In the *San Francisco Chronicle*, Joseph Henry Jackson likened the book to "an historical ballet," and congratulated its author for producing "one of the most brilliantly conceived and executed pieces of historical writing in our day." Clifton Fadiman, in the *New Yorker*, praised the book's "complexly orchestrated symphony of narratives," welcomed it as not only "good history" but "at its best, drama and poetry," and recommended DeVoto for Pulitzer Prize consideration. By July 1, the book had sold nearly 10,000 copies.[25]

Scholars who reviewed the book saw similar merits in the narrative, but they criticized the overarching interpretation. Frederic Paxson was impressed by DeVoto's conducting of a "chronological symphony," but he thought the book oozed "*obiter dicta* and at times acid," and he suggested that "1846 was perhaps merely the year between 1845 and 1847." Richard Hofstadter labeled DeVoto a "latter-day poet of Manifest Destiny with a sense of humor," but he argued that "if the Civil War was in any sense inevitable, it is not particularly important to know exactly when it became so, one wants to know why, and only a small part of the answer can be found here." William Hesseltine thought the volume needed to be "divested of . . . pseudo-philosophical gibberish," but he saw it as providing a "skillful synthesis." Henry Nash Smith admired the ways in which DeVoto's literary skills and critical judgments distinguished him from professional scholars, but he thought the thesis somewhat "overstated." Ralph Henry Gabriel viewed the narrative parts of the book as an "outstanding achievement." He also objected to the word "inevitable" as too strong, but in doing so he used terminology that must have turned DeVoto apoplectic: "if history is made by men, as DeVoto affirms, the War Between the States might have been avoided at some time between 1846 and 1861."[26]

Several other historians, DeVoto's friends, privately expressed their admiration for the book. Henry Steele Commager, who was trying to convince DeVoto to write a volume for the New American Nation series, told him that he had read his fiction and read his history and thought the latter to be the best. Paul Buck informed him that "whatever you have been in the past, my boy, you are a historian now—one of the fraternity and one of the best." And Frederick Merk thought it an "excellent book," one that "puts you even more firmly than your *Mark Twain's America* among the despised class of historians. . . . I have liked your judgments. They seem to me to be sound, though sometimes you state them more vigorously than I would have. . . . As an historian you have no fears, either of man or of the devil."[27]

DeVoto felt gratified by the personal encouragement of these scholars, whose work he respected deeply. But the private judgment of another leading historian and intimate friend turned his joy to bitterness. Arthur Schlesinger Sr., whose works DeVoto praised as models of the new social history and whose whistle DeVoto kept wet during Prohibition, apparently thought *The Year of Decision* was "not history." Furthermore, DeVoto believed that Schlesinger voted against him for the Pulitzer Prize because, in a footnote, DeVoto had sided with Walter Webb against Fred Shannon, whose 109-page critique of Webb's book *The Great Plains* (1931) was commissioned by Schlesinger. Whatever the truth of the allegation, DeVoto was convinced of it and, at a moment of creative triumph, he felt as alienated from the historical profession as from literary circles. He told Commager that the "historians in Cambridge regard me as a phony, a charlatan, and a menace to the public peace and dignity of considerably more horrifying aspect than the one the literary critics have drawn."[28]

Whatever the opinion of some professional historians, DeVoto would have even greater public success with his next two works of history: *Across the Wide Missouri* won the Pulitzer and Bancroft Prizes and *The Course of Empire* won the National Book Award. And yet DeVoto's histories slid quickly from night table to carrel to office bookcase. The process began the moment scholars tried to unravel the book for its thesis and it accelerated as the context that shaped the making of the book shifted. There is nothing unique about this in DeVoto's case. To greater and lesser degrees other books from DeVoto's time have travelled the same route: Miller's *New England Mind* (1939), Matthiessen's *American Renaissance* (1941), Schlesinger's *Age of Jackson* (1945). To be sure, the "theses" of these volumes are widely discussed, but are the books read? Are they devoured and appreciated as historical literature, as carefully wrought wholes designed with the care of a novelist whose argument cannot be separated from text and context anymore than thread from carpet?

Scholars seized on one thesis in *The Year of Decision*, the idea that expansion to the Pacific made the Civil War inevitable, and they balked at it. It is not that they were wrong to do so. DeVoto's "social energies" and "lines of force" (p. 5) do not explain much and he never developed his discussion of "the logic of geography, . . . economics, . . . and desire" (p. 495) into an answer for the "why" question. But in objecting to inevitability, scholars yanked at one central thread and overlooked, or at least discounted, the context that nurtured DeVoto's use of that word.

If books are written with purpose, two of the purposes behind DeVoto's book were to refute Civil War revisionists and rebuke World War II isolationists. For DeVoto, the Civil War released the nation's future from the stranglehold of the past; not only was it inevitable, it was a damn good thing. So too with American involvement in World War II. *The Year of Decision* is a World War II book in ways that go well beyond what we now see as an almost formulaic celebration of cultural experience, national character, and democratic institutions. It even goes beyond the analogies in the book to "refugees . . . [fleeing] Hitler" (p. 78), the Indians' "Teutonic brag" (p. 157), and "the limpid logic of the German mind" (p. 349). DeVoto sought to eradicate any comparisons that might be made between Polk's War with Mexico and Hitler's invasion of Poland ("a favorite trick of Goebbelsian oratory," admonished one commentator). At a luncheon sponsored by the American Booksellers Association, DeVoto observed that "Germany invaded self-governing civilized peoples. We occupied 750,000 square miles practically uninhabited—a vast waste."[29]

"Practically." Almost no one at the time expressed resentment over the attitude toward native populations and cultures that DeVoto let slip with that word. Unfortunately, in his descriptions of Indians and Mexicans, DeVoto was pinioned in his time. He referred to the Apache and Comanche as "terrible savages," "professional marauders and murderers," and "practicing sadists" (pp. 249–50). He thought little better of the Blackfeet, Sioux or Cheyenne. "In sum," he stated, the Indians were a "neolithic people" (p. 305). DeVoto's view of Mexicans is equally offensive: a "simple, childlike, gay people" (p. 333). "Gang politics" was all they were capable of (p. 72). When DeVoto uses the word "greaser" to characterize Frémont's attitude toward a particular Mexican, it seems to come with author's endorsement (p. 73).

These contexts and prejudices date the book and enlarge our understanding of the work, but it would be too easy to argue that the book fell victim to its prowar urgency and proconquest mentality. Even if we consider other factors—the apparent decline of a popular audience for history, the deepening chasm between amateur and professional historians, the postwar return to a faith in objective, empirical, scientific scholarship and a second turn toward searching for sophisticated theories of historical causation, the marginalization of Western history within the academy and the proliferation of monographs on Westward expansion and the coming of Civil War—even with all this we still only partially fathom the postpublication history of *The Year of Decision*.[30]

Perhaps asking why the book lost its audience, why it quickly depreciated in value, is to ask the wrong question, for that is a scholar's question that leads us to pick at the book for its interpretation, its argument, its thesis, and then discard the remains. It is also a question that assumes some books do not die in pieces, that some books are continually read and enjoyed whole. Much as I wish this were true, I do not believe it. DeVoto's carefully crafted works of historical literature stand as models of literary and historical holism, but we look first at the parts, if we look at all.

There has been much recognition and much discussion in the past decade of the dilemma of professional and epistemological fragmentation, and the ways in which we read should be included in that discussion. This general re-examination of why, how, and for whom we practice history has been exciting and exasperating. Exciting because every generation must address for itself the same intractable problems that bedeviled earlier generations—the problems of narrative, knowledge, interpretation, and audience. Exasperating because, for all the talk of relativity, it has been a discussion certain in its condescension to past debates, the debates of the 1930s and 1940s, as naive and unsophisticated. It has been a discussion that, for all the talk of recapturing a public audience, takes place in scholarly journals and relies on nearly incomprehensible, inaccessible terms. It has been a discussion that, for all the talk about language, shows little joy in words, and for all the talk about literature, shows little pleasure from reading. Indeed, it is surprising the extent to which the debate over writing history in the 1980s has failed to focus on the issue of how readers, particularly academics, read.

If it is misleading to inquire why historians come to neglect a book, it is equally unavailing to suggest reasons to read one, whether it be *The Year of Decision* or any other title that appears, if anywhere, on supplemental reading lists in graduate seminars. To be sure, it is striking how DeVoto's themes, recast into current parlance, still permeate interpretations of the antebellum period. But that is no cause to relish a 500-page book. Nor should the book be hawked as a model for the formidable task we currently set for ourselves — the inclusion of multiple perspectives, experiences, and approaches in a single work.

We should read *The Year of Decision*, if at all, because DeVoto creatively addressed fundamental problems in the writing and meaning of history. We should read it because he sought to eradicate the pernicious distinction between popular and academic history, between amateur and professional historian. We should read it cover-to-cover because he wrote it like a novel. We should read it because he told the "story of some people who went West," and the writing of history is no more simple and no more complicated than that. We should read it because, with DeVoto, it is our job to "read all the books that explain America to itself." And we should read it for the same reason that Garrett Mattingly thought we should think and care about history in the first place: it does not "matter at all to the dead whether they receive justice at the hands of succeeding generations. But to the living, to do justice, however belatedly, should matter."[31]

Louis P. Masur, Department of History, University of California, Riverside, is the author of Rites of Execution: Capital Punishment and the Transformation of American Culture, 1776–1865 *(1989) and "Stephen Jay Gould's Vision of History,"* Massachusetts Review *(Autumn 1989).*

I am grateful to Mark DeVoto, Wallace Stegner, and Margaret Kimball, Archives and Manuscript Librarian of the Stanford University Libraries, for permission to quote from DeVoto's papers. I should also like to thank Daniel Aaron, James Goodman, Douglas Greenberg, Robert Hine, Russell Jacoby, and Thomas Slaughter for their comments on earlier drafts of this essay.

1. Bernard DeVoto, "Letter From Santa Fe," *Harpers* 181 (August 1940): 334. For Schles-

inger's recollections of the trip, see his "Foreword" to the American Heritage Library edition of *The Year of Decision: 1846* (1989), pp. xi–xii.

2. DeVoto, "Notes From a Wayside Inn," *Harper's* 181 (September 1940): 445; "Letter From Santa Fe," p. 336.

3. For a superb biographical study of DeVoto, see Wallace Stegner, *The Uneasy Chair* (1974; 1988). See also the recollections of Catherine Drinker Bowen, Edith R. Mirrielees, Arthur Schlesinger, Jr., and Wallace Stegner in *Four Portraits and One Subject: Bernard DeVoto* (1963). DeVoto to Garrett Mattingly [1937], DeVoto Papers, Stanford University Library Special Collections. DeVoto and Mattingly met at Northwestern in the early 1920s and remained friends and correspondents until DeVoto's death in 1955. Mattingly provided an early assessment of DeVoto's work in *Bernard DeVoto: A Preliminary Appraisal* (1938).

4. DeVoto, "Fossil Remnants on the Frontier," *Harpers* (April 1935), reprinted in *Forays and Rebuttals* (1936), p. 41; on DeVoto and Harvard, see Stegner, *The Uneasy Chair*, esp. pp. 160–76 and 198–200. On the American Civilization Program, see DeVoto's editorial "Enlightened Research," *Saturday Review of Literature* (April 10, 1937): 8, and his essay "Interrelations of History and Literature," in William Lingelbach, ed., *Approaches to American Social History* (1937), pp. 34–56.

5. DeVoto, "But Sometimes They Vote Right Too," *Harper's* (November 1950), reprinted in *The Easy Chair* (1955), p. 192; DeVoto to Franklin J. Meine, March 18, 1933, DeVoto Papers.

6. Carl Becker, "Everyman His Own Historian," *American Historical Review* 37 (January 1932): 221–36; Charles Beard, "Written History as an Act of Faith," *American Historical Review* 39 (January 1934): 219–31; Arthur Schlesinger, "Amateur History," *Saturday Review of Literature* (December 19, 1936) (see also response by Louis Hacker in the issue of March 20, 1937); Maurice Mandelbaum, *The Problem of Historical Knowledge: An Answer to Relativism* (1938). For an overview, see Peter Novick, *That Noble Dream: The "Objectivity Question" and the American Historical Profession* (1988), esp. pp. 250–78.

7. Allan Nevins, "What's the Matter with History?" *Saturday Review of Literature* (February 4, 1939): 3, 4, 16. Fifteen years later, Nevins would contribute to the creation of *American Heritage*. See Roy Rosenzweig, "Marketing the Past: *American Heritage* and Popular History in the United States," in Susan Porter Benson, et al., eds., *Presenting the Past: Essays on History and the Public* (1986), pp. 21–49.

8. DeVoto, "What's the Matter with History?," *Harper's* 179 (June 1939): 109, 110.

9. DeVoto, "The Skeptical Biographer," *Harper's* (January 1933), reprinted in *Forays and Rebuttals*, pp. 197–98; DeVoto, "The Easy Chair," *Harper's* 198 (April 1949): 55.

10. DeVoto, "The Easy Chair," *Harper's* 198 (April 1949): 53.

11. DeVoto to Madeline McQuown, January 3, 1947, in Wallace Stegner, ed., *The Letters of Bernard DeVoto* (1975), pp. 287–89 [hereafter cited as *Letters*].

12. DeVoto, "How Not To Write History," *Harper's* (January 1934), reprinted as "Thinking About America," *Forays and Rebuttals*, p. 177; "What's the Matter With History?," pp. 111, 112.

13. DeVoto, "Exile's Return," in *Forays and Rebuttals*, p. 321; Pareto's book originally appeared in Italian in 1916. Beginning in the Fall of 1927, DeVoto studied the French edition, *Traité de Sociologie Générale* (1919). Starting in 1932, he participated in a Harvard seminar on Pareto that lasted for two years and was attended by, among others, Crane Brinton, Robert Merton, Talcott Parsons, and Joseph Schumpeter. See Stegner, *The Uneasy Chair*, pp. 138–44, and Barbara Heyl, "The Harvard 'Pareto Circle'," *Journal of the History of the Behavioral Sciences* 4 (October 1968): 316–34.

14. See DeVoto's essays, "A Primer for Intellectuals," *Saturday Review of Literature* (April 22, 1933): 546; "Sentiment and the Social Order: An Introduction to the Teachings of Pareto," *Harper's* 167 (October 1933): 571; "The Importance of Pareto," *Saturday Review of Literature* (May 25, 1935): 11. Part of Pareto's appeal was among intellectuals seeking an alternative to Marxian socialism. Since Mussolini trumpeted Pareto, it seemed clear to some that the popularity of the Italian sociologist was a sign of growing affection for facism among conservative intellectuals. See George E. Novack, "Vilfredo Pareto: The Marx of the Middle Classes," *New Republic* (July 19, 1933): 258–61, and the exchange between DeVoto and No-

vack in the *New Republic* (October 11, 1933): 244–45. By the late 1930s, DeVoto's fascination with Pareto began to wane, though there is little doubt that he continued to use Paretian terms. An insightful critique that helps to explain why the Pareto fad among intellectuals passed quickly is offered by Benedetto Croce in "The Validity of Pareto's Theories," *Saturday Review of Literature* (May 25, 1935): 12–13. For an eye-opening analysis of the shifts in DeVoto's political ideology, see Arthur Schlesinger, Jr., "The Citizen," in *Four Portraits*, pp. 41–77.

15. DeVoto, "What's the Matter With History," p. 111; DeVoto to Mattingly, December 28, 1945 in *Letters*, p. 283; Meyer Belsky to DeVoto, May 1, 1944 and Devoto to Belsky, May 3, 1944, DeVoto Papers.

16. DeVoto, "What's the Matter With History," p. 112. See also DeVoto's editorial, "The Second Step," *Saturday Review of Literature* (February 5, 1938): 8: "When you have realized its [the past's] complexity, acquired dependable information about it, and perceived that its parts are related to one another, you have begun to make progress in history"; DeVoto to Mattingly, June 15, 1938, DeVoto Papers; Typescript copy of "Three Lectures Broadcast on Historical Fiction," 1937, Lecture III: The Materials of History, p. 30, DeVoto Papers.

17. DeVoto to Madeline McQuown, January 3, 1947, *Letters*, p. 289; *Saturday Review of Literature* (July 22, 1933): 4; DeVoto, "Fiction Fights the Civil War," *Saturday Review of Literature* (December 18, 1937): 3; DeVoto to Lewis Gannett, November 10, 1940, DeVoto Papers. For additional expressions of rage by DeVoto on this subject see his *Harper's* essays "The War of the Rebellion" (February 1946) and "The Confederate Anachronism" (March 1946), reprinted in *The Easy Chair*, pp. 151–66; and DeVoto to William Sloane, December 3, 1948, in *Letters*, pp. 307–8.

18. DeVoto to Garrett Mattingly, May 10, 1933[?], in *Letters*, p. 266; DeVoto to Mattingly, Summer 1933, in *Letters*, pp. 266–67; DeVoto to Franklin Meine [1933], DeVoto Papers.

19. One reader informed DeVoto that " 'The General Reader' is not a 'non-existent person': I am it—in testimony whereof I want to tell you how much I have enjoyed 'The Year of Decision.' " Fannie Hardy Ecksturn to DeVoto, May 5, 1943, DeVoto Papers.

20. Following the publication of the award-winning *Across the Wide Missouri* (1947), DeVoto wrote ". . . from now on some kinds of history can be written satisfactorily only by methods which I have used in all three of my books, and may possibly have been the first to have used them, methods which I can designate roughly as the test-boring and the focus on simultaneousness." DeVoto to Madeline McQuown, January 3, 1947 in *Letters*, p. 288.

21. DeVoto to Madeline McQuown, January 3, 1947, in *Letters*, p. 288. DeVoto was more confident of the form after publication than before. In 1941 he sent Mattingly a draft of the first chapter and asked him whether he found "the method intolerable" and the "whole scale preposterous?" "My effort," he said, "is to tell even the reader who knows this stuff something he didn't know before—that it was all happening at the same time. . . . I am deliberately working toward a total effect." DeVoto to Mattingly, October 13, 1942, DeVoto Papers.

22. DeVoto, "Manifest Destiny," in *Harper's* 182 (April 1941): 560; Typescript of Lecture series entitled "American Empire, 1846: Manifest Destiny and the American Frontier," delivered at the Lowell Institute between November 13 and December 11, 1941. Lecture Eight, p. 23, DeVoto Papers; DeVoto to Alexander Cowie, September 23, 1943, DeVoto Papers.

23. DeVoto to Ted Weeks, August 4, 1942, DeVoto Papers. See also DeVoto to Clifford Dowdey, October 7, 1945, DeVoto Papers.

24. DeVoto to Henry Seidel Canby, July 19, 1942, in *Letters*, p. 228. See also DeVoto's essays "The West: A Plundered Province," *Harper's* 179 (August 1934): 355–64, and "The West Against Itself," *Harper's* 194 (January 1947): 1–13.

25. As one might expect, Stegner provides fascinating insight into DeVoto as historian as compared to novelist. See *The Uneasy Chair*, pp. 242–45 and passim; *Time* (April 19, 1943): 98; *The New York Times*, March 23, 1943; *San Francisco Chronicle*, March 21, 1943; *New Yorker* (March 27, 1943): 61–62; Alfred McIntyre to DeVoto, July 20, 1943, DeVoto Papers.

26. Paxson's review appeared in the *American Historical Review* 49 (October 1943): 120–21; Hofstadter's in the *New Republic* (May 3, 1943): 610–11; Hesseltine's in the *Wisconsin Magazine*

of History 27 (September 1943): 97–99; Smith's in *New England Quarterly* 16 (September 1943): 497–500; and Gabriel's in *The New York Times Book Review*, March 28, 1943, front page.

27. Henry Steele Commager to DeVoto, November 30, 1946, DeVoto Papers. See also DeVoto to Commager, April 29, 1946 in *Letters*, pp. 283–84; Paul Buck to DeVoto, March 12, 1943, DeVoto Papers; Frederick Merk to DeVoto, March 27, 1943, DeVoto Papers. See Merk to DeVoto, August 1, 1951 for a discussion of Frederick Jackson Turner. DeVoto disagreed profoundly with a Turnerian emphasis on the role of individualism in the frontier experience, believing instead that cooperation was more evident and significant. But, like Turner and Merk, he sought a balance between the role of geographic determinism and human choice in history. Merk told DeVoto that he once asked Turner "which of the two—the geography or the people—he believed to be the primary force in producing the section. He squirmed and he did not like to have the question put to him in that bald and brash form. But the substance of his answer was that the people shaped their destiny."

28. See, for example, DeVoto's review of *The Rise of the City*, *Saturday Review of Literature* (March 4, 1933): 464; according to Schlesinger, Jr. "Benny DeVoto was the family bootlegger," "Foreword," p. xi; Schlesinger Sr.'s attitude to the book is mentioned by Stegner in *The Uneasy Chair*, p. 237 and in his article "Historian by Serendipity," *American Heritage* 24 (August 1973): 32. On the issue of the Pulitzer Prize, see Stegner, *The Uneasy Chair*, p. 429n2. The ironies here run especially deep, for, in 1937, DeVoto criticized the selection process for the Pulitzer Prize in History and endorsed the selection of a committee of fourteen historians who, when surveyed, said they would have awarded the Prize in 1934 to Schlesinger for *The Rise of the City*. DeVoto, "The Pulitzer Prize in History," *Saturday Review of Literature* (March 13, 1937): 14. DeVoto's less pleasant side is evident from his resentment at the book that won the Pulitzer Prize in 1944. See his "Introduction" to Wallace Stegner, *Beyond the Hundredth Meridian* (1954, 1982), p. xv. On the Webb-Shannon controversy consult Novick, *That Noble Dream*, pp. 201–2; DeVoto to Henry Steele Commager, April 30, 1944, in *Letters*, p. 271.

29. See Philip Gleason, "World War II and the Development of American Studies," *American Quarterly* 36 (Bibliography 1984): 343–58; John Chamberlain, *The New York Times*, March 23, 1943; DeVoto quoted in the *New York Herald Tribune*, April 7, 1943. DeVoto was an interventionist, but he took offense at those who, based on a reading of the book, called him an imperialist. He considered himself an "anti-imperialist" who was prepared to oppose those who represented "the dangerous, the explicitly Nazi side of American expansionism." DeVoto to Ted Weeks, August 4, 1942, DeVoto Papers.

30. On the historical profession following World War II, see Novick, *That Noble Dream*; DeVoto inveighed against the "automatic dismissal of Western history as merely sectional, not national, history." See his introduction to Stegner, *Beyond the Hundredth Meridian*, p. xviii.

31. DeVoto, "The Centennial of Mormonism," *Forays and Rebuttals*, p. 81. Garrett Mattingly, *The Armada* (1959), p. 375. For an appreciation of Mattingly that discusses this quote, see J. H. Hexter, *Doing History* (1971), pp. 157–72.

"ROOTS OF MALADJUSTMENT" IN THE LAND: PAUL WALLACE GATES

Jon Gjerde

The land made an indelible imprint on the American republic during the nineteenth century. It was a vast resource which provided real and fabled opportunity for the white American settlers who took it from its native occupants. It was a shaper of American myth: the land was transformed into a garden by the individualistic yeoman pioneer whose interaction with it in turn helped form the character of the nation. It was a means by which the federal government could be financed during its formative years. It led to the creation of farm families and, by implication, population growth throughout the century. The land, in short, was invested with indispensable meaning for the nation throughout the first century of its existence.

Despite a continued romanticization of farmers and their soil in the years that followed, the promise of the land faded. Although land was believed to be a means of mobility for countless Americans, tenancy was increasing by the late nineteenth century at a disturbing rate, especially in regions such as the Middle West that had once been celebrated as sites of opportunity.[1] Although the countryside was supposed to provide an idyllic environment in which children were nurtured to serve as the pillars of "American" urban and rural society, turn-of-the-century observers became increasingly alarmed by the "moral decline" in the country as tenants and migrant labor inexorably altered the rural social landscape.[2] Although family farmers were presumed to be stewards of the soil, vast clouds of dust swallowed up entire states during the Depression as the Dust Bowl became synonymous with the Great Plains.[3] The promise of the land had apparently been betrayed.

It was amidst the ambiguities and apprehensions of the early twentieth century that Paul Wallace Gates began his life-long reassessment of American land policy and the impact of land law on the American nation.[4] Given the state of agriculture in the 1930s, it is not surprising that he condemned the consequences that land law had on the nation. Under the tutelage of James B. Hedges, Gates wrote a doctoral thesis that was published in 1934 as *The Illinois Central Railroad and Its Colonization Work*. In that same year, already troubled by the effect of land law on American development, Gates was summoned to serve on the Land Policy Section of the Agricultural Adjustment Administration.[5] While working with other rural historians, sociologists, and economists, Gates was struck by the incongruities in the design and operation of American land law. He articulated those weaknesses in a series of articles published in the mid-1930s. In focusing on the Homestead Act of 1862, Gates argued that "roots of maladjustment" in land policy had created a system rife with fraud and fraught with systemic handicaps for yeoman settlers. The system, in short, belied the Jeffersonian rhetoric that sustained it.[6]

In the decades that followed, Gates refined—and in some cases revised— his fundamental criticism of land disposal in the United States. Since the field of land law was vast, Frederick Merk observed, "intensive cultivation of it was possible only in segments."[7] Accordingly, Gates used case studies to examine specific aspects of land policy, disposal, and the social consequences that resulted. In *The Wisconsin Pine Lands of Cornell University: A Study in Land Policy and Absentee Ownership*, published in 1943, he illustrated how Ezra Cornell's investment in scrip in Wisconsin enriched Cornell University and advantaged speculators in relation to small-scale settlers. Eleven years later, Gates's attention turned to land disposal in Kansas. In *Fifty Million Acres: Conflicts over Kansas Land Policy, 1854–1890* (1954), he wove the weft of the misfortunes of Indian and poor white landowners into the woof of large-scale economic interests of railroad magnates and distant land speculators to create a tapestry of social and political development of a western state. Perhaps his crowning achievement was *History of Public Land Law Development* (1968), an overview of American land law commissioned by Milton A. Pearl, director of the Public Land Law Review Commission.[8] The volume, over 800 pages in length, is sweeping in its coverage and trenchant in its criticisms of the policies of the United States toward its land.

Gates published other works that focused more generally on American agriculture.[9] Nonetheless, as a result of his magisterial volumes on land alienation and privatization, his greatest contributions to American historiography were related to central issues of American land policy. His intellectual growth during the turbulent thirties, moreover, served as a great influence which led him to question the work of earlier historians at the same time that it limited his vision, leaving him vulnerable to attack by scholars who followed him.

In style and substance, Gates's scholarship clearly set a course that differed from that which had been charted by Frederick Jackson Turner. Unlike Turner, who stressed the independent yeoman farmer as a singular, positive force in American society, Gates focused on a land law which produced two inextricably interrelated—but nonetheless clearly "un-American"—types.[10] The first was the land speculator who was able, due to ill-conceived land policy, to engross vast tracts of agricultural resources. This, in turn, gave rise to a second party: the tenant farmer, whose predicament resulted from the antisocial actions of the speculator. Out of the relationship of speculator and tenant there emerged an agricultural society ill-prepared to care for itself politically or socially or for the land.

At the root of the failure of American settlement, Gates argued, was the manipulation by land speculators of "mistaken land policies which were once thought to be establishing a democratic system of land ownership."[11] The public domain was a vast resource with the potential to create "economic democracy" for the people and revenue for the government. Unfortunately, the latter concern won out. Since only those with capital could purchase land, the poor were effectively disfranchised of land-owning opportunities. No attempt was made, moreover, to limit the size of sale to single individuals until after 1862. Speculators, as a result, were able to acquire much of the choice land in the West and to partake in an orgy of "land monopolization." "Land-hungry settlers," on the other hand, "were practically denied the right of ownership."[12]

The negative consequences of land speculation were illustrated by Gates in a study of northern Indiana published in 1939. Whereas the southern portion of the state escaped widespread speculation, the northern areas had fallen into the hands of speculators who took vast tracts on the Indiana prairies and launched enormous cattle farms which brought them income while they anticipated the profits that would accrue from the appreciation of their ventures. At an opportune moment, the speculators sold the land to secondary promoters who brought much of it into grain production. Nonetheless, it was too late for what Gates calls "democratic ownership": the prices for land now exceeded fifty dollars an acre and would-be farmers were caught in a cycle of tenancy.[13] "The first generation of speculators," Gates concludes in a scathing criticism of American land policy, "contributed *nothing* to the development of the prairie country."[14]

Tenancy thus was a direct result of land speculation, and for a number of reasons. At first, land speculators, such as Henry W. Ellsworth, who eventually owned about 125,000 acres, offered land for lease to tenants who cleared and improved the land and thereby increased its value.[15] As the land increased in value in part as a result of tenant improvement, poorer families were effectively priced out of the market when the speculators finally sold their caches of land. Many tenants thus were not young farmers who were climbing an "agricultural ladder" to freeholding. They were rather a permanent landless class given the unwelcome choice either to remain as tenants in the country or to join the massive dislocation of farm folk and move to the city.

If land speculation promoted tenancy, Gates contended, the combination of speculators and tenants in turn fostered social and economic conditions detrimental to the development of the nation and its people. Gates, in effect, was concerned about the negative externalities—the capacity of individual decision-makers to displace costs onto others—which resulted from land speculation and larger farms, absentee ownership and widespread tenancy. In the first place, the development of local communities was stunted by absentee ownership and widespread tenancy. Absentee owners were reluctant to pay those taxes that provided essential revenue to local governments, since those taxes provided services that did not directly benefit speculators. As a result, large landholders in Indiana, Gates observed, consistently delayed payment of taxes assessed of them, sometimes for as long as eight years. The absentee speculators thus not only kept land out of the hands of settlers but forced actual settlers either to forgo internal improvements or to tax their own property more heavily and thus put themselves at greater financial risk in order to "compensate for the unimproved lands of the nonresidents who paid little or nothing into the treasury."[16]

Nor was the behavior of small speculators blameless. Gates noted that "settler-speculators" purchased more land than they could bring into immediate production in order to sell at a profit. Although their investments would be lucrative, they nonetheless were forced to shoulder a larger proportion of the costs of infrastructure development than their neighbors who owned what they could farm. If, as was often the case, the local investor in land refused to accept the burden of taxation, roads were not built and children were not adequately schooled. In addition, Gates argued, large local landholders retarded the development of their own cultural institutions, such as churches and libraries, as their unimproved land lay idle and their neighborhoods remained sparsely populated.[17] Greed in all forms had its hidden costs.

Land speculation not only frustrated the quality of life in local society, it also exacted a high price from society in general. The development of a transportational infrastructure, most notably the railroad, was impeded, both directly and indirectly, by land engrossment. On the one hand, land speculators—large and small alike—objected to bond issues that would sanction the construction of railroads. Gates suggested that large landholders of the pine lands of Wisconsin, for instance, repeatedly opposed bonds that would have provided for railroad construction. Similar circumstances transpired on the Indiana prairies where railroad schemes which depended on local aid failed and thereby increased the transportation costs of the settlers.[18] Sparsely populated tracts, a direct result of speculation, on the other hand, gave railroad developers pause.

Perhaps worst of all, the agriculture of land speculation and tenancy in concert misused the soil, America's most vital resource. In the early years of settlement, speculation and tenancy actually slowed the bringing of land into production. Wet lands in Indiana initially lay unused because speculators were unwilling to invest further in land improvements, on the one hand, and tenants had little capital and were disinclined to improve land with their labor since they could be dispossessed at any time, on the other. If the land had been "democratically owned," Gates believes, cooperative ditching systems would have been feasible and the lands would have been cultivated much sooner.[19] Some years later, as large cattle farms were broken up in Indiana and crops became the major source of income, absentee landowners and their tenants contributed not to an underuse of land, but to its abuse. The landlords, who wanted immediate returns, "forgot that land is not inexhaustible." The result was a soil depletion, a problem that would continue to beset American agriculture.[20]

In sum, Gates argued that the problems which plagued American agriculture in the twentieth century had deep roots. He contended in particular that the incongruities of American land law led Americans down a slippery slope of speculation, tenancy, and ultimately of social injustice and resource misuse. "The evolution of our national land system," he argued in a brief, but trenchant, passage, "has consisted of a series of slow and bungling changes to which may be ascribed the large-scale speculation in lands, the early development of tenancy, uneconomic farm units, misuse of the lands, reduction in carrying capacity to the range, wasteful treatment of the timberlands, misguided settlement, and misery for thousands of farm families."[21] The abuse and misallocation of the United States' most valuable resource was not a blessing for many Americans but rather a curse, a curse that inexorably thwarted the possibilities for democratic ownership in the United States.

The socioeconomic landscape of Gates's rural worlds was informed by the climate of opinion during which he wrote. His convictions about land law after all were formulated during a period when capitalist agriculture (and capitalism in general) was undergoing its most serious failure and the system faced its most serious scrutiny. Nor is it without significance that Gates wrote from a Progressive perspective that excoriated the monopolists and championed the masses. Throughout much of his work, moreover, one detects a sense of American exceptionalism, a conviction that inequalities of wealth are indeed "un-American," and a confidence in the American agrarian myth. If Gates disagreed with Turner about the various types that were found in rural regions, they both recognized common "American" intents nonetheless.

Farming was a way of life; land was a means toward that end; and the behavior of the elite—speculators and legislators alike—often was detrimental to the process.

Gates's interpretation of land law and agricultural development found many followers.[22] Following World War II, however, as American agriculture underwent a period of unparalleled industrialization, corporatization, and enlargement in farm size, a group of scholars launched a counterattack against the basic foundations that sustained his argument. Importantly, the revisionists affirmed Gates's contention that the land speculator and tenant farmer were integral parts of an elaborate social equation in rural America. Yet their work asserted a more sanguine outcome of the relationship. A reevaluation of landowning patterns revealed that tenancy was not a permanent plight for most. Indeed, the agricultural ladder from tenant to farmer, the revisionists contended, worked. It worked, moreover, in part *because* of the behavior of the very speculators that Gates castigated so pointedly. The corollary followed: if speculators facilitated the acquisition of land among small-holders, the land law which sustained them perhaps was not so exploitative after all.[23]

These new economic historians focused on the relationships between large landholders and tenants and contended that they were normal operations in a market that distributed goods and services in a quite sensible and relatively equitable fashion. In fact, neither the claim that speculators had cornered the land market nor the notion that they were overly avaricious, they insisted, were warranted. The abundance of government land prevented land buyers from acting as monopolists. If they could not control the market, speculators had to adjust to its constraints. Their capital tied up in land, moreover, was an asset that could be invested elsewhere if other ventures appeared more profitable. An inability to control an immense land market in concert with a wide array of investment opportunities encouraged land speculators not to hold land off the market because the capital opportunity costs often exceeded the expected profits from land sales. After all, they were realtors who gained from the rapid turnover of land so land was sold soon after it was acquired.[24] If speculators sold quickly, they also found it difficult to garner substantial profits, in large part because the land market was so fluid. Stanley Lebergott calculated that settlers who bought their land from speculators who acquired land in bounty warrants spent only 4.7 percent more than that paid directly to the government.[25] For those who did rent land, the rates, seen from a worldwide perspective, were hardly usurious. When compared with European societies, Lebergott figured that land rents on the nineteenth-century American frontier, which varied from 1 to 7 percent of farm income, were at least five times lower than those in Britain.[26]

Since land speculation failed to disadvantage the landless, the revisionists insisted, tenancy was for most only a temporary condition. A key consideration for Gates was the degree to which land law, and the wealthy who used that law to their advantage, handicapped the poor. The fact that federal land law prior to 1820, for example, required a minimum purchase of 320 acres at two dollars an acre excluded a significant proportion of the citizenry from owning land. The crucial issue between Gates and his critics was the degree to which speculators prohibited or facilitated land ownership within the structure of the law. Revisionists argued that land speculators in effect lowered the transactions costs to create a veritable partnership with those who sought land. Large land owners publicized their land and, by so doing, enlarged the information available to potential migrants and thereby promoted settlement. And since they provided credit to buy land, land speculators, rather than encouraging tenancy, actually promoted "democratic ownership" of land. Reluctant to foreclose on delinquent land buyers, the speculator land sellers inadvertently provided a buffer to their customers against foreclosure and forced tenancy.[27]

Tenants thus were not victims of speculation and incongruous land policies. Rather, tenancy was simply a stage in the life cycle, a rung on a ladder that led to land ownership. Many recent studies have stressed the difficult but often successful upward mobility of rural folk that began with tenancy.[28] Donald L. Winters, for example, traced Iowa tenants over time in the late nineteenth century and found one-fifth later living as landed farmers.[29] Indeed, revisionists have gone so far as to argue that a land alienation that required an exchange of assets was "superior" to one that fostered squatting in the backcountry. The negative rents paid by squatters as they awaited an efficient transportation system to envelop them diverted resources from the United States and imposed years of "hardship and misery" on the squatters themselves.[30] The tables have been turned: recent historians, in direct opposition to the scholarship of Gates, have taken the black hat off the land speculator and have placed it on the erstwhile victim: the squatter.

These new economic historians have incisively criticized Gates and have forcefully demonstrated his tendency to overstate the negative effects on land law in the relationship between speculator and tenant. Land speculators were not necessarily bogeymen, only businessmen who profited more from marketing land than from holding it off the market for speculative purposes. Since they lowered transaction costs, speculators eased, rather than prohibited, "democratic ownership" of land. Likewise, Gates apparently erred with regard to tenancy and the efficacy of the agricultural ladder. If questions about the rural opportunity structure have not been definitively answered, recent studies in economic history have repeatedly stressed that tenants in the Middle West frequently became landowners, rather than the other way around.[31]

Indeed, Gates himself seemed to temper his arguments in recent years. In 1973, for example, he observed that despite a "malfunctioning" of "an intended democratic system of land disposal," the story is one of "relative success." "If Jefferson could have seen the results of the public land system," Gates concluded, "he would have been convinced that . . . the policy had worked reasonably well."[32]

Those who attacked Gates were detached from Progressive historiography and from the agrarian myth. They addressed the issues of land alienation from a neoclassical framework and prided themselves in their use of "rational" economic models.[33] Yet their conceptualizations, which concentrated on the relationship between land buyer and land seller, tended to give short shrift to exogenous factors outside of their models. If their economic models of agricultural development were well-conceived, they often failed to stress the systemic ramifications of land-selling and land-buying. And here we return to the negative externalities associated with the process of land alienation and agricultural settlement. What additional costs and benefits did the market-driven relationship between seller and buyer have on agricultural community development and on land use?

It is true that Gates's revisionists did grapple with the effects of land policy within a larger framework of rural economic and cultural development. Yet if they insisted that little evidence existed to illustrate deleterious effects of the American system of land alienation, one senses a hesitation in their conclusions.[34] Tenant farmers, for example, are not seen as more inefficient than their land-owning neighbors in large part because neither were good stewards of the soil. Few farmers or tenants practiced crop rotation; few applied commercial fertilizers.[35] The farm outputs of each group, moreover, was "virtually equal," according to Winters, which suggests that "tenancy did not undermine agricultural development and slow economic growth."[36] Nor have recent scholars viewed speculators as impediments to cultural development. Utilizing a tax roll sample from Poweshiek County, Iowa in the 1850s, Swierenga calculated that one-half of the tax burden was assumed by absentee landowners. Nonresident landowners, moreover, were not any less delinquent than resident farmers in paying their taxes. Rather than hampering rural development, Swierenga argued, they contributed "substantially to the material progress" of Iowa and, by implication, the rural Middle West. "They were more," Swierenga concludes with graphic metaphor, "than mere leeches fattening on the blood and sweat of honest agriculturists."[37]

Perhaps so. Yet numerous studies have raised serious doubt about positive effects of large landholders on rural communities. Indeed, a bridge exists between Gates (and his Progressive colleagues in the 1930s) and recent agricultural critics who both have underscored the societal costs which resulted from tenancy and large ownership.[38] Gates was not the only researcher who stressed the negative relationship between absentee ownership and social organization. Herbert Quick argued in 1925, for example, that the "two types of mind among pioneer farmers" included one which looked upon the farm as a "means of making money," the other as "a piece of soil out of which to produce a living for the family." The former, which speculated on land, was "fundamentally . . . anti-social"; the latter was "the impulse of the citizen who builds up society."[39] Walter Goldschmidt's classic study later illustrated such contrasts in two California communities with varying land ownership patterns.[40] The region characterized by "industrial agriculture" replete with large-scale, absentee ownership of land suffered in comparison with a community typified by owner-operated farms. The latter enjoyed greater retail trade, greater educational opportunity, more parks, religious institutions, and civic organizations. Significantly, similar findings have been reported in contemporary rural communities. Nor are they isolated instances. A recent federal study has discovered a relationship between farm size and rural poverty even in the wealthiest agricultural counties.[41] A local investigation of rural Nebraska, moreover, has argued that the number of farms is a better indicator of such indices of "quality of life" as school enrollment and service establishments than farm output.[42] Sociologist Dean MacCannell succinctly sums up the modern rural relationship: "as farm size and absentee ownership increase, social conditions in the local community deteriorate."[43]

Analogous questions are posed about the relationships between farmers and the soil. Recent studies have underscored the link between soil erosion and absentee ownership. In one study, erosion rates for cropland and pasture were 40 percent greater on rented land than on owned land. Another investigation discovered that owner-operators were more likely to invest in conservation than were those who did not own the land they farmed.[44] Examples of land-use in a modern agricultural system, of course, differ profoundly from the farm operations in years past. Nonetheless, based on these findings, one is struck both by the common critique of land use patterns and the construction of the relationships between land law, land ownership, and community development among Progressives such as Gates and recent rural reformers alike.

If Gates stressed the global societal costs of speculation and tenancy, his construction of rural economic relationships also pointed to problems that resulted simply from the capitalization of land. Gates, as a Progressive with a Jeffersonian cast, wrote of farming as a mode of life and, as such, distinguished land-owning from farming. The latter used a variety of production inputs—including land—to create wealth; the former usually profited from land's tendency to increase in value. If the farmer used the land to feed his family and provide for his children upon his retirement, the speculator used the land to amass paper wealth. Gates overstated the degree to which the speculator inhibited the process by which families could become farmers. Nonetheless, he outlined the quandaries that arose when land became capitalized. As land became more of a commodity for speculative investment, farmers as farmers were forced to compete in a land market that made it increasingly difficult to enter farming and increasingly contentious within families. True, landowning farmers could sell their land at a profit, but they, and especially their children, also faced constraints if they wished to remain in farming. The scarcities of soil within a capitalist land market, in short, created the potential for a deterioration of the social fabric of rural communities. As land speculation increased profits, it did not necessarily improve quality of life for those who were committed to living in a rural world. Gates's mythic worldview might be criticized as one of romanticism rather than rationality. Yet by distinguishing farmers *qua* farmers from farmers *qua* landowners, as Gates did, we are provided with a critique of developments in the American rural world, a critique that is resonant in many of the writings of recent critics of agricultural policy. A capitalized land market was at best a double-edged sword.

The substantive and historiographical influence of the scholarship of Paul Wallace Gates has thus been profound. His work consistently underscored the significance of landed property in forming and informing the American ethos. His concern about the American public domain, which contained *billions* of acres and was divided into *millions* of farms in the nineteenth century, and the legal code which dispensed it, served to highlight perhaps the most remarkable factor in the development of the American republic. Whereas historians of late have featured the urban republicanism of Tom Paine at the expense of the rural republican world of Thomas Jefferson, it is well to review Gates's work on central economic and cultural forces of land that deeply colored American development in the country *and* city.

An examination of Gates's work, moreover, provides us with a depiction of the Progressive worldview under which he operated. As such, his villains and heroes provided the gist for those who followed him to attack his findings. Yet his work is much more than a period piece. It cautions us against viewing issues from an exclusively economic perspective that isolates the question from the context. If the circumstances of the speculator and the tenant were created out of a "rational" market, perhaps the rural world they created was not as sound. If farming was viewed as a way of life, perhaps land law and the land market did create a system incongruous with the context of those who labored on American soil. Perhaps it is only during economic shocks, as during the thirties and eighties, that the nation realizes "the errors it permitted to develop in its land use pattern."[45] Perhaps the work of Gates, recently discounted by economic historians, has much to tell us still.

Jon Gjerde, Department of History, University of California at Berkeley, is currently completing a manuscript on the sociocultural development of the rural Middle West in the nineteenth and early twentieth centuries.

I am grateful to Lawrence Glickman and Anita Tien for their thoughtful reading and incisive comments on an earlier draft.

1. The proportion of tenant-operated farms in Nebraska increased from 18.1 percent in 1880 to 36.9 in 1920; in Iowa from 23.8 percent in 1880 to 37.8 in 1910. On contemporary concern about tenancy, see Benjamin H. Hibbard, "Tenancy in the North Central States," *Quarterly Journal of Economics* 25 (1911): 710–29.

2. The result was a Country Life Movement. See L. H. Bailey, *Country Life Movement in the United States* (1911).

3. An excellent summary of the concerns that the Dust Bowl created is found in Donald Worster, *Dust Bowl: The Southern Plains in the 1930s* (1979).

4. Gates's significance in the field has been a focus of earlier essays. Excellent treatments of his career include Margaret Beattie Bogue and Allan G. Bogue, "Paul W. Gates," *Great Plains Journal* 18 (1979): 22–32; Frederick Merk, "Foreword," in David M. Ellis, *The Frontier in American Development: Essays in Honor of Paul Wallace Gates* (1968); and Donald L. Winters, "Agricultural Tenancy in the Nineteenth-Century Middle West: The Historiographical Debate," *Indiana Magazine of History* 78 (1982): 128–53.

5. Merk, "Foreword," p. xii.

6. Paul W. Gates, "Recent Land Policies of the Federal Government," in *Certain Aspects of Land Problems and Government Land Policies*, Part 7 of the *Report on Land Planning*, Land Planning Committee of the National Resources Board (1935), pp. 60–85; "The Homestead Law in an Incongruous Land System," *American Historical Review* 41 (1936): 652–81.

7. Merk, "Foreword," p. xiv. Gates's most important essays are made accessible in a collection entitled *Landlords and Tenant on the Prairie Frontier: Studies in American Land Policy* (1973).

8. Gates also published extensively on arrangements of land in California, including the book, *Ranchos and Farms, 1846–1862* (1967).

9. For example, Gates, *The Farmer's Age: Agriculture, 1815–1860* (1960), and *Agriculture and the Civil War* (1965).

10. See, for example, Gates, "Frontier Estate Builders and Farm Laborers," in Clifton B. Kroeber and Walker D. Wyman, eds., *The Frontier in Perspective* (1957), pp. 143–63; and Gates, "Frontier Landlords and Pioneer Tenants," *Journal of the Illinois State Historical Society* 38 (1945): 142–206. Gates himself used the term "un-American"; see "Land Policy and Tenancy in the Prairie Counties of Indiana," *Indiana Magazine of History* 35 (1939), p. 19.

11. Gates, "The Role of the Land Speculator in Western Development," *Pennsylvania Magazine of History and Biography* 66 (1942), p. 314.

12. "Land Policy and Tenancy in the Prairie Counties of Indiana," p. 3; "Land Policy and Tenancy in the Prairie States," *Journal of Economic History* 1 (1941), p. 60.

13. "Land Policy and Tenancy in the Prairie Counties of Indiana," p. 25.

14. Ibid., my emphasis.

15. Ibid., pp. 19, 14–15.

16. Ibid., p. 19.

17. "The Role of the Land Speculator in Western Development," pp. 316–17.

18. Gates, *The Wisconsin Pine Lands of Cornell University*, and "Land Policy and Tenancy in the Prairie Counties of Indiana," p. 22.

19. "Land Policy and Tenancy in the Prairie Counties of Indiana," pp. 21–22.

20. Ibid., p. 25.

21. Gates, "Recent Land Policies of the Federal Government," p. 85.

22. See, for example, LaWanda F. Cox, "Tenancy in the United States, 1865–1900: A Consideration of the Validity of the Agricultural Ladder Hypothesis," *Agricultural History* 18 (1944): 97–105; and Fred A. Shannon, *The Farmer's Last Frontier: Agriculture, 1860–1897* (1945).

23. Many of the revisionists were students of or students of students of Gates. For example, Margaret B. Bogue, *Patterns from the Sod: Land Use and Tenure in the Grand Prairie, 1850–1900* (1959); Allan G. Bogue, *From Prairie to Corn Belt: Farming on the Illinois and Iowa Prairies in the Ninteenth Century* (1963); Robert Swierenga, *Pioneers and Profits: Land Speculation on the Iowa Frontier* (1968); Seddie Cogswell, Jr., *Tenure, Nativity and Age as Factors in Iowa Agriculture, 1850–1880* (1975); and Donald L. Winters, *Farmers Without Farms: Agricultural Tenancy in Nineteenth-Century Iowa* (1978).

24. Swierenga calculates that the timespan between initial sale to speculator and resale was 31.6 months per acre (*Pioneers and Profits*, p. 219); Edward H. Rastatter, "Nineteenth-Century Public Land Policy: The Case for the Speculator," in David C. Klingaman and Richard K. Vedder, *Essays in Nineteenth-Century Economic History: The Old Northwest* (1975), pp. 118–35.

25. Stanley Lebergott, " 'O Pioneers': Land Speculation and Growth of the Midwest," in David C. Klingaman and Richard K. Vedder, eds., *Essays on The Economy of the Old Northwest* (1987), pp. 47–48. Moreover, the higher price paid to speculators, Lebergott argues, was a result of the superior lands that they engrossed.

26. Ibid., pp. 42–43.

27. Swierenga, *Pioneers and Profits*, pp. 215–26; Winters, *Farmers without Farms*, p. 18.

28. See M. B. Bogue, *Patterns from the Sod*, pp. 102–3, 162–65; A. G. Bogue, *From Prairie to Corn Belt*, p. 56; Winters, *Farmers without Farms*, pp. 78–91; Jeremy Atack, "The Agricultural Ladder Revisited: A New Look at an Old Question with Some Data for 1860," *Agricultural History* 63 (1989): 1–25.

29. Winters, *Farmers without Farms*, pp. 79–88.

30. Terry L. Anderson, "The First Privatization Movement," in Klingaman and Vedder, *Essays on The Economy of the Old Northwest*, pp. 59–73.

31. See Winters, "Agricultural Tenancy in the Nineteenth-Century Middle West"; and Jeremy Atack, "The Agricultural Ladder Revisited."

32. Gates, "Introduction," *Landlords and Tenants on the Prairie Frontier*, p. 12.

33. See, for example, Winters, "Agricultural Tenancy in the Ninteenth-Century Middle West," pp. 149–52.

34. See, for example, ibid., p. 146.

35. See M. B. Bogue, *Patterns from the Sod*, pp. 180–81; A. G. Bogue, *From Prairie to Corn Belt*, p. 62; Winters, *Farmers without Farms*, pp. 92–105.

36. Winters, *Farmers without Farms*, p. 98.

37. Swierenga, *Pioneers and Profits*, pp. 220–27, at 225.

38. Among the latter, see Marty Strange, *Family Farming: A New Economic Vision* (1988).

39. Herbert Quick, *One Man's Life* (1925), p. 131. Quick concluded that the speculator "has the better chance to get rich; but this is owing to *certain maladjustments of society* by which he profits" (my emphasis).

40. Walter Goldschmidt, *As You Sow* (1947).

41. U.S. Congress, *Technology, Public Policy, and the Changing Structure of Agriculture: Volume 2—Background Papers*, (1986), cited in Strange, *Family Farming*.

42. Larry D. Swanson, "A Study of Socioeconomic Developments: Changing Farm Structure and Rural Community Decline in the Context of the Technological Transformation of American Agriculture," (Ph.D. diss., University of Nebraska, 1980), cited in Strange, *Family Farming*.

43. Dean MacCannell, "Agribusiness and the Small Community," (unpublished ms., University of California at Davis, n.d.), cited in Strange, *Family Farming*.

44. David E. Ervin, "Soil Erosion Control on Owner-operated and Rented Cropland," *Journal of Soil and Water Conservation* 37 (1982): 285–88; and Donald Baron, *Landownership Characteristics and Investment in Soil Conservation* (1981), cited in Strange, *Family Farming*.

45. Gates, "The Role of the Land Speculator in Western Development," p. 48.

THE IMAGE:
THE LOST WORLD OF DANIEL BOORSTIN

Stephen J. Whitfield

If the contemporary United States is, in Susan Sontag's phrase, "the quintessential Surrealist country,"[1] shooting out juxtapositions that go beyond contrapuntalism, spinning into paradoxes that seem to defy explanation, and shattering into discontinuities that keep rearranging contexts into freak shows and that turn so many Americans into amnesiacs, then one challenge of the historian is to convey the peculiar texture of such experience, in which a mass-mediated "reality" seems to have transformed sense and sensibility. To fathom the meaning of changes—in epistemology and psychology, in tastes in the arts and in patterns of behavior, in politics and economics—requires an omnivorous appetite for reading in a variety of fields and subjects that need to be connected, and incessant attentiveness to the stimuli of the very environment that is both transformed and transforming.

Three decades ago Daniel J. Boorstin tried in *The Image* to make contemporary life intelligible, by drawing upon "my personal experience: the billboards I have seen, the newspapers and magazines I have read, the radio programs I have heard, the television programs I have watched, the movies I have attended, the advertisements I receive daily through the mail, the commodities I have noticed in stores, the salesmen's pitches which have been aimed at me, the conversation I hear, the desires I sense all around me. The tendencies and weaknesses I remark in twentieth-century America are my own." *The Image* is thus a commonplace book, exploring the meaning of "the trivia of our daily experience [which] are evidence of the most important question in our lives: namely, what we believe to be real."[2] Here then is a rarity: a historian's work that can be validated or qualified or rejected not only according to its deployment of salient documentation or to the internal consistency and plausibility of its argument, but in the light of phenomena that his readers face daily. The world that we know and have made—which Boorstin implies has largely superseded a world we have lost—can falsify the claims of his book, which the immediacy of his readers' own surroundings and stimuli can test.

This particular reader doubts that the passage of thirty years has dimmed the luster of Boorstin's observations. Indeed, so savvy are the insights sprinkled throughout *The Image* that the landscape now seems Boorstinian. The emerging and exasperating phenomena that he traced have continued to spread like an oil slick across the American scene, so that a new law of historical motion has needed to be formulated; Jean Baudrillard and Umberto Eco have proposed "hyper-reality." Boorstin himself was less sophisticated. "Because I cannot describe 'reality,' " he conceded at the outset, "I know I risk making myself a sitting duck for my more profound philosopher–colleagues."[3] (But they have since become birds of a feather. Having rejected the correspondence theory of truth, many of those colleagues have themselves given up trying to define "reality.")

His book instead boldly claims only to know what "reality" is not. The term is not apt in characterizing the nation that, he had argued only three years earlier in *The Americans: The Colonial Experience,* was founded in "givenness." Our consciousness in the meantime had become flooded with shadows; for we were living in an "age of tautological experience,"[4] preferring the ersatz to the authentic, the artificial to the spontaneous, the remote to the direct. To Heidegger's famous question (earlier Leibniz's) of why there is something and not nothing, Boorstin answered, in effect, that mass culture gives no guarantee that there is not nothing. But he spurned the open invitation of German thought—let's get metaphysical—in favor of a democratic approach to his readers that presumes no prior knowledge (not even historical knowledge), no technical language nor "idiolect," no authority except a certain sensitivity to the consequences of what he called the Graphic Revolution.

For the core of *The Image* is organized around the theme of declension. The chapters on journalism, fame, and travel start with a historical baseline when neither press agents nor interviews had been imagined, when greatness was related to deeds and talents, when poor folks did not visit museums or travel, before experience became synthetic and fabricated. The epic of America therefore becomes a breach of promise, a downward trajectory that has confronted its befuddled citizens with "the menace of unreality. . . . We risk being the first people in history to have been able to make their illusions so vivid, so persuasive, so 'realistic' that they can live in them. We are the most illusioned people on earth," having flunked the Jeffersonian test of civilization, which is happiness. Since we "have fallen in love with our own image," we are doomed to frustration: "Nearly everything we do to enlarge our world, to make life more interesting, more varied, more exciting, more vivid, more 'fabulous,' more promising, in the long run has an opposite effect."[5] In "the Age of Contrivance," we have confirmed Freud's view by paying the price of civilization, which is unhappiness.

General reviewers mostly praised this gloomy message as trenchant and entertaining, though the professional historians who addressed it in the *Mississippi Valley Historical Review* and the *American Historical Review* managed to restrain their enthusiasm ("tiresome," "trifling," "impressionistic"). A critic in the *Canadian Forum*, one H. M. McLuhan, accused Boorstin of a "tendency to substitute moral disapproval for insight" and "to look at the oncoming electronic culture from the fixed point of the receding mechanical culture."[6] It is true that *The Image* arrived a little too early to catch the centrality of television. But McLuhan was wrong to discern the "moral disapproval" animating Boorstin's text, which is no jeremiad warning that American culture was going down the tube. His foreword soothingly insists that the book is written from "an affection for America and an amazement at America."[7] But he was not, at least openly, appalled at America. No outrage is expressed because his fellow citizens seem to echo the plea of Blanche DuBois: "I don't want realism. I want magic!" Nor does his disapproval extend as far as Neil Postman's *Amusing Ourselves to Death*, which would find that the very procedures of rational discourse are imperilled when seeing is believing.[8] Writing when the "oncoming electronic culture" (outasight, outamind) was much less dominant, the future Librarian of Congress had not imagined that the Book itself — that artifact which UNESCO defined as a "non-periodical printed publication of at least 49 pages excluding covers"[9] — was being measured for a coffin.

In Boorstin's own canon, the place of *The Image* is likely to remain equivocal, however. While his other books have been subjected to considerable professional attention and criticism (whether for the complacency of *The Genius of American Politics*, 1953, or for the capriciousness of *The Americans* trilogy), *The Image* has been left largely undisturbed. No *Historikerstreit* has swirled around it. J. R. Pole's critique of Boorstin's writings, for example, devotes only two paragraphs to *The Image*, even though it "represents a grave departure from the confidence that marked Boorstin's earlier thought. As another critic has observed, the corruption and the threat are now within the community itself and cannot be ascribed to the temptations of alien ideology."[10]

And indeed that may be why Boorstin himself has evaded the melancholy implications of his own book. Not until the fifth chapter does he elaborate upon his title, classifying images as synthetic, passive, simple and ambiguous — by contrast with (earlier) ideals, which are depicted as good. But his appeal for ideals conflicted with his customary exaltation of America for having repudiated the need for them. Boorstin "locates the splendor of America in its mindlessness, hails vagueness and ignorance as sources of our social health, and rejoices in the pervasiveness of our anti-intellectualism," Kenneth S. Lynn complained in 1966.[11] But whatever the fairness of this charge against Boorstin's work (at least beginning in the 1950s), it does not take into account *The Image*, which valorizes reflection and perspicacity (though not, of course, theory or ideology) in emancipating us from our illusions.

The tone of *The Image* manifestly collides with the zippety-doo-dah boosterism of everything from *The Genius of American Politics* forward. The "consumption communities" so breathlessly depicted in *The Decline of Radicalism* (1969) and *The Democratic Experience* (1973) are diagnosed as "suffer[ing] from social narcissism" in *The Image*,[12] where the author works the night shift so briefly that even he cannot seem to remember what it was like. *Hidden History* (1987), the only one of his six books of essays that reprints chapters from previous books and thus represents a special monument to his scholarship, almost treats *The Image* as an homage to the new world that Americans have so creatively fashioned. "Behind these scenes of experiment and enterprise, we glimpse 'The Momentum of Technology' " is how three chapters abridged from *The Image* are introduced. "Amid the surprising delights of our self-made world, the Momentum of Technology becomes ominous. 'Pseudo-events'— experiences of our own contriving—begin to hide reality from us, to confuse our sense of reality, taking us headlong from the world of heroes to a world of celebrities, transforming us from travelers into tourists."[13] This nervous interruption is barely allowed to detract from the upbeat spiel of the tour guide.

Only two years before *The Image* was published, Boorstin had asserted that "if the historian has any function . . . it is to note the rich particularity of experience, to search for the piquant aroma of life. . . . The historian as humanist is a votary of the unrepeatability of all experience."[14] That role could not be squared with the imminent argument of *The Image* that experience had become homogenized, impoverished, devoid of piquancy, operating on remote control. The imaginative bravura of *The Image* therefore becomes even more impressive because its thrust contradicted its author's most characteristic impulses and outlook. The star-spangled dustjacket of the hardcover edition gave no hint of its subversive contents, which may be why the subtitle that was substituted in the paperback (1964) and later editions ("A Guide to Pseudo-Events in America") can only spike the force of ". . . What Happened to The American Dream."

Such reassurances went beyond packaging. For the text sought to italicize the conservatism to which Boorstin was otherwise committed. "We expect too much of the world," he warned (as though American thought in the 1950s was afflicted with the fatal abstraction of utopianism!). Nor did he recommend the search for blame in the market forces which promote those images (that are really plugs for products), in the corporations that provided Americans with information: "Our real problem is personal."[15] As the citizen threatened to become reduced to a consumer (including a consumer of political commercials), and the representative institution began to shift from the city hall to the shopping mall, Boorstin tended to resist the most worrisome implications of his own insights. What Boorstin saw as "the thinner things of life," others would see as anorexic, the result of artificial sweeteners added by the very enterprises whose inventiveness and improvisatory power he elsewhere praised.

But *The Image* shows that, in America anyway, the sharpest critics are very often former radicals, trained in the fervent heterodoxy that equipped them not for revolution but for writing. The book also suggests that perhaps only a conservative—indeed a venturous conservative—could be so attuned to the novelty of his surroundings, could calibrate the thoroughness with which an earlier world had vanished. Upholding a standard of authenticity, and depicting a more heroic past, *The Image* gives the bum's rush to those who might cite earlier instances of the atmospherics of deception and artifice: "Such acolytes of the familiar avoid recognizing the consequences of their own blindness [to novelty] by saying it is quite normal to be blind."[16]

For all of Boorstin's own attentiveness to the distinctively new ambience that made experience itself "tautological," *The Image* also belongs to its time, when it was widely assumed—and not only by conservatives—that material problems had largely been licked. Social criticism in this era could be summarized as a respectable version of Yogi Berra's approach to baseball: "90 percent of this game is half-mental." Boorstin's observation that "we are haunted, not by reality, but by those images we have put in place of reality"[17] had its analogues in Betty Friedan's description of "the feminine mystique" as the numbing problem of the suburban housewives whom she interviewed, in Paul Goodman's insistence that young males were growing up absurd because of an equally vague and undefinable longing for worthy vocational purpose, in John Kenneth Galbraith's sense that "the conventional wisdom" impeded understanding of the need to correct private indulgence.

Because Boorstin in *The Image* comes closer than any of these critics to the abyss, to the politics of cultural despair, it is more closely affiliated with radical perspectives than with the optimistic conservatism with which he usually aligned himself. Walter Benjamin's essay on "The Work of Art in the Age of Mechanical Reproduction," which was not translated until 1968 (and is not cited in the bibliographic essay in *The Image*), anticipates Boorstin's fourth chapter. Indeed the entire argument of his book is closer to Herbert Marcuse's *One-Dimensional Man* (1964), and to the Frankfurt School's criticism of the triumph of technology and the emptiness of mass culture, than to either pragmatic thought or political conservatism of a generation or so ago. The intellectual pedigree of *The Image* is not explicit, and Boorstin's evasion of any large philosophical problem seems to be typically American. But the spoor to continental thought can be tracked more readily than the author may acknowledge. Already by 1843, soon after the invention of the camera, Feuerbach labelled "our era" one that "prefers the image to the thing, the copy to the original, the representation to the reality, appearance to being." Marx and Engels's query in *The German Ideology* ("Is the *Iliad* possible when the printing press and even printing machines exist?") hinted at Boorstin's emphasis upon the Graphic Revolution in reshaping the configurations of discourse.[18]

But the value of *The Image* derives less from the intellectual antecedents that it builds upon than from the pertinent features of American culture that the book describes and anticipates. The changes that the author noticed, and that he weighed against a historical standard, have accelerated in their velocity. Perhaps a few illustrations can spotlight the trends that he detected.

1. "The rise of advertising," *The Image* claims, "has brought a social redefinition of the very notion of truth." For "all of us . . . are daily less interested in whether something is a fact than in whether it is convenient that it should be believed. . . . What seems important is not truth but verisimilitude," with how it will play in Peoria, where, in effect, "it is more important that a statement be believable than that it be true."[19] Hoaxes quite obviously depend for their success upon verisimilitude; and it was a humiliating moment for the historical profession when the eminent author of *The Last Days of Hitler* fell for a fraudulent Hitler diary in 1983. H. R. Trevor-Roper's credulousness ("I'm staking my reputation on it") could at least be judged against a recognizably scholarly norm—unlike a presumably respectable magazine like *Newsweek*, which proclaimed in its cover story on the release of the "diary": "Genuine or not, it almost doesn't matter in the end. . . ."[20] The erasure of the line between truth and falsehood is a symptom of cultural loss, a capitulation to an advertising notion of truth.

2. What Boorstin called "the dissolution of forms" has gotten more closely connected to this capitulation than his book had foreseen. Take, for example, the response to Alex Haley's *Roots* (1976)—the biggest "nonfiction" bestseller in U.S. publishing history (unless the Bible is counted), with over six million copies sold in hardcover, and with translations into thirty-seven languages. It won not only a special National Book Award but a special Pulitzer Prize as well. It was initially hailed for its painstaking historical research. But then Haley was successfully sued for having plagiarized a novel (Harold Courlander's *The African*), and the genealogy that so stirred readers could not withstand the scrutiny of several historians and journalists. (If Kunta Kinte ever

existed, he could not have been Haley's ancestor, having landed in Annapolis four years too late to "be" Toby Waller.) The author then defended himself by referring to *Roots* as "faction" that blended research with the genre of fiction,[21] and ABC decided to play it safe by announcing that its television version was "based on the novel by Alex Haley." Where that left the Pulitzer Prize jury, which did not believe that it was honoring fiction, isn't clear. It is as though the jury was also proclaiming: it almost doesn't matter.

3. Though published before the appearance of *People* Magazine and its imitators, *The Image* adumbrated the endemic confusion not only between fact and fiction, but between the hero and the celebrity. Boorstin's definition of the latter—a "human pseudo-event" "who is known for his well-known-ness"—should be compared to C. Wright Mills's earlier description of glitterati who "are celebrated because they are displayed as celebrities."[22] The display is ubiquitous now. A "*Time* Magazine Television Special" at the end of 1990 promised viewers "an hour of heroes, villains, complicated plots and surprise endings." The one villain depicted in the advertisement is Saddam Hussein; while the only heroes are not heroes at all, not even celebrities, but the cartoon Simpsons—as though they operated on the same plane of reality and interest. "This year the most compelling drama wasn't a drama," *Time*'s ad eerily asserts. "It was real life."[23] When cartoon characters are considered as "real," as worthy of attention, as the Iraqi dictator, the best way to interpret—and criticize—the cultural atmosphere that Americans inhale and may take as "natural" is Boorstinian. A decade ago children aged four to six were asked whether they like television or their fathers better, and 44 percent replied in favor of television.[24]

4. The proliferation of "pseudo-events" is why Ronald Reagan could be deemed the fulfillment of What Happened to The American Dream, in the precise sense of Boorstin's original subtitle. When Larry Speakes was asked on October 5, 1984, if the President had read the congressional report on the Beirut truck bombing, the White House spokesperson replied: "I don't think he's read the report in detail. It's five-and-a-half pages, doubled spaced." But twenty days later Reagan boasted of "read[ing] every comic strip in the paper." Perhaps the only interesting remark that he ever made—a politician who revised the Socratic credo by proving that the unexamined life *is* worth living—was his claim, in an interview at the end of his second term, that far from wondering how an actor could be President, he wondered "how you could do this job and *not* be an actor."[25] The stress on celebrity and on pseudo-events has soaked up the notion of seriousness, undoubtedly contributing to political inertia. Voter turn-outs have continued to decline alarmingly, and perhaps the sense that "there is no there there" fuels the malaise.

Though Reagan did not invent stagecraft as a substitute for statecraft, his administration's addiction to images was unprecedented. "Now that every sewer commissioner campaigns on smoke and mirrors," journalist Charles Krauthammer noted in 1982, "Ronald Reagan has made the empty gesture the touchstone of a Presidency—and succeeded." Adroitness in media manipulation has come largely to determine eligibility for civic life. "In the hands of those in power, practitioners of symbolic politics, it has made gesture a substitute for policy," Krauthammer complained. "In the hands of dissidents, practitioners of political metaphor and mime, it has made gesture a substitute for argument. And in the minds of citizens, practitioners of the art of spectatorship, it has made politics a form of entertainment."[26] Hence the irony of Larry Speakes's last speech as a public servant, enunciating the hope—before the National Press Club in 1987—that policy would be based on what's best for the American people, not on what looks good on television: "Let's not write a TV script and then create an event designed for the evening news." He received a Presidential Citizens Medal.[27]

5. The Reagan years culminated to date a process that requires the sort of analysis that *The Image* foreshadowed. Consider its assertion that "freedom of the press" is often a euphemism for the prerogative of reporters to produce their synthetic commodity."[28] By 1989 television prime-time news programs were staging "re-enactments" of events to boost ratings. NBC's *Yesterday, Today and Tomorrow* combined professional actors as well as some of the original participants themselves (like the pilot and flight attendant from a near-crash in 1972) to show viewers what happened (more or less). CBS's *Saturday Night with Connie Chung* mixed interviews with re-creations, blurring the line between what may have happened and what is simulated.[29]

Even the most significant historical encounter between the press and the presidency can be subjected to a Boorstinian analysis. To make *All the President's Men* effective on the screen, Robert Redford was involved in helping Bob Woodward and Carl Bernstein to conceive their book about uncovering the Watergate scandal—their own account of what they did—before they had begun writing it.[30] The Warner paperback did not show photos of the reporters on the cover but instead the movie stars who played them. At one showing of the film, about a decade after the scandal itself, a Harvard undergraduate asked her professor: "You mean 'Deep Throat' was Hal Holbrook?" It is amusing to add that Jonathan Boorstin (a son of the historian) became associate producer of the film version.

6. In the three decades since publication of *The Image*, popular culture continues to follow a Boorstinian script by jumbling the ordering and sequencing of genres, by impugning the very notion of hierarchy and significance, by trivializing what it touches, by confusing the line between the original and the copy. What do such conditions mean for real novelists? Satirist Russell

Baker once imagined how Tolstoy would have had to operate in the quest for "big rubles," with his agent telling him to begin with submitting a *Reader's Digest* condensation, then (since this version is an unwieldy 575,000 words) to do a scenario—also unworkable (because the movie script would have meant producing a thirty-seven hour film), then with a comic book version of *War and Peace*. "Then," the agent assures him, "we will hire a composer to write the [soundtrack] music for the smash-hit film soon to be made on which the comic book is based, and point out that when the movie is finished it will be based on the full-length best seller soon to be written."[31] And so on. Indeed, as Paul Boorstin (another of the historian's sons) explained, after he and his wife Sharon had secured movie rights to a novel before they had signed a publishers' contract to write the book (which they had not yet written): "The new trend in Hollywood is to finance the writing of the novel by buying the movie rights. It makes sense."[32]

And what of "the last star," as a biography of Elizabeth Taylor is entitled? In 1982 she filed suit to stop an unauthorized TV movie about her life, which she defined in a way that inadvertently confirmed the Marxist "fetishism of commodities": "I am my own industry. I am my own commodity." Not her talent nor her activities but her very life was reduced to a product that had not just a value but a price, a zany capitalist version of transubstantiation.[33] But *The Image* did not consider the possibility of pathological sickness when the hero (or villain) blurs with celebrity. A century ago one killer supposedly boasted of having personally enforced a social code that stigmatized criminality and punished the criminal (who was famous): "I shot Jesse James!" In 1980 the boast of an autograph hound, Mark David Chapman, was senseless and nihilistic, barren of meaning except in the perverted democracy of celebrityhood: "I shot John Lennon!"

Faced with the insidious effects of popular culture, the embattled members of the Frankfurt School offered their writings as pieces of resistance, as contributions to "the great refusal." Faced with the problem of entrenched stereotypes, Walter Lippmann's *Public Opinion* (a work commended in *The Image*) proposed the solution of greater thoughtfulness through the institution of an "intelligence bureau." Faced with the illusory consequences of the Graphic Revolution, Boorstin supplied no remedy except vigilance—a deeper awareness of our predicament, beginning with the realization that it *is* a predicament. "The task of disenchantment is finally . . . the reader's," the writer concluded. "Each of us must disenchant himself, must moderate his expectations, must prepare himself to receive messages coming in from the outside. The first step is to begin to suspect that there may be a world out there."[34] Images therefore are not just to be seen, but to be seen through. Or as Willie Stark's attorney-general, Hugh Miller, puts it in *All the King's Men*: "History is blind but man is not."[35]

That is why *The Image* is invaluable, and why students of the past are increasingly pursuing the agenda that Boorstin advanced in his "Suggestions for Further Reading (and Writing)." In identifying fresh topics for exploration for historians and specialists in American Studies, he championed the need for histories of news and communications, American photography, histories of the book and printing, and histories of television (before Erik Barnouw became the Braudel of broadcasting). Biographies of the likes of Capone, Valentino, Chaplin, Sinatra, Monroe, and Presley, the author added, would make "a parable for our time," and "would teach us more about ourselves than many of the more lengthy studies of less significant but more conventionally 'important' minor figures in our political, literary, and academic life." Boorstin wrote *The Image* without knowing "of a regular course on the art of the movies in a department of literature in a single major university, although there may be such," in contrast with "numerous courses on the far less significant . . . works . . . of minor playwrights."[36] He also advocated a linguistic turn, even as the neologism that he coined—"pseudo-event"—would enter the language, especially alongside its variant of "media event."[37] In the rearview mirror of history, objects may appear larger than they were at the time. Retrospect allows us to see the significance of what contemporaries may dimly have noticed or understood. *The Image* itself now looks less eccentric, though no less ingenious, than it did three decades ago.

It is so rare for a historian to be clever that Boorstin's astonishing erudition at least dampens the suspicion that he is *only* clever. His books yield surprising and obscure information, related with such sprightly wit and vividness that many a larcenous lecturer has cherished them for introductory courses (and beyond). Boorstin's zest to transmit knowledge of the past served him well as a cultural critic in *The Image*, which is enhanced with an argument that is more taut and coherent than in *The Americans*. In 1960 he had asserted that "our greatest historians—whatever else they may have done—have somehow added to our understanding of what it meant to be alive at a particular time and place in the past."[38] That is what this book does—for the present. It deserves to be pondered, and extended, and known for more than its wellknownness.

Stephen J. Whitfield, Department of American Studies, Brandeis University, is the author of The Culture of the Cold War *(Johns Hopkins University Press, 1991).*

1. Susan Sontag, *On Photography* (1977), p. 48.
2. Daniel J. Boorstin, *The Image: Or What Happened to The American Dream* (1962), pp. 264–65. (Though that is the date on the title page, the author's copyright is recorded as 1961.)
3. Ibid., p. viii.
4. Ibid., p. 115.
5. Ibid., pp. 241, 255, 257.
6. H. M. McLuhan, review of *The Image*, *Canadian Forum* 42 (July 1962): 90.

7. Boorstin, p. vii.

8. Neil Postman, *Amusing Ourselves to Death: Public Discourse in the Age of Show Business* (1985), pp. 74, 76.

9. Daniel J. Boorstin, *The Discoverers* (1983), p. 524.

10. J. R. Pole, "Daniel J. Boorstin," in Marcus Cunliffe and Robin W. Winks, eds., *Pastmasters: Some Essays on American Historians* (1969), p. 237; David W. Noble, *Historians Against History* (1965), pp. 173–75.

11. Kenneth S. Lynn, review of *The Americans: The National Experience, Kenyon Review* 28 (January 1966): 117.

12. Boorstin, *The Image*, p. 257.

13. Daniel J. Boorstin, *Hidden History* (1987), p. xi.

14. Daniel J. Boorstin, *America and the Image of Europe: Reflections on American Thought* (1960), p. 66.

15. Boorstin, *The Image*, pp. vii, 3.

16. Ibid., p. 289.

17. Ibid., p. 6.

18. Ludwig Feuerbach, *The Essence of Christianity* (1843), quoted in Sontag, p. 153; Karl Marx and Friedrich Engels, *The German Ideology* (1972), p. 150.

19. Boorstin, *The Image*, pp. 212, 227, 289.

20. "Hitler's Secret Diaries," *Newsweek* 101 (2 May 1983): 52, 60.

21. Richard Nelson Current, *Arguing With Historians: Essays on the Historical and the Unhistorical* (1987), pp. 153–56; Leslie A. Fiedler, *The Inadvertent Epic: From Uncle Tom's Cabin to Roots* (1979), pp. 71–85.

22. Boorstin, *The Image*, p. 57; C. Wright Mills, *The Power Elite* (1956), p. 74.

23. *Time* 136 (24 December 1990): 7.

24. Lance Morrow, "The Politics of the Box Populi," *Time* 113 (11 June 1979): 95.

25. Quoted in Paul Slansky, *The Clothes Have No Emperor: A Chronicle of the American 80s* (1989), pp. 111, 116, 271–72.

26. Charles Krauthammer, "Lights, Camera . . . Politics," *New Republic* 187 (22 November 1982): 22.

27. Slansky, p. 186.

28. Boorstin, *The Image*, p. 29.

29. Richard Zoglin, "TV News Goes Hollywood," *Time* 134 (9 October 1989): 98–99.

30. Jack Hirschberg, *A Portrait of All the President's Men* (1976), pp. 28–31.

31. Russell Baker, "Hey, Ruble!", in *So This is Depravity and Other Observations* (1980), pp. 168–70.

32. "Running the Film Backward," *Time* 115 (24 March 1980): 86.

33. Greil Marcus, *Lipstick Traces: A Secret History of the Twentieth Century* (1989), pp. 106, 108.

34. Boorstin, *The Image*, pp. vii, 260.

35. Robert Penn Warren, *All the King's Men* (1946), p. 462.

35. Boorstin, *The Image*, pp. 274, 282–83.

37. William Safire, *Safire's Political Dictionary* (1978), pp. 576–77.

38. Boorstin, *America and the Image of Europe*, p. 67.

INDUSTRIAL SLAVERY AND
THE TRAGEDY OF ROBERT STAROBIN

Alex Lichtenstein

Robert S. Starobin was a promising New Left historian whose life and career were cut short by suicide in 1971. Part of a generation of students trained by Kenneth Stampp at Berkeley,[1] his scholarly engagement in the reevaluation of African-American history was eventually joined to his political commitment to the black liberation movement. His monograph, *Industrial Slavery in the Old South*, published in 1970, contributed to the burgeoning literature on slavery that came in the wake of the upheavals of the 1960s. Given the current interest in examining the legacy of the New Left's entry into the profession, this seems an appropriate moment to reconsider *Industrial Slavery* as one of the lasting works from that period.[2]

Historiographically, *Industrial Slavery* addressed head-on some still unresolved issues in the history of slavery, the South, and African-Americans. Starobin entered into the debate over the political economy of slavery by demonstrating that slave labor was perfectly compatible with industrial enterprises. Two decades later southern historians still pursue the questions addressed by his work: was slavery suited only to plantation agriculture? Did the southern commitment to slavery impede economic and industrial development? Did the adaptation of slavery to urban and industrial settings indicate the demise or the resilience of unfree labor?[3] The book also has much to say about the always controversial question of slaves' resistance and accommodation to their condition.

In his brief career as a political activist and radical scholar, Robert Starobin made every stop on the New Left's itinerary. A "red diaper baby"—indeed, son of the foreign editor of the *Daily Worker*—he believed the task of his generation of radicals was to carry the torch of the Old Left, while transcending its limitations. As a student activist, he cut his political teeth in the Free Speech Movement at Berkeley; as a young faculty member he moved on to

antiwar work in Madison, and by the end of the 1960s was a partisan of the
Black Panther party at a time when white leftists were increasingly less welcome in black nationalist movements. In addition to further estranging him
from the Old Left tradition championed by his father, this latter commitment
both shaped his scholarship and contributed to his own personal and political
confusion about the appropriate role of the scholar-activist.[4]

Until the time of his death at the age of thirty-one, Starobin's commitment
to an academic career did not appear to flag—his 1968 dissertation was published by Oxford University Press in 1970 as *Industrial Slavery;* that same year
he published a collection of documents on the Denmark Vesey insurrection
in Charleston, which demonstrated the existence of a carefully planned revolt.[5] He had also begun work on a pathbreaking collection of slave letters,
in an attempt to let the protagonists of black history speak for themselves,
rather than through the evidence left by their white oppressors.[6] Like so many
others in the student left, academic life seemed the career path most compatible with his political radicalism.

In a period when the Right likes to bash the sixties in the culture at large,
and in the academy in particular, it is refreshing to recall the major contribution made by historians who came of age in this period, and whose political
commitment informed their scholarship without distorting it. Solid pieces of
scholarship like *Industrial Slavery* readily refute the charge that the sixties
eroded academic "standards." Moreover, radical intellectuals carried their
principles with them into the very institutions they had often confronted as
students, and insisted that African-American history, women's history, and
the history of working people be taken seriously. Pioneer New Left historians
like Robert Starobin demonstrated that with a sharp eye for important un-
asked questions, and prodigious research in the conventional sources, radical
scholarship could be produced by traditional critical methods.

In essays written for the *Journal of Contemporary History* and *Radical America,*
Starobin consciously staked out his own historiographic ground to the left of
his mentor's generation of liberal scholars of slavery and African-American
history. Acknowledging Stampp's important role in "demolishing" traditionalist views of plantation slavery, Starobin nevertheless went on to characterize most liberal revisionist historiography in the field as elitist, assimilationist,
and skewed toward celebrating the achievements of the black bourgeoisie.
Yet he also sharply distinguished his generation's approach from the Old Left
historiography of Herbert Aptheker and Philip Foner, who he felt engaged
in hero-worship of their own. The "Marxists . . . have more in common with
liberal scholars than they would be willing to admit, and less in common with
the radical historians of the 1960s than one might suppose," he claimed.[7]

Starobin began his scholarly career in the late 1960s, when disillusionment with the inability of the Civil Rights Movement to uproot racism and challenge the nation's discriminatory political economy had reached high tide. This led radical scholars, black and white alike, to an increasingly nationalist and radical position. For historians, this entailed placing slavery and racism at the heart of American political and economic history, rather than on the periphery as a peculiar "moral lag" which could be rectified by the power of good intentions. Thus, Starobin noted, Staughton Lynd rewrote the history of the Constitutional Convention as a debate over slavery; Eric Foner and Eugene Genovese restored slavery to its proper place in understanding the Republican party, secession, and southern nationalism; and black scholars like Vincent Harding viewed "racism as a functional component in American development."[8] And Starobin himself suggested that slavery was a flexible and dynamic institution, which if wedded to industrial development, might have been a formidable foe for the northern bourgeoisie. As Frank Freidel suggested in *Saturday Review*, *Industrial Slavery* "erased the last remnant of optimism" that the bonds of slavery were loosening in the 1850s.[9]

Despite his sense of playing the intellectual radical to an essentially liberal historiographic revolution wrought by Stampp and others, in retrospect Starobin's book sits firmly midstream of the broad current of revisionist work on slavery that began with *The Peculiar Institution* (1956) and perhaps culminated with Lawrence Levine's *Black Culture and Black Consciousness* (1977) two decades later.[10] Indeed, *Industrial Slavery* bore the imprint of the author's dissertation advisor and his work. A glance at *The Peculiar Institution* reveals that the topics addressed by Stampp—the conditions of labor, resistance, repression, "maintenance, morbidity, mortality," and profitability—set the agenda for *Industrial Slavery* (as one reviewer of the latter remarked).[11] Moreover, Starobin's dissertation and resulting monograph were in great measure an extended study of a question touched on briefly in Stampp's book, but clearly left for others to explore. Stampp treated the question of slave labor in industry in a mere four pages, but boldly concluded that "it is doubtful . . . that slavery in any decisive way retarded the industrialization of the South." Starobin's task was to search for evidence for that provocative assertion.[12]

And search for it he did. What is most striking about *Industrial Slavery* is the astonishing breadth of research that went into the book. Starobin visited thirty-eight archives, from Madison to Mobile, from the Huntington to Harvard's Baker Business Library, and consulted nearly every significant holding in the South. His bibliography lists almost 300 manuscript collections. Even reviewers doubtful about some of his cruder calculations, or who quibbled with his conclusions, expressed admiration for the "formidable" research.[13]

Not surprisingly, the book's most significant and lasting contribution is documentary: *Industrial Slavery* still represents the most complete compendium of southern slave-based industry. The opening chapter of the book provided an overview of the diverse industrial pursuits to which slave labor was applied in the antebellum South. While even by Starobin's reckoning only 5 percent of the slave population was engaged in industry by the 1850s, both the diversity and concentration of this labor force made it significant. Slaves worked in nearly every nonagricultural economic sector, including manufacturing, mining, forest industries, transportation, and agricultural processing. In contrast to the postbellum period, when blacks were excluded from the mills, southern textile operators were willing to rely on slaves. Tobacco and hemp factories also sought out a bound labor force; by 1860 80 percent of Richmond's tobacco factories worked ten or more slaves, and nearly one-third of them had over ninety-five bondspeople. According to Starobin, the antebellum turpentine industry "was entirely dependent on slave labor" (p. 26). Slaves were also used in the emerging southern coal and iron industry.[14] The 10,000 slaves employed at southern ironworks guaranteed that "the manufacture of iron was . . . heavily dependent upon slave labor" (p. 14).

Some reviewers felt that the book was overly indulgent with the definition of "industrial" in an effort to inflate the economic versatility of slavery.[15] The inclusion of rice-milling, sugar cane grinding, cottonseed oil pressing, and other processes one step removed from plantation agriculture, appeared to some as more of a blow to Starobin's case than supporting evidence. Yet Starobin's insistence that adjuncts to the plantation regime, such as the sugar mill, be considered as "an emerging industrial pursuit" (p. 19) has proved a useful heuristic device. The most recent work on sugar and slavery has made a convincing case for the fundamentally "industrial" character of investment, labor, and production on sugar plantations.[16]

This survey of industrial slavery suggested two other important features of the institution. First, Starobin was careful to point out that industrial slavery was quite distinct from urban slavery, and that the conclusions drawn by historians about the supposed liberality of the latter were inapplicable to the industrial sector. Second, he concluded that only one-fifth of industrial slaves were hired; the rest were the bondspeople of the owners of the industrial enterprise in which they worked. This fact directed attention away from the question of slave-hiring, and toward the interesting question of what Starobin called "slave capitalization."

Building on these observations, Starobin used the data he collected to view the most pressing questions of revisionism through the lens of industrial slavery, and to put forth a compelling brief for the compatibility of slavery and industry. The chapters that followed were organized thematically, ascending, in a materialist fashion, from what is now called "the point of production" to the economic and political implications of slave-based industry.

He began by considering the conditions of work, and the provision of food, shelter, and clothing. Long hours, determined by production schedules rather than agrarian rhythms, inadequate clothing, erratically supplied food provided at subsistence level (obviously more difficult to acquire than on a farm), and extremely hazardous working conditions, characterized the life of the industrial slave. Thus, in Starobin's view, industrial slavery combined the harshest features of early industrial labor and bondage itself. In particular, he sought to challenge the views of scholars who suggested urban slavery and the practice of slave-hiring—both subsidiaries of, but as Starobin correctly noted, not identical to, industrial slavery—undermined the peculiar institution.[17] To the contrary, slaves who worked in industry endured the most extreme conditions, and were worse off than those who continued to labor in agriculture. Far from serving as a "twilight" realm between slavery and freedom, industrial labor tightened the bonds of slavery even further.

Perhaps the most suggestive aspect of the discussion of conditions focused on industrial accidents and slave insurance. While not fully developing an analysis, Starobin argued that "by spreading slave losses among large numbers of slave users, [insurance] promised to underpin valuable investments in industrial slaves" (p. 72). Here, it seems, was a significant instrument that could conceivably accommodate slavery to industrial capitalism through risk-sharing and by limiting liability. This, as well as explorations of legal disputes brought on by slave casualties in industry, are still promising avenues for further investigation.[18]

Starobin then moved on to discuss the methods of labor "discipline" employed by slaveowners and the forms of resistance developed by slaves. Rejecting the notion that industrial slaves were more content with their status, or the suggestion that "privileged" slaves showed reluctance to rebel, he catalogued the by now familiar patterns of "day-to-day resistance to slavery." As with plantation slaves, negligence, slow work, sabotage, arson, theft, and flight, were all part of the industrial slave's arsenal. Outright rebellion or conspiracy was, of course, far less common. Yet in the slave revolts that did occur in the antebellum South Starobin observed "the striking fact that almost all rebel leaders and many followers actually were . . . artisans or industrial slaves" (p. 88), including Vesey and his comrades, the leaders of the 1811 revolt in Louisiana's sugar parishes, and the suspects in the 1856 "conspiracy" of slave ironworkers in the Cumberland Valley.[19]

Starobin paid far less attention to the unique position of hired slaves, who found themselves able to manipulate the potential conflicts of interest between their owner and their temporary employer to their own advantage. Other scholars of industrial slavery, particularly Ronald L. Lewis and Charles B. Dew, have taken issue with the unremittingly harsh nature of the institution portrayed in *Industrial Slavery*, in part by emphasizing the appeal to paternalism made possible by slave-hiring. Similarly, where Starobin argued that holidays, payment schemes, and other incentives were used "to control . . . industrial slaves and to increase their productivity" (p. 97), Lewis and Dew suggest that industrial slavery required masters to accommodate and conciliate their workforce to an unusual degree. Dew went so far as to insist that the industrial slave, at least in ironworks, "had considerable influence over his working conditions, his family arrangements, and the course of his everyday life."[20]

Of course this was a matter of emphasis, rather than outright disagreement: where Starobin saw sticks his detractors saw carrots. But this difference takes on special significance when it is applied to the question of payment for "overwork," cash incentives paid (or promised) to slaves for labor beyond a fixed task. The entry of wage labor relations into the slave economy might have had profound effects on the institution. But Starobin explicitly dismissed historians' earlier view of this payment as "a developing wage system" (p. 99). As a long-standing practice in slave industry, the task and "overwork" system had always been used to improve discipline and extract additional labor from recalcitrant slaves, Starobin claimed. Perhaps these "wages" gave slaves more of a stake in the industrial labor they were forced to perform, but at bottom cash incentives "were not a step towards emancipation, but rather a technique of slave control" (p. 99). Ironically, now the pendulum has swung back again, as historians have recently demonstrated the opportunities for accumulation provided to slaves who worked by the task in agricultural as well as industrial pursuits. In the light of Starobin's persuasive critique of task labor, the repressive aspects of this form of labor organization deserve renewed attention.[21]

Indeed, one might ask, if industrial slavery was an incipient form of free labor, why did industrialists seek out a slave labor force at all? In a fascinating account of the relationship between free (white) and slave labor in southern industry, Starobin pointed to several factors militating against "conversion" to free labor in slave-dominated sectors, even as slave prices began to rise. In addition to subscribing to proslavery ideology, many industrialists found the reliability of slave labor compelling. Free white workers, particularly immigrants, were regarded as prone to quit, strike, or riot. As one Alabama coal operator complained, "no reliance whatever can be placed upon" (p. 125) free labor. Through an inventive use of business records (frequently overlooked by social historians), Starobin also illustrated the flexible and adaptive nature of industrial slavery. Hired or purchased slaves could replace unskilled laborers or even be "coupled" with skilled free workers when needed in key areas of production or in emergencies. Moreover, Starobin showed that free and slave labor worked side by side in some instances. At the Tredegar iron works, skilled white workers helped train the slaves who eventually came to displace them. Finally, Starobin compiled figures that indicated the cost advantages of slavery over free labor, though he misleadingly referred to this as "efficiency" (p. 155). Firms that relied on an industrial slave labor force were able to reduce their labor costs, and "most . . . whose records are available matched or exceeded an annual rate of return of about 6 percent" (p. 148), Starobin's benchmark for profitability.

In short, slavery provided a viable, profitable, and above all, flexible labor force for southern industry, particularly when compared to the available options. Yet the poorly developed free labor market that made slavery attractive may have been a result of slavery itself. Few historians would dispute that forced labor conceivably could have been applied to virtually any productive process with short-term success. But if slavery was compatible with antebellum industry at the level of the individual firm, workplace, or task, this begged the question of its long-term effects on the southern economy and labor market. Starobin argued against the view that slavery *per se* hobbled investment in industry and capitalist development. Slaveholders used slaves as a flexible and mobile form of *capital*, which could be invested (planters subscribed to railroads and even iron works by providing a labor force), hired out, shifted between agriculture and industry, or liquidated when necessary. The relative weakness of the industrial sector below the Mason-Dixon Line could be attributed to limited markets, unfavorable balances of trade, competitive disadvantages, and "the ability of southern agriculture to outbid industry for investment capital" (p. 186). Even if a commitment to slavery contributed to these weaknesses, it was not the primary cause of backwardness. In fact, it was the struggle to make southern industry competitive against the odds that attracted industrialists to the "specific competitive advantages" (p. 163) of bound labor in the first place.

Industrial Slavery was almost universally well-received as "an excellent study."[22] But despite the "extraordinary and diligent research," the forceful arguments, and the pungent observations, the book is certainly not without its flaws.[23] At times, Starobin fails to fully explore how reliance on bound labor actually shaped working conditions in industry. Moreover, in his vivid descriptions of southern industrial workplaces, it is not always clear that the enterprises he described employed slaves. Frequently *Industrial Slavery* substitutes qualifiers such as "many" or "most" when measuring the overall sig nificance of slave labor in southern industry. This tendency is then wedded to occasional sweeping but unsubstantiated claims, such as "slaves . . . continued to dominate most occupations" (p. 116). Reviewers in economic history, in particular, were troubled by the supposed "lack of theoretical and statistical underpinning" for Starobin's economic analysis.[24]

Ironically, further econometric research by Fred Bateman, one of his critics, demonstrated that if Starobin's numbers and economic theory were shaky his general conclusions were not: "by market dictates, industrial expansion should have occurred" in the antebellum South, Bateman concluded in his own study.[25] Slavery was perfectly compatible with a profitable and competitive industrial sector. If historians were to explain the "failure" of industrialization in the South, the alleged unprofitability of slave-based industry was not the answer. As Kenneth Stampp himself pointed out, Starobin had demonstrated, without sophisticated econometric techniques, "the adaptability of slavery to industrial activities" four years before *Time on the Cross* (1974).[26]

Yet, in the final analysis, Starobin's Marxian assessment was that slavery and full industrialization were ultimately incompatible. He simply maintained that the point of contradiction had not been reached during the antebellum period. This was both the most compelling and controversial question raised by *Industrial Slavery*. Far more significant than patterns of investment, labor cost, and return was the political question raised by industrial slavery: the contested verity of Eugene Genovese's view that "the cause of southern industrialization demanded above all the destruction of the slave regime" and the liquidation of its dominant class, the southern planters.[27] For Genovese, southern industrialists who threw in their lot with the slave regime were blindly committed to a social order that ran contrary to their class interests. In contrast, Starobin found the accommodation of slave-owning industrialists to secessionist politics far less problematic. Indeed, in the final chapter of *Industrial Slavery* he suggested that there had been successive campaigns for slave-based industrialization in the Old South which coincided with declining cotton prices, fears of political impotence, impediments to the geographical expansion of slavery, and southern dreams of autarky and national independence. This vision culminated in a declaration of southern sovereignty which of necessity expressed the confidence of the slaveholding class that industrialization could occur on its own terms.[28]

To be sure, Starobin was perfectly aware that the southern oligarchy could ill-afford the development of an indigenous bourgeoisie or white working class. But he argued that in their drive for regional self-sufficiency slaveowners were able to contain these dangers. Even as industrial slavery was encouraged, certain sectors of both the skilled and unskilled labor markets were reserved as an exclusive sphere for whites. Working-class objections to slave competition resulted in specific color bars, not total racial exclusion from southern industry. Here, in fact, may be the antebellum origins of what has come to be called the "segmented" labor market, which stamped the industrial economy of the New South, and indeed, the United States as a whole, with a persistent racial division of labor. As for the threat of a rising bourgeoisie, Starobin insisted that the expansion of slavery into industry strengthened the southern commitment to the peculiar institution and assured that the slaveholding class would "maintain their hegemony" (p. 231) even in the face of industrial development. This argument was essentially an adaptation of Barrington Moore's much-maligned "Prussian Road" thesis, which Starobin alluded to in the final footnote of his text.[29]

One otherwise sympathetic reviewer, Harold Woodman, chided Starobin for this "unhistorical" suggestion; at bottom, an industrial slaveowning class was an impossible paradox, Woodman maintained.[30] While Genovese himself appears not to have publicly sharpened the differentiation between Starobin's position and his own on this question, southern historians still dispute if— and more reasonably, when—slavery and industrial capitalism were mutually exclusive elements of southern political economy.[31] As the econometricians Fred Bateman and Thomas Weiss note, "whether an entire industrial system based on slave labor could have evolved remains an intriguing question."[32] Unfortunately, Starobin's narrative halted at the very moment the possibility was put to the test. For the answer, if there is one, likely is to be found in an industrial history of the Confederacy. War made state-sponsored industrial development imperative. Some historians have noted the significance of this development, but few have evaluated the direct contribution of slave labor to the process of rapid military industrialization.[33]

The historiography of the New South, as well, frequently revolves around the putative relationship between bound labor and economic backwardness. Jonathan Wiener has argued that "Genovese's analysis of the slaveowners applies equally well to their postwar heirs" in the agricultural sector, where a commitment to extremely coercive labor relations supposedly entailed hostility to industrial development.[34] The implications of *Industrial Slavery*, however, suggest that historians might consider the ability of postbellum industrialists to accommodate unfree labor relations to their vision of southern modernization. Starobin's view that the competitive disadvantages restraining southern industry simultaneously encouraged reliance on a bound labor force in the sectors that did develop, might apply equally to the postbellum political economy. Advocates of a New South based on industry came up against familiar constraints: weak home markets, lack of capital and infrastructure, a poorly developed and isolated labor market, and a national industrial economy dominated by northern firms.[35] Frequently the best way for southern industry to gain an edge was to keep wages low, severely restrict the power and mobility of labor, and even promote a new form of "industrial slavery": convict labor.[36]

Starobin himself never had much of an opportunity to further this debate, both because he quickly moved on to other issues and because of the tragic end of his career. But his turn to new sources and new questions in 1969 and 1970, raised sensitive historiographic and political issues. Starobin was acutely conscious of the fact that the "traditional sources available for the study of slavery," on which *Industrial Slavery* relied, "present slavery entirely from the white man's point of view." Consequently, he began to devote himself to the study of documents which could provide "an approach to black history from the point of view of the blacks."[37] This emphasis on "bottom up" sources coincided with his growing commitment to the cause of the Black Panther party. His second book, *Denmark Vesey: The Slave Conspiracy of 1822* (1970), was dedicated to Fred Hampton and Bobby Seale, and the royalties were contributed to the Panthers. Yet as his political radicalism increased, his scholarly interpretation of the slave correspondence he had unearthed became less compatible with the black nationalist perspective he sought to embrace. In contrast to his focus on resistance in *Industrial Slavery*, he began to consider the delicate issues of slave accommodation, privilege, and betrayal.

In a controversial paper (later published in *The Journal of Social History*) presented at the 1969 Wayne State Convocation on the Black Man, he used slave letters to demonstrate the accommodative role of black slavedrivers and houseservants. At a time when militant blacks frequently challenged the fitness of whites to teach or write African-American history, Starobin's emphasis of slave loyalty to slaveowners evoked hostile criticism from the black scholars on the panel. Possibly the painful dilemma of a white historian teaching and writing black history mirrored his ongoing struggle to reconcile professionalism and revolutionism, the personal and the political. In a eulogy for Starobin, Julius Lester, one of the Wayne State panelists, openly lamented that he had not later reminded him that "there is no contradiction" between scholarship and revolutionary commitment, between being white and supporting black liberation: that "to be a good scholar is to be constantly involved in committing revolutionary deeds."[38]

As historians begin the process of evaluating the sixties, and the impact of that era on U.S. history, the historical profession, and their personal lives, the tragedy of Robert Starobin continues to reverberate. Some may still regard him as one of the casualties of the excesses and confusions that beset the New Left in its latter days. Beyond this contested ground, however, his work speaks to some of the most enduring and valuable intellectual and cultural legacies of the movement. Starobin and other New Leftists who entered the academy believed that partisan scholarship was no less rigorous and no more compromised than the tradition of alleged neutral "objectivity." Much of his generation's work has demonstrated the essential truth of this claim, and American historical writing is much the richer for it. Furthermore, as Starobin and others hoped, there is a growing recognition that the diverse experiences of African-Americans, women, and other minorities deserve not just a place in the American historical narrative, but are central to it. And in order to rewrite American history from this perspective, historians now routinely consult evidence that speaks directly from that experience, in the voice of its protagonists. Finally, this appreciation of subjectivity has been extended to scholars themselves, and to the efforts of women and minorities to claim a right to define their history on their own terms. Certainly historians still struggle with the unresolved issues of scholarship and race raised by Starobin's antagonists at Wayne State two decades ago.[39] But as the renewed and more mature debates about identity, intellectual authority, and difference illustrate, it is well worth asking how personal experience shapes historical writing, and how selfhood shapes historical consciousness.

The revisionist historiography of slavery was in the vanguard of these transformations, in part because slavery and race have been such powerful undercurrents in the nation's history and yet were so glaringly absent from white historical consciousness. Through *Industrial Slavery* and his other work, Robert Starobin made a small but significant contribution to this field. Despite his desire to empathize with and champion the cause of the historical burden of those who endured bondage, his ultimate assessment of slavery was characteristically pessimistic. In bleak words, Starobin wrote, "those who think that slaves could not be used in industry misunderstand the versatility of bondage. Those who think that repression of men is impossible without force misjudge the relationships between rulers and ruled."[39] Indeed, his work still stands as a powerful corrective to the notions that bound labor only appears in societies fully committed to agrarianism, and that the history of racial oppression will end as a result of human progress.

Alex Lichtenstein, Department of History, Florida International University, Miami, is author of " 'That Disposition to Theft With Which they Have been Branded': Moral Economy, Slave Management, and the Law," Journal of Social History 21 *(Spring 1988): 413–40, and is completing a manuscript on convict labor in the New South.*

I would like to thank Sybil Lipschultz for suggesting that I write this essay, and for her helpful comments along the way. Thanks also to Greg Bush, Dan Cohen, Jim O'Brien, Brian Peterson, Joyce Peterson, and Darden Pyron for their timely help.

1. Robert H. Abzug and Stephen E. Maizlish, eds., *New Perspectives on Race and Slavery in America: Essays in Honor of Kenneth M. Stampp* (1986). This *Festschrift* was dedicated to the memory of Robert Starobin.

2. On the entry of New Left scholars into the profession, see Jonathan Wiener, "Radical Historians and the Crisis in American History, 1959–1980," *Journal of American History* 76 (September 1989): 399–434; Peter Novick, *That Noble Dream: The "Objectivity" Question and the American Historical Profession* (1988), pp. 415–68; Paul Buhle, ed., *History and the New Left: Madison, Wisconsin, 1950–1970* (1990).

3. Peter J. Parish, *Slavery: History and Historians* (1989), p. 98.

4. Much of this background is gleaned from Ira Berlin's perceptive foreword to Robert S. Starobin, ed., *Blacks in Bondage: Letters of American Slaves* (1988, rpt. of 1974 edition), p. v, and the full biographical account in Linda R. Forcey, "Personality in Politics: The Commitment of a Suicide," Ph.D. diss., State University of New York, Binghamton, 1978, esp. pp. 49–50, 67–69. For a moving discussion of the broken links between Old and New Left, and the possible relationship to Starobin's suicide, see Joseph R. Starobin, *American Communism in Crisis, 1943–1957* (1972), pp. xiii–xv.

5. Robert S. Starobin, ed., *Denmark Vesey: The Slave Conspiracy of 1822* (1970); see also the review by Eric Foner, *New York Review of Books*, 4 November 1971, pp. 38–40.

6. Later published as *Blacks in Bondage*.

7. Robert S. Starobin, "Racism and the American Experience," *Radical America* 5 (Mar.-April 1971): 93–111, p. 98. See also "The Negro: A Central Theme in American History," *Journal of Contemporary History* 3 (1968): 37–53 for an earlier version of this essay.

8. Starobin, "Racism and the American Experience," p. 99; Staughton Lynd, *Class Conflict, Slavery, and the United States Constitution* (1967); Eric Foner, *Free Soil, Free Labor, Free Men: The Ideology of the Republican Party before the Civil War* (1970); Eugene D. Genovese, *The Political Economy of Slavery: Studies in the Economy and Society of the Old South* (1965), and *The World the Slaveholders Made: Two Essays in Interpretation* (1969); Vincent Harding, "Beyond Chaos: Black History and the Search for a New Land," in *Amistad 1* (1970), pp. 267–92. On the shift to "nationalist" claims to black history in the late 1960s, see Novick, *That Noble Dream* pp. 472–91. For a recent powerful restatement of the necessary centrality of race to American historiography, see Nathan I. Huggins, "The Deforming Mirror of Truth: Slavery and the Master Narrative of American History," *Radical History Review* 49 (Winter 1991): 25–48.

9. Frank Freidel, review in *Saturday Review*, 18 July 1970, pp. 32–34; see also V. Jacques Voegeli, review in *Yale Review* 60 (Spring 1971): 449–53, p. 449, for a similar observation.

10. Three recent treatments of slavery historiography are: Charles B. Dew, "The Slavery Experience," in John B. Boles and Evelyn Thomas Nolen, eds., *Interpreting Southern History: Historiographical Essays in Honor of Sanford W. Higginbotham* (1987), pp. 120–61; Parish, *Slavery: History and Historians*; August Meier and Elliot Rudwick, *Black History and the Historical Profession, 1915–1980* (1986), pp. 239–76.

11. Voegeli, *Yale Review* 60 (Spring 1971): 449–53; see also Forcey, "Personality in Politics," p. 154.

12. Kenneth M. Stampp, *The Peculiar Institution: Slavery in the Antebellum South* (1956).

13. See, e.g., Eric Lampard, review in *Economic History Review* 2d ser., 25 (May 1972): 379–80.

14. The iron industry has served as the focus for most other studies of industrial slavery. See, e.g., Charles B. Dew, *Ironmaker to the Confederacy: Joseph P. Anderson and the Tredegar Ironworks* (1966), "Disciplining Slave Ironworkers in the Antebellum South: Coercion, Conciliation, and Accommodation," *American Historical Review* 79 (April 1974): 393–418, and "David Ross and the Oxford Iron Works: A Study of Industrial Slavery in the Early Nineteenth-Century South," *William and Mary Quarterly* 3d ser., 31 (April 1974): 189–224; Ronald L. Lewis, *Coal, Iron and Slaves: Industrial Slavery in Maryland and Virginia, 1715–1865* (1979).

15. Lampard, *Economic History Review* 2d ser., 25 (May 1972): 379–80; Harold D. Woodman, review in *Journal of Southern History* 36 (Nov. 1970): 602–03.

16. Sidney Mintz, *Sweetness and Power: The Place of Sugar in Modern History* (1985), pp. 47–61.

17. The review in *Journal of American History* pointed to this revisionism as his major contribution to the literature. Richard O. Curry, review in *Journal of American History* 58 (December 1971): 747–49.

18. Mark Tushnet, *The American Law of Slavery, 1810–1860: Considerations of Humanity and Interest* (1981), pp. 170–88, suggests, however, that bourgeois legal instruments were incompatible with the use of slaves in industry.

19. On Vesey, see Starobin, *Denmark Vesey*; on Louisiana, Herbert Aptheker, *American Negro Slave Revolts* (1943), pp. 249–51; on the Cumberland Valley "conspiracy," see Charles B. Dew, "Black Ironworkers and the Slave Insurrection Panic of 1856," *Journal of Southern History* 41 (1975): 221–38.

20. Dew, "Disciplining Slave Ironworkers in the Antebellum South," p. 394; Lewis, *Coal, Iron and Slaves*, p. 82.

21. For positive assessments of task work in industry, see Clarence Mohr, *On the Threshold of Freedom: Masters and Slaves in Civil War Georgia* (1986), pp. 179–81; and Dew, "Disciplining Slave Ironworkers in the Antebellum South," pp. 405–06; in agriculture, Philip Morgan, "Work and Culture: The Task System and the World of Lowcountry Blacks," *William and Mary Quarterly* 3d ser., 39 (Oct. 1982): 563–99. Leslie S. Rowland, "The Politics of Task Labor and Independent Production in Lowcountry South Carolina and Georgia," unpublished paper presented at "Cultivation and Culture: Labor and the Shaping of Slave Life in the Americas," Conference at the University of Maryland, College Park, April 1989, offers a critique of this approach and emphasizes instead exploitation over autonomy.

22. F. N. Boney, review in *American Historical Review* (Dec. 1970): 2117–19.

23. Woodman, *Journal of Southern History*.

24. Fred Bateman, review in *Business History Review* 44 (Autumn 1970): 411–13.

25. Fred Bateman and Thomas Weiss, *A Deplorable Scarcity: The Failure of Industrialization in the Slave Economy* (1981), pp. 159–60.

26. Kenneth S. Stampp, "A Humanistic Perspective," in Paul A. David, et al., eds., *Reckoning With Slavery: A Critical Study in the Quantitative History of American Negro Slavery* (1976), p. 13.

27. Genovese, *The Political Economy of Slavery*, p. 181.

28. It should be noted that despite disagreements on the specifics of hiring, treatment, and capitalization of industrial slave labor, Ronald Lewis seems to agree with Starobin's conclusion when he writes that the slaveholding class believed that "if industrialization was necessary to maintain the South's social institutions then slavery must be adapted to industrial expansion" (Lewis, *Coal, Iron and Slaves*, p. 234).

29. Barrington Moore, Jr., *Social Origins of Dictatorship and Democracy: Lord and Peasant in the Making of the Modern World* (1966). On the applicability of the "Prussian Road" to capitalism in the U.S. South, see Genovese, *The Political Economy of Slavery*, pp. 206–07; Jonathan Wiener, "Class Structure and Economic Development in the South, 1865–1955," *American Historical Review* 84 (December 1979): 970–92, and Harold D. Woodman's comment, p. 998; Jonathan Wiener, "Review of Reviews: Barrington Moore's *Social Origins of Dictatorship and Democracy*," *History and Theory* 15 (1976): 146–75; Lawrence Powell, "The Prussians are Coming," *Georgia Historical Quarterly* 71 (Winter 1987): 638–67; Michael O'Brien, "The 19th-Century American South," *The Historical Journal* 24 (September 1981): 751–63; Alexander Lichtenstein, "The Political Economy of Convict Labor in the New South," Ph.D. diss., University of Pennsylvania, 1990, ch. 1.

30. Woodman, *Journal of Southern History*.

31. For a strong recent restatement of the basic antagonism between slavery and industrial development, see Barbara J. Fields, *Slavery and Freedom on the Middle Ground: Maryland During the Nineteenth Century* (1985), pp. 55–57.

32. Bateman and Weiss, *A Deplorable Scarcity*, p. 33.

33. Raimondo Luraghi, *The Rise and Fall of the Plantation South* (1978), pp. 112–32; Mohr, *On the Threshold of Freedom*, pp. 120–89.

34. Jonathan Wiener, *Social Origins of the New South: Alabama, 1860–1885* (1978), p. 206.

35. Gavin Wright, *Old South, New South: Revolutions in the Southern Economy Since the Civil War* (1986).

36. Dwight B. Billings, Jr., *Planters and the Making of the "New South": Class, Politics and Development in North Carolina, 1865–1900* (1979); Philip J. Wood, *Southern Capitalism: The Po-*

litical Economy of North Carolina, 1880–1980 (1986); Stanley Greenberg, *Race and State in Capitalist Development: Comparative Perspectives* (1980); Gerald Jaynes, *Branches Without Roots: Genesis of the Black Working Class in the American South, 1862–1882* (1986); Ronald L. Lewis, *Black Coal Miners in America: Race, Class and Community Conflict, 1780–1980* (1987), ch. 2; Lichtenstein, "Political Economy of Convict Labor."

37. Starobin, ed., *Blacks in Bondage*, pp. xv–xviii.

38. Robert S. Starobin, "Privileged Bondsmen and the Process of Accommodation: The Role of Houseservants and Drivers as seen in their own letters," *Journal of Social History* 5 (Fall 1971): 46–70. See Meier and Rudwick, *Black History and the Historical Profession*, p. 292; Novick, *That Noble Dream* pp. 475–76; Forcey, "Politics and Personality," pp. 158–66; Julius Lester, "On the Suicide of a Revolutionary," in *All is Well* (1976), pp. 279–83 (first published as a eulogy for Robert Starobin in *Liberation*, Spring 1971), for accounts of this significant encounter. See Forcey, "Politics and Personality," esp. pp. 196–214, on Starobin's suicide.

39. Robert S. Starobin, "Disciplining Industrial Slaves in the Old South," *Journal of Negro History* 53 (April 1968): 128.

WILLARD HURST, CONSENSUS HISTORY, AND
THE GROWTH OF AMERICAN LAW

Aviam Soifer

At the end of the 1950s, John Higham identified a new trend among American historians: a search for "a placid, unexciting past" as part of "a massive grading operation to smooth over America's social convulsions."[1] What Higham called the "Cult of the American Consensus" appealed to homogeneity, continuity, and national character as it assaulted the Progressive interpretation of history. Both Higham's influential 1959 essay in *Commentary* and Richard Hofstadter's extended reflection on consensus history in *The Progressive Historians* (1968) claimed that one could date this sea-change to around 1950. The tide then began to run out on economic and regional conflict as the reigning historical motif and to shift massively toward consensus history.[2]

Higham and Hofstadter agreed that Louis Hartz and Daniel Boorstin were the consensus trend-setters. If Louis Hartz actually decried the absence of dissent and diversity as he described a liberal consensus, Daniel Boorstin exemplified the celebration of conservative complacency in the era of McCarthyism for which consensus history is remembered today. Boorstin celebrated the very limitations in American political thought that Hartz sought to understand. In fact, Boorstin so identified with what he promoted as the distinctive American genius of democracy that Hofstadter could proclaim, "Boorstin is the American eagle himself, flourishing in his proper habitat."[3]

Boorstin's undifferentiated Americans had discarded stale European models, employed naive practicality to unite in a stable way of life, and remained largely untroubled by divisive principles or practices. If Boorstin's model seemed a significant departure from the bulk of American historiography prior to 1950, his approach actually echoed American legal history before that date. There are numerous personal and political explanations for Boorstin's journey from Oxford and Yale law degrees and his publication of *The Mys-*

terious Science of the Law (1941) to his role as preeminent consensus historian. But it is deeply ironic that, around 1950, the dominant interpretations of American history and American legal history switched places almost completely.

It was in 1950 that Willard Hurst's *The Growth of American Law* made it clear that to be a legal historian would mean thereafter that "You're either a Hurstian or a reviser of Hurst."[4] With this book, Hurst changed forever how remembering law ought to be done. Unquestionably, *The Growth of American Law* "represented something new," "dissolved constraints," and helped start Hurst's campaign to expose "the hitherto invisible ways in which the apparently most commonplace incidents of a legal order illuminate social values."[5] The legal process approach began to supersede legal realism in American law schools in the wake of World War II, but Hurst's book actually was the first sustained example of legal realist history. Initial reviews recognized it as a pioneering effort. If anything, time has enhanced Hurst's achievement, though Hurst's own role is often forgotten. He is the legal historian who broke out of the limits of traditional legal history. His work made him "the leading exponent and practitioner of an external historiography."[6]

Hurst's approach moves far beyond the traditional box of autonomous legal doctrine; he concentrates instead on economic and social factors that continuously interfere with any and all efforts through law "to order men's affairs according to rational weighing of values and the means of achieving them" (*The Growth of American Law*, p. 25). His tale actually is a grim account of both crucial regulatory omissions and actions that undercut whatever creativity and commonwealth ideals remained from the eighteenth century. Hurst notes, moreover, that in legal planning and responses since about 1870 there has been precious little creativity, and virtually no success. Thus, "[t]he law has no very proud story to tell of itself" (p. 17).

Even as the trend in American history moved toward Boorstin's celebratory American exceptionalism, Hurst's book first took American legal history outside and away from the conservative, consensus-driven mode.[7] It is paradoxical that Willard Hurst's great innovative work is now often inaccurately categorized—and dismissed—as an example of consensus history. Moreover, most American historians ignored Hurst's work and hardly discovered the category of legal history beyond the courts for several more decades.[8]

Forty years later, it is necessary to puncture some myths about the book and its author. In particular, the dragons now to be coaxed from their caves are the prevalent assumptions: (1) that Willard Hurst assumes consensus in American legal history, and (2) that he celebrates it. Actually, Hurst tells a tale of dissensus. Hurst offers a detailed declension history in which he concentrates on vital influences on law from outside the doctrinal cubbyholes that dominate legal thought. The book has a vivid undertone of understated jeremiad. Hurst critiques developments in American law outside courthouses and beyond familiar tales of great lawyers and judges. He tracks missed opportunities. Yet, in the tradition of the Wisconsin historical school, Hurst remains a committed reformer rather than a cynical observer.

Pictures and paradoxes illuminate the statistical detail and painstakingly gathered evidence central to *The Growth of American Law*. Hurst's remarkable attention to, and appreciation for, institutional details is a noteworthy part of his achievement. Here, certainly, is an extraordinary scholar: a master of both the microscope and the telescope. Paradoxically, he is able to combine incredible attention to detail with direct treatment of some of the biggest questions society confronts. It is worth exploring how this doubting optimist achieved the extraordinary feat of quietly, studiously establishing a new paradigm.

James Willard Hurst: Some Biographical Notes

Origins and Mysteries

Though he will not see the point, it is worth talking about this man, as well as about the book and the myth that Hurst's work is generally representative of consensus history. Hurst is a man who never seemed ambitious for prestige or power. He repeatedly had unusual opportunities to demonstrate this quality in real life, as well as in theory.

J. Willard Hurst was born just across the Wisconsin border in Rockford, Illinois. His father was in the business of showing movies while Willard was growing up. The week of Willard's birth on October 6, 1910, newspapers reported an air race from Chicago to New York; a republican revolution in Portugal; the discovery of a new star by a woman working at the Harvard Observatory; impending arrests in the bombing of the *Times* Building in Los Angeles; and turmoil over socialists, Democrats, suffragists, and the world oil market. Charles Evans Hughes let it be known that he was about to leave the New York governorship to take a seat on the United States Supreme Court, and Justice William Moody announced that he was about to resign, thereby giving President Taft another Supreme Court appointment; want ads for other job openings specified "a girl (white)" or "reliable, settled German or Scandinavian woman for housekeeping."[9]

In October 1910, Louis Brandeis's battle with the Taft administration over environmental protection in the Pinchot-Ballinger congressional hearings had ended formally only a few months earlier, but Brandeis was busier than usual. He was struggling to resolve the long New York garment industry strike while remaining immersed in preliminary railroad rate hearings, a crucial round in his nine-year battle against the New Haven Railroad. This was also the time when Brandeis first became friendly with the LaFollettes. In December, Robert LaFollette sent Brandeis a confidential draft of the statement announcing the creation of the National Progressive Republican League.[10] Lest anyone maintain an overly romantic view of Jeffersonian yeomen in the good old days supporting one another while assiduously protecting civil rights and liberties, it should be noted that in Hurst's home town, Rockford, Illinois, approximately one hundred immigrant workers were arrested for failure to register for the World War I draft. Dozens faced deportation after they were released from jail more than a year later.[11]

Willard Hurst is remarkably self-effacing. Though personal details are scarce, it is well-known that he went east to attend Williams College. This apparently was entirely his own decision, inspired by reading Emerson and Thoreau as a high school student. His parents took him on a trip to visit eastern colleges, and he was immediately smitten with Williams. There, he was influenced by his history and economics professors. He credits mandatory chapel only with instilling his appreciation of Bach, but he concedes that he often heard Reinhold Niebuhr as a guest preacher and was impressed by him.[12] Hurst went on to great success at Harvard Law School, and graduated in 1935. Before he clerked for Justice Brandeis in the 1936 Term, Hurst worked for a year as a research assistant to Felix Frankfurter at Harvard. Though Hurst took Harvard by storm, he remains critical of his own legal studies. He told one interviewer that Harvard Law School was "like a high grade school for plumbers"[13] and told another that, though he attended law school from 1932–35, he could recall hearing the Depression mentioned "only two or three times" in law school classes.[14]

Distinguishing Brandeis

In many respects, Willard Hurst is the Brandeis clerk who most nearly followed the advice of the man known in Washington as "Isaiah." Repeatedly, scholarly studies of Brandeis rely heavily on Hurst's talent for perceptive observation, his remarkable recall, and his basic sense of fairness. Because of the recent Brandeis biography boomlet, Hurst's recollections are familiar to many. But notes of an interview of Willard Hurst done by Samuel Konefsky in 1951 reveal more about Brandeis—and Willard Hurst.

In that interview, Hurst was less critical of Brandeis than David Riesman had been two days earlier. Riesman, who clerked for Brandeis the year before Hurst did, had just provided Konefsky with a startlingly negative portrait of Brandeis.[15] Hurst acknowledged Brandeis's starkly austere habits and the distance Brandeis maintained from his clerks. Unlike Riesman, Hurst did not attribute these traits to miserliness or to rigidity, but saw them as related to

Brandeis's dedication to making it respectable to be "a man of ideas" in the eyes of the common man and to his pursuit of "the secret joys of a thinker." Hurst himself is surely an exemplar of a rare species in academia, a truly modest man. Still, like Brandeis, Hurst clearly aspires to think and write for the ages. Enhanced status for the thinker is vital. "[L]ife in community may become both a source and a guaranty of the full realization of the individual human spirit"[16] only if the university succeeds in the study of the particular for the sake of the general.

After his clerkship, not only did Willard Hurst return to a university in the hinterlands (as Brandeis repeatedly urged promising young people to do), but he listened to Brandeis's specific suggestion that he contact Dean Lloyd Garrison about a teaching job at the University of Wisconsin.

Hurst planted himself in Wisconsin, the place Brandeis and other Progressives considered the model for their vision of experimental federalism. Elizabeth Brandeis Raushenbush, an economist at the University of Wisconsin, played a major role, along with her husband, Paul, in creating and publicizing Wisconsin's pioneering unemployment insurance scheme. Justice Brandeis not only took great pride in his daughter's accomplishments, but he repeatedly invoked Wisconsin as a model while he advised President Roosevelt and other New Dealers about how to cope with the Depression. Hurst signed on directly to "the Wisconsin idea"—the faith that academics at Wisconsin put into gathering facts, thereby learning of and acknowledging limitations, yet remaining committed both to education and to reform as crucial duties. Affirmative engagement in one's community was crucial to make life worth living.

For Willard Hurst, as for Brandeis, the function of government involved "a positive duty through cooperative aid to set men free from the tyrannies that otherwise might be imposed by nature and other human beings."[17] A central point throughout Hurst's work was that by supplying order in any form, government involved numerous series of choices. In frontier communities and New Deal agencies alike, fundamental normative decisions established the crucial legal framework within which groups and individuals made further, relatively fettered choices. Therefore, the obligation of the academic was to learn about and become involved in reforming government.

In a wonderfully characteristic letter Hurst wrote to Felix Frankfurter early in 1938—a letter Hurst obviously typed rather badly himself, using the same method he still uses to give students and colleagues meticulous single-spaced pages of comments on their drafts—Hurst listed and discussed nine factors he had considered as he weighed an offer to go to Yale Law School at a higher rank and nearly twice the salary he was receiving at Wisconsin.[18] The letter is noteworthy for its lack of sycophancy that Frankfurter, a self-styled master of "personalia," tended to receive as well as to dish out.

Hurst discounted salary concerns because "I have no one to support except myself, and not the slightest immediate possibility of marrying." (It is unclear when Hurst began commuting to see Frances Wilson on a single car, gas-powered train from Madison to Rockford—with a stop at Beloit for the train-man's dinner—but they married in 1941). Hurst conceded that professional recognition would be easier to achieve at Yale. Yet he worried that one "may be encouraged to bask in the reflected prestige." He added, "I suppose it is on the whole desirable to want professional recognition; quaere if there may not be more of a spur to winning it honestly where one's product won't bear in the background the reassuring trademark, made-in-New Haven." It was another factor, however, that seemed crucial in a letter that reads more as a statement of why Hurst already had decided to stay at Wisconsin than the musings of someone seeking advice to follow.

Hurst considered Wisconsin "just about an ideal 'laboratory' situation fromthe [sic] standpoint of studying the legislative process: a state in which there is a long tradition of political experiment, which seems to go on pretty well even when there is not a La Follette ascendency; and some first rate civil service people . . . within a ten minute walk of the campus." Connecticut, in contrast, "isn't a live or progressive state legislatively (if, indeed, it is any respect other than as a commuters' reservation)." So Willard decided to stay in Madison for a few more years "particularly because of this extraordinarily interesting state government machinery here on the doorstep."

It is hardly surprising, therefore, that the case study that Willard Hurst and Lloyd Garrison chose to pursue through the first volume of their pioneering *Law in Society* casebook of 1941 involved various ways that law in Wisconsin intersected with a widow's claim for damages after her husband, a carnival worker, was crushed beneath a company tractor. The casebook includes wit-nesses' accounts that vividly portray the gory scene as Gervase Hannon's guts literally poured out before his death. But this prototype for the law and society movement was designed to equip undergraduates as well as law students with enough sophistication about law to realize that neither legislative, ju-dicial, nor administrative treatment of Hannon's case—nor of any other case large or small—is inevitable or in itself commanded by law.

There was no claim to neutrality here. *Law in Society*, and more vividly Hurst's later work, represent elements of a radical reformist, one might even say utopian, agenda. Facts may always caution and generally suggest decline rather than improvement over time, making the use of "Growth" in the title of several of Willard's books seem problematic at first glance. Yet, with a combination of Holmesian toughness and faith, Hurst is an educator. The facts matter. Facts set severe limits, yet change must still be attempted. With Holmes, he has "no belief in panaceas and almost none in sudden ruin."[19] At best, growth leads to decline and death, yet growth still merits attention and care.

In a 1942 article setting forth a "Research Program" for legal history, Hurst doubted that each generation learns much from its predecessors. "But," he continued, "civilization is a minority affair. To believe in education is to believe that there are opportunities to apply informed, humane reason to influence the course of events."[20] Almost immediately, Hurst was off to Washington to serve in the general counsel's office of the Board of Economic Warfare. He negotiated hard to use the wartime contracting power to improve the working conditions of Bolivian miners and the like. Soon thereafter, he joined the Navy and was appointed to work on the famous *Cramer* treason case, which ultimately led to his first published work in legal history, a detailed study of the origins of the law of treason.[21]

As early as 1945, Hurst argued that there seemed "no reason except tradition, never itself adequately founded, why legal history should be narrowed to a study of the resolution of social conflicts by litigation."[22] In an essay analyzing books written by nonlawyers about Wisconsin, Michigan, Montana, and Oklahoma, Hurst noted that perceptions about the relative role of legal institutions in history by laymen "may be the fresher and the more unbiased."[23] He emphasized what he called the colonial relationship of raw material-producing states to older regions, the persistent tension between debtors and creditors in American history, and "the surge of clashing interests of all kinds."[24] Even in 1945, he focused on the repeated "failure," "default," "do-nothing line," and "inertia" of government. To help explain the failure of legal controls, Hurst explored the distinction between an unhealthy balance of power on one hand, and social inertia and simple failure of intelligence on the other. Ranging from attention to the dogmatic application of the crop-farm ideal in Montana to the rise of the Ku Klux Klan in the 1920s that suggested "that the victory of reason and decency is precarious and open to constant challenge," Hurst hardly proclaimed an upbeat American consensus. He even doubted progress. Instead, he stressed the wasteful exploitation of natural resources; "waves of agrarian, lower-middle, and middle-class revolt;" and "public acquiescence in, and even approval of, shortsighted taking of public wealth for immediate private gain."[25]

Though in this review the nexus of law and the economy emerged as the most pervasive interrelation, Hurst insisted that more attention ought to be paid to the effects of other types of power on legal institutions. He specifically mentioned the impact of family, church, education, and technology. Even within the law, he claimed, a narrow focus on litigation seemed "particularly absurd" in an age facing the central problem of "whether men will be able to use the power of the politically organized community to secure the basic conditions of a decent life for the individual, without thereby destroying the very values they are trying to realize."[26]

Hurst's vigorous doubts were not tailored to fit the exuberant fashion of post–World War II America. Instead, he called for an entirely new approach. And the rest *is* history: our best legal history still follows the background theory initially sketched and then developed by Willard Hurst.

The Scholarly Activist and the Artist

How are we to evaluate Willard Hurst's extraordinary scholarly career? Let us begin with Winslow Homer. Surely neither the analogy nor even the relevance to Willard Hurst is immediately clear—beyond the initial(s) similarity. But some readers may be persuaded that the analogy is illuminating: Winslow Homer is almost universally acclaimed as the greatest American artist of the nineteenth century. Moreover, it has proved difficult to assign influences to his work or to pigeon-hole him. Winslow Homer developed an original American vision by breaking with convention and emphasizing modernity and nationalism in his scrupulous attention to ordinary people in commonplace acts and places. He also emphasized the importance of the fugitive, transitory effects of natural light.[27]

Winslow Homer was the second son of a marriage that merged old, somewhat threadbare New England family lines. He was born in Boston in February 1836. That same month, Jason Lathrop set up a crude printing press on a stump on the western shore of Lake Michigan and printed the record and short constitution of "The Pike Creek Claimants Union."[28] Through Willard Hurst, Lathrop and his comrades will always be linked with use of the legal order—even by a group of "illegal" squatters—to promote the release of energy against a backdrop of a threatening physical and social environment.[29] And Winslow Homer's work, particularly the work that came after his portraits of the middle class at leisure in the 1870s, concentrates on a struggle against nature, often presented from the unusual perspective of the hunted, rather than the hunter.[30] Both Hurst and Homer offer powerful, gloomy perspectives on the post–Civil War period, when "an unpatterned, radically important drift and default of policy"[31] became the norm and when innocents became the obvious, but largely unnoticed, victims.

Homer got his start doing lithographs for a well-known Boston firm. He became known as an unusually skilled illustrator, and did etchings of the Civil War for the era's leading magazines that had begun to cater to a burgeoning middle-class readership. Homer's Civil War sketches were outside the canon in several senses: he concentrated on enlisted men, not their officers, for example, and he drew the dreary routine of daily camp life rather than dramatic battle scenes. Moreover, this period marked the beginning of his lifelong commitment to drawing models in the natural light of out-of-doors, rather than in the studio. Homer's credo was, "If a man wants to be an artist, he must never look at pictures."[32]

It already may be possible to glean at least some resonance between Homer's renowned attention to democratic details and Willard's own artistry. ("Resonance" is so conveniently vague and distensible a term, covering so many analytic sins, it is just the sort of word to make even mild-mannered Willard Hurst angry.) Hurst's credo, and more unusually also his work, push us outside the judicial framework. He wants us to concentrate on affirmative efforts to use law to supply a better framework to resolve societal conflicts, despite a long national history of drift. Legal institutions are not to be found within the four corners of appellate decisions, which are primarily the museums and galleries of the wealthy and well-connected.

Willard Hurst is like Winslow Homer in another way: he is able to convey the mood and personality of individuals in the context of their environments with unusual sympathy but without actually sketching in the details of their faces. Both are adept at conveying identification with victims, albeit generally without personal details. Homer's legendary insistence on privacy and his withdrawal from urban art centers to the rugged, isolated coastline of Prout's Neck, Maine enhanced the power of his art. (But Hurst is certainly no recluse. Frances and their children, as well as countless students, followers, and friends demonstrate that here any Homeric analogy breaks down.) Moreover, the bleakness of Homer's *The Fox Hunt* (1893), *Undertow* (1886), *The Gulf Stream* (1899) or *Right and Left* (1909) find no parallel in Hurst's work. In these paintings, Homer was almost obsessed with the imminent threat or actual moment of death. He conveyed a painful fact of life with gripping imagery. Willard Hurst also wrestles repeatedly with harsh evidence without flinching, yet he somehow remains gentler and more optimistic than Homer. Winslow Homer died on September 29, 1910, exactly one week before Willard Hurst began his Midwestern sojourn. I express no views on reincarnation.

Virtually all of Willard Hurst's work demonstrates the difficulties and limitations of reform. Yet he remains entirely committed to the effort to gather the facts to help liberate us from past mistakes. More basically, Willard Hurst believes with quiet passion that law can be used to push back our limits somewhat, and that such an effort is worth a lifetime's dedication.

Prairie Home Companion
Why do the Hursts seem to belong so convincingly in a prairie-style house, designed in the Frank Lloyd Wright style by one of Wright's students? Per-

haps because the entire house revolves around a solid center, the equivalent of "middle-class values" in Hurst's work. Because its efficiency and clear lines obviously appealed to them. And because Wright and his students may be associated with building beautiful, relatively reasonably-priced and practical homes that fit comfortably into the environment. Their designs paid attention to interior as well as exterior details, considered empty spaces along with solid structures as building blocks in design, and did not try to isolate either interior or exterior from their natural surroundings. So it is no surprise that the man who has carved a scholarly home in a context that previously went unnoticed is very much at home in this home in his community. Hurst has pointed out patterns in what seemed an unapproachable wilderness of social and economic forces that create law. This pioneer showed that hedges and walls could not exclude the world from law. Moreover, he suggested that they should not.

Frederic Maitland keenly comprehended English legal history not merely through his unmatched archival work, but also because he wrote with understanding about his own ancestral lands and the community in Gloucestershire where he lived. Similarly, Willard Hurst knows much about optimism accompanying daily struggle with the environment because he so intimately knows the American Midwest and its people. There are echoes of Carl Becker and Frederick Jackson Turner in Hurst's work. That they all climbed Bascom Hill at the University of Wisconsin may suggest the force of environmental influence they all championed.[33]

An aspect of Willard Hurst's work that speaks directly to our current concerns, but that has been largely overlooked, is his repeated emphasis on the growing importance of groups. Yet he also sounds a characteristic warning: "Since our thinking did not keep pace with the increasing group emphasis in our life, it was not surprising that shrewd men could warp individualistic symbols of the constitutional ideal to sanction unchecked organized power."[34] But the University of Wisconsin, and the Law School in particular, stand out in American higher education for their longstanding attention to group identification, tracing back to Thorstein Veblen and John R. Commons and emphatically forward until today. These are institutions where groups of scholars repeatedly pierce individualistic cant.

As the personal is also political, the institutional is also individual. By all reports, Willard Hurst has been a vital institutional citizen. On a personal level, he has quietly supported people and scholarly projects with strength and sensitivity. With his help, this community, this group of strong, often prickly individualists, has done a great deal to fulfill both sides of a vital Hurstian paradox: "Individuals realize their humanity only in society, but they realize their individuality only in self-awareness, which consists in some sense of separateness."[35] The University of Wisconsin is different; Willard Hurst is unique. Together, they have done much to "realize their humanity."

The Growth of American Law: **The Book**

The extent to which *The Growth of American Law* departs from the legal history that had come before it, and was not a legal history in any conventional sense, is difficult to recapture, largely because so many of us have been influenced by the work of Willard Hurst, whether or not we are conscious of the impact. In numerous reviews published soon after the book appeared, reviewers repeatedly noted that the book, because it was more physiology than anatomy, said something new and provocative about American law.[36] Perhaps some have forgotten how Willard Hurst achieved his breakthrough. It is worth recalling the book's careful, innovative structure, and then briefly considering its message, which is more jeremiad than apologetics.

Physiology, Not Anatomy

Willard Hurst believes that "[t]he deeper we probe to explain shifts in legal doctrine, the less we are satisfied with what at first seem the practical answers" (*Growth of American Law*, p. 12). Therefore, he examines law from as far outside the doctrinal box as he can get.[37] In doing so, he discovers that the reality underneath the toughness of institutional structure is that "law has been more the creature than the creator of events" (p. 6). His analysis proceeds through the impact of physical, technological, and social facts on law in the United States.[38] He does not deny that ideas matter, however. Hurst insists that "ideas tie in closely with habits of action, and both change institutions" (p. 14). In fact, this pioneer about the impact of economic and social forces on legal institutions maintains that men are the essential moving causes behind change. The key issue is "what they have in their minds, whether they are thinking things through more or less consciously, or are acting out of habit" (p. 15). This hardly seems consistent with the commonplace portrait of Hurst as a pure functionalist, nor with Talcott Parsons's later criticism of Hurst's work for "failing to distinguish three closely related but still . . . importantly different categories, namely the legal, governmental, and the political."[39]

One of the most significant innovations in the book is the structure, which departs from the usual analysis of the three branches of government. Hurst studiously seeks to avoid the customary excessive focus on appellate judicial opinions or on the impact of great individuals or great cases. Instead, the book analyzes five legal institutions: the legislature, the courts, the constitution makers, the bar, and the executive.

Each of these five divisions may be read as a separate essay, but they have common themes, developed quite schematically within each section as well as in the book's introduction and conclusion. While there is some overlap, there is little repetition. Hurst's clear writing style moves the reader along at a nice clip. Sprinkled throughout the book are marvelous nuggets of buried information from a remarkable array of sources, along with Hurst's clear interpretations. He repeatedly indicates when there is substantial evidence for the general points he makes and when there is not, and he is hardly shy about sharing his judgments.

This meticulous scholar does not hide behind the screen of scholarly neutrality, yet he is more judicious than most scholars and judges who do.[40] Moreover, one can clearly find him anticipating some of the most important subsequent contributions in legal scholarship since 1950, such as Guido Calabresi's work on accidents and social cost (p. 12); Charles Reich's ideas about new property being created by judges out of procedural protections (p. 91); and Morton Horwitz's thesis about the *sub rosa* subsidization of the powerful through judicial decisions and so-called private legal ordering (pp. 72–73, 242–44).

A careful reading of the book discloses flashes of dry humor (e.g., "[t]he earlier casebooks were as bare of assisting or amplifying footnotes as a Dissenters' chapel of sacred ornament," p. 265), and Hurst's fascination with irony helps make the book seem both contemporary and like a product of the late eighteenth century. Even if it is not the case that "There is nothing like a paradox to take the scum off the mind,"[41] Hurst's examination of numerous paradoxes in the main currents of American thought is particularly intriguing. Perhaps the United States has been an unusually legalistic society, for example, because people "were looking for beliefs to which they could hold fast, in a country of change; they also wanted change which would fulfill the promise of a new continent and advance their personal fortunes" (p. 357). And "the extent to which Americans put issues into legal terms and tried to use and control the legal agencies reflected a lesser role for the law" (p. 4). Unlike many of us, however, Hurst does not use paradox to avoid revealing his own position. To the contrary, he is unusually frank about what he believes the facts to be and what he makes of them.

It may be useful to consider one of the book's sections in some detail both to get a sense of where Hurst comes out on the questions he addresses and to begin to examine the criticism that misses the critical fire smoldering beneath Hurst's low-key writing style and his kindly disposition. Section 5, "The Bar," probably constitutes Hurst's most radical scholarly departure. Nobody had ever done such a synthesis before or considered the many ways in which lawyers are a separate institution worthy of examination. While we have had much excellent historical work on the bar since,[42] Hurst's chapter remains one of the very best analyses of the bar's role in American society.

The Bar: "Real Points for Moral Indictment"

Hurst begins this chapter, "The Character of the Lawyer in United States Society," by describing ambivalent popular attitudes toward lawyers. He briefly reviews the central role of lawyers in typical American success stories, along with longstanding, widespread antilawyer sentiment. Hurst then makes a revealing move. He condemns popular criticism for missing "the more real points for moral indictment." These are: first, "the intellectual dishonesty" with which influential lawyers supported private against public interest; next the "inertia" of lawyers despite blatant defects in the administration of justice, "though such defeats robbed ten thousand of their due for every one whose money was misappropriated by a faithless counselor." Finally, Hurst points out that criticism of lawyers for pursuit of their own economic interest "comes with poor grace from generations that subscribed to the ambitions they saw in others" (p. 252).

One should not be misled. In his customary fashion, Hurst builds his generalities from scrupulous attention to details that range from the structure of law firms to education and admission to the bar and include the exceedingly conservative role of bar associations representing a profession whose members on the whole "were among the most unthinkingly and stubbornly individualistic members of the loosely organized American society" (p. 285). Moreover, Hurst does a wonderful job of exploring the tensions within the concept of being a professional in a society dominated by middle-class attitudes—a nation, that is, "characteristically distrustful of speculative thought and the grand manner in action; a society which was interested in what could be accumulated, counted, and used; a society that had concern for righteousness, but under a scale of values formed in a period highly individualistic and competitive in its measure of a man" (pp. 305–06).

At times, Hurst's indictment sounds like some of the best of the contemporary critique of possessive individualism. Any dismissive view of Willard Hurst and of *The Growth of American Law* itself presents something of a mystery. Why isn't Willard Hurst read, or at least claimed as a progenitor, by vehement critics on the Left or the Right in legal education today?

The primary reason, I think, is that Willard Hurst eschews flamboyant passion to such an extent that his passionate criticism has been buried. (Another reason, of course, is that many people do not read the books they talk about, but this is a kind of Hurstian reality test that has little to do with academic arguments.) There is a commonplace, faulty assumption that Willard Hurst is either an extreme, unsophisticated functionalist or one of those post–World

War II apologists for the status quo now generally lumped under the label "consensus historians."[43]

It is true that over and over Hurst suggests an American mainstream. But he hardly celebrates it.[44] The mainstream is a torrent of old forms and beliefs ill-adapted to control the selfish and the powerful. The American character he examines is remarkably short-sighted. At least since 1870, Americans have been recklessly exploiting the environment and one another. All the while, as Hurst puts it, Americans "have demanded their 'rights' and at the same time concerned themselves in fixing the other man's 'duties' " (p. 3).

Additionally, Hurst's work is overlooked or rejected precisely because he downplays the drama of individual lives. He believes that such drama increases our temptation to attribute too much weight to individual contributions. And he can be justifiably criticized for concentrating so much on the facts and faults of the mainstream that he hardly touches upon the unique problems of discrete and insular minorities. There is little about African-Americans, for example, though he does note their omission from the American society he describes, and nothing about Native Americans. But these omissions hardly mean that he embraces the status quo, or that he does not believe deeply that individuals ought to try to resist the trends he decries.

The Growth of American Law is a tale of no easy successes, of towering limitations, and of great complexity. That Hurst offers no panacea does not mean that he is satisfied. Nor does his adamant refusal to engage in conspiracy theorizing connote complacency about the tragic consequences wrought by the largely unplanned combination of overemphasis on production and private power, lack of long-range responsibility, and unconcern for facts. The growth of American law, as Hurst describes it, has not been positive growth. Driven by social and economic forces, unconcerned about conservation, unaware of rampant exploitation, Americans and therefore American legal institutions grow increasingly out of control.

In fact, there is something almost utopian in Willard Hurst's faith in the discovery of facts as the basis for improvement in the face of all the details and trends he has discovered. He recognizes that the political progressivism behind the Wisconsin idea "had the weakness of believing too much in the power of facts and disinterested expertness" (p. 65). Yet Willard Hurst's program remains closely linked to the Progressives, and shares with them a belief in the affirmative obligation of government to act for the general welfare. Nevertheless, he concludes *Growth of American Law* with a pessimistic assessment. He observes: "(1) a diminished political sensitivity, and (2) a growing impersonality in people's dealings with one another. Both worked to give undisciplined freedom to particular interests at the expense of the individual and community life" after 1870 (p. 440).

The book's conclusion, entitled "To . . . Promote The General Welfare," concentrates on the breakdown of the sense of community. Hurst thereby anticipates much of the current debate about republicanism and interest group pluralism and he clearly sides with those who aspire to civic virtue and republicanism. Like them, he has not solved the problem of interdependence; unlike many of them, his vision comes to grips with the sobering lessons of history. While he states that "[g]roup interest was the most dynamic force that played on our law," Hurst somewhat surprisingly invokes John C. Calhoun and the danger Calhoun accurately noted of different interests combining to produce "a spurious expression of majority policy" (pp. 439–40). Where once there was a sense of belonging, and of connection to a community, Hurst sees preoccupation with private business; lack of interest in the efficiency of public institutions; and reduced involvement in, and even appreciation for, politics. Unlike constitutional law scholars who have led the revival of republicanism during the 1980s, however, Hurst does not turn to the courts as a likely source for promoting the general welfare. If he has any hope at all in contemporary legal institutions, it is the possibility of some movement on behalf of the general welfare made by the executive branch of federal and state governments. In this respect, painful experience reminds us how many years ago this book was written.

More fundamentally, Willard Hurst believes in education as crucial and in the gathering of facts as the essence of power. As Keats once said, however, "A fact isn't true until you love it."[45] But Hurst is somewhat a Populist as well as a Progressive. Despite all, Hurst remains a believer somehow in the basic good of humankind. He decries romanticism and demands that the historian, even the generally rugged Holmes, not forget to "respect[] the stubborn resistance of the raw materials."[46] In responding to some of his critics, Hurst declares himself the kind of legal realist who is concerned with the deficiency of political processes and the fragmentation of policy-making into responses to organized groups. He views his Wisconsin forest history as the story of "failure to fulfill commonwealth criteria of rational public policy through adequate accounting for social income and cost, to the detriment of the long-term vitality of the whole society."[47] Behind all the ledger-sheet rhetoric, however, there lurks an engaged, even a quietly enraged, moralist.

Hurst's own values may be evident in his quotation of words used by Felix Frankfurter in praise of Florence Kelley. Frankfurter wrote:

> There are two kinds of reformers whose chief concern has been that earning a living shall not contradict living a life. One type is apt to see evil men behind evils and seeks to rout evil by moral fervor. Florence Kelley belonged to the other, the cooler and more calculating type. Not that she was without passion. But passion was the driving force of her mind, not its substitute. She early realized that damn-

ing facts are more powerful in the long run than flaming rhetoric, and that understanding is a more dependable, because more permanent, ally than the indignation of the moment. . . .[48]

Hurst praised Brandeis because Brandeis "took the oratory out of liberalism . . . [and] put fact in."[49] In a sense, justice and law clerk somehow absorbed so much flinty Yankee reserve while at Harvard that they joined in making it a virtue. As with Winslow Homer, it became part of their artistry and their lives.

Hurst also noted, however, that Brandeis believed that the Supreme Court should be "a sort of Holy Synod, untouchable" and stressed the symbolic aspect of the institution. Hurst's enthusiasm for the power of facts has battered down the symbolic redoubt of the Court, and he has gone beyond the Brandeisian-Wisconsin faith in detached facts and experts. In what seems a neat application of Niebuhrian irony, Hurst instead makes a leap and embraces engaged factfinding and democratic politics without manipulating symbols as the last, best hope.

In many ways, Willard Hurst is the last, best legal realist. He has been the most consistent over time, the legal realist best able to bridge the gap between finding the facts and trying to do something in the real world once the facts are known. In Willard's career there may be no prescription for how to achieve utopia, or even lasting reform, but there is surely an exemplary answer to the charge that legal realism really is nihilism.

Across forty years, *The Growth of American Law* speaks directly to some of our most important academic debates. Discussion of both legal realists and ideas of community and commonwealth again fill academic journals. But many of the debates over the past forty years seem reminiscent of the forty dreary years of wandering in the desert following the exodus from Egypt. Willard decided long ago not to use the J. (for James) in his name. That initial might better fit him if it stood for Joshua. Not the Joshua who was able to get the sun to stand still, nor the Joshua whose trumpet made the walls of Jericho come tumbling down—perhaps those Joshua roles are more fitting for the Richard Posners and Duncan Kennedys of this world. Rather, it is Joshua the scout whom Willard resembles. In the biblical story, there were twelve spies who visited the Promised Land, and found it brimming with milk and honey, but also heavily defended by gigantic warriors. The first ten spies accurately reported what they had seen and were immediately killed by God's plague, apparently for emphasizing the impossibility of the task ahead.[50] Joshua and one other spy also brought back bleak truths about Canaan. But they told that truth with hope. Therefore, only they lived to struggle forward into the promised land.

Aviam Soifer, Boston University School of Law, is most recently the author of "On Being Overly Discrete and Insular: Involuntary Groups and the Anglo-American Judicial Tradition," Washington and Lee Law Review *48 (Spring 1991).*

This essay is an expanded version of a talk given in October 1990 as part of a conference held in Madison, Wisconsin to mark the fortieth anniversary of the publication of *The Growth of American Law* and Willard Hurst's eightieth birthday. Participants discussed Hurst's work and his influence and joined in the hope that Willard Hurst might live to Moses's allotted 120 years, and yet witness struggling steps toward his commonwealth ideal somewhere in this bountiful land.

1. John Higham, "The Cult of the 'American Consensus,' " *Commentary* 27 (1959), pp. 93, 94.

2. Richard Hofstadter, "Conflict and Consensus in American History," in Hofstadter, *The Progressive Historians: Turner, Beard, Parrington* (1968), pp. 421–66. Hofstadter made the important, but often-forgotten, point that consensus history need not be associated with the particular conservative climate in which it originated. Indeed, Hofstadter claimed that his own assertion of consensus history in 1948 in *The American Political Tradition* had its sources in the Marxism of the 1930s (p. 452n9). Two decades later, however, Hofstadter expressed considerable ambivalence about his own position *vis a vis* consensus history. The consensus approach remained useful, Hofstadter claimed, in a way analogous to a picture frame: "it sets the boundaries of the scene and enables us to see where the picture breaks off and the alien environment begins; but it does not provide the foreground or the action, the interest or the pleasure, the consummation itself, whether analytical or esthetic" (p. 453).

3. Hofstadter, *Progressive Historians*, p. 449. The rise of consensus history is complex, of course, and should not be glibly or exclusively connected to the political atmosphere of the early Cold War period. See Michael Rogin, *The Intellectuals and McCarthy: The Radical Specter* (1967).

4. Lawrence Friedman, quoted in David Margolick, "At the Bar," *New York Times*, Mar. 23, 1990, at B5, col. 1. According to Fred Konefsky, most of the scholarship in American legal history since Hurst's *Law and the Conditions of Freedom in the Nineteenth Century* (1956) constitutes footnotes to that book. John Kidwell, "John C. Stedman—An Appreciation," *Wisconsin Law Review* (1984), pp. 567, 569 (quoting Konefsky).

5. Robert Gordon, "Introduction: J. Willard Hurst and the Common Law Tradition in American Legal Historiography," *Law & Society Review* 10 (1975), pp. 9, 45, 54. Gordon's study remains an exemplary overview of American legal historiography, as well a particularly insightful commentary on Hurst's contributions. For a neat companion piece, illustrating the importance of Hurst's work by criticizing and expanding upon it, see Harry Scheiber, ibid., p. 57. A good Hurst bibliography through 1975 is available in the same volume of *Law and Society Review*, pp. 326–33; another accompanies a *festschrift* in his honor published in *Wisconsin Law Review* 1093 (1980).

6. *Wisconsin Law Review* 1093 (1980), p. 12. These days, the very idea of an "outsider's perspective" is controversial, see, e.g., Marc Galanter's book review of Robert Burt, *Two Jewish Justices: Outcasts in the Promised Land* (1988), *Law and Social Inquiry* 14 (1989), pp. 507. Gordon is surely accurate, however, when he stresses how innovative Hurst was in adopting an outsider's perspective in contrast to previous legal historians. Nevertheless, Hurst has been subject to criticism for not adequately attending to the perspective of those outside his primary concern with the routine business, institutions, and ordinary people of society. Thus, rebels and outlaws, ethnic and racial minorities are rarely subjects for Hurst's scholarly attention. For critical commentary see, e.g., Eugene Genovese, "Law and the Economy in Capitalist America: Questions for Mr. Hurst on the Occasion of His Curti Lectures," *American Bar Foundation Research Journal* (1985), p. 113; Sidney Harring & Barry Strutt, "Lumber, Law, and Social Change: The Legal History of Willard Hurst," *American Bar Foundation Research Journal* (1985), p. 123; and sources cited *infra* note 37.

7. See generally Morton Horwitz, "The Conservative Tradition in the Writing of American

Legal History," *American Journal of Legal History* 17 (1973), p. 281; Stanley Katz, "Looking Backward: The Early History of American Law," *University of Chicago Law Review* 33 (1966), p. 867.

8. That discovery is probably best symbolized by the decision to award the 1978 Bancroft Prize to Morton Horwitz's *The Transformation of American Law* (1979). A recent indication of the extent of previous neglect is Peter Novick's *That Noble Dream: The 'Objectivity Question' and the American Historical Profession* (1988). For all that book's meticulous research and breadth of coverage, it discussed legal history only in the recent context of the Critical Legal Studies movement of the late 1970s (pp. 555–57). Novick did devote a few pages to the Legal Realism movement of the 1920s and 1930s (pp. 145–50, 288–89), but he discussed the Realists for their parallels with historical relativism, and not for any of their views of legal history.

9. *New York Times*, Oct. 6–10, 1910.

10. Philippa Strum, *Louis D. Brandeis: Justice for the People* (1984), pp. 133–95.

11. William Preston, Jr., *Aliens and Dissenters* (1963), pp. 90, 253–55.

12. Hurst also says he was greatly influenced by Karl Polanyi's *The Great Transformation* (1944). Author's conversations with Victor Brudney, Clark Byse, Stanley Kutler, and Willard Hurst, October 1990.

13. Samuel Konefsky, Interview Notes, Sept. 14, 1951, Book 1, pp. 6–11, graciously made available to me by his son, Fred Konefsky.

14. William Moore, "Profile: Emeritus Professor Willard Hurst," *Gargoyle* 16 (1986), pp. 3, 4. Hurst recalled, "I was pretty much given the notion that the law was as much a separate and distinct piece of reality as, let's say, astronomy." Reminiscing last October about Harvard Law School in the mid-1930s, Willard and Carl Auerbach traded stories about the noticeable absence of realists and about how students incurred the wrath of Dean Pound for daring to invite Karl Llewellyn to speak at the Law School Forum. Conversation with author, October 1990.

15. Konefsky Interview, Sept. 12, 1951, Book 1, pp. 1–5. Riesman recently published an autobiographical sketch, "Becoming an Academic," in Bennett Berger, ed., *Authors of Their Own Lives: Intellectual Autobiographies by Twenty American Sociologists* (1990), in which Riesman presents a toned-down, still quite negative, recollection of his year clerking for Brandeis.

16. J. Willard Hurst, "Legal History: A Research Program," *Wisconsin Law Review* (1942), pp. 323, 324.

17. Donald Richberg, "The Industrial Liberalism of Mr. Justice Brandeis," in Felix Frankfurter, ed., *Mr. Justice Brandeis* (1932), p. 138.

18. Stanley Kutler found this letter, dated January 3, 1938, in the Frankfurter Papers, Manuscript Division, Library of Congress, and graciously made it available to me. This marks only the first of many attempts by Yale and Harvard Law Schools to lure Willard Hurst, including using the possibility of the deanship at Yale. See, e.g., Laura Kalman, *Legal Realism at Yale: 1927–1960* (1986).

19. J. Willard Hurst, *The Growth of American Law: The Law Makers* (1950), p. 209, quoting Holmes.

20. J. Willard Hurst, "Legal History: A Research Program," *Wisconsin Law Review* (1942), pp. 323, 324.

21. *Cramer v. United States*, 320 U.S. 730 (1943). The *Harvard Law Review* articles Willard produced out of that wartime experience were republished, with additional material, in J. Willard Hurst, *The Law of Treason in the United States* (1971).

22. J. Willard Hurst, "The Uses of Law in Four 'Colonial' States of the American Union," *Wisconsin Law Review* (1945), p. 577.

23. Ibid., p. 579.

24. Ibid.

25. Ibid., p. 589.

26. Ibid., p. 577. Hurst was careful to note that these opinions were those of the author, not of the United States Navy "with which he is at present connected."

27. See Nicolai Cikovsky, Jr., "An Original Form of Art Speech," *Winslow Homer* (1990), pp. 35–47. See also James T. Flexner, *The World of Winslow Homer, 1836–1910* (1966).

28. J. Willard Hurst, *Law and the Conditions of Freedom in the Nineteenth-Century United States* (1956), pp. 3–6.

29. It may be worthy of note that only eighteen years after the Pike's Creek, squatters sought both legal and extralegal means to secure their property in the place that became Racine, Wisconsin. Racine was where a fugitive slave, Joshua Glover, was captured by a slave owner from Missouri. Glover's capture and rescue led to the dramatic tale of interposition by Wisconsin legal authorities against federal slave law and their defiance of federal judicial power, made famous by Chief Justice Taney's unanimous decision asserting broad federal *habeas corpus* jurisdiction in *Abelman v. Booth*, 62 U.S. 506 (1859)

30. Theodore E. Stebbins,, Jr. et al., *A New World: Masterpieces of American Painting, 1760–1910* (1983), p. 332. See also L. Goodrich, *Winslow Homer* (1944); and Cikovsky. I leave to others discussion of Homer's important series on African-Americans in the South, drawn after his visit to Virginia in 1875. But his "Cotton Pickers" in particular seems to capture dignity in the face of oppressive working conditions in a unique way, just as the full sketch of the faces of the two women was unique in Homer's artistic career. See generally Mary Ann Calo, "Winslow Homer's Visits to Virginia During Reconstruction," *American Art Journal* (Winter 1980): 5.

31. Hurst, *Law and the Conditions of Freedom*, p. 53. Through this default and drift, Hurst continued, "the legal order profoundly affected a new challenge of social environment to liberty."

32. Cikovsky, p. 35.

33. See Carl L. Becker, "Kansas" and "Frederick Jackson Turner," *Everyman His Own Historian: Essays on History and Politics* (1935). Though Turner decried the rise of American conformity, in 1926 he still hoped that the West "may yet make new contributions to America, by its union of democratic faith and innovation with a conservative subconsciousness" (Frederick Jackson Turner, *The Significance of Sections in American History*, 1932, p. 255). See generally Merle Curti and Vernon Carstensen, *The University of Wisconsin* (1949).

34. J. Willard Hurst, *Justice Holmes on Legal History* (1964), p. 39.

35. Ibid., p. 15.

36. For particularly snappy examples of the general enthusiasm for the book, see, e.g., John Frank, *Yale Law Journal* 59 (1950), p. 1381; Frank Horack, Jr., *Harvard Law Review* 64 (1951), p. 866; Robert Hunt, *Iowa Law Review* 35 (1950), p. 730; and John Roche, *University of Pennsylvania Law Review* 99 (1950), p. 263. Many others, including Max Radin, Thomas Reed Powell, Philip Kurland, and Phil Neal from the law schools, and a smattering of political scientists, historians, and sociologists, heaped praises on what they repeatedly called a pioneering book. A compilation of these early reviews is available in *Law and Social Inquiry* 10 (1976), p. 330. There were a few exceptions to the general run of rave reviews. The most interesting were those by Mark DeWolfe Howe, who derided Hurst's "faith in statistics" and criticized his "cavalier dismissal of the law that was created in the colonies before 1750" (*New York Herald Tribune Book Review*, July 2, 1950, p. 6); by Erwin Surrency in *Temple Law Quarterly* 24 (1951), p. 509, who gave the book a mixed review, since he considered it "a great contribution to the field of political science," but questioned the book's standing as history; and by Ford W. Hall in *Texas Law Review* 28 (1950), p. 992, who noted Hurst's lack of adequate attention to the influence of treatise writers on states, such as Texas, that were settled in the latter two-thirds of the nineteenth century, but who presciently observed that Hurst "provides a view of a sizeable portion of the forest."

37. Hurst's ability to break entirely outside the box is central to Robert Gordon's discussion of his work (note 5). Critics of Hurst's work have challenged his ability to do so and suggest that he is actually at times an apologist for the status quo who seems to write winners' history. For perceptive criticism that focuses primarily on Hurst's magisterial lumber book, see Harring and Strutt (note 6), as well as an article by Eugene Genovese and Hurst's brief response in that American Bar Foundation Research Journal Review Symposium. Other important articles at least partially critical of Hurst's work include Harry Scheiber,

"At the Borderland of Law and Economic History: The Contributions of Willard Hurst, *American Historical Review* 75 (1970), p. 744; Mark Tushnet, "Lumber and the Legal Process," *Wisconsin Law Review* (1972), p. 114; and Stephen Diamond, "Legal Realism and Historical Method: J. Willard Hurst and American Legal History," *Michigan Law Review* 77 (1979), p. 784.

38. Those who attack Hurst as a consensus historian tend to concentrate on his later *Law and Economic Growth: The Legal History of the Lumber Industry in Wisconsin, 1836–1915* (1964). Hurst's critics claim that because of his concern with large issues and dominant institutions, his lumber book omits crucial elements of conflict of interest, corruption, and class confrontation. For example, Harring and Strutt (note 6), detail a dramatic series of clashes between John Deitz, a part-time employee and farmer, and the Weyerhauser lumber "pool" on the upper Chippewa River in Wisconsin. After years of legal confrontations and sporadic violence, a posse of forty men shot it out with Deitz and his family on land the lumber company wanted for a dam. Deitz subsequently got a life sentence for murder, but he went to jail a hero, sent off by a receiving line of hundreds of supporters and national press coverage. The story of the Deitz affair—the shootout occurred the month Willard was born—is not included in the lumber book. Willard's response was that such clashes were marginal, and that his book focuses on "conflict typically among contenders for the stakes in fast exploitation of the forest" (p. 138).

39. Talcott Parsons, "Hurst's *Law and Social Process in United States History*," *Journal of the History of Ideas* 23 (1962): 558, 562. Parson's review of Hurst's 1960 book nevertheless was overwhelmingly favorable and proclaimed that Hurst "may be claimed to stand in the best sociological tradition" (p. 561). Parsons described Hurst's work as "very illuminating, not simply to those interested in American history, but to all social scientists who are concerned with the society and hence must pay attention to the historical background of the problems they study" (p. 558).

40. Hurst's work anticipates G. Kitson Clark's well-known advice to anyone who seeks to generalize: "do not guess, try to count, and if you cannot count, admit that you are guessing" (G. Kitson Clark, *The Making of Victorian England*, 1962, p. 14).

41. As Holmes put it in Mark Howe, ed., *Holmes-Laski Letters: The Correspondence of Mr. Justice Holmes and Harold J. Laski, 1916–1925* (1953), p. 389.

42. See, e.g., Jerold Auerbach, *Unequal Justice: Lawyers and Social Change in Modern America* (1976); Maxwell Bloomfield, *American Lawyers in a Changing Society, 1776–1876* (1976); Gerald Gawalt, *The Promise of Power: The Emergence of the Legal Profession in Massachusetts, 1760–1820* (1979); Robert Stevens, *Law School: Legal Education in America from the 1850s to the 1980s* (1983); Robert Ferguson, *Law and Letters in American Culture* (1984); Robert Gordon, "The Independence of Lawyers," *Boston University Law Review* 68 (1988): p. 1.

43. For a recent discussion of the consensus approach, describing it as the counterprogressive trend that dominated postwar American historical writing, see Novick, "A Convergent Culture" pp. 320–60. Novick notes that the University of Wisconsin remained "something of a Progressive redoubt" and a "besieged outpost" for historians "holding out against postwar tendencies" (pp. 345–47). Novick never mentions Hurst, however, and pays scant attention to legal history.

44. Perhaps in this sense, Hurst echoed Richard Hofstadter's early statement of the consensus idea of America as "a democracy in cupidity rather than a democracy of fraternity," (*The American Political Tradition*, 1948, pp. xxxvi–xxxvii), but he was not part of a general consensus approach that involved "an attempt to give some positive content and direction to the essentially negative and critical counterprogressive venture" (Novick, p. 334). In some of his later work, Hurst did sound less critical at times, e.g. his preface to *Law and Economic Growth* (1964, p. xv), referring to "affirmative situation-shaping uses of political process . . . characteristic of the general development of economic and social organization and productive capacity in the nineteenth-century United States." But the thrust of that book, too, was essentially an account of short-sightedness and failed aspirations that produced unfortunate, unintended results.

45. Shelby Foote, quoting Keats's letter, in Mark Muro, "Shelby Foote Makes His Presence Felt in PBS Epic," *Boston Globe*, Sept. 26, 1990, Living Sec., p. 47.

46. J. Willard Hurst, *Justice Holmes on Legal History* (1964), p. 61. Hurst criticizes the normally tough-minded Holmes for romanticizing the social sciences, and for failing to perceive the effort of history to "grasp the whole event" in contrast to the abstraction of the social scientist's attempt to limit and control variables.

47. J. Willard Hurst, Author's note, *Law and Economic Growth: The Legal History of the Lumber Industry in Wisconsin, 1836–1915* (1984 ed.), p. xviii.

48. Frankfurter, quoted in J. Willard Hurst, *Law and the Conditions of Freedom in the Nineteenth-Century United States* (1956), pp. 106–07.

49. Konefsky Interview, p. 9. Brandeis clearly was a major influence on Hurst, but Hurst has grown quite skeptical about many of Brandeis's specific ideas. Though Frankfurter once noted "the indispensable collaboration of Mr. Willard Hurst, research fellow" in his acknowledgments, (in *The Commerce Clause under Marshall, Taney and Waite*, 1937), Frankfurter neither ranks as role model nor major intellectual influence on Hurst. Author's conversations with Victor Brudney, Clark Byse, Stanley Kutler, and Willard Hurst, October 1990.

50. Numbers XIV, 37 Joseph H. Hertz, *The Pentateuch and Haftorahs* 629 (1961, 2d ed.).

THEORY AND PRACTICE IN THE "NEW" HISTORY: REREADING ARTHUR MEIER SCHLESINGER'S *THE RISE OF THE CITY, 1878–1898*

Terrence J. McDonald

In his 1963 autobiography, Arthur Meier Schlesinger[1] wrote that his first clear recollection of happenings outside of his hometown of Xenia, Ohio involved the World's Columbian Exposition in Chicago in 1893 when he was five years old. His parents both attended the fair and brought back "prized souvenirs," but the "sharper remembrance" of that event arose "from seeing a strange glow in the skies one night which my playmates and I promptly attributed to the fair's reflected lights. It was in vain for our elders to tell us that it was the aurora borealis."[2]

That glow was still present in Schlesinger's mind exactly forty years later when the fair's "White City" formed the dramatic high point of his 1933 book, *The Rise of the City, 1878–1898*. Schlesinger found "both the visual evidence and the promise of a new stage in American civilization" in the White City:

> On the shore of Lake Michigan a rough, tangled stretch of bog and dune was transformed into a dream of loveliness. No one who set foot within the Court of Honor, the crowning glory of the whole, could fail to be thrilled by the beauty of the spectacle. . . . The exposition was visited, in great part, by average men and women, particularly from the Middle West, whose lives had hitherto been colorless and narrow, many of whom indeed had never before seen a large city. . . . They came, saw, and like countless other rural folk were moved to tears by the compelling power of its beauty. (pp. 284–86)

Schlesinger's second encounter with the White City was influenced not only by his first, but by many other details of his early life that locate his formative years firmly in that pregnant time we have come to call the Progressive Era. When Schlesinger was born in 1888, his father, a loyal Democrat, had wanted to name him "Grover," after Grover Cleveland (he later seemed grateful to his sisters for vetoing this choice). He gave the valedictory address to his high school class on themes taken from Bellamy's *Looking Backward,* a book that would influence him long after. The minister of the church he attended while an undergraduate at Ohio State was the great exponent of the social gospel, Washington Gladden. His most influential professors in graduate school at Columbia included Charles A. Beard, James Harvey Robinson, and Edwin R. A. Seligman, men who towered over pre–World War I American social science. While at Columbia he dined with Morris Hillquit and Upton Sinclair and in 1912 he once stood in line at Carnegie Hall for two hours waiting to hear "Fighting Bob" La Follette expound on the issues of the presidential campaign, only to be turned away—along with four or five thousand others—for lack of room.[3]

That time in American politics and its voice in American historiography is long gone now, along with overflowing houses at Carnegie Hall to hear lectures on presidential campaigns. For most American historians Schlesinger is today remembered—if he is remembered at all—as he was portrayed by critics writing in the 1960s and 1970s as a sort of Moses of American social history, a historian who saw into the promised land of a history of society, but who lacked the theory of society necessary to get him there. The harsh epitaph for the social history of his generation was written by Richard Hofstadter in a 1968 evaluation of the History of American Life series of which Schlesinger was coeditor and to which he contributed *The Rise of the City.* According to Hofstadter, the series was "nothing better than a stillbirth" because its authors were "trying to write a kind of sociological history without having any sociological ideas."[4]

So much for the Francis Lee Higginson professor of history at Harvard; author of nine books of his own and coauthor or editor of twelve more (not counting the thirteen volumes of the History of American Life Series); president of the American Historical Association in 1942; founding representative of the American Historical Association to the Social Science Research Council and president of the council itself from 1930–1933; advisor to sixty-nine doctoral dissertations at Harvard and Radcliffe, including those of some of the most distinguished historians of their generations; and through the work of his students, a scholar claimed to be, at various times, the "father" of both the history of American cities and American "social and intellectual" history.

To some extent the lack of a clearer impression of Schlesinger's work is the natural result of the passage of time. Schlesinger, after all, retired from Harvard in 1954 and died in 1965 and his academic career had begun more than fifty years before his death. He finished his course work for the doctorate at Columbia in 1912 (the same year he began teaching at Ohio State) and he actually received the degree in 1918. He offered his first course on "The Social and Cultural History of the United States" at the University of Iowa in 1922. His most popular—and probably most influential—book *New Viewpoints in American History* was published in that same year. He joined the faculty at Harvard in 1924.

But Schlesinger's reputation has also suffered because his work became entangled in the politics of subfield legitimation in the 1950s and 1960s. Freud might have warned historians of the dangers of historiographical fatherhood: one is no sooner acknowledged as the "father" of a field than he must feel the hot breath of the oedipal rage of his "sons." As the putative "father" of so many fields, Schlesinger was a prime target for a younger generation active in separating "intellectual" from "social" history; the "new" social history from the "old"; and the "new" urban history from both the "old" urban history and the "new" social history.

There were many signs of Schlesinger's broad influence in the early 1950s. When John W. Caughey surveyed American historians in 1952 to discover their choices for the "best" books in American history published between 1920 and 1935, only thirty-six works received more than six votes and only three historians had written more than one of those works: Frederick Jackson Turner, Samuel Eliot Morison, and Arthur Meier Schlesinger. Schlesinger's *New Viewpoints in American History* finished tenth in the poll, with thirty-two votes. *The Rise of the City* was listed among twenty-two other works on the poll's ballot that had received from six to nineteen votes. Furthermore, in 1951 and 1952, essays credited Schlesinger with nurturing *both* urban and intellectual history. Writing on "The Rise of American Intellectual History" in the *American Historical Review* of 1951, John Higham noted that the "most impressive contribution" cumulatively to intellectual studies came from the students of Schlesinger, "who was turning out a sizable share of the best Ph.D.s in United States history." The next year in the same journal Blake McKelvey claimed Schlesinger as the founder of "American Urban History Today." For McKelvey Schlesinger's *Rise of the City* "first revealed the dominant role played by urban developments in late nineteenth-century America," while his "seminal" 1940 essay on "The City in American History" weighed "the cumulative effect in time of the problems and achievements of many cities within a given society."[5]

But these essays were also markers of changing times because neither ranked Schlesinger among the current adepts in either field and both authors were clearly endeavoring to move the field in a more specialized direction away from the work of the "master." (Here the man of the hour was Oscar Handlin, whose *Boston's Immigrants* was claimed by both McKelvey and Higham as an exemplar of their fields.) Indeed, if read back-to-back the essays implied that Schlesinger was a sort of jack-of-all-trades and master of none.

A more straightforwardly critical attitude was developing among the "newer" social historians who would cut their teeth against the allegedly "un-systematic" social history of Schlesinger and his colleagues. As early as 1941 William Diamond had criticized the definitional vagueness of Schlesinger's work, attributing it, in part, to his failure to make use of new theoretical work on the city developed by the Chicago School of Sociology. Thomas Cochran elaborated this critique more broadly in 1954, when he declared in *The Social Sciences in Historical Study* that up until then there had been "many 'social' accounts of American historical data but few sociological interpretations" be-cause earlier historians like Schlesinger had not made enough use of social science theory. Richard Hofstadter continued this line of criticism in the 1968 essay quoted above where he also denounced the idea of social history as a series of volumes moving rapidly in sequence from one "sociological subject to the next . . . without a firm conceptual framework upon which to order the whole."[6]

Meanwhile, two essays published in the early 1960s set the terms for a sim-ilar debate within the field that revered Schlesinger the longest, American urban history. In "The City in History—Some American Perspectives" Schles-inger's student, Richard C. Wade, carried on the agenda that Schlesinger set in his 1940 essay. Focusing, as Schlesinger did, on the "American experience with the city" Wade declared that an urban approach "does furnish the his-torian with many valuable and interesting perspectives." But it was precisely this approach that Eric Lampard rejected in his 1961 essay on "American His-torians and the Study of Urbanization." There—and in a series of essays that followed this one over many years—Lampard built upon the insights of Di-amond a critique that decried the confused state of urban history and its focus on "problems" within cities and "impacts" of cities on American society rather than a focus on what he deemed to be the central process at work, urbani-zation itself, defined in terms of the so-called "ecological complex" developed by sociologists.[7]

As the field developed, much of urban history was, in fact, written under the Schlesinger/Wade aegis, but the theoretical and historiographical "high ground" continued to be taken by the more structural and ecological ap-proaches, which held out the hope of discovering what was distinctively "ur-ban" in both the urban historical experience and urban historiography. For better or worse, one of the monuments to the latter approach was the 1981 *Philadelphia* collection edited by Theodore Hershberg and it is worth noting that there was no mention of Schlesinger whatsoever in Hershberg's intro-ductory survey of the field. Not surprisingly, given all the above, for most social historians trained in the 1970s an assignment to read a volume of the History of American Life series then was likely to be regarded either as an insult or a joke.[8]

No one would have been less surprised by this than Schlesinger, himself.

Having studied with both Beard and Robinson, Schlesinger was a "card-car-rying" member of the so-called "new" history, and as such he believed fully that the frameworks for historical inquiry would change both in response to the changing present and to the impact of the social sciences. In an important essay on historical method published in 1929 Schlesinger urged historians to use theory to hunt for the "underlying forces . . . with which to explain the motivation of events," and also warned that work in the social sciences would always "be conditioned by the 'climate' peculiar to the period in which the student does his work."[9]

But how did a man who believed these things write history that was as atheoretical, formless, and "stillborn" as his critics claimed? In fact, he didn't! There is a provocative, wide-ranging, witty, and yes, theoretical mind at work in Schlesinger's many essays and books. This is as true in *The Rise of the City* as in his other works. With *The Rise* Schlesinger had the miserable fate to have written a book that was found wanting not because it is pointless or atheo-retical, but because it was shaped by the historical and theoretical preoccu-pations of one era and judged by those of others.

To understand the theoretical framework of—and limitations upon—*The Rise of the City* we must begin with a look at Schlesinger's more intellectually revealing previous book, *New Viewpoints* (1922), a collection of twelve wide-ranging interpretive essays on topics from "The Influence of Immigration on American History," to "The Riddle of the Parties," many of which still repay reading. Schlesinger described *New Viewpoints* as an attempt to "bring to-gether and summarize, in non-technical language, some of the results of the researches of the present era of historical study and to show their importance to a proper understanding of American history" (p. viii), and his abundant bibliographical notes to these essays essentially codify the theoretical, his-toriographical, and substantive state of the art of Schlesinger's social history. Three things stand out there that are relevant here: the goal of Schlesinger to deploy theory to penetrate to the "deep structure" of social life, the centrality of "economic" theory in this endeavor, and, the role of economic change as the motor of social transformation.

For example, the bibliographical note to his essay on "Economic Influences in American History" makes clear that Schlesinger had no interest in pro-ducing what he called a "mere chronicle"—like that of John B. McMaster—that simply portrayed the "life of the masses with a profuseness of detail that gave new realism to the old story." On the contrary, his goal was to "account for the mainsprings of social conduct" and to do it by applying "economic analysis to American history" (pp. 69–70). The absence of focus on these ec-onomic influences in other works was puzzling to Schlesinger given what he saw as the centrality of economic change in his essay on what he called the

"Foundations of the Modern Era." For him the two "epochal events" that opened the "modern" era in America were the Civil War, which both destroyed slavery and discredited the doctrine of state sovereignty, and the "great economic revolution which swept through the nation at high tide from about 1860 to 1880" (p. 246). According to Schlesinger this economic change threw up the industrial cities, encouraged specialization and competition both in the economy and society, created both enormous riches and "the labor problem," attracted men of a "practical stamp" (rather than great orators or statesmen) into late nineteenth-century politics, and helped to generate a new political philosophy. For while laissez faire was "well adapted to the conditions prevailing before the economic revolution, when land and natural resources were plentiful and cheap," Schlesinger wrote, the increasing complexities generated by the economic transformation and its byproducts had produced the feeling that "liberty and opportunities of the individual can be properly safeguarded only by the protective oversight of the government . . . and the dominant thought of Americans is agreed that intelligent social control furnishes the best preventive of ruthless individualism, on the one hand, and of government paternalism on the other" (p. 263).[10]

Schlesinger's notion of an economic development that led inexorably toward this moderate solution of the pressing issues of the late nineteenth century comported well with the thought of some major figures of turn-of-the-century social science, who, as Dorothy Ross has recently pointed out, recovered from what she has called the "crisis of the gilded age" by discovering in the operations of the capitalist economy itself the potential for a society of both abundance and relative equality.[11] Schlesinger took a course at Columbia with one of the most influential of these social scientists, Edwin R. A. Seligman and he was deeply impressed with Seligman's 1902 book, *The Economic Interpretation of History,* from which he borrowed the terminology he used in *New Viewpoints* and which he called there the "best critique by an American of the economic theory of historical development" (p. 71).

What Schlesinger took from this little book was not its "critique," but its elaboration of what Seligman himself called an economic theory of history in a "reasonable and moderate sense of the term." According to Seligman, it was the economic interpretation that taught historians to "search below the surface," in the knowledge that "the chief considerations in human progress are the social considerations, and that the important factor in social change is the economic factor." Having gone beneath the surface, however, historians would learn, Seligman wrote, that economic changes transformed society by "slow and gradual steps," that private property "is a logical and salutary result of human development," that "with every improvement in the material condition of the great mass of the population there will be an opportunity for the unfolding of a higher moral life," and that "a more ideal economic adjustment" would be reached "when science shall have given us complete mastery over means of production." Seligman's theory had, as he put it, nothing in common with socialism; going beneath the surface led primarily to the discovery of the abundant potential of capitalist economic development subjected to "intelligent" social control.[12]

Seligman's theory also provided historians like Schlesinger with both a crucial explicit legitimation for a kind of history that went both beyond and beneath political history and a method for doing that history by identifying events, processes, and movements as either "dynamic" (i.e., moving in line with the presumedly progressive direction of economic change) or "static." But what Seligman did not provide was a well-specified theory of the linkages between economic and social or political power or a well thought out method for making these all-important linkages. He admitted as much, writing that historians were now seeking to "gauge the influences of factors" which "turn out to be exceedingly elusive" by employing a "social science whose very principles have not yet been adequately and permanently elaborated."[13]

New Viewpoints made it abundantly clear that having penetrated the surface of "fife and drum history" Schlesinger had unleashed a riot of poorly defined social historical "forces," "factors," and "influences" which he was hard pressed to define (e.g., what was the difference between a "factor" and an "influence"), to differentiate from one another (e.g., what was the difference between an "economic" and a "geographic" factor), or to link with other historical developments. He was, however, by no means alone in this problem. For example, Ellen Nore has noted the same thing about Schlesinger's mentor, Beard, who also took the writings of Seligman to be "axiomatic," but whose explanations of the dynamics of social history "tended all too frequently to be vague and indefinite." And John Higham has argued that other historians of this period "often made cautious, implicit use of economic interpretations in organizing their material" but their "attempt to be comprehensive and eclectic without specifying the locus of power gave their work a largely descriptive cast."[14]

Given the predilections that Schlesinger revealed in *New Viewpoints*, then, we might expect that *The Rise of the City* would attempt to go "beneath" the surface of political history to look for the "dynamic"—i.e. progressive—aspects of the urbanization process while at the same time offering only general linkages between those aspects and changes in the rest of society. And that is exactly what it does. In some ways, in fact, it may be said that Schlesinger set out in *The Rise* to do with the city what Seligman had done with the economy; to locate the late nineteenth-century urbanization process and the city itself on an evolutionary scale leading toward the triumph of rationality over necessity. In his autobiography Schlesinger wrote that his youthful reading of Bellamy and his personal and academic encounters with socialism at Columbia had not turned him into a socialist, but had convinced him that socialists "discharged a needed function" by holding up "to the country a brave and clearly conceived goal." There is little doubt that he saw something quite similar in the broad avenues of the White City.

Taking his cue from Adna Weber's pioneering *Growth of Cities in the Nineteenth Century*, Schlesinger portrayed the city, at bottom, as a phenomenon of economically driven population concentration, meticulously charting the rate of concentration and the increase in points of concentration for each section of the United States, as well as detailing the depopulation of some rural areas. Indeed, it was for this reason that he started—somewhat improbably—with chapters on the South and West. Having already triumphed in the Northeast, the urbanization process was most dramatic in the period he covered in the areas where it had been least advanced up to that time.[15]

All other aspects of his book flow from this population concentration either as a direct causal effect or because the density of types of persons made more visible an issue which was not specifically related to population density in general. For example, density of population directly stimulated invention, required the development of "a spirit of impersonal social responsibility," and facilitated organized efforts for "cultivating the life of mind and spirit" (p. 80). Because crowded living required better communication, transit, architecture and lighting, the period was "a golden age of invention" that saw development of, among other things, the telephone, trolley, and skyscraper. The social problems generated by crowding overwhelmed the "rural spirit of neighborliness" and required new public and private efforts to tackle questions of "pure water, sewage disposal, and decent housing for the poor" (p. 120). In the cities the artistic misfit "starved in his rural isolation" might find the sympathy, encouragement, and criticism necessary to refine "talent into genius," experience the energizing effect of living "in the midst of great affairs," as well as live close to publishers, art dealers, and wealthy patrons (p. 247).

With these direct effects of urbanization in place, other kinds of agglomeration effects would become visible. The "woman question" of the period was focused on the cities because it was there that more women were more visibly active both in paid work outside the home and in the leading roles in social welfare work against urban problems. Education throve on the density, talent, and excitement of the urban place, and it was no coincidence, according to Schlesinger, that with one or two exceptions all the "large, progressive, prosperous institutions of higher learning were to be found in or near urban districts" (p. 215). In the cities the question of what to do with increasing leisure time was "dramatically posed and answered" with higher membership in fraternal orders, wider patronage for theater, and increasing support both for what he called "popular songs" and "serious music" (pp. 288–90).

As a result of all these developments the rise of the city meant also the division of the United States into two cultures: "one static, individualistic, agricultural, the other dynamic, collectivistic, urban" (p. 53). And in the conflict between the two the former was "a stag at bay," doomed both because rural population was migrating to the cities and because "urban" amenities were taking over the country. The "urban" culture was fated to triumph because it was the "dynamic" culture, the one with a "close correlation" with the social, economic, and intellectual forces that were bringing about "new horizons, new attachments of interest, new views and new men" (p. 415). Symptomatic of its victory, on the national level at least, was the transformation of the central issue of political conflict from "how much authority the general government possessed" to "the alternative uses to which the expanded powers should be put" (p. 416).

Ironically, the "urban" culture was not triumphant in the big cities where it was blocked by the "worst city government the country had ever known." The political problem in the cities, too, began with the pace of urbanization itself. Americans, Schlesinger argued, had no experience in the political management of "densely packed urban centers" and as a larger proportion of the population annually "hived in cities" human relations "were rendered more complex, new social maladjustments appeared, and governmental services and safeguards were required that were unknown to the earlier and simpler days of the republic" (p. 389). The press of population caused conscientious municipal officials to "flounder" and provided opportunities for those "not actuated by upright motives" to command their price.

For Schlesinger the "commanding position of the city in cultural life" made its failure as a political organism all the more tragic," not because the best men did not enter politics, but because the "cesspool under nearly every city hall" kept city government from moving in the same progressive directions in which the "urban" culture was moving and in which state and national governments had moved (pp. 390, 393). The "outpouring of legislation for educational and humanitarian welfare" was evidence that by means of corrupt practices acts and in other ways state "legislative corruption was the exception rather than the rule," while at the national level via civil service and other reforms the government "had purged itself of the bribery and wrongdoing which had come with the moral backwash of the Civil War," and had moved to extend the power of the national government at the expense of state power in "the most striking political phenomenon of the times" (pp. 395–96). Until city governments adopted measures to stem their own corruption and learned that they were not so much "little states but large corporations" they themselves would block the triumph of "urban" culture at its origin.

This contradiction between the culture and politics of the cities was one of the things that led Schlesinger to render a mixed positive verdict on both the period and the process that were the foci of the book. For Schlesinger the "mists and shadows" that gathered over America in the beginning years of the fin de siècle had "always been streaked with light for those with eyes to see" (p. 428). During the same two decades that "capitalistic greed ground the faces of the poor under its iron heel," there was "a great advance on the part of the American people in gaining freedom from bread-winning toil" (p. 287); philanthropy, education, and culture "attested to the essential humaneness of the American character"; and new technology along with the increasing role of private and public agencies in everyday life improved the position of the common man. The Columbian Exposition (again) "revealed to a wondering world the summit of American accomplishment in the fine arts and graces of life" (p. 428), at the same time urban progress, he had written in an earlier chapter, was "experimental, uneven, often accidental." The people were, as yet, "groping in the dark" and what most impressed him about the period was the "lack of unity, balance, planfulness, in the advances that were made" (p. 120). All the socioeconomic elements for the quantum leap into the rational utopia that both Seligman and Schlesinger longed for were there, but the political drive to make the leap was still developing.

It does some injustice to Schlesinger to flatten *The Rise* into this brief summary of its causal structure, but the historiographical issue of the lack of a framework requires this focus. Missing in this account must be the breadth of concern, sparkling wit, and prodigious research that make this book so much worth another reading. There is no doubt that Schlesinger captured the dynamism and multiplicity that were—and always will be—the hallmarks of the American city. He also both claimed too much for urbanization and specified that process too little; he saw a positive logic in urban development that led him to underestimate the misery and conflict that were an inevitable part of the urbanization process in those years; he trusted too much in the power of the "urban culture" to overcome the obvious obstacles to "intelligent social control." He did all these things under the aegis of a theoretical framework that left a lasting impression on the historians of his generation and, in part because of this framework, when he declared that "in the eighties urbanization became a controlling factor in national life" (p. 79), he knew exactly what he meant.

Dixon Ryan Fox was absolutely right, therefore, when he wrote in the editor's introduction to *The Rise of the City* that Schlesinger's purpose was "not merely to make live again a phase of American life that has half-faded from memory," but rather to describe and appraise the city as "the new social force which waxed and throve while driving the pioneer culture before it" (pp. xiii–xiv). And if Schlesinger's book had arrived when scheduled there is a high probability that it would have been received as a masterpiece. Schlesinger and Fox had signed the contract to produce the History of American Life series in 1923, assuming that the whole project would come to fruition in about three years. Schlesinger began work on *The Rise* that summer hoping to be on the same schedule.

Alas for Schlesinger and the book it appeared on the desk of reviewers ten years later in the dreadful winter of 1933, a time that Bernard De Voto called in his review "the most painful winter of our national existence." Now the most apt urban symbol was the "Hooverville" and the difference between that and Schlesinger's White City both measured the astonishing distance the country had travelled economically since 1923 and marked the fact that the political economic hopes and theories of a generation had gone down in the crash along with the stocks and bonds and banks.[16]

This change was evident in the mixed reviews that the book received. While almost all the reviews of *The Rise* were respectful and most praised Schlesinger's diligence of research and breadth of focus, most also criticized the book's lack of an "interpretation" generally and its handling of the economy in particular. These criticisms were closely related because what some reviewers wanted by way of "interpretation" was more recognition on Schlesinger's part of the deadly parallels between the 1890s and the 1930s and therefore, a more critical focus on the economic aspects of the history of urbanization.

Part of this criticism was based on the original decision of Fox and Schlesinger to divide the series' coverage of the years 1878–1898 into two volumes, Schlesinger's on the city and Ida Tarbell's on the economy (*The Nationalizing of Business, 1878–1898*, which did not appear until 1936). In his review, for example, Henry Steele Commager decried the editorial decision to divide the period because "economics is the warp upon which the social patterns of these decades was woven," and De Voto wrote that the lack of central focus on the economy was "at first something of a shock—it is not 'Hamlet' without the prince, but it is certainly 'Uncle Tom's Cabin' with Legree left out."[17]

But part of this criticism also represented a rejection of what Schlesinger did say about the economy. The economy was not absent from *The Rise*, but present in the Seligmanian sense discussed above. Schlesinger's account of the urbanization process was predicated upon certain kinds of economic transformation of which he was well aware and the most crucial outcomes of that process (e.g., progress toward the "urban" collectivist culture) were based upon an improving standard of living. As his writings on economic history made clear, Schlesinger was by no means unaware of the cyclical tendencies in the American economy, but on the whole for him capitalist economic development was a progressive force and this gave his narrative a progressive cast. Again De Voto, who was Schlesinger's friend and labored mightily to defend the book in his review, captured this theme: "Mr. Schlesinger is probably no more optimistic than the next one, but his narrative covers such an astonishing and unpredictable advance in civilization, such an endless series of problems somehow solved, or partly solved, and dangers somehow averted or partly averted, that the reader irrationally projects the line into the future." For many reviewers that line did not seem at all to extend into the future and Schlesinger's failure to note this meant that there was no interpretive line in the book at all.[18]

Reviewers as different otherwise as sociologist Robert Lynd, political scientist Albert Lepawsky, economist Louis Hacker, and historians Commager and Beard agreed that the book had no interpretation. Hacker wrote that Schlesinger had let his "zeal for presenting half-forgotten curiosities dull his critical facilities" and had produced a "monotonous cataloguing of men and events with no effort to point up the significant and dismiss the trivial."[19] Beard, who had been one of Schlesinger's most inspiring teachers in graduate school, declared dismissively that Schlesinger apparently thought that "interpretations are wrong, that none is possible, and that impressionistic eclecticism is the only resort of contemporary scholarship."[20]

As Schlesinger might have put it, for "those with eyes to see" there was, indeed, an interpretation in the book. The White City, which had arisen out of the ashes of the depression of 1893, spoke the same message in the winter of 1933. It said: "This, too, shall pass." But it must also be said that Schlesinger did not emphasize this point. There were no references to the crash or depression in either *The Rise* or Fox's editor's introduction to it. The American reviewers might have been too close to their own tragedy to hear this message in any case. The only unqualified rave review appeared outside of the United States, in the *Times Literary Supplement*. The anonymous author there declared that the book was a "model of diligent research, sound judgment, and lucid exposition," and, in a phrase that must have pleased the author, said that he had "penetrated below the surface of current events" and "discerned the profound significance of this period for American civilization." The summary of the book's argument followed very much along the lines of that offered here, with a focus on the effects of the urbanization process on the rest of American society.[21]

Schlesinger's silence on the issues of 1933 may be explained by many things, but the most obvious explanation is that he was not a presentist. His belief in the everchanging nature of history led not to a sort of instrumental view of history, but to the position that historians have "an obligation to appraise human behavior according to the standards of the times." To fulfill this obligation to him we need note further only that in *The Rise* Schlesinger took both his theoretical interests and empirical energy far beyond the limits of the conventional historical practice of his day. If it is not the history of the city that we need today it is still the place to start for a refreshing sense of the possibilities that the American city once represented. If we no longer see those possibilities it may be less the result of our improved historical practice than of the diminishing size of our moral universe.[22]

Terrence J. McDonald, Department of History, University of Michigan, is the author, most recently, of "Faiths of Our Fathers: Middle Range Social Theory and the Remaking of American Urban History 1940–1985," forthcoming in Kathleen Neils Conzen, Michael H. Ebner, and Russell Lewis, eds., American City History: Modes of Inquiry *(1992).*

1. A word about "nomenclature" is necessary at the outset. Countless such references to the contrary notwithstanding, there is, strictly speaking, no such person as Arthur Meier Schlesinger, *Senior.* Arthur Meier Schlesinger did not refer to himself in this way, probably in part because the man we now know as Arthur Meier Schlesinger, Jr. was actually born Arthur Bancroft Schlesinger and changed his name to his father's only at the age of 15 when he applied for a passport. Throughout this essay, then, I will refer to the elder Schlesinger as Arthur Meier Schlesinger. For details on the name change of Arthur Bancroft Schlesinger, see Arthur Meier Schlesinger's autobiography, *In Retrospect: The History of a Historian* (1963), p. 157.

2. Schlesinger, *In Retrospect*, p. 16.

3. Schlesinger, *In Retrospect*, passim.

4. Richard Hofstadter, "History and Sociology in the United States," in Seymour Martin Lipset and Hofstadter, eds., *Sociology and History: Methods* (1968), p. 8.

5. John W. Caughey, "Historians' Choice: Results of a Poll on Recently Published American History and Biography," *Mississippi Valley Historical Review* 39 (1952): 289–302; John Higham, "The Rise of American Intellectual History," *American Historical Review* 56 (1951): 453–71; Blake McKelvey, "American Urban History Today," *American Historical Review* 57 (1952): 919–29.

6. William Diamond, "On the Dangers of an Urban Interpretation," in Eric F. Goldman, ed., *Historiography and Urbanization: Essays in Honor of W. Stull Holt* (1941), pp. 67–108; Social Science Research Council Committee on Historiography, *The Social Sciences in Historical Study* (1954), p. 166; Hofstadter, "History and Sociology," p. 8.

7. Richard C. Wade, "The City in History—Some American Perspectives," in Werner Z. Hirsch, ed., *Urban Life and Form* (1963), pp. 59–79; Eric E. Lampard, "American Historians and the Study of Urbanization," *American Historical Review* 67 (1961): 49–61.

8. Theodore Hershberg, "The New Urban History: Toward an Interdisciplinary History of the City," in Hershberg, ed., *Philadelphia: Work, Space, Family, and Group Experience in the Nineteenth Century* (1981), pp. 3–35.

9. Arthur Meier Schlesinger, "History," in Wilson Gee, ed., *Research in the Social Sciences: Its Fundamental Methods and Objectives* (1929), pp. 209–40.

10. John Bach McMaster, *A History of the People of the United States*, 8 vols. (1883–1913).

11. Dorothy Ross, *The Origins of American Social Science* (1990), pp. 53–64.

12. Edwin R. A. Seligman, *The Economic Interpretation of History* (1907), pp. 67, 106–07, 133, 155, 163–64. Although this book was originally published in 1092 Schlesinger used this later edition.

13. Seligman, *Economic*, 164.

14. Ellen Nore, *Charles A. Beard: An Intellectual Biography* (1983), p. 68; John Higham, *History: Professional Scholarship in America* (1983), pp. 118–19. Higham's account of the "new"

history remains the best, I believe, although he attributes these problems to the attempt to achieve a broad "synthesis" while I understand them to have more to do with the application of theory.

15. Adna Ferrin Weber, *The Growth of Cities in the Nineteenth Century* (1899). Schlesinger's understanding of the urbanization process is very similar to that of Hope Tisdale, "The Process of Urbanization," *Social Forces* 20 (1942): 311–16, an article which many believe to be a classic statement of the process as having to do with population concentration. Both Tisdale and Schlesinger were influenced by Weber.

16. Bernard De Voto, "American Life," *Saturday Review of Literature* 9 (1933): 464.

17. Henry Steele Commager, "Transition," *New Republic* 75 (1933): 215; De Voto, "American Life," p. 464.

18. De Voto, "American Life," p. 464.

19. Robert Lynd, "Only Day-Before-Yesterday," *Survey Graphic* 22 (1933): 331; Albert Lepawsky, review, *American Journal of Sociology* 39 (1933): 252–53; Commager, "Transition"; Louis Hacker, "The American City," *The Nation* 136 (1933): 236.

20. Charles A. Beard, review, *American Historical Review* 39 (1933): 779–80.

21. "The Rise of the American City," *Times Literary Supplement*, June 8, 1933, p. 389.

22. Arthur M. Schlesinger, Jr., quotes this sentiment in a discussion of his father's ideas on historical practice in the "Introduction" to *Nothing Stands Still: Essays by Arthur M. Schlesinger* (1969).

LEE BENSON AND
THE CONCEPT OF JACKSONIAN DEMOCRACY

Daniel Feller

In an influential essay published in 1957 entitled "Research Problems in American Political Historiography," Lee Benson decried "the impressionistic approach long dominant in American political historiography" and called for the adoption of "systematic research methods" in history. This would be a first step toward "the attainment of genuinely objective historical interpretations of systematic, well-described, known data; that is, interpretations which can be described accurately as consistent with scientific procedures."[1] Four years later Benson offered a view of what the new history would look like in *The Concept of Jacksonian Democracy: New York as a Test Case.*

The Concept of Jacksonian Democracy left its imprint upon an entire generation of American political historians. Important studies by Ronald P. Formisano, Samuel P. Hays, Michael F. Holt, and Paul Kleppner credited Benson's influence. Allan G. Bogue and Joel H. Silbey dedicated books to him. In 1977 a poll of historians ranked *The Concept of Jacksonian Democracy* third, behind Richard Hofstadter's *The Age of Reform* and *The American Political Tradition* and ahead of Arthur Schlesinger's *The Age of Jackson* and C. Vann Woodward's *Origins of the New South,* among the most influential books in American political history to appear since World War II.[2]

The Concept of Jacksonian Democracy energized an army of disciples; it also galvanized squads of critics. While enthusiasts hailed what Allan G. Bogue called Benson's "virtuoso efforts" to unite history with the technique and theory of the social sciences, David Hackett Fischer condemned *Concept* for combining "the worst of both methodological worlds." A quarter-century after the book's publication, historians were still writing to expose its errors. But even skeptics acknowledged it as a "pathbreaking study."[3]

The impact of Benson's work reflected its ambitious purposes. In *The Con-*

cept of Jacksonian Democracy and contemporaneous essays, Benson levelled a comprehensive indictment against the prevailing narrative mode and "progressive" viewpoint in American political history, as exemplified in books like Schlesinger's *Age of Jackson*. Historians of American politics, Benson charged, had substituted artful rhetoric, hoary mythology, and brazen partisanship for conceptual rigor, evidentiary proof, and intellectual detachment. They had accepted an "economic determinist" view of politics, blithely assuming that economic interests determined partisan loyalties (p. 165). Historians had also adopted, without verifying, an instrumentalist model of popular voting which enabled them to accept election results as referenda on the particular issues set forth by rival candidates and parties. (For instance, in the 1844 presidential election the main new issue was Texas annexation, which Democrats favored and Whigs opposed. The Democrats won; ergo "a majority of the American people" wanted Texas, p. 256.) Historians had interpreted election results without regard to context and without disaggregating the returns to determine exactly who had voted for whom. They had treated campaign rhetoric uncritically, branded parties with poorly defined, often anachronistic labels, and posited dubious continuities between political groupings over different eras.[4]

As Benson saw it, the substantive errors produced by this historiography were inseparable from its methodological and conceptual defects. Historians had reached the wrong conclusions because they had followed the wrong procedures, and they had followed the wrong procedures because they had not thought clearly what they were about. They had "not as a group tended to view analytically and study systematically the problems inherent in the construction and use of their concepts" (p. vii). Benson not only demanded a reexamination of old shibboleths like "Jacksonian Democracy"; he wanted historians to adopt a new way of thinking and of writing, and indeed a new purpose.

Conceived as "essentially an essay on the clarification of historical concepts," *The Concept of Jacksonian Democracy* would show them how. It was a "test case" in a dual sense, not only of New York as a microcosm of the nation, but of the results to be obtained by applying "sustained, systematic work on general conceptual problems" and the precise research methods and analytical tools of the social sciences to the study of history (p. vii).

Still *The Concept of Jacksonian Democracy* began with a methodologically conventional, though highly revisionist, history of New York state politics in the formative years of the Jacksonian party system. In six chapters Benson dynamited the foundations of a half-century's historiography portraying Andrew Jackson and his party as the vanguards of an egalitarian, democratic, and liberal movement in politics. In New York, Benson found, the proto-

Jacksonian "Albany Regency" faction headed by Martin Van Buren did not lead the campaigns for universal male suffrage and popular election of the president, for social reforms such as abolition of imprisonment for debt, or for the eradication of economic privilege. The impulses behind these reforms either came from groups opposed to the Regency (most notably the Antimasons) or else pervaded the entire polity. Benson found no evidence for a class interpretation of Jacksonian politics: Whig and Democratic parties drew their leadership from the same strata of society, and neither bore any real resemblance to the bygone Hamiltonian Federalists and Jeffersonian Republicans. Operating in a political environment democratized and energized by the "Transportation Revolution," both parties espoused an egalitarian ideal and championed economic development, albeit through different means.

Not all of Benson's points have stood up, and his use of literary sources was inherently no more convincing than that of his predecessors. All the same there was great creativity in this work of demolition. Benson's careful separation of the various types of reform movements and his strictures against carelessly linking them through anachronistic labels rescued Jacksonian historiography from a hopeless rhetorical muddle. Presumably no one will ever again call Democrats and Whigs "liberal" and "conservative" without explaining precisely what they mean. Benson also cast a prudently jaundiced eye at partisan class-war rhetoric that historians had sometimes accepted at face value, and for which he coined the famous phrase "campaign claptrap" (p. 81). Yet at the same time he grasped the psychological effectiveness of exaggerated attacks on political foes. "To track down and slay monsters was politically rewarding" (p. 52). In this, and in his explication of the appeal of the Antimasons and nativists, Benson anticipated the insights of the later "republican" school of historians. By showing, for instance, how the Antimasons could mount a popular crusade against exclusivity and privilege, only themselves to face accusations of moral and religious tyranny, Benson showed how adaptable and available antiaristocratic rhetoric was in what he dubbed "The Age of Egalitarianism." Against this demonstration, simplistic formulations of Jacksonian politics as a struggle between Democratic "masses" and Whig "classes" crumbled.

But all this debunking was mere prelude to Benson's real goal of erecting a new understanding of Jacksonian politics upon sounder foundations. With the rubble of past historiography cleared away, Benson returned to first questions—"who voted for whom" and why (p. 123).

Taking a presidential race as his starting point, Benson first compared the New York state returns in 1844 to those in previous and subsequent elections. They showed almost no change. "The most revealing thing that happened in the 1844 election was that so little happened" (p. 137). In fact, voting patterns had reached an "equilibrium point" (p. 131) in 1832 and remained stable until 1853, with the electorate nearly evenly divided between the two parties. So much for the Democrats as the "popular party" (p. 133), and so much for the 1844 election—and by extension, any ordinary election—as a referendum on any particular issue posed in the campaign. To explain his findings Benson invoked the concept of a voting cycle, consisting of a stable phase during which voting patterns changed little, demarcated at either end by a fluctuation phase in which they changed rapidly.

Inspecting the 1844 electoral data at the county and town level, Benson further found no relationship between party strength and the wealth or occupation of voters. On this basis he rejected "an interest group theory of politics" rooted in "economic determinism" (pp. 164, 140). What then did shape voting behavior? The catchword "ethnocultural" belies the complexity (and sometimes the confusion) of Benson's answer. Warning against rigid classification schemes, Benson sketched a picture of overlapping layers of religious, ethnic, and attitudinal influences upon political preference. While some groups (for instance, blacks and Irish Catholics) aligned solidly with one party or another, white Protestants, who constituted most of the electorate, tended to split between "puritan" Whigs and "nonpuritan" Democrats—a distinction more of temperament than of creed.

Benson proceeded to reshape his empirical findings into evidence for "a general theory of American voting behavior" (p. 277). Drawing upon Richard Hofstadter's *The American Political Tradition* and Louis Hartz's *The Liberal Tradition in America* to certify Americans' broad agreement upon the fundamentals of political economy, Benson posited that the absence of serious conflict between economic classes or interest groups freed voters to employ their ballots for other than policy purposes. Among those purposes were to declare their identities and to strike at their enemies, both identities and enemies being usually in the American experience defined in ethnic, religious, and cultural, not socioeconomic, terms.

Thirty years later, much of Benson's particular analysis of Jacksonian politics still stands. Among the themes stressed in *The Concept of Jacksonian Democracy* were the newly democratized political environment of the 1820s and hence the essential differences between Jacksonian-era parties and their Federalist-Jeffersonian predecessors, the transformative effect of economic development upon political institutions and practices, the genuine popular appeal of a Whig program coupling economic advance with moral improvement, the cultural and religious tensions that found expression in party conflict, the depth of party loyalty and hence the stability of voting patterns, and the pervasiveness of egalitarian rhetoric and antiaristocratic appeals in political discourse. Most of these points are routinely accepted today even by historians who still stress class divisions in Jacksonian politics.

But it was the so-called ethnocultural thesis which made *The Concept of Jacksonian Democracy* both influential and controversial, to the point that Benson's other accomplishments and innovations were often either overlooked or credited to someone else. A whole generation of historical scholarship, and of scholarly criticism, flowed from a single "sweeping proposition" in *Concept*: "that at least since the 1820's, when manhood suffrage became widespread, ethnic and religious differences have tended to be *relatively* the most important sources of political differences" (p. 165). And here substance and method merged, for Benson's new understanding of American politics rested upon what he claimed was a superior, "scientific" approach to the study of history itself.

The analysis of voting behavior supporting the ethnocultural thesis in *The Concept of Jacksonian Democracy* came dressed in all the trappings of social science. Assumptions, propositions, hypotheses, theories, and models decorated its pages. But while Benson summoned historians to adopt the methods and attitudes of the social scientist, he did not mimic the dry tone of the neutral, detached observer of human behavior. Benson was on a crusade, and to wage it he chose a style that was assertive and highly personal. In 340 pages of text, the word "I" appeared ninety times. Benson's rhetoric made exciting reading; yet its insistency jarred with his demand for a cooperative, progressive approach to historical inquiry and his frequent disclaimers of conclusiveness in his own findings.

Concept's combative style enthused some and enraged others. Either way, it worked. Jabbing italics, bolstered by an imposing display of social science terminology and numerical data, intimidated even where they did not persuade. Historians unaccustomed to encountering such artillery surrendered readily to Benson's claims of superior accuracy and precision.

Indeed, the impact of *The Concept of Jacksonian Democracy* owed much to its crusading spirit. Enthralled by Benson's assault on his muddle-headed predecessors and enraptured by the prospect of "scientific" history, Benson's converts set out to fortify and broaden his findings. In the next few years, a spate of monographs established the ethnocultural thesis as the prevailing explanation of American politics. Already by 1967 the political scientist Walter Dean Burnham could describe the idea that ethnicity has always been "basic" to American political divisions as "axiomatic."[5]

Yet *The Concept of Jacksonian Democracy* inspired bitter dissent as well as emulation. Some historians worried over how Benson's approach to voting analysis, focusing on behavioral patterns and continuities, could be reconciled with a traditional historiography stressing ideas, issues, policies, and outcomes as the stuff of politics. Integrating the ethnocultural model of voting into a narrative of events seemed all but impossible, yet divorcing them meant splitting the historical universe of politics in two. But the most searching questions about Benson's findings concerned not their implications, but their basic validity. Accepting his own prescriptions for rigorous formal analysis, critics subjected Benson's logic and evidence to withering scrutiny.[6]

They discovered that what looked at first reading like sure proof often appeared, on closer inspection, to be something else. Benson's analysis of the 1844 election returns produced a "startling gap between the traditional claims about New York voting behavior and the findings revealed by systematic collection and ordering of the data" (p. 150). Yet his techniques of "systematic examination of the data" (p. 146) included adopting certain counties as "representative examples" without in any way demonstrating their representativeness, and erecting conclusions upon a precarious base of assumptions and estimates. Some of Benson's assumptions were whoppers—for instance, "since the United States is highly heterogeneous, and has high social mobility, I assume that men tend to retain and be more influenced by their ethnic and religious group membership than by their membership in economic classes or groups" (p. 165). The United States has had high religious mobility too, especially in the era of the Second Great Awakening. Benson assumed precisely what needed to be proved.

Showing the primacy of cultural over economic motivations for voting required, in some instances, artificially severing circumstances that Benson's own evidence showed to be connected—for instance, class, social status, and moral values. Benson reported that "stripped of their more extravagant features, scaled down and reformulated," Horace Greeley's Whig editorials "indicated party differences in *moral attitudes and ways of life*," not in "the class composition of parties." But the editorials Benson quoted clearly indicated both. They denounced Democratic "ignorance and vice," but also characterized Democrats as "loafers around the grog-shops" who "have idled and squandered," while "the thrifty, the thoughtful, the industrious" had "earned and saved." It took dexterity to read class out of these comments, or out of Philip Hone's report that "nine tenths of 'our respectable citizens,' the merchants, the professional men, the mechanics and workingmen, those who went to church on Sunday," voted Whig in 1844 (pp. 198–99). Benson performed the same legerdemain on a larger scale in comparing agricultural and lumbering towns. Since he could "think of no 'economic' reason why men engaged in lumbering should prefer one party to the other," he ascribed loggers' Democratic allegiance to "moral attitudes and values commonly held by lumbermen" and concluded that the comparison "discredits rather than supports economic determinism" (p. 205).

One central tenet of the ethnocultural thesis—that "the Catholic Irish voted overwhelmingly Democratic wherever they lived and whatever their occupation"—appeared first in *The Concept of Jacksonian Democracy* as something to "be shown later" and to "be demonstrated below." A chapter later it was a fact that must be "recognized" (pp. 173, 141, 144, 146). The proof of this fact consisted of a two-page discussion of observations in county histories, correspondence, and newspapers.[7] Some of Benson's most intriguing formulations rested on nothing more "scientific" than a careful study of editorials in the *New York Tribune*. Curiously, in these cases Benson's methodological claims disguised what was actually a novel reading of traditional literary sources.

Where *The Concept of Jacksonian Democracy* did venture into data manipulation it deployed techniques that were, at best, primitive. This was partly a matter of necessity, partly of preference. Lacking good data on voting patterns and ethnic breakdowns (a defect he would later help remedy through his work with the Inter-University Consortium for Political Research), Benson resorted to plain guesswork, presenting precise estimates of percentages with the disarming comment that the figures were "not intended to be taken literally" but "seem to be of the right order of magnitude" (pp. 167, 343).[8]

Benson promised a "multivariate analysis" to sort out the various determinants of voting behavior. Yet in the technical sense, there was no multivariate analysis in *The Concept of Jacksonian Democracy*. There were no correlation coefficients, no significance tests, no regression equations. Instead Benson relied on a largely intuitive procedure that one critic called "gestalt correlation."[9] The choice here was deliberate; Benson shunned complex statistical procedures which abstracted historical explanation from the concrete reality of men and events. But his simpler method could not do what he claimed for it—namely, control for one variable while measuring the effects of another. It could not, for instance, separate out the categories "Irish Catholic" and "working class" to determine whether Irish Catholics voted Democratic regardless of their class, or workers voted Democratic regardless of their ethnicity and religion, or neither.

Perhaps most damaging to Benson's credibility was a logical discrepancy which jeopardized his whole analysis. Benson selected the 1844 election for detailed scrutiny because that was the year that "group voting patterns . . . crystallized" in New York state (pp. ix, 123). But elsewhere in *The Concept of Jacksonian Democracy*, Benson held that "New York voting patterns crystallized" not in 1844 but in 1832, the year that inaugurated the "stable phase" of the state's voting cycle (pp. 62, 128). Benson claimed the stable voting of 1844 was "irreconcilable with the Jacksonian Democracy assumption that socioeconomic principles and policies primarily determined political cleavages," since "party differences over *socioeconomic* issues did not have sufficient impact to alter voting patterns already fixed by 1832" (p. 292). But what fixed them in 1832? On Benson's own showing, the Bank War did.

In other words, if Benson's theory of voting cycles was correct, then the place to seek the original, primary determinants of voting behavior was at the moment when that behavior assumed the shape it would hold for the remainder of the voting cycle. That happened in 1832, not 1844. Benson had analyzed the wrong election.

The point in reviewing these shortcomings is not to revive old controversies, but to show that accepting the ethnocultural thesis on the basis of the evidence presented in *The Concept of Jacksonian Democracy* required something approaching an act of faith. That so many historians did accept it was a tribute to the forcefulness of Benson's presentation. But it was also testimony to a growing disillusionment with the prevailing view of Jacksonian politics as a class struggle, and with the frank partisanship for the Democrats that often accompanied that view. Richard Hofstadter and Louis Hartz had already cleared the way for a new approach by questioning the depth of partisan differences over political economy. Then in 1957 Bray Hammond's *Banks and Politics in America from the Revolution to the Civil War* and Marvin Meyers's *The Jacksonian Persuasion* warned, in different ways, against accepting politicians' own statements of what they were about. By 1960 the time was ripe for a new master explanation of Jacksonian, and beyond that American, party politics.

The Concept of Jacksonian Democracy supplied that explanation, and powered it with the superior cognitive claims of "social science history." In retrospect both the explanation itself and its scholarly reception clearly reflect certain intellectual trends of its day. Benson's dismissal of Whig and Democratic beliefs as mere variants of liberal egalitarianism, his conviction that the rhetorical strife of party politics concealed a real world of economic consensus and cultural antagonisms, found ready concurrence among historians swimming in the wake of Hofstadter and Hartz. "It is true," said Benson, "that the major New York parties differed distinctly over principles and policies, but seen in perspective, their differences were relatively narrow in scope" (p. 292). It depends upon whose perspective. Benson's disparagement of Jacksonian policy debates reflected his own generation's predispositions and worldview as much as it did any compelling force of historical evidence or logic. The proposition that mere "clashes over the positive state, locus of government power, role of different government branches, and foreign policy" could not have been enough to provoke "really sharp cleavages" in the electorate seemed simply self-evident to many historians thirty years ago. But it does not seem self-evident today; nor, one suspects, would it have seemed so in Jacksonian America.

In its disinclination to take Jacksonian policy differences seriously, *The Concept of Jacksonian Democracy* was both product and emblem of a time which has passed. But its importance has outlasted that time. Regardless of the fate of the ethnocultural thesis or any other of his particular findings, Benson's attack upon traditional modes of explanation in political history presented a challenge no later scholar could ignore. Allan G. Bogue has observed that "narrative political history today . . . reflects the influence of social science historians to a far greater extent than many exponents of the narrative form either admit or realize."[10] This is true, and the primary agent for transmitting the concerns, methods, and vocabulary of statistical social science to American political history was *The Concept of Jacksonian Democracy.* Today even scholars who contest Benson's conclusions play in his ballpark; they employ, and try to improve, his methods to dispute his results. The preeminent work on Jacksonian politics before Benson, Arthur Schlesinger Jr.'s *The Age of Jackson,* contained not a single table, statistic, or data analysis in five hundred pages of text. After *Concept,* Schlesingerian viewpoints resurfaced in books by Donald B. Cole, James Roger Sharp, J. Mills Thornton III, and Harry L. Watson, all of which analyzed election returns and displayed batteries of tables, graphs, and computations.[11] The very language of this essay, with its talk of "data" and "variables" and "determinants of voting behavior," reflects Benson's inescapable influence.

But for Benson himself, refining historians' language and perfecting their techniques of measurement were merely intermediate goals. The ultimate purpose of *The Concept of Jacksonian Democracy* was to furnish a brief for what he once called "a genuinely scientific history"—a history based upon "the scientific style of analysis, i.e., explicit conceptualization, theory construction, model building, systematic comparison, standard criteria of measurement." This would be not only a more precise and accurate history, but a new kind of history. And it would serve a higher function: it would build upon historical knowledge to discover and verify "general laws of human behavior."[12]

It was this larger purpose that shaped the distinctive mode of analysis in *The Concept of Jacksonian Democracy.* That mode moved always from the unique to the universal—from an event (for instance, the election of 1844) to the behavior that produced the event, and from there to a generalization about American voting behavior. Implicit in this structure of explanation was a search for something more than an understanding of events in their particularity. If individual historical occurrences could be accounted for empirically, without laws or models, then Benson's generalizing tools—the concepts, theories, hypotheses, and propositions—were so much dead weight. What justified their presence was Benson's desire not just to explain history, but to transcend it.

And here both *The Concept of Jacksonian Democracy* and Benson's concept of the usefulness of history ran into a wall. Benson's method danced a dialectic between behavioral theory and historical fact, between the general and the particular. Benson invoked theory to explain events, while the events in turn validated the theory. Conceding that his findings were tentative and incomplete, Benson refrained from asserting more certainty than he could sustain. Over and over in *The Concept of Jacksonian Democracy* he abjured any claims of finality for his propositions; he offered only preliminary support, and claimed only potential verifiability and *"reasonable* credibility" (p. 290). When he used words like "proof" and "facts," he put them in quotation marks.

Yet for a historian seeking to develop general laws of human behavior, the problem of verification could not be so easily dodged. At some point a historically rooted science of human behavior must go beyond the formulation and preliminary testing of hypotheses. Eventually the buck must stop; the theory must be proved if it is to furnish explanatory or predictive power. Laws are laws. Benson did not reach the point of proof where theory became law. More importantly, he did not show that it could be reached. His theories remained as hypotheses. But as long as they did so, additional cases (past or future) could not truthfully be said to be governed or predicted by the theory. Instead they serve as further evidence to sustain or discredit the theory. The process of theory validation never ends; the goal of a proven theory recedes interminably before us; and scientific historians, like other mortals, beat on, boats against the current, borne back ceaselessly into the past.

The Concept of Jacksonian Democracy thus bequeathed a divided legacy. Benson's prescriptions for doing better history have endured, but the greater dream that propelled them, of erecting a transhistorical science of human behavior, has been abandoned and nearly forgotten. Heeding Benson's criticisms, historians of American politics still strive for greater coherence, accuracy, and intellectual honesty in their grasp of the past. But not many still hope to use history in order to escape from history into the eternal present of the social sciences. Few would if they could. Historians no longer crouch for enlightenment at the feet of behavioral theorists, and the edicts that issued with such sweeping grandeur from psychology, sociology, and political science a generation ago now seem painfully culture-bound and historically naive.

Today the vision of the historian's future that inspired *The Concept of Jacksonian Democracy* appears as the most archaic feature of a brilliantly original work. As a historical revisionist, Lee Benson pushed the study of American politics toward a new level of precision and sophistication. As the champion of a historically rooted science of human behavior, he pointed forward down a dead-end road.

Daniel Feller, Department of History, University of New Mexico, is the author of "The Election of 1836" in Arthur M. Schlesinger, Jr., and Fred L. Israel, eds., Running for President *(forthcoming).*

Thanks to Lawrence F. Kohl, Howard N. Rabinowitz, and Richard H. Sewell for their help with this essay.

1. Lee Benson, "Research Problems in American Political Historiography," in Benson, *Toward the Scientific Study of History* (1972), pp. 8, 11, 80—a compilation of Benson's historiographic and programmatic essays.

2. Ronald P. Formisano, *The Birth of Mass Political Parties: Michigan, 1827–1861* (1971); Samuel P. Hays, *American Political History as Social Analysis* (1980); Michael Fitzgibbon Holt, *Forging a Majority: The Formation of the Republican Party in Pittsburgh, 1848–1860* (1969); Paul Kleppner, *The Cross of Culture: A Social Analysis of Midwestern Politics, 1850–1900* (1970); Allan G. Bogue, *Clio & the Bitch Goddess: Quantification in American Political History* (1983); Joel H. Silbey, *The Partisan Imperative* (1985). Poll results are in Bogue, *Clio,* pp. 113–14. A concise statement of Benson's influence on political historians is in the Introduction to Silbey, Bogue, and William H. Flanigan, eds., *The History of American Electoral Behavior* (1978).

3. Bogue, *Clio,* p. 46; David Hackett Fischer, *Historians' Fallacies* (1970), p. 113; Richard B. Latner and Peter Levine, "Perspectives on Antebellum Pietistic Politics," *Reviews in American History* 4 (March 1976): 15.

4. Benson's critique was developed most extensively in "Research Problems" and other essays in *Toward the Scientific Study of History.*

5. William Nisbet Chambers and Walter Dean Burnham, eds., *The American Party Systems: Stages of Political Development* (1967), p. 285. In addition to the titles cited in note 2 above, see Richard Jensen, *The Winning of the Midwest: Social and Political Conflict, 1888–1896* (1971); Robert Kelley, *The Cultural Pattern in American Politics: The First Century* (1979); Paul Kleppner, *The Third Electoral System, 1853–1892* (1979); and William Gerald Shade, *Banks or No Banks: The Money Issue in Western Politics, 1832–1865* (1972).

6. Richard L. McCormick, "Ethnocultural Interpretations of Nineteenth-Century American Voting Behavior," in *The Party Period and Public Policy* (1986), pp. 29–63; J. Morgan Kousser, "Must Historians Regress? An Answer to Lee Benson," *Historical Methods* 19 (Spring 1986): 62–81. Several reviews of books influenced by Benson—including Kousser, "The 'New Political History': A Methodological Critique," *Reviews in American History* 4 (March 1976): 1–14; Latner and Levine, "Perspectives on Antebellum Pietistic Politics"; and James E. Wright, "The Ethnocultural Model of Voting: A Behavioral and Historical Critique," *American Behavioral Scientist* 16 (May-June 1973): 653–74—raised questions also applicable to Benson's own work.

7. *Concept,* pp. 171–73. This statement may seem startling, for Benson asserts the fact of Irish Catholic Democratic voting so frequently that one assumes it has been proved. That is just the point.

8. On Benson and the IUCPR, see Bogue, *Clio,* chs. 2, 5.

9. *Concept,* pp. ix–x (a supplementary note added to the paperback edition); Kousser, "The 'New Political History,' " pp. 5–6.

10. Bogue, *Clio,* p. 14.

11. Donald B. Cole, *Jacksonian Democracy in New Hampshire* (1970); James Roger Sharp, *The Jacksonians versus the Banks* (1970); J. Mills Thornton III, *Politics and Power in a Slave Society* (1978); Harry L. Watson, *Jacksonian Politics and Community Conflict* (1981). It was perhaps the absence of what we regard in the post-Benson era as the stuff and substance of political history that led Cole to characterize *The Age of Jackson* as "a work of intellectual history" in *"The Age of Jackson*: After Forty Years," *Reviews in American History* 14 (March 1986): 154.

12. Benson, *Toward the Scientific Study of History,* pp. 200, 83–84.

THE INVENTION OF RACE:
REREADING *WHITE OVER BLACK*

James Campbell and James Oakes

We write our books and articles and if we are lucky our colleagues pay attention. We wait a year or two for reviews. After a while we show up in footnotes.
A couple of lines, maybe even a paragraph, in the latest textbook registers
the influence our scholarship is having on the field. That's the way it normally
works. But that is not what happened to Winthrop Jordan's *White Over Black*
when it was published in 1968. The big reviews came out right away, followed
by big prizes. Everyone noticed; everyone raved. Chapters were reproduced
in academic anthologies; an abridged version became a staple in undergraduate surveys. Yet for all its monumental proportions, the book cast a curiously
slender historiographical shadow. Unlike, say, Gordon Wood's *The Creation
of the American Republic,* published only a year later, Jordan's work did not
become the centerpiece of a long and fruitful scholarly debate. It sits on our
shelves, the proverbial book we read in graduate school.

Even in its time the book seemed more the end of an older discussion than
the beginning of a new one. The method of choice was social, not intellectual,
history. At a time when historians struggled to recover the experience and
agency of African Americans, *White Over Black* treated them primarily as problems in the "white mind." It was also Jordan's singular misfortune to produce
a history of racial attitudes at the very moment when Americans were beginning to look beyond racism to the political and economic sources of social
inequality. The "real" issue was class, not race. In the wake of *White Over Black*
came a score of studies arguing that race and racism were not "ultimate realities" at all, but screens for other, usually material, interests.

Reception of *White Over Black* was also overly determined by the famous
Handlin-Degler debate about the origins of slavery and racism in America.
In a pathbreaking essay of 1950, Oscar and Mary Handlin argued that Afri-

cans in seventeenth-century Virginia were not initially singled out for enslavement, but were treated pretty much like English indentured servants. It
was only under the pressures of the New World environment that Africans
came eventually to be associated with the condition of slavery. And it was
this association which led, over time, to the development of a historically
specific ideology of black inferiority. Several years later Carl Degler challenged the Handlins' thesis. Citing evidence of European and very early
American contempt for Africans, Degler argued that blacks were subjected
to uniquely discriminatory treatment right from the start. Economics may
have given rise to slavery and racism may have developed only later but prejudice against blacks was nevertheless crucial in the decision to enslave Africans, Degler argued. Indeed, in more than one venue he suggested that
prejudice has been so widespread in human history as to be nearly universal.
Unfortunately, the subtleties of the Handlin-Degler debate quickly gave way
to a crude dichotomy that caricatured both positions and forever shaped the
way *White Over Black* was read. By 1968 many readers approached Winthrop
Jordan's book looking for a definitive answer to the question: Did slavery
cause racism or did racism cause slavery?

But Jordan had in fact rejected these alternatives, offering an interpretation
of the origins of racism that was at once distinct from the Handlins' and even
more depressing than Degler's. Unlike either the Handlins or Degler, Jordan
argued that white prejudice did not crystallize into racism in the seventeenth
century but in the late eighteenth century, and not as a simple byproduct of
slavery but in response to the specter of emancipation. Indeed, of *White Over
Black's* nearly six-hundred pages, five hundred cover the years after 1700.
Jordan's discussion of the American Revolution begins about halfway
through the book, which means that 50 percent of his text is devoted to the
last half of the eighteenth century.

Jordan's emphasis on the radical transformation of the late 1700s is only
one of the ways that *White Over Black* resonates with more recent scholarship.
Rereading the book a quarter century after publication, what stands out is
not its obsolescence but its prescience. Historians are fascinated by the social
and cultural "construction" of reality, the complex processes that produce the
"common-sense" categories of everyday life. In this setting, *White Over Black*
commands our attention as the definitive history of the long and agonizing
process by which Americans invented the idea of race. As do today's "New
Atlantic" historians, Jordan recognized that the American colonies were embedded in a wider economic and intellectual world, that events in London
and Paris and Port au Prince reverberated through Boston and Charleston.
And well before historians discovered Benedict Anderson, Jordan understood that the process of building an American nation involved the "imag-

ining" of a community, and that this process entailed exclusion as well as inclusion. In surprising ways the quintessential book of the 1960s reads like a primer for the 1990s.

The best way to appreciate this is by carefully reconstructing the book's complex argument, beginning with the well-known opening chapters on Elizabethan England and seventeenth-century America. Notwithstanding Jordan's strong emphasis on the late eighteenth century, his first hundred pages deserve special attention. They are among the most tightly argued and establish several of Jordan's most persistent themes. They are the most widely reproduced pages of the book, and the most egregiously misread.

Chapter 1, "First Impressions," examines the explosion of commentary that attended England's first sustained "face-to-face" encounter with sub-Saharan Africans in the sixteenth century. Four things struck the English with peculiar force. First, they described Africans as *black*—"an exaggerated term" freighted with negative connotations—inaugurating a long tradition of speculation on the causes of skin color. Second, but far more impressive to the English at the outset, Africans appeared to be "heathens." Unlike Catholics or Muslims, they seemed to have no religion whatsoever. Third, Africans appeared to be devoid of civilization, to be "savage." This attribute they shared with Native Americans, though observers were prone to draw different conclusions in the two cases. Finally, Africans struck the English as peculiarly lewd and libidinous, almost bestial, an ancient association that acquired new saliency in the sixteenth century.

Each of these impressions was critically ambiguous; none led automatically to the enslavement of Africans by Englishmen. The encounter with "black" people spurred the development of cultural relativism as much as prejudice, Jordan writes. The same Protestants who were appalled by heathenism tended also to be moved by the spirit of Christian universalism. Englishmen generally considered savagery a cultural curiosity produced by the environment; not until the eighteenth century did they invoke it as a justification for enslavement. Even skin color was often seen as a consequence of climate and as such subject to change. In short, Elizabethan attitudes toward African blacks did not constitute racism and cannot explain the origins of slavery in North America. They certainly did not add up to a vision of innate, ineradicable inferiority, rooted in the body, which forms the core of Jordan's conception of racism.

Yet many readers took "First Impressions" as definitive proof that English colonists were racist from the outset. Barbara J. Fields, the book's most severe critic, read *White Over Black* that way, accusing Jordan of treating racism as a transhistorical phenomenon, embedded in the white psyche, rather than as an ideological construction that masked underlying class relations. In fact Fields's criticism hinges on a misreading of the central argument of *White Over*

Black. Jordan is scrupulous in insisting that what is at issue in the first chapter is not race or racism but a conception of difference, registered along a variety of axes, only one of which was skin color. Seventeenth-century perceptions of Africans, however derogatory, were still too inchoate, too ambiguous about the sources and meaning of perceived differences, to provide a firm justification for enslaving blacks.

For Jordan English prejudices are interesting primarily for what they reveal about the English. The central theme of chapter 1, and indeed of the entire book, is that white attitudes were anything but the unmediated reflections of an objective physical or social reality. The important question is why the English suddenly took so much interest in exploring the differences between themselves and Africans. Having passed through a Protestant reformation and a Puritan revolution, Jordan argues, pious Englishmen were inclined to fall into fits of intense self-scrutiny. They were also obsessed with social order as they confronted the first dramatic stirrings of capitalist development. "Tudor England," Jordan explains,

> was undergoing social ferment, generated by an increasingly commercialized economy and reflected in such legislative monuments as the Statute of Apprentices and the Elizabethan vagrancy and poor laws. . . . Literate Englishmen generally (again not merely the Puritans) were concerned with the apparent disintegration of social and moral controls at home; they fretted endlessly over the "masterless men" who had once had a proper place in the social order but who were now wandering about begging, robbing, raping. They fretted also about the absence of a spirit of due subordination—of children to parents and servants to masters. (p. 42)

In this "charged atmosphere" the English looked at Africans as "social mirrors" and "were especially inclined to discover attributes in savages which they found first but could not speak of in themselves" (p. 40). In the lexicon of today's anthropologists, Africans became the "other," a negative reference for Englishmen struggling to reconstruct their own sense of identity. This was even more true in America, Jordan argues, where the English colonists confronted a wilderness which simultaneously evoked the dream of freedom and the specter of complete social breakdown. By selectively isolating a host of physical and cultural differences between Africans, Native Americans, and themselves, the English were able to triangulate their own position thereby recovering the sense of order and control they so desperately craved.

Thus for Jordan the white encounter with blacks always was a psychological as well as a social transaction; it engaged not only conscious interests but unconscious fears and obsessions. Jordan's emphasis on the unconscious and irrational is most evident in his careful investigation of the enduring linkages between racial prejudice and sexual insecurity. He suggests, for example, that the colonists' feverish discussion of black sexual potency provided a way of externalizing their own buried anxieties about sexual license, figuratively chaining "the blackness within." This preoccupation with the white psyche has irked a number of Jordan's critics, who maintain that it obviates class distinctions and conduces to a consensus vision of American history. Yet nothing in Jordan's formulation precludes class analysis, or the possibility that prejudice could be used instrumentally to advance or obscure class interests. On a number of occasions, in fact, Jordan makes precisely that point.

Ultimately, however, Jordan locates the origins of slavery not in the white psyche but in the material interests of English colonizers. At the outset of chapter 2, "Unthinking Decision," Jordan carefully distinguishes two questions often conflated by historians: What caused slavery? and Why were some groups enslaved rather than others? To the first question, Jordan's unambiguous answer is: economics, or more specifically, the labor shortage. "It may be taken as a given that there would have been no enslavement without economic need, that is, without the persistent demand for labor in underpopulated colonies" (p. 91). This premise leads Jordan, like the Handlins before and Edmund Morgan after him, into an examination of the English class structure of the late sixteenth and early seventeenth centuries. At the moment of settlement, Jordan points out, the English knew of three very different ways of getting some people to work for others: wage labor, indentured servitude, and slavery. Each had a distinct history; each had its own prospects for success or failure in America. Given the availability of land, few settlers would voluntarily sell their labor for wages to another. So very early on, the English turned to indentured service, a relatively new form that grew out of the apprenticeship system. A response to the social turmoil of the sixteenth century, indentured servitude combined feudal elements of coercion with a recognition of certain basic rights presumed to accrue to all Englishmen. As such, indentured service was very different from slavery—at least as the English understood it.

While the practice of slavery had long since died out in Britain, the concept endured in English law and to a lesser extent in English imaginations. In a discussion that anticipates subsequent work by M. I. Finley and Orlando Patterson, Jordan pieces together contemporary understandings of what it meant to be enslaved. Unlike the medieval villein, the slave's loss of freedom was total. And unlike indentured servitude, slavery was perpetual, usually hereditary. Slavery, Jordan writes, was "somehow akin to a loss of humanity," the loss being symbolized in the widespread belief that slaves were captives of war whose physical lives had been spared in return for the loss of social life. Finally—and again unlike the indenture system or wage labor—

slaves were "others," which in the seventeenth century generally meant non-Christians.

All of which raises the second question: Why were some groups enslaved and others not? The answer, for Jordan, lay in a constellation of factors. English settlers were well aware that the Spanish and Portuguese were enslaving Africans on both sides of the Atlantic, that fellow Englishmen were doing the same thing in the West Indies, and that the Dutch were constructing a robust trade in Africans. Equally important, English impressions of Africans dovetailed neatly with their concept of the slave: Africans were captives, apparently devoid of civilization and religion, and resoundingly un-English. By the same logic Native Americans were vulnerable to enslavement, and many were in fact enslaved, though certain practical difficulties—the relative ease of escape, appalling morbidity, and the ever-present threat of retaliation—kept their numbers relatively small. The English were also accustomed to treating the Scottish, Welsh, and Irish differentially, often barbarically, but there were powerful inhibitions against enslaving fellow Christians. Thus indentured servants were often brutalized, degraded, and subjected at times to harsher treatment than slaves, but they were never stripped of all their freedom and as such were never actually enslaved. Thus Jordan's cryptic chapter title—"Unthinking Decision"—may be partly explained by his sense that the English "choice" of Africans was overdetermined. They were vulnerable, available, and they fit colonists' "rough" ideas about slavery quite well. "On every count," Jordan concludes "Negroes qualified" (p. 56).

But the decision was "unthinking" in another sense as well. In the specific conditions of seventeenth-century America, Jordan argues, it was easy for whites to enslave Africans without resorting to racial arguments—or to any other arguments, for that matter. Probably the most striking feature of the process is the virtual absence from the documentary record of any attempt by seventeenth-century Virginians to justify or reason through the implications of their handiwork. This absence underscores Jordan's claim that a coherent ideology of racism did not exist at the moment the English began enslaving Africans in North America. Indeed only in the early eighteenth century—after mass enslavement had begun and after social and economic conditions had given rise to slavery in every North American colony—did skin color replace religion as the chief distinction the English made between themselves and their African slaves. Difference of color, Jordan concludes, was not a reason for enslaving Africans; it was the rationale for it, after the fact.

Part 2 of *White Over Black* examines the process by which this rationale was elaborated during the first half of the eighteenth century. The material realities of slavery propelled this development. Slave population was reaching significant proportions in northern cities as well as southern colonies. Controlling the slaves on a day-to-day basis was proving difficult. Slave rebellion, especially in the wake of uprisings in South Carolina and New York City, became a very real concern. Colonists also confronted a dramatic increase in the population of Christian Africans, further undermining the distinction between heathen and Christian that initially served as a rationale for the specific enslavement of Africans. And there were other problems as well. What was the place of free blacks? What about the children of "mixed" couples? All of these issues forced whites to think about blacks more systematically than they ever had.

As they did so whites drew on two secular traditions, the Great Chain of Being and the Linnean system of biological classification. Although the former was ancient and hierarchical and the latter modern and horizontal, both were influenced by the eighteenth-century zeal for scientific categorization, itself a part of what Jordan sees as the "gradual secularization of thought" in the Western world as a whole. Together, he argues, these trends led to "the naturalization of man," the elevation of the ancient science of anatomy into something entirely new: the use of the human body as a basis for distinguishing between different groups of people. Precisely which physical differences mattered was, as Jordan points out, a highly selective affair. Thus blacks were placed beside apes in biological classifications, even though factors such as bodily hair (and even skin color) might just as well have placed whites in that position.

Again, Jordan is careful to distinguish this preoccupation with physical distinctions from racism. To be sure, the building blocks for what would later become racism were being gathered. But even in 1750, he argues, more than a century removed from Elizabethan England, with African slavery long since established up and down the North Atlantic coast, American colonists could not have instituted recognizably modern forms of racial segregation, in part because "until the latter part of the eighteenth century . . . there was no explicit racist doctrine in existence which could have served as rationale for separate water pumps" (p. 131). Consider those words carefully: "*no explicit racist doctrine in existence*" until "*the latter part of the eighteenth century.*"

The critical shift to racism began with the American Revolution, which constitutes the fulcrum of Jordan's book. It was no small coincidence that the slave economy faltered as America declared its independence. The implications for the place of blacks in the new nation were immense. During the American Revolution the principle of human equality leaped beyond its traditional religious boundaries and became a secular ideal in American political culture. Environmentalism became the accepted form of explaining human differences, while everywhere in revolutionary America the basic sameness of all humans was emphasized. And it was in these years that Americans became conscious of "prejudice." Antislavery and humanitarian ideas sprouted rapidly in the soil of a moribund slave economy. Many of the harshest features of the slave codes were eliminated. Every northern state instituted some plan of emancipation. A wave of manumissions swept the upper South. In Delaware and certain parts of Maryland and Virginia the free black population increased tenfold, outstripping the population of slaves.

Unfortunately, the era spawned other processes as well, which would eventually help contain the Revolution's libertarian impetus. As Jordan notes, the last quarter of the eighteenth century witnessed a remarkable crystallization of racial thought. It is difficult to unravel this process because the discussion of "race" took place in many registers and was often embedded in larger debates about hierarchy, national identity, and the endowments of nature. Jordan, characteristically, frames the issue in terms of "self-scrutiny," suggesting that white Americans were forced, in the very act of declaring themselves free and independent, to account for those in their midst who were neither. Whatever the sources, the result was an explosion of speculation about African Americans (and to a lesser extent Native Americans), most of it couched in the deceptively transparent language of natural science. By the early 1800s the ideological building blocks that had been gathering for centuries had been assembled into the coherent conviction that blacks were innately inferior to whites, and that the two "races" could never live together as equals. Here, at last, was "racism," and Jordan devotes nearly three-hundred pages to its development in the wake of the American Revolution.

He divides his discussion of postrevolutionary America into two lengthy parts, beginning, as always, with economic, political, and cultural context. The economic revival of slavery in the lower South was the starting point, but only that. The rapid rise of the cotton economy in the 1790s, after slavery had been abolished or languished elsewhere, effectively created a momentous sectional division at the very moment that America was defining itself as a nation. The decline of revolutionary antislavery organizations, Jordan writes, "dovetails with the timing of economic changes in the South and the development of American nationhood" (p. 342). Political and social turmoil spawned the impulse to restrict the contagion of liberal egalitarianism. Conservatives reacted sharply to the political upheavals of the 1780s and the French Revolution. The racial dimension of such fears, long smoldering below the surface, burst into flames with the outbreak of slave revolution in Haiti. The slave rebellion in Virginia in 1800, led by Gabriel Prosser, struck even closer to home. "To trace the spread of Negro rebellion in the New World," Jordan writes, "and to examine American responses to what they saw as a mounting tide of danger is to watch the drastic erosion of the ideology of the American Revolution" (p. 375).

Although Jordan sees revolutionary ideology as overwhelmingly libertarian in its implications, he is also sensitive to its internal contradictions. "[T]he absence of any clear disjunction between what are now called 'human' and 'property' rights," he notes, "formed a massive roadblock across the route to abolition of slavery" (p. 351). The inability of most antislavery advocates to consider the place of emancipated blacks was yet another indication of the "limits of antislavery" in the Age of Revolution. Nowhere were these internal limits more evident than in the environmentalist critique of slavery. Antislavery scholars such as Samuel Stanhope Smith and Benjamin Rush, two key players in Jordan's narrative, insisted that African Americans were capable of improvement, that their degraded condition was a reflection not of innate inferiority but of a stultifying environment. Yet in making this argument both Smith and Rush accepted "whiteness"—both physical and cultural—as the norm. And both partook of the era's naturalistic temper, blithely assuming that the effects of the environment could be read where it most mattered: in the body. Thus Smith not only argued that African Americans' mental and moral faculties were improving through exposure to the American environment, but insisted that this improvement was registered physically in both sharpening of countenance and lightening of skin. Similar premises underlay Rush's notorious suggestion that blackness was a tropical disease akin to leprosy which would, when cured, leave blacks white. Such concessions fatally weakened environmentalism's antislavery thrust. It was only a matter of time before proponents of black inferiority began proffering their own environmental explanations, arguing, for example, that long exposure to luxuriant tropical climes had rendered blacks constitutionally indolent, mentally torpid, and thus unfit for freedom.

Widespread fear and loathing of free blacks was itself a crucial component in the development of racist ideology. It was the prospect of emancipation, after all, that provoked Jefferson's appalling outburst in the *Notes on the State of Virginia*. Indeed, one of the central ironies of *White Over Black*, and of the period itself, is that the enlarged population of free people of color, perhaps the chief product of the revolutionary "contagion of liberty," was itself one of the proximate causes of postrevolutionary racism. "In retrospect," Jordan writes, "it is easy to see that [the existence of free blacks] constituted an invitation to development of a new rationale which would tell white men who they were and where they stood in the community—the rationale of racial superiority" (p. 134).

The revival of the slave economy, the spread of Jacobinism, the internal weakness of antislavery, and the growth of the free black community converged in the late eighteenth and early nineteenth centuries to sustain the powerful conservative upheaval (Jordan is reluctant to call it "reaction" but the terminology hardly matters) that issued in a modern ideology of racism.

A familiar pattern of segregation emerged: black testimony was increasingly restricted from American courtrooms; black schools were separated from white; blacks were consigned to the galleries of white churches. Radical environmentalism was dead. Even the most ardent opponents of slavery came to argue that emancipation had to be accompanied by the removal of blacks from the United States. "What American intellectuals did in the post-Revolutionary decades was, in effect, to claim America as a white man's country" (p. xiii). This claim was based on a critical premise that was widely assumed but only occasionally articulated: that blacks were not simply inferior to whites, but that they were inherently inferior and that they would therefore never be equal.

By Jordan's account it took hundreds of years to reach that conclusion. It follows, then, that Jordan cannot believe that racism caused slavery; the very opposite of what his book is often said to argue. He does not even argue that slavery caused racism—at least not in the straightforward way the phrase seems to imply. And contrary to his critics, Jordan does not see racial attitudes as independent entities; they exist only in wider historical contexts that give them meaning and which change over time. He does not see "race" as a transhistorical category; he does not see racism as an "ultimate reality." Indeed, what is most striking about *White Over Black*, a quarter-century after its publication, is how easily it fits among the more recent attempts to demonstrate the historically or culturally constructed nature of powerful social categories. Long before anyone was writing about the invention of sex, Winthrop Jordan wrote a brilliant book about the invention of race.

At a time when the consensus interpretation still had considerable residual power among historians, *White Over Black* argued, first, that the American Revolution was a radical social transformation and, second, that it was followed by a major period of conservative reaction. Since 1968, however, our understanding of the radicalism of the Revolution and of the subsequent period of conservatism has become considerably more sophisticated. Two issues stand out: first, it would be impossible today to explain the rise of racial ideology in the late eighteenth century without paying far more attention than Jordan did to the transforming influence of capitalist development. Second, a new version of *White Over Black* would have come to terms with the work of scholars—among them Linda Kerber, Henry May, Drew McCoy, and David Brion Davis—whose explorations of postrevolutionary reaction provide a vital context for the study of emerging racial ideology.

There are other flaws. Jordan is rarely explicit about the historically specific definitions of race and racism that he is using, a failure which invites misreading. (A short "note on the concept of race" only compounds the problem by seeming to suggest that race may, after all, be biologically real rather than

the historically constructed category the rest of the text shows it to be.) Inconsistencies and obscurities, particularly in the book's second half, raise still
other questions: How, precisely, do pre- and postrevolutionary patterns of
segregation differ? Was Thomas Jefferson "an effective sounding board for
his culture" (p. 429) or was his "the most intense, extensive, and extreme
formulation of anti-Negro 'thought' offered by any American in the thirty
years after the Revolution" (p. 481)? The sheer density of evidence, combined
with Jordan's refusal to resort to simple explanations, imparts an almost Del-
phic quality to parts of the analysis.

There are other aspects of Jordan's analysis that would undoubtedly be
treated differently twenty-five years later. Aside from an insightful discussion
of the linkages between Jefferson's racism and his misogyny, *White Over Black*
generally neglects women and gender. Yet recent work in American and European history suggests some striking parallels between the evolution of
ideas about race and gender. Even as the concept of innate racial difference
crystallized in the late eighteenth century, an ideology of sexual difference
acquired new rigor, and for many of the same reasons: the collapse of patri-
archal social and political structures, the universalistic implications of liberal
ideology, and the explosion of natural science, with its zeal for classification.
Obviously the two processes were not identical. The doctrine of "separate
spheres," for example, never applied to African Americans; nor did anyone
ever argue that women had no place in American society and should thus be
removed by colonization at the earliest possible convenience. Nonetheless,
it is no coincidence that two of the major groups explicitly excluded from the
revolutionary compact were the subjects of intense scientific scrutiny in the
late eighteenth century, scrutiny which served to "fix" their physical nature
and rationalize a distinct social role.

Even less satisfactory is Jordan's treatment of African Americans themselves. When he wrote *White Over Black* historians were wringing their hands
over the "Elkins thesis." They did not yet have the benefit of the tremendous
studies of slave culture that would, by the mid-1970s, leave Elkins's argument
in tatters. Jordan's book occasionally reveals the traces of an older view of
African American life, one that bemoaned the degree to which slavery had
stripped Africans of their cultural heritage, leaving them more or less helpless
in a cultural void. As a result Jordan has trouble confronting the agency of
blacks in the history of white racial attitudes. Indeed, one of Jordan's most
powerful arguments—that white attitudes about blacks tell us more about
what's going on among whites than they do about the realities of African or
African American life—inadvertently reinforces this weakness in *White Over
Black*. Yet evidence of black agency surfaces again and again throughout the
book: the pattern of daily resistance among slaves, serious outbreaks of slave

rebellion, and the steady determination of blacks to claim their freedom whenever possible and to assert their rights as free men and women. Indeed African Americans were among the most avid participants in the late-century debates on race, slavery, nature, and the compass of revolutionary ideals. *White Over Black* would have been greatly enriched by a deeper appreciation of the complexities of African American life, and of the degree to which white attitudes were the product not simply of an internal crisis within white society but also of a sustained cultural encounter between whites and blacks.

These shortcomings notwithstanding, there is reason today to appreciate more than ever the central thrust of *White Over Black*. We live in an age when public commentators respond to seemingly intractable social problems by denying the existence of "the social" as a meaningful category of analysis. Crime, unemployment, homelessness, are commonly reduced to individual failures of character or, more ominously, to genetic predisposition. Distinguished sociologists casually interpret statistical correlations as evidence that blacks have inherited their lower IQ scores or that they commit violent crimes because they are born with extra Y chromosomes. That no geneticist has ever located a gene for either "intelligence" or "aggression" suggests the continued power of racial ideology in the interpretation of statistical data. To appreciate the point, turn the tables: imagine a scholarly search for a gene that predisposes prosperous white men to embezzle funds from savings and loans, violate SEC restrictions against insider trading, cheat on their tax returns, and pad their expense accounts—all on the basis of strong statistical correlations between white-collar crimes and white skin. If such racialist leaps of logic are palpably absurd when the subjects are white men, it must be asked why the absurdity is less striking when comparable arguments are made about African Americans. To answer that question, there is no better place to begin than the masterpiece Winthrop Jordan published twenty-five years ago.

James Campbell, Department of History, Northwestern University, is the author of Our Fathers, Our Children: A History of the African Methodist Episcopal Church in America and South Africa, *to be published by Oxford University Press. James Oakes, Department of History, Northwestern University, is the author of* Slavery and Freedom: An Interpretation of the Old South *(1990). His current project is tentatively entitled* Created Equal? A Social History of American Political Thought.

DESTINY AND AMNESIA: THE VISION OF MODERNITY IN ROBERT WIEBE'S *THE SEARCH FOR ORDER*

Kenneth Cmiel

Which of us has a book in print twenty-five years after publication? The life span of academic opinion is so short, and the churning mass of publication so great, that most of our books get lost in just a few years. "Never try to use a book more than ten years old in any class," a bookseller once told me after a futile search for a fourteen-year-old text. Good advice, on the whole, and advice that makes the longevity of Robert Wiebe's *The Search for Order* even more impressive. Published in 1967, in the past couple of months I have spotted it in bookstores in Chicago, Iowa City, the San Francisco Bay area, and even Budapest, Hungary.

The genius of *The Search for Order* is its synthesis. Wiebe took a number of themes that historians and social scientists had been working on for some years and brought them together into a very readable story. Neither political history nor social history, *The Search for Order* is the history of a civilization. Like Jacob Burkhardt's *Civilization of the Renaissance,* it weaves together politics, culture, and society—in extraordinarily graceful prose. Just a few years before, historians had been debating whether Theodore Roosevelt was a "conservative" or not. After Wiebe's book such a discussion seemed beside the point.

Such success creates its own problems: everyone "knows" what the book is about; its contents become a few catch-phrases. By taking a close look at *The Search for Order* twenty-five years after publication I hope to help save the book from that fate. For if you listen carefully to the words themselves, I will argue, you will find *The Search for Order* a much sadder book than is normally thought, one that paints a rather grim, even bleak, picture of life in the twentieth century.

The Search

Almost every American historian still knows the thesis of *The Search for Order*, at least in broad outline. By the 1870s, the United States was a distended society. The eruption of modern social and economic forces brutally undermined the autonomy of small-town America. International markets, a national credit system, the railroads, the mass movement of peoples from all over the globe to urban areas—these were some of the forces trampling what Wiebe called "island communities," those small self-contained towns and neighborhoods that had organized the life experience of most Americans until the years after the Civil War. The story of the book is how the United States eventually shed its nostalgia for the island community and began constructing the bureaucratic nexus needed to order a modern society (*The Search for Order*, p. xiv). Central to the change, according to Wiebe, was "the new middle class," those professionals and modernizing businessmen intent on curbing the unruly disorder but at the same time not fogged by any romantic ennui for the older ways of life.

Although not mentioned in the text, the intellectual background to *The Search for Order* was modernization theory. In the 1950s and 1960s, liberal social scientists argued that the whole world was moving from static, traditional societies toward modern, dynamic ones. The social theory of Talcott Parsons and Edward Shils provided critical background for this thinking, but literally hundreds of articles and monographs spelled the theory out in concrete application. Daniel Lerner's influential *The Passing of Traditional Society* (1958) was one such text; Seymour Martin Lipset's *The First New Nation* (1963) another. In 1966, the year before Wiebe's book was published, an array of synthetic books appeared trying to outline the modernization process.[1]

How much Wiebe consciously used this theory versus how much he just picked up from what was in the air is of little matter. The bottom line is this: the characteristic assumptions of modernization theory color nearly every page and theme of *The Search for Order*. It is often remarkable how specific the parallels are. Like all modernization theory, Wiebe made the development of mass communication a central part of his story.[2] Just as the sociologist James Coleman did, Wiebe argued that the pragmatic, rational attitudes toward social problems so important to modernization meant that bureaucracies would have to perpetually respond to new issues. There would be no final resolution.[3] Like Edward Shils, Wiebe spoke of the shifting relationship between periphery and center of society.[4] As a number of social scientists had claimed, Wiebe thought that successful modernization generated some order in society, an order built on interest-group politics.[5]

Robert Wiebe is an excellent historian. *The Search for Order* was more nuanced to the individualizing details of U.S. history than some of the more procrustean social science of the day. In fact, one of the dangers of having this book become a classic is that it can be reduced to the "modernization thesis," an interpretation ignoring the richness of the actual text. Unlike what some current glosses of *The Search for Order* claim, Wiebe was well aware that society was not perfectly "rationalized" by 1920, the endpoint of his book. The closing pages indicate the tentativeness with which the new order was grasped, the inability of elites to understand fully what they were doing, the huge demographic pockets that bureaucratic rationality did not reach. "The large majority of wage earners lived beyond its influence," Wiebe commented, "untouched by its values and largely free from its discipline." Similarly, a "great many in the countryside had also escaped the bureaucratic web." The "enduring rural localism," fueled by "old village values," underwrote the fury of the Eighteenth Amendment (p. 301, also see p. xiv).

Yet there is good reason why a myth has arisen that *The Search for Order* ended with bureaucratic rationality imposed. Wiebe relentlessly organized his whole book around the *search* for order (not the establishment of order) but there was no doubt that the search would succeed. Wiebe took for granted the eventual arrival of modern, integrated, administrative and bureaucratic systems that would bring peace to the body politic. And plotting the book in terms of the direction of history was not accidental: it was a central tactic of modernization theory that hinted at even deeper intellectual debts. *The Search for Order,* like all modernization theory, was a direct descendant of nineteenth-century philosophies of history.

First, like nineteenth-century theory, say in Hegel or Marx, modernization theorists claimed that nothing less than the whole of world history could be understood by grasping the essential drift toward modernity. The theory was the most recent stab at a universal history of mankind.[6] And modernization theorists, like Hegelians of the nineteenth century, often intimated that there was something necessary, inevitable, about this process. On one thing, at least, both Hegel and Talcott Parsons would agree—there were evolutionary stages to history.[7]

But such connections, noted in passing by numerous scholars, have remained murky and unexplored.[8] There were a number of reasons why modernization theorists were unable to recognize their own similarities to earlier philosophies of history. One critical problem was that of will, of the role of human agency in history. By the 1950s, it seemed that earlier philosophies of history denied the role of human *praxis* in the making of history. A thinker like Hegel saw history unfolding in a particular direction regardless of where historical actors thought they were going. The "chaotic interplay of particular self-interests and passions" wound up creating a history that was both rational and progressive. The real was the rational, as Hegel put it. Human actors were the "tools of history," so to speak. This was what Hegel called the "cunning of reason."[9]

Scholars of the 1950s and early 1960s often portrayed history as having a direction and logic that sucked in all participants. As one leading social scientist put it: "Modernization and aspirations to modernity are probably the most overwhelming and most permeating features of the contemporary scene. Most nations are now caught in its web." For another scholar it was a "universal tendency" for modernized societies to "penetrate" traditional ones regardless of whether the latter willed it or not. As Daniel Lerner put it in his 1958 study of the Middle East, against the "rationalist and positivist spirit. . . . Islam is absolutely defensless."[10]

Nevertheless, modernization theorists usually denied any connections with earlier philosophies of history and were far more ambiguous about the question of agency.[11] Their faith in historical progress included less *Geist* than Hegel, more bureaucracy than Spencer, and, most important, less class conflict than Marx. Modernization theorists saw themselves as modern and scientific, implicitly exemplifying the best of the rationalization process. By the 1950s, the older philosophies of history smacked of a period where the division of labor had not yet touched intellectual life. It seemed either too old-fashioned or too Marxist to speak so openly of the unfolding of history, of the necessary stages that the whole world went through, although, that was, in fact, what modernization theory was presenting.

The Search for Order is implicated in all of this. Like so many of his contemporaries, Wiebe tried to distance himself from evolutionary philosophies of history. To Wiebe, people like Edward Bellamy, Lester Ward, and Walter Rauschenbusch were romantics trying to reconstruct community on a national level. They owed much to Hegel, Wiebe said at one point (p. 140); their preordained stages of history represented a "cast of mind" that was actually a "prison" (p. 144). Teleological theory "never reconciled human control with a predetermined progress" (p. 144). It was only when more functional thinking surfaced, thinking well-suited for bureaucratic management, that modernization would proceed.

Yet if Wiebe would not say so directly, and perhaps did not even think it consciously, his prose nevertheless kept referring back to an autonomous and inevitable flow to history. At critical moments—summaries of the argument, titles of chapters, keywords employed—Wiebe's own language intimated that modernization has a logic all its own, that against the rationalist and positivist spirit the island community was defenseless. The title of the chapter on the 1890s, "The Fate of the Nation," implied inevitability. Elsewhere Wiebe wrote that during World War I the "pieces for a pattern seemed to appear by magic," that they "fell into place with a neatness almost no one could have predicted," indicating some preexisting place for the pieces to fall to (pp. 293, 296). Wartime rationalization "seemed to be following a prearranged schedule," Wiebe wrote, again hinting that some "order" existed independent of the people who made it (p. 296).

One way the text did this work was by abstracting social concepts from the people who made them up. Terms like "community" and "nation" occasionally take on a life of their own, something Wiebe himself negatively associated with nineteenth-century evolutionary theory. "The health of the nineteenth-century community rested on two things," Wiebe wrote, "its ability to manage the lives of its members, and the belief among its members that the community had such powers" (p. xiii). In this passage the term "community" becomes an "it" that performs action. But who, in actual fact, could have been doing the managing except members of the community? Wiebe's words impute some sort of personality to the community itself, above and beyond its constituents. One could alternatively think of the community as made up of people who interact in various ways, some with duly constituted authority, some without. In this view the community is not ordering its members, but people have arranged lives in such a way as to constitute a community. Instead of the abstraction ruling its citizens, the actions of people define the abstraction.

The same sort of reification appears elsewhere. For instance, although World War I had brought the outlines of a new order to America, that order remained "indefinable." But if people did not yet understand the new system, Wiebe claimed that in "a general sense, the nation had found its direction" (p. 301). It is not that people don't understand the implications of their actions (nothing unusual there), but that Wiebe can in the same breath claim that "the nation" (at this point apparently disconnected from any real people) has "found" its way. Here is the sense that the nation is an independent personality, doing things regardless of whether people want it or not. Here too is the notion of a direction to history. This is Hegel's cunning of reason.[12]

At times Wiebe's language can be deeply ambiguous, quickly shifting back and forth, first seeming to grant autonomy and agency and then pulling it away. Such an ambiguity surfaces in one of the most famous sentences of the book. "The heart of progressivism," Wiebe wrote "was the ambition of the new middle class to fulfill its destiny through bureaucratic means" (p. 166). *Ambition* here conjures up free will and action. The new middle class is taking charge. But just as quickly the term *destiny* tugs the other way. The new middle class is only fulfilling some plan, doing what it had to do to find its place in a grander historical scheme. Hegel, it might be added, spoke very similarly about "world-historical figures," those Napoleans and Alexanders who managed to take humanity to the next stage of civilization.[13]

That Wiebe's analysis leads in this direction is lent more support by his argument that the new middle class did not yet see what it was creating. As late as 1920 the new order was still "undefinable," the new middle class still laboring in "confusion" (pp. 301–02). Woodrow Wilson, his advisers, and Congress did a remarkable job managing the nation during World War I, Wiebe thought, but no one "could pretend . . . they followed a master plan" (p. 221). The new thinking was "exceptionally vague" about the nature of leadership, Wiebe thought. "In fact, fuzziness in crucial matters constituted its gravest weakness" (p. 162). This was not a class fully aware of its own purpose, both the subject and object of history. To the contrary, the class succeeded because it rode the crest of modernity. "Often confused," Wiebe wrote, the new middle class nevertheless "did represent a new society" (p. 132). *Praxis* here disappears; and modernity begins to look more like a destiny than a creation.

The vision of history behind *The Search for Order* also helps explain Wiebe's rendering of violence and conflict. One common misperception about *The Search for Order* is that violence is missing. This is just empirically wrong. Wiebe saw conflict and did not mince words about it. Western mine operators "shot and beat, trampled the strikers' rights as citizens" (p. 38). Southern whites attacked African Americans with "viciousness" (p. 110). The suppression of strikes before 1917 was "ferocious"; the violations of civil liberties during the war, acts of "inhumanity" (pp. 290, 301). And what was the establishment's response to Haymarket? "Sanctity of human life had certainly not been the issue; within a few hours after the event police had indiscriminately killed at least as many as the bomb" (p. 79). By the 1890s, Wiebe argued, the United States was a nation riven by its "pathological" divisions (pp. 95–96).

Wiebe did not ignore conflict: brutality, chaos, and venality appear and reappear. But just as with the assertion that *The Search for Order* ended with rationality imposed, there is a reasonable basis for the mistaken claim that Wiebe did not include conflict. And similarly, this is unpacked through Wiebe's implied philosophy of history. For conflict appeared not in its own right in terms of its historic mission. The discord and violence were structured in ways that appear to soften their blows.

First, Wiebe denied that class conflict could explain much (pp. 13–14). Instead, discord was understood as part of the strain of modernization. Conflict in *The Search for Order* is multidimensional, racial at one point, class-driven at another, antimodern and rural at still a third. But in *The Search for Order*, there are no constant enemies, no sustained sets of opponents. Wiebe associates discord with disorder rather than warfare, chaos rather than the ongoing struggle of well-defined social enemies.

There is also a purely textual dimension to the softening of conflict's force. Since Wiebe folds brutality and supression into the larger story of modernization, he does not linger on the details. There are no descriptive pictures of any act of inhumanity; no incidents discussed in any depth. Instead, some brutality is announced, assimilated into a larger story, and then is gone. The result for any reader is that oppression appears fleetingly, only in passing.

At bottom, then, Wiebe's treatment of violence contains the following paradox: because he understood modernization in a particular way, discord was central to his story—it revealed the strains of transition. At the same time, because he saw the process as heading toward resolution, violence and oppression take on a passing character in the text—produced by historical situations instead of evil people, they exemplify the cunning of reason.[14]

This too rings similar to nineteenth-century philosophies of history. Wiebe's folding of violence into the logic of change sounds very much like Hegel's sense of history as a slaughterbench. "Every philosophy of the cunning of reason," Luc Ferry has noted, "cannot help justifying war." Such theories are "necessarily dialectical in the sense that peace must always be realized through its opposite," and "sociability through unsociability." To understand history dialectically is to see how violence contributes to the progress of humanity.[15]

By the time Wiebe's book appeared in 1967, attacks on modernization theory were already appearing.[16] One important complaint was that the theory misunderstood conflict in several specific ways. Conflict, it was claimed, was more than a transitional disorder, it was the catalyst of change itself. Thus Barrington Moore, in The Social Origins of Dictatorship and Democracy (1966), argued that a violent break with the traditional past was a necessary precondition for the emergence of stable democratic regimes. A related charge was that modernization theory made tradition and modernity far too neatly packaged, with none of the messiness that was the reality of actual history. In response to this attack, writers sympathetic to modernization theory, scholars like Reinhard Bendix, Samuel Huntington, Clifford Geertz, and S. N. Eisenstadt, were by the mid-1960s trying to recast the theory to include a more complex sense of conflict and tension. Dislocation and disorganization were being understood as part of modernity proper as much as the modernizing process.[17]

Both of these changes—that violence is a catalyst of change and that discord continues after modernity triumphs—came from those committed to some theory of modernization. Neither appear in The Search for Order. In this respect the book is one of the last major statements of the earlier form of modernization theory that sees discord as transitional and assumes bureaucratic rationality will bring some stability to the social system.

For Order

Nineteenth-century philosophy of history understood the ideal to be bound up in the real. For Hegel, only immature minds thought of a total transformation of society; the "adult's way of looking" understood the rough "harmony between 'is' and the 'ought to be.' "[18] This same effort of reconciliation to reality is operative in *The Search for Order*. "Idealism" and "realism" were terms that Wiebe himself used constantly, and idealism, he claimed, had to adjust to mass, industrial society. Wiebe argued that all sorts of groups committed to small-town mores were out of touch, unable to grasp the emerging urban-industrial order. Only by breaking through such "idealistic" thinking could a more "realistic" approach surface. And realism was bureaucracy.

A writer like Hegel had great faith in history because he saw it as the unfolding of God's will. "The state," Hegel wrote, "is only the march of God through the world."[19] When Hegel claimed that the ideal must capitulate to the real, then, this was something more complicated than twentieth-century realism. The "ideal" that must bend was the *human* ideal, the longings of a people at any given time. And these human longings could not stray too far from what "was" because God directed the course of history. He watched over it and gave it shape. The wicked as well as the good were a part of God's handiwork, all designed for the best. For Hegel, above the human ideal that had to bend to reality was the Absolute Ideal that gave shape to reality.

One hundred years later, however, God was dead. And this changed the meaning and consequences of Wiebe's capitulation to the "forces" of modernity. For Hegel, history marched toward freedom. This was, to be sure, not freedom understood in terms of simply doing what you want, but freedom as the reconciliation of rational desire with the course of history. Nevertheless, the goal was something called "freedom." For Wiebe, however, nothing so inspiring remained. Without a God, all that was left was "order." Wiebe's modernity is far grimmer than that pictured in nineteenth-century philosophies of history.

Again and again, Wiebe stated explicitly that the goal was order, control, discipline. The author's own language was as bleak as any used by Foucault in the 1970s. The "fevers of war constituted just one chapter," Wiebe wrote, "in the developing campaign to discipline American society" (p. 287). Taft, in 1912, "thought of reform in terms of control" (p. 217). All three candidates, in fact, thought of national "guidance" in "bureaucratic terms" (p. 217). Bureaucratic thinking "obliterated the inner man," Wiebe wrote elsewhere. Education became "the guidance of behavior with social processes," or "social engineering" (pp. 148–49, also p. 209). Still elsewhere: "The old problems of establishing and maintaining order, then, continued without pause," producing a sense of "chaos" in the late nineteenth century, "a more conscious sense of individual helplessness" in the twentieth (p. 187). At one point Wiebe did mention that bureaucratic management might lead to "social release" as well as "social control" (p. 223), but this wasn't followed up anywhere in the book. Instead, readers were treated to continuing allusions to order, discipline, restraint. On the book's last page was still one more reference to men "imposing order upon the nation" (p. 302).

That Wiebe was writing about a search for *order* should be confronted squarely and its implications explored. In *The Search for Order* there is not a sustained passage on the quality of life. Poverty is addressed in passing but Wiebe does not say that the end result of order is a better standard of living. Nor is it freedom or democracy. There is no discussion of a new kind of fraternity or of a refigured, national community. Wiebe, it should be emphatically emphasized, was not rewriting the story of reform invented by such people as Herbert Croly, Jane Addams, or John Dewey. The story for Wiebe is bureaucratic rationality pure and simple.

The Search for Order owed a lot to the modernization theory of the 1950s, but it owed just as much to early-twentieth-century writers skeptical of democratic pieties. The spirit of Max Weber, Sigmund Freud, and especially Walter Lippmann runs through Wiebe's book. Through bureaucratic rule, accomplished via constant negotiation among elites, some social consensus would be preserved. But even "consensus" should be understood more as the absence of a negative than a strong positive, one way that *The Search for Order* looked like Lippmann's *Public Opinion*. Wiebe used the terms "cooperation" or "coordination" to describe successful rule, terms putting the emphasis on the bureaucratic process instead of common values. When Wiebe spoke about "social consensus," on the other hand, he viewed it as one of the fuzzy "idealistic" notions that persisted in a futile effort to bring "cohesion" to American society. As with Lippmann, chaos would be eliminated by expertise and elite negotiation, not by some shared sense of purpose in the populace at large.[20]

It would be very wrong to assume that Wiebe thought there was anything noble about these changes. Words with positive valence appear throughout the text, but associated with the fading order, all things which had to pass. Typically, the term *community* is used in this way.[21] So too is *democracy* and its cognates.[22] Moreover, the word *democracy* was conspicuously absent whenever Wiebe described the new urban-industrial order. The implication was clear. It was not that democracy was being refigured to the new ways of the world; it was that democracy was in decline. At times Wiebe made the contrast directly, setting the two systems against each other. As he put it in one such passage, socialists elected to union offices acted just like their non-socialist opponents, shelving "plans for democratic unionism in favor of a centralized command" (p. 174).[23]

Wiebe's realism seemingly undermined all ideals. Woodrow Wilson spoke "platitudes about equality and individualism" (p. 218); the objective of the new civil service reform was "efficiency rather than moral purity" (p. 171); T. R. ruled with "the magician's skill" (p. 192). The very notion of a people ruling itself was suspect, the point where Wiebe's links to Lippmann seemed the strongest. Notions like "the people" or the "rational public" existed only as a "mystic coherence," an "article of faith," while the real politics took place at the bureaucratic level (pp. 162–63, 222, 283). The use of vague civic symbols to manipulate mass attitudes was a major theme of Lippmann's *Public Opinion*.

The contrast between democracy understood as local control and modernity understood as elite management was something else Wiebe shared with Lippmann.[24] The vacuous and manipulative blather of modern civic rhetoric, the negotiation (manipulation?) behind the scenes, the connection of this to modern mass communication—this was Lippmann's analysis as much as Wiebe's. *The Search for Order* was 1960s modernization theory, but with a dark edge found in only a small part of that era's scholarship.

Wiebe's tortured pages on progressive theories of leadership highlight his hesitations about the new system. These theories, which posited bureaucrats as directly fulfilling the will of the people, were "immediately and persistently attacked as undemocratic." Wiebe was gentle on the reformers' motives but chilling about the reforms' effects. Although the new middle class "trod so close to elitist rule," Wiebe wrote, they thought they were "modernizing, not destroying democracy." And if he could say that the "theory was not as boldly authoritarian as it sometimes appeared" (what a compliment!), he also made clear that it left the question of leadership very confused. What did the new bureaucratic thinking create: leaders with "an ominous freedom of action," where "communion with the masses suggested the lockstep of totalitarianism," or elites who were "highly intelligent coordinators," responding "to all manner of rational public demands" (pp. 161–62)? Wiebe bitingly noted that some progressives thought Mussolini "a somewhat peremptory democrat" (p. 155).

But if there was darkness in *The Search for Order*, it was the author himself who kept it at the edges. The dismissal of idealism, disdain for civic rhetoric, and the preoccupation with order might have sounded like Lippmann, but Wiebe's great faith in interest-group negotiation sounded very much like the social science of the 1950s and early 1960s. Woodrow Wilson's legislative program, the "Wilsonian compromise," Wiebe called it, "covered an impressive range." Among other things, "no well-organized group was denied" (p. 221). At moments like this, Wiebe seemed confident about "the assumptions of a bureaucratic order: a society of unceasingly interacting voluntary groups assisted in their course by a powerful, responsive government" (p. 222).

Depending on where one looked, you could find either optimism or pessimism, either 1960s modernization theory or early-twentieth-century "realist" criticism of progressive democratic theory. The blend gives *The Search for Order* much of its distinctive flavor.

Wiebe's hesitation to condemn reflected, I think, his own generous spirit. He didn't like to moralize. But just as much it reflected his sense of modernity's inevitability. To rail against the new was beside the point, and it got in the way of securing order as well. Just as much as Max Weber, Wiebe saw us trapped in the "iron cage" and, if his words weren't as brutal or as frank as Weber's, they still hinted at an "icy darkness" laying ahead of us all.[25] After 1907, Wiebe wrote, the "movements for control remained much cooler—more calculated—for a much longer period. The greater emphasis on enticements and compromises, showed a much defter hand, as if Machiavelli had taken the helm from Savonarola" (p. 209).

At the same time, however, Wiebe's hesitancy about judging blocked an even icier interpretation of his own material. I find *The Search for Order* a darker, more nihilistic portrait of modernity than Wiebe was willing to claim. In fact, I think it reads even darker today than when it was first published. It is a picture of modernity closed in on itself, incapable of reflecting on its mission. Wiebe's portrait very logically leads to the conclusion that the "end of history" had arrived, but unlike Hegel's, an end that could promise only order instead of freedom.

For Wiebe, bureaucratic thinking was critical to modernization. This orientation, as Wiebe portrayed it, broke all thinking into pieces, compartmentalizing social problems the better to treat each in a manageable fashion. Every issue became part of a "complex social technology," Wiebe wrote. Change was no longer seen as evolutionary but as the perpetual "interaction and adjustment" of the different pieces of the puzzle (p. 146). The continuous management of problems replaced thinking about the next stage of history. In *The Search for Order*, bureaucratic thinking replaces evolutionary thought (pp. 145–63).

Reinhart Koselleck has suggested that the notion of a modern age first appeared when expectations drifted beyond experience. Modernity, in other words, began when people wanted more than they could get. For Koselleck, the decline of eschatological history between the fifteenth and eighteenth centuries was matched by the rise of various philosophies of history. The latter were critical to the emergence of modernity. Their talk of the "goal of history," of human "progress," of the material and spiritual "improvement" of the world—all created horizons of expectation reaching past lived experience.[26]

But Koselleck also pointed out a second type of posteschatological thinking about the future. This he calls "rational prognosis," tracing its origins back to Machiavelli and Guicciardini. It refers to the effort to manage problems as they arise. It is the "delicate art of political calculation." Unlike philosophies of history with their long-term projections, political calculation does not look beyond the most immediate future. Its job is to neutralize the unexpected. Rational prognosis, in other words, tries to contain the future instead of opening up its possibilities.[27]

Rational prognosis, bound so close to actual experience, can potentially black out any distant expectations opened up by the philosophy of history. This is exactly what happens in *The Search for Order*: Wiebe presents a picture of evolutionary theory being replaced by bureaucratic thinking that is a pure form of political calculus, the constant adjustment to new forces, an effort to negotiate some check on the potential "chaos" of indeterminacy.

The result, however, if pursued to its logical conclusion, was to bind all thinking to the present. There was no room for dreaming in Wiebe's modernity; all residual idealism was treated with Lippmannesque cynicism.[28] For Wiebe, modernization meant the perpetual work of control. By arguing that idealism had to disappear, replaced by constant political calculation, Wiebe's modernization reunited lived experience with human expectations. By assuming that this would succeed, Wiebe in effect suggested an end to history.[29]

For Wiebe, bureaucractic thinking was the mechanism for order, the way to reconcile the ideal to the real. But if Wiebe's analysis was right, bureaucratic thinking would serve another purpose, one he did not explore. It would generate an institutionalized amnesia. There would be no way to orient oneself in time, something that Koselleck has shown to be central to modernity's sense of progress. One would be precluded, in other words, from seeing other ways of being.

Moreover, with serious thinking broken up into the scattered pieces of the specialists, even a coherent snapshot of the current state of things would be gone. If Wiebe was right, and instrumental thinking so thoroughly dominated, there would be no thought that tried to bore into the essence of modernity. We would be reduced to thinking about how things might be used instead of looking at what they were. Not only would other ways of being be concealed, but we would not even know it.[30]

This would be modernity triumphant, but without any guiding faith. Here the Lippmann-like cynicism with which Wiebe treated public references to "the people" or "rational public" was especially chilling, suggesting that the civic language expressing "faith" in the regime was not to be taken seriously. Instead of a faith in democracy that oriented us to the future, "faith" for Wiebe had become a form of false consciousness, a way of evading any confrontation with what we actually had become (see esp. pp. 162–63). Bureaucratic thinking, the success of modernity, the end of history—all prove to be a form of nihilism.

Here too contrasts with Hegel are illuminating. Like Wiebe, Hegel saw what is now called "state-building" as critical to the "solution" to history. Like Wiebe, Hegel was skeptical of easy references to "the people." And just as Wiebe found the new middle class the catalyst for order, Hegel argued that the civil servant was the key to modernity. For both Wiebe and Hegel, the civil servant marked the end of history.

Yet there were differences. To Hegel, the civil servant was important because he was a member of the universal class. Free from any position in the social struggle, the civil servant would tirelessly work toward the good of the whole. Such heady and naive optimism was gone from Wiebe. Indeed, a precondition for Wiebe's modernity is to disconnect thinking from any notion of totality, to accept interest-group negotiation as standard practice, and to treat discrete social problems in functional terms. Wiebe's civil servants do not tirelessly work to realize the freedom of citizens, do not reconcile the subjective and the objective. Their historical mission is to maintain order and sever any need for this reconciliation. They manage the world. And by turning thought into "techniques of constant watchfulness and mechanisms of continuous management" (p. 145), they closed off the possibility of even raising "the present age" as a category to be explored.

It is then not surprising that none of the protagonists in *The Search for Order* can grasp the new system emerging, that neither leaders nor followers can see what is going on. Their very mode of thinking would preclude it. The end of history owes its emergence not to a higher stage of consciousness, as Hegel thought, where the whole can be surveyed, but to an institutionalized amnesia, where a whole can't even be imagined.

Yet if nihilism runs through *The Search for Order*, it also suggests how Wiebe overstated his case. Wiebe's own account of the triumph of bureaucratic thinking is contradicted by *The Search for Order* itself. Wiebe argued that modern social thought would be content with subdividing social analysis into discrete parts. But *The Search for Order*, rooted in an evolutionary philosophy of history, does not do this at all. It is a broad sweep of a whole civilization. Management is never enough, the need to understand, to place oneself in a frame, is just as important. And it is just this enframing that *The Search for Order* was meant to provide. Readers turn to the book not to find aid in managing any discrete part of the "social technology," but to get a broad sense of how the world they live in was put together. They turn to it, in other words, to help make sense of their lives.

Considering how people make sense of their lives might have led Wiebe in directions he did not take. The histories of friendship, love, family, neighborhood, work—indeed, of all those face-to-face practices by which people orient themselves in the daily world—were not addressed in *The Search for*

Order. Wiebe might have explored how bureaucratic systems corrupted these lifeworlds.[31] He might have looked at the ways that people manipulated the system to their own ends.[32] Or he might have seen bureaucratic systems as imperfectly correcting the brutalities of daily life.[33] But Wiebe turned down none of these avenues. So preoccupied was he with the system-building itself that he ignored the ways that the system interacted with human beings.

Nor did Wiebe explore alternatives to order. Entrepreneurial thinking, still a potent force in American culture, celebrates a modernization valuing risk over routine.[34] Christopher Lasch has uncovered a whole tradition of thinking condemning the modern concept of progress and substituting a religious sense of "hope" or "redemption" to look to the future.[35] And postmodern writers champion "play," the transgression of established borders, hoping to articulate a means of raising possibilities in a manner different from the philosophy of history.[36]

But we need not turn to formal social thought to find alternatives to order. Everytime someone compulsively drops a couple of hundred into the slots at Reno, or two people in a fit of lust have sex in the back seat of a car (sans protection), or a man or woman gets drunk and burns a tattoo into their skin — there the stochastic, the passionate, and the impulsive are in revolt against comfortable routine. Every Sal and Dean and Thelma and Louise on the road is engaged in what might be called a search for disorder. This too has a history, although most historians, so close to the genteel end of the middle class, do not generally think about such things. But they are there. There are more things in the world than order. And perhaps we can thank God for it.

The brilliance of *The Search for Order* was its synthesis. But for me the most engaging part of the book a generation after its publication is Wiebe's confrontation with modernity. Wiebe's modernization theory had a bitterness in it, verging on a film noir version. In the more optimistic modernization theory, Henry Fonda would have been cast as the Great Progressive Hero. Wiebe, I like to think, would have argued for Robert Mitchum.

I find much to commend in this picture. When reflecting on the cynicism that dominates our own politics, on the sense of futility that "the people" have about the system, on almost everyone's inability to take political rhetoric seriously, and on the role that contemporary mass communication plays in all this with its spin-doctors, network analysts, and correspondents, I still see Wiebe as definitely onto something.

And if *The Search for Order*'s hints of an unavoidable modernity seem naive twenty-five years later, they strike me as no more or less naive than contemporary manifestoes for research evoking agency or everyday resistance. In *The Search for Order* there are details that were wrong, important questions not pursued. No doubt about it, the book would be written differently today.

Still, each time we confront some part of the "system" that seems to act stupidly or cruelly (as we all do), remember, Wiebe was talking about *order*, not happiness. And that, after twenty-five years, is exactly what continues to give the book its bite. Think of *The Search for Order* as a very gentle man confronting some very dark forces.

Ken Cmiel, Department of History, University of Iowa, is the author of "A Broad Fluid Language of Democracy: Discovering the American Idiom," Journal of American History *(December 1992).*

1. C. E. Black's *Dynamics of Modernization: A Study in Comparative History* (1966); S. N. Eisenstadt, *Modernization: Protest and Change* (1966); Myron Weiner, ed., *Modernization: The Dynamics of Growth* (1966); Talcott Parsons, *Societies: Evolutionary and Comparative Perspectives* (1966).

2. Compare Daniel Lerner, "Modernization: Social Aspects," *International Encyclopedia of the Social Sciences* (1969), 10: 386; and Wiebe, *Search for Order*, pp. xiii, 19, 96, 209, 217, 296.

3. James C. Coleman, "Modernization: Political Aspects," *International Encyclopedia of the Social Sciences* (1968), 10: 395–96. Or as another writer put it, a "willingness to accept continuous change on the plane of both an individual and social structure"—James O'Connell, "The Concept of Modernization," *South Atlantic Quarterly* 64 (1965): 554; compare with Wiebe, *The Search for Order*, pp. 145, 193, 195.

4. Edward Shils's essays are collected in *Center and Periphery: Essays in Macrosociology* (1975); *Search for Order*, p. 37.

5. Seymour Martin Lipset, *Political Man: The Social Bases of Politics* (1960); and *The First New Nation* (1963), pp. 25–29; *The Search for Order*, pp. 145–48, 221–23, 293–99.

6. See, for example, Black, *Dynamics*, p. 1.

7. Talcott Parsons, "Evolutionary Universals in Society," *American Sociological Review* 29 (1964): 339–57.

8. One purpose of this essay is to take a closer look at the connections between modernization theory and earlier theories of historical evolution. Among those who have in passing noted the connection, see O'Connell, "Modernization," p. 560; Samuel P. Huntington, "The Change to Change: Modernization, Development, and Politics," *Comparative Politics* 3 (1971): 290–93 (Huntington's brief comments are especially helpful in placing modernization theory in intellectual history); Christopher Lasch, *The True and Only Heaven: Progress and Its Critics* (1991), pp. 160–61; Francis Fukuyama, *The End of History and the Last Man* (1992), p. 68. Arthur M. Wilson has looked at the similarities between modernization theorists and eighteenth-century theories of progress—see Wilson, "The *Philosophes* in the Light of Present-Day Theories of Modernization," *Studies in Voltaire and the Eighteenth Century* 58 (1967): 1893–1913.

9. Luc Ferry, *The System of Philosophies of History* (1992), pp. 37–46, at p. 39.

10. Eisenstadt, *Modernization*, p. 1; Marion J. Levy, Jr., "Patterns (Structures) of Modernization and Political Development," *Annals of the American Academy of Political and Social Science* 358 (1965), p. 30; Daniel Lerner, *The Passing of Traditional Society: The Modernization of the Middle East* (1958), p. 45. Lerner is actually quoting someone here, but the context makes clear that he subscribes to the view.

11. For an example of skepticism toward nineteenth-century predecessors, see Parsons, *Societies*, p. 115. Parsons, of course, developed his theory as a "voluntaristic" alternative to Marx. At the same time, he thought "democracy" was an "evolutionary universal"—see Parsons, "Evolutionary Universals." Jeffrey Alexander points out that criticism of Parsons often comes from two quite opposite directions. One group claims that Parsons holds an unrealistic form of voluntarism, the other that Parsons is a voluntarist in name only while a determinist in practice. Alexander argues that the roots of these criticisms lie in the am-

biguity of Parsons's own thought—Jeffrey Alexander, *Theoretic Logic in Sociology: The Modern Reconstruction of Social Thought—Talcott Parsons* (1983), pp. 301–08.

For another good example of this tension between agency and determinism, see H. Stuart Hughes, *Consciousness in Society* (1958), pp. 330–35, where Hughes praises Max Weber's social theory for salvaging a modified place for will while noting a couple of pages away that Weber thought we were trapped in the "iron cage" of modernity. Hughes relied heavily on Parsons for his interpretation of Weber.

12. For another example, see p. 165, where *society* is personified in the same fashion: "Most of them [the new middle class] lived and worked in the midst of modern society and accepting its major thrust drew both their inspiration and their programs from its peculiar traits." Here again the use of "its" gives something called "society" the means to act; middle-class reformers do not shape change but succeed by adjusting themselves to the "thrust" of society.

13. Georg Wilhelm Friedrich Hegel, *The Philosophy of History* (1956), pp. 30–31.

14. For an exceptionally clear example of this, see the discussion of the "inhumanity and supression" of labor during and after World War I (p. 301).

15. Ferry, *System of Philosophies*, pp. 46–50, 105–11, at p. 109.

16. Joseph Gusfield, "Tradition and Modernity: Misplaced Polarities in the Study of Social Change," *American Journal of Sociology* 72 (1967): 351–62; C. S. Whitaker, Jr., "A Dysrhythmic Process of Political Change," *World Politics* 19 (1967): 190–217.

17. Clifford Geertz, *Agricultural Involution: The Process of Ecological Change in Indonesia* (1963); Samuel Huntington, "Political Development and Political Decay," *World Politics* 17 (1965): 386–430; Reinhard Bendix, "Tradition and Modernity Reconsidered," *Comparative Studies in Society and History* 9 (1967): 292–346; Eisenstadt, *Modernization*, p. 20.

18. Hegel, *Hegel's Logic: Being Part One of the "Encyclopedia of the Science"* (1975), p. 291.

19. Hegel, *Selections*, J. Loewenberg, ed. (1957), p. 443. On the broader role of religion in nineteenth-century German historical thinking, see Georg Iggers, *The German Conception of History: The Nationalist Tradition of Historical Thought from Herder to the Present* (1968), pp. 14, 174–75, 184, 185, 270–71.

20. Lippmann argued that the modern "common will" was created not by democratic deliberation that generated agreement on a common aim, but by elites manipulating symbols that were so vague that people with very different aims would interpret them to suit their own "realities"—Walter Lippmann, *Public Opinion* (1922), pp. 125–58; compare with *The Search for Order*, pp. 156–59, 162–63, 293–94, 296, 297.

21. For some examples, see *The Search for Order*, pp. 55, 287, 301.

22. I am excluding here, of course, references made to the Democratic party.

23. For *democracy, democrat,* or *democratic* used in association with earlier practices or ideals, see pp. xiii, 2, 36, 37, 91, 100, 113, 167; used in direct contrast to bureaucratic order, see pp. 60, 74, 152, 174; used to describe the phoniness of old ideals under the impact of modern forces, see pp. 38, 77, 227; used to describe the progressives' confusion of "democracy" with order, see pp. 155, 161.

The only place that Wiebe used the term democracy in connection with "modern" forces was when describing the attitudes of urban reformers like Frederic Howe or Tom Johnson. Even here, however, Wiebe saw a gap between attitude and action. Once in office, this group lost touch with the "people" they were supposed to represent—see pp. 132, 142, 167, 176, 196, 212–13. On p. 170 Wiebe used *community* in conjunction with these reformers.

24. Lippmann, *Public Opinion*, esp. pp. 169–74, 195–97, 233–62.

25. Max Weber, *The Protestant Ethic and the Spirit of Capitalism* (1958), pp. 181–83; H. H Gerth and C. Wright Mills, eds., *From Max Weber: Essays in Sociology* (1946), p. 128.

26. Reinhart Koselleck, *Futures Past: On the Semantics of Historical Time* (1985), pp. 267–88.

27. Ibid., pp. 12–16.

28. *The Search for Order*, pp. 155–59, 162–63.

29. I use the phrase "end of history" not to mean that nothing more will happen, but that there is no further "stage" of history, no new horizons that will appear. Future events then are the working out of the details of this final stage of history. This is Hegel's meaning of

the phrase. For a recent argument that no more advanced stages of history will appear, an argument made in the wake of communism's collapse (and paying homage to modernization theory as a flawed precursor), see Francis Fukuyama, *The End of History and the Last Man* (1992).

30. See Martin Heidegger, "The Question Concerning Technology," in *The Question Concerning Technology and Other Essays* (1977).

31. Jürgen Habermas, *The Theory of Communicative Action, vol. 2: Lifeworld and System: A Critique of Functionalist Reason* (1987).

32. James C. Scott, *Domination and the Arts of Resistance* (1991); John Fiske, *Understanding Popular Culture* (1989); Michel de Certeau, *The Practice of Everyday Life* (1984).

33. This is a theme of some of the best feminist scholarship. For example, Linda Gordon, *Heroes of Their Own Lives: The Politics and History of Family Violence* (1988).

34. Milton Friedman, *Capitalism and Freedom* (1962).

35. Lasch, *The True and Only Heaven*.

36. Jean-François Lyotard, *The Postmodern Condition: A Report on Knowledge* (1984).

GILBERT H. BARNES AND DWIGHT L. DUMOND: AN APPRAISAL

Merton L. Dillon

As graduate students in the late 1920s, Gilbert H. Barnes and Dwight L. Dumond probably read Charles A. and Mary Beard's *The Rise of American Civilization* (1927)—almost everyone, it seems, did. But for those two, acquaintance did not bring acceptance. Unlike many other young historians at the time, Barnes and Dumond resisted the explanatory power of material interest and technological change. They never would be numbered among the progressives. The Beards's explanation of the Civil War struck them as particularly unconvincing.

At the watershed of the Beards's narrative stood the great conflict that they called The Second American Revolution. Traditionally slavery and antislavery, together with the moral issues inherent in them, figured large in accounts of Civil War causation, but not for the Beards. They credited "the economic processes of the age" with moving the nation toward war. "Slavery was but one element," they explained, "and if the number of abolitionists is any evidence, a minor element, in the sweep of political and economic forces that occupied the attention of statesmen throughout the middle period and finally brought on the irrepressible conflict." The moral and religious aspects of slavery, although much agitated, had been of small consequence, except to veil material interest. Not surprisingly, the origins of abolitionism little interested scholars for whom economics supplied the dynamics of history. When the Beards did try to account for abolitionism, which they agreed helped cause 1830s discord, their interpretative genius faltered: "The sources of this remarkable movement are difficult to discover."[1]

By redeeming this lapse, Barnes and Dumond would dramatically alter the prevailing understanding of the Civil War and its origins, invite reappraisal of the influence of religion throughout American history, and contribute to recognition of the permeating effect of racism and slavery in this country. In so doing, Dumond, in particular, would offer one of the profession's vivid examples of history employed for didactic purposes.

Both men wrote dissertations under the direction of Ulrich B. Phillips, who then was considered the preeminent student of slavery and a major interpreter of the Old South. Although both Barnes and Dumond acknowledged his inspiration, their work diverged far from his in nearly every respect.

As early as 1915 Barnes came upon the activities in western New York of the revivalist Charles G. Finney and the reform movements his revivals fostered. The labors of Theodore Dwight Weld, a Finney convert who until Barnes's discoveries was practically unknown, struck Barnes as having been far more effective in promoting antislavery than those of William Lloyd Garrison, the presumed leader of the movement. Sometime in the next decade Barnes located a trove of correspondence of Weld and his wife, Angelina Grimké, and of her sister, Sarah. From this rich material he constructed a narrative that led from Finney's evangelism to Weld's abolitionism, and thence ineluctably to anti-slavery electoral politics and, finally, to Civil War. Barnes believed that in enthusiastic religion he had found the source of abolitionism that would remain mysterious to the Beards. Economics played no role in Barnes's fast-paced drama. Neither did Garrison, except as an evil genius whose egotism and radicalism, Barnes charged, hampered the work of the true reformers, the majority of them Weld's converts and close associates.

Barnes's account moved the center of antislavery from New England, which had been its presumed focus, to New York and the West. Although on the face of it this shift, like the demotion of Garrison, appeared iconoclastic, probably few found the change truly surprising. This was a time when Frederick Jackson Turner's views of frontier influence reigned supreme, when historians were more likely to find initiative and creativity emanating from the West than from New England. In approaching his studies of the South, Phillips, Barnes's dissertation adviser, had charged New England's historians with systematically distorting the South's record and the complex events that he later termed "The Course of the South to Secession." Having designed his own work as a corrective to such warp, Phillips could take satisfaction that his student had struck yet another blow at New England's hegemony.[2] In due time Dumond's publications would have a similar effect.

Barnes's most striking contribution lay in the motives and character he ascribed to those western abolitionists whose methods he approved. His dissertation, completed in 1930 and published in 1933 as *The Antislavery Impulse, 1830–1844*, was peopled with men and women (mostly men) of uncommon religious zeal. According to Barnes, abolitionism, having originated in Finney's revival, was itself a great religious crusade aimed at ending slavery through awakening white Americans to the sin of slaveholding. There

was something novel about taking such an idea seriously in 1930, and presenting it as respectable, for religion as a force in American history had long been
neglected. The Progressive historians, in particular, found no room in their
analyses for so immaterial an element; neither, at the time Barnes's book
appeared, did sophisticated Americans hold evangelism and professions of
religious conviction in very high esteem. They were likely even to find them
embarrassing. The Puritans and Puritanism, together with their alleged off-
spring, Prohibition, had come to be objects of derision; Biblical conservatism,
as represented in the Scopes Trial and interpreted by H. L. Mencken, and
evangelists, as caricatured by Sinclair Lewis in *Elmer Gantry*, represented
ignorance and chicanery. To the many persons holding such attitudes, religious intensity as exemplified by the abolitionists seemed alien and suspect. It
is not surprising, then, that some reviewers at the time, and critics afterward,
read Barnes's book as an exposure of a flagrant instance of religious extremism,
this one having the tragic consequence of civil war.[3] Nonetheless, *The Antislavery Impulse* was recognized as an innovative and important work, even
though some continued to judge its animus toward Garrison extreme, while
others could not bring themselves to view even the western faction of the
abolitionists, whom Barnes extolled, as being anything other than fanatics.
Reaction in the South was notably ambivalent. The Civil War and Reconstruction were still near enough in time and the South still possessed sufficient
regional pride to give appreciative accounts of the antislavery movement
power to revive old debates and resurrect old anger. Dumond, in particular,
would find that this situation continued for many years to come.[4]

Even before *The Antislavery Impulse* appeared, Barnes and Dumond began
to edit the Weld-Grimké letters. These were published in 1934 under the
auspices of the American Historical Association, as Barnes's book had been.
The volumes' introduction repeated Barnes's understanding of the close causal
relation between the revivals, the antislavery movement, and the Civil War,
and explicitly rejected an economic interpretation of the conflict.[5] The editors
apparently assumed that these matters exhausted the documents' significance.
They missed the implications of the fact that, as a reviewer noted, "The writers
of these letters seemed unaware that Andrew Jackson was president or that
they lived in the stirring period of Jacksonian Democracy."[6] In later years, as
historians extended the scope of their concerns, the Weld-Grimké letters came
to serve as an invaluable source for social history, including most recently the
history of women. Scholars also would find in them material clues to cultural
and psychological aspects of reform that did not occur to Barnes and Dumond,
nor, it is fair to add, to many others at that time.

Except for infrequent book reviews, Barnes published nothing more, but
spent the rest of his career (he died in 1945) teaching economics at Ohio

Wesleyan College. It was Dumond who expanded upon the work Barnes had begun.

Although many scholars' early publication holds the seeds of their later work, this is conspicuously not true of Dumond's. Nothing in his first book, *The Secession Movement, 1860–1861* (1931), still the only comprehensive treatment of its subject, would lead a reader to predict either the tone or interpretation that characterized its author's mature work. Improbable as it now may seem in light of Dumond's eventual reputation, some readers detected in its restrained prose untoward sympathy for southern positions. *The New York Times*'s reviewer went so far as to label him "a Northerner with Southern principles [who] purports to give a history of the secession movement. The danger of his book is the oily, silky way in which he writes it, which gives the uninformed an impression of sobriety and impartiality." The point seemed proved when Joseph G. de Roulhac Hamilton at the University of North Carolina found "manifest in it, fairly clearly, strong sympathy with the point of view of the South in the period treated."[7]

When the book appeared, and for some years afterward, Dumond apparently did indeed view himself as a southern historian in the Phillips mold. He would be one of the organizers of the Southern Historical Association and would serve on its first board of editors. But soon, from holding views compatible with those of Phillips (when Phillips accepted an appointment at Yale, Dumond succeeded him at Michigan), Dumond went his own way. He cut his ties with the SHA, and by the late 1930s emerged as one of the profession's harshest critics of slavery and the slaveholders' policies.

Perhaps no historian of recent years has felt more earnestly the scholars' duty to take a moral stance toward their subject and toward related events in their own time. In his introduction to *The Letters of James Gillespie Birney, 1831–1857* (1938), selections from a large antislavery collection he had discovered, he abandoned dispassion. Beginning with that essay and continuing without abatement, he expressed his opinions in forceful, often unqualified language, seldom leaving doubt as to his position. To most readers it must have been obvious that he had moved far from the decidedly southern sympathies of his mentor. Yet Dumond always insisted, though without much evidence, that had Phillips lived, he would have arrived at a similar position with respect to slavery and the antislavery movement. "As for Phillips, he was closer to me than my own father," Dumond wrote in 1965. "No man knew him better or respects his memory more. I shall say what I please about his work, secure in the knowledge that were he here, he would be in perfect accord."[8]

Dumond was born and grew up in Ohio, and as a young man had considered training for the ministry. These facts may help explain why his absorption in the Weld-Grimké and Birney papers—both of them permeated with profound religious commitment and indignation at slavery—so influenced him. As more than one critic observed, reading Dumond was equivalent to reading an abolitionist tract: "the editor has become a member of the Weld-Grimké-Tappan-Finney Holy Band," commented a southern reviewer of the Birney letters.[9] But to be overwhelmed by Dumond's unbounded empathy is to risk missing other salient aspects of his analysis.

Research on the secession movement had given him an appreciation of the finespun constitutionalism of its advocates. Now, in the papers and published writings of Birney, a slaveholding lawyer turned abolitionist and presidential candidate of the Liberty Party in 1840 and 1844, Dumond encountered the powerful legal and constitutional arguments that politically oriented abolitionists turned against slavery, arguments that in the Weld-Grimké papers and in Barnes's account were decidedly subordinate to evangelism. Dumond's grasp of the secular and institutional basis for antislavery likewise led him to emphasize its pre-evangelical phase. Whereas Barnes neglected American antislavery before 1830 while crediting British influence, Dumond pointed to continuities with the Revolutionary and Early National periods. There he found important sources for abolitionism in the natural rights theories of the Enlightenment.

In his Commonwealth Foundation Lectures, delivered at the University of London and published as *Antislavery Origins of the Civil War in the United States* (1939), Dumond presented an extended interpretation of the causes of the war. His emphases somewhat differed from those of Barnes, but more noteworthy was his revising of the progressive historians, who viewed the war as a struggle over sectional economic interests, and of the revisionists, who found the war "needless" on the ground that it resulted from the blunders of politicians who failed to defuse the "unreal" issues agitated by extremists, North and South. Slavery as a matter of moral urgency did not enter either progressive or revisionist analysis. For Dumond, in contrast, slavery was the only thing that did matter.

Barnes had ended his study in 1844, the year that Weld, the central figure in abolitionism as Barnes understood it, retired, and when antislavery unmistakably established itself as a force in Congress. Dumond, extending the chronology, made explicit the ties of antislavery with political developments of the 1840s and 1850s. The abolitionists' campaigns of the 1830s, he found, shaped electoral politics in the next decades and finally formed the basis for the Republican party. Dumond was not a political historian, however, and it would be left to others to explore the complex upheavals that destroyed the Second American Political System.[10]

To Dumond the Civil War was as irrepressible as it was to the Beards, but for different reasons. He believed with the abolitionists that slavery was an iniquity that had to be destroyed if the nation were to be true to its avowed principles. Slavery's defenders, Dumond argued, not its critics, bore ultimate responsibility for the war. To protect the institution, they suppressed civil liberties—freedom of speech, press, and assembly—first in their own section and then throughout the nation. Right-minded southerners would have brought about the end of slavery peacefully and at an early date had they remained free to discuss it. Instead, slaveholders harried their critics out of the South or otherwise silenced them, leaving the section helpless to negotiate peaceful change. At this point, Dumond insisted, armed conflict between slavery and freedom became inevitable.

By destroying the rights of white Americans as well as the rights of slaves, slaveholders set the stage for an American Armageddon. They were abetted in their malevolence by the churches, which refused to condemn slaveholding unequivocally, and by government officials, North as well as South, who refused to protect free speech. For slavery and the iniquities it produced, Dumond argued, the Constitution offered ample remedy. Contrary to Garrison and southern rights advocates, the Constitution never was intended to be a proslavery document. It had been written to embody the spirit of the Declaration of Independence and always should be construed in that light. It was the antislavery element's historic mission to gain political control and then destroy slavery by interpreting the Constitution as the Founding Fathers intended.

Antislavery Origins met a mixed reception. Its narrative of events from abolitionism to Civil War was too schematic for some to accept, and some faulted its inattention to the complex social and economic developments of the 1840s and 1850s. Yet, the cogency of its argument and the eloquence of its style prevented out-of-hand rejection. Even the Georgia historian E. Merton Coulter, a defender of most things southern, mustered grudging approval: "This book is an interesting example of abolition doctrines polished up with modern American scholarship, which, nevertheless, in many of its interpretations is bold and sometimes wise." Hard for many to forgive, nevertheless, was the book's most obvious feature—its close correspondence to the abolitionists' view of history. Thus, Theodore Clarke Smith, himself a northern student of antislavery and a sharp dissenter from Charles A. Beard's recent critique of the presumptions of scientific, objective history, found little in it to commend. He thought it "incredible" that the book "should actually be published in 1939."[11] To this point Dumond's scholarship seemed remote from contemporary social concerns: he was engaged only in professional debate over Civil War causation. But events in the 1940s and 1950s invited application of his scholarly interests to issues of heated controversy, first, as fears of internal subversion led to restrictions on free speech, and second, as the civil rights movement intensified. Dumond made the most of both opportunities.

In his presidential address at the Mississippi Valley Historical Association's 1949 meeting in Madison, Wisconsin, he delivered a ringing endorsement of academic freedom, which he saw as imperiled by the loyalty oaths, legislative investigations, and speaker rules that accompanied the early stage of the Cold War. He likened official repression on college campuses to attempts made a century earlier to silence abolitionists. The specific cure for all societal ills, he declared, was free inquiry and free discussion. He intended his defense of free speech to register beyond the convention hall: "What I have to say about it is addressed not alone to members of this Association, but to all who have in their keeping the destinies of our schools, our press, our churches, and our public forums."[12] Here was the scholar as advocate, frankly employing history for contemporary purpose. Absent was even the pretense of objectivity. The Beards might have approved; those who heard him certainly did. The speech was followed by thunderous applause and a standing ovation. According to the official account of the annual meeting, "The presidential address . . . was the high point of the program. For more than an hour he held his listeners spellbound."[13]

By that time, Dumond already was well along in preparing the full-scale history of the antislavery movement that he regarded as his life's work. Much of *Antislavery: The Crusade for Freedom in America* (1961) would be written during the contentious years that followed the Supreme Court's decision in *Brown* v. *Board of Education*, and would bear the imprint of that circumstance. It is a history of the antislavery movement, but it also is unmistakably a brief for civil rights.[14] Few scholarly books, long in preparation, are published at so opportune a moment—when public preoccupation and topic so neatly coincide.

By the early 1960s schismatic professional debates over Civil War causation had subsided, leaving a residual certainty that, whatever else the war involved, it indeed was about slavery and race, as Barnes and Dumond always insisted. Nevertheless this understanding seemed likely to be obscured for the general public by the romanticism, pageantry, and sentimentality that surrounded the commemorations of the war's centennial then underway. At the same time the impassioned controversy accompanying the civil rights movement focused attention on African Americans, past and present, as seldom before. Celebration mingled with anxiety and social tension.

For this tension *Antislavery* offered no balm and no concessions. Dumond reminded readers who may have been bemused by the Civil War centennial that the war was not a pageant. It was about race and freedom and about the future of the Republic. And he sobered contemporaries with the warning that they faced the same issues as their forebears, and evaded them at their peril. *Antislavery* embodied the spirit of civil rights in its most uncompromising, least temporizing form, and it endorsed the movement's goals without reservation. Something of the passion of those years is preserved in Dumond's stark description of slavery and the degree to which it poisoned the nation's life, and in his admiring account of those who struggled to end it. An unswerving commitment to liberal values pervades the entire book as does indignation that Americans in the 1830s, or at any time since, failed to adhere to them. Few scholarly works ever have set forth with such power the all-pervading influence of slavery, the ideas behind it, the social relationships it produced, and, perhaps most important to say in 1961, its persisting effects. All of these, Dumond charged, resulted from "belief in the biological inequality and racial inferiority of the Negro. . . . *Slavery was not the source of the philosophy.* It merely enshrined it. . . ." Nor, he insisted, casting an eye on the present, did the philosophy die with Emancipation. The freedmen and women soon were reduced "to a second-class citizenship, which is and always has been a modified form of slavery from colonial times to the present" (p. 3, italics in original). Dumond called for the end of racial prejudice and discrimination in the 1960s as forthrightly as any abolitionist in the 1830s had called for the end of slavery.

Dumond had promised a thorough, authoritative treatment of antislavery. He delivered on the promise with an encyclopedic work of some 250,000 words; yet, for many the book was a disappointment. Paradox abounds. The undisputed scholarly contributions of *Antislavery* are matched by grave liabilities. Probably no prior historian of the subject had so mastered the sources or mined them so diligently. *Antislavery* preserves the names and achievements of abolitionists so obscure that one encounters them no place else. It treats at length aspects of the subject that previously had gone unattended. It is not bare narrative nor mere compendium but sets forth sharply defined, closely reasoned theses. Basic to all is restatement of an already familiar premise: economic interest can not account for either slavery or antislavery. Following Phillips, Dumond holds that slavery was less an economic system than a system of racial adjustment, a means of maintaining white dominance over a people judged inferior and dangerous, and was so defended. In turn, antislavery was a religious and moral crusade unsullied by ulterior motives. A decades-long struggle over ideas and ideals, not over material interest, culminated in the Civil War.

Dumond, as strong a proponent of the Higher Law as were the abolitionists, argues that government and churches were designed by their founders to be bastions of immutable principles of freedom and would have been so had misguided or evil forces not intervened. The American Constitution, grounded in the eternally valid principles enunciated in the Declaration of Independence, provided ample weapons to destroy slavery. But the slave power succeeded in dominating the nation, making those weapons unusable, and endangering freedom for everyone. Against great odds, antislavery forces eventually marshalled support sufficient to rescue liberal values, but only at the cost of war. The rescue proved impermanent, however, because, although slavery was destroyed, the idea of racial inequality, which sustained it, survived and lived on to restrict freedom in the present. To some readers, accustomed to more complex analyses, this drama, with its strong, uncomplicated narrative line, no doubt resembled a medieval morality play. To Dumond, it embodied incontestable truth.

The concept of the slave power (or the slavocracy), a staple of antebellum discourse, had dropped from use before Dumond resurrected it to thread the pages of *Antislavery* with its machinations. While many still no doubt would shy from the term and even from the concept, no less an authority on the South than David Potter conceded that Dumond presented the extent of southern political and cultural influence in such a way as to require future historians to reckon with it. Evidently this is so, for a prominent historian of the antebellum South recently has written with apparent ease of the "slavepower."[15]

Despite its intensity, *Antislavery* conveys a conservative message. It does not call for new values but for implementation of old, well-endorsed ones. Probably neither Dumond nor Barnes before him was temperamentally disposed to look favorably on a radical analysis of American society and institutions or on radical proposals to change them. Thus they uniformly denounced Garrison's anarchism and nonresistance and his predilection for causes they considered extreme. To them, abolition was reform, not revolution. Dumond could discuss Gabriel's and Denmark Vesey's conspiracies for slave revolt with tolerance, and could write sympathetically even of Nat Turner—slavery had driven these men to desperate measures. Free men and women, however, should act more responsibly. Thus, he does not mention John Brown's raid nor the numerous white advocates of violence in the antislavery cause. Dumond's hatred for slavery has no limits; his endorsement of civil rights goals is unreserved. But the means he allows for their attainment are circumscribed by his total faith in reason, in the virtue of ordinary people, and in the democratic process. The proper modes of reform are religious argument—to persuade sinners of wrongdoing—and political organization—to garner votes in order to work within the system. Fortunately for him, *Antislavery* appeared when integration and civil rights attained through moral pressure and legislation were still the movement's articulated means and goals. In constructing his argument, he did not have to reckon with the jolt that urban riots occurring outside the South and calls for black power and separatism surely would have administered to his moral universe.

The "ever-expanding antislavery movement, going back to Revolutionary days, had been *political*," Dumond explains, as he prepares to discuss—and to defend—the Liberty Party. "The impulse it had received from Christian benevolence in the decade ending in 1839 was now exhausted" (p. 285, italics in original). His unalloyed endorsement of electoral politics may suggest that he could not grasp the reasoning that led Garrisonians to eschew political action and, instead, to persist in agitation to promote antislavery commitment. But this is not the case: "The failure of the churches [to continue preaching the sin of slaveholding] . . . forced the country to turn to political action against slavery, and political action destroyed slavery as a system but left the hearts of the slaveholders unregenerate and left oppression of the free Negro little less of an evil than slavery had been" (p. 344). If the words *white Americans* were substituted for *the slaveholders*, Garrison could have agreed. Despite this congruence, *Antislavery* otherwise continues the vendetta against Garrison that Barnes initiated and that Dumond never abandoned.[16] He softened his criticism, however, by concluding that Garrison was not so much harmful to the cause as simply irrelevant. He also disposed of suggestions made elsewhere that Garrison's extremism retarded an incipient southern emancipation movement: "there was nothing to retard" (p. 173).

Dumond's animosity toward Garrison, Harriet Beecher Stowe, and many other New England abolitionists, however inexplicable it may be, is perhaps only an idiosyncracy any strong-minded historian must be allowed. Unfortunately the book suffers from more serious deficiencies that reviewers did not hesitate to note, which have impeded its continued authority.

The contrast with the fate of Barnes's *Antislavery Impulse* is striking. Although scholars have shown Barnes's thesis to be overstated and some of his central interpretations to be flawed, his book nevertheless occupies a secure place among antebellum studies.[17] Dumond's more comprehensive and more closely argued work has dropped from sight almost as though it never were. It seldom appears in bibliographies, is rarely cited, and, one suspects, is not read.

By 1961 overt apologists for slavery were scarce, and abolitionists were rid of the obloquy that once clothed them; yet few professional historians found tasteful, to say nothing of convincing, the praise that Dumond heaped on all abolitionists (Garrisonians excepted) and the contrasting shame to which he consigned all who disagreed with them. He apparently saw no gradations of good and evil. And, though none ventured to say so, some reviewers may have found his depiction of slavery as unmitigated horror overdrawn and his assumption that slavery alone accounted for abolitionism implausible.[18]

Equally serious, it was thought, because they violated canons of scholarship rather than only of judgment, were some of the book's other conspicuous qualities. It can not be emphasized enough, however, that in committing these violations, Dumond knew exactly what he was doing. They were the result of calculation and conviction, not of carelessness.

Antislavery is written almost exclusively from the sources—pamphlets, official reports, newspapers, and other contemporary printed material. Dumond evidently did not think it useful to explore manuscripts beyond those he had edited (the Weld-Grimké and Birney collections), probably because their principals constituted the central points of the movement as he understood it. Dumond knew the abolitionists from the face they presented to the world through their published writings as perhaps no one else ever has. But with their other, more private aspects, he felt no need to become acquainted. Thus he left a tempting lacuna that others soon would rush to fill.

Most of *Antislavery*'s reviewers noted, too, its author's failure to cite secondary literature, except for the writings of some of his students and a very few others, not many of them recent.[19] This isolation from current scholarship, like the restricted sources, resulted from decision, not from mindless neglect. Dumond believed that almost everyone who wrote on the subjects that engaged him were mistaken on central points. Only a select few besides himself properly understood slavery, antislavery, and the Civil War. He refused to risk contamination of his judgment by becoming overly familiar with the seductive, interpretative errors which he was convinced marred most scholars' work.

Antislavery stands in isolation in another respect as well. Dumond's unconcern with social, cultural, and economic forces, to say nothing of psychological theory, appears to place the antislavery movement in a setting without perspective. But this limitation, grave though it appears, is intrinsic to his thesis: "the reform movement was an intellectual and religious crusade for social purpose," he declares, and he writes also of "man's fierce passion for individual freedom and equality of opportunity" as the engine driving reform. Finally, he asks, as though certain of assent, "Need one look beyond these impulses for the intellectual ferment of the three decades before the Civil War?" (pp. 155, 156, 157). Dumond was sure that slavery itself accounted for opposition to it. Search for more remote explanation was unnecessary. As though in answer to those who later would find that the reform movements were the product of modernization, rather than of slavery and other social ills, and were encouraged by entrepreneurs as a means of social control, he contends that on the contrary "reform activity was the beneficiary of business activity and business expansion" (p. 156). In short, *Antislavery* relates the abolitionists to nothing except the imperatives of religion and natural law on the one hand and to the evil of slavery on the other. For Dumond, these were sufficient. To many other historians, however, their exclusiveness resulted from lack of perception. An entire literature has been produced to remedy what some consider his shortsightedness in this regard.[20] By pursuing his eccentric convictions, however justified they were in his sight, Dumond resisted a new concept of social history that was changing the way historians thought about the past and their responsibilities in recovering and explaining it. Venerable categories of causation were dismissed as naive by those who sought ever more sophisticated modes of historical explanation and ransacked the social sciences to find them. Impatient with what they regarded as simplistic interpretations, they would stud their critiques with the hitherto rare word *reductionist.*

Elitism remained for the most part an unrecognized offense in the early 1960s, and the charge was seldom levied. But it might have been. Dumond described the antislavery movement as *"an intellectual and moral crusade for social reform and common decency in human relationships, initiated and carried on at great personal sacrifice by men of property and high social position in religious and educational institutions, in public life, and in the professions"* (p. 94, italics in original). Dumond doubtlessly assumed that by asserting the abolitionists' high economic and social status he somehow secured for them an elevated place in history, but, of course, he miscalculated. It is not likely that many today would be comfortable offering such a depiction, even if they believed it true.[21]

Antislavery is a testament to its author's absolute faith in liberal values, but, as the above indicates, its integrity in this regard provided no immunity to critical assault. Dumond's profound knowledge of the antislavery movement and his intense commitment to a cause that many other historians shared, could not, by themselves, satisfy new expectations nor compensate for scholarly deficiencies and peculiarities. C. Vann Woodward characterized *Antislavery* as "a modern primitive, a Henri Rousseau of historiography," which, he wrote, "successfully avoids engagement with the contemporary mind. . . ."[22] However that may be, neither Dumond nor his scholarship can be so easily dismissed. The final appraisal may be left to a historian with whom Dumond may have felt little kinship but whose views of slavery and the planter class resembled his own. Although in his review of *Antislavery* Herbert Aptheker identified some of the same limitations others noted, he also saw a quality most failed to mention: it was "the single most devastating assault yet made in American historiography on the various forms of defense of or apologia for slavery that have hitherto defamed the craft." He continued, "No white professor in an accredited American university has ever delivered so devastating an attack upon the moonlight-and-magnolia school of historiography as has Professor Dumond . . . ; no such individual in the discipline of history ever before so unequivocally attacked racism and white supremacy."[23] At the time of his retirement Dumond drafted his own evaluation of his career: "he has been, through the years, a foremost champion of the theory that human history is essentially moral history, and that historians must assume the responsibility not only of describing events but of discovering motives and making judgments."[24] And, he might have added, citing himself as example, the responsibility of censuring their own times and attempting by means of their scholarship to move society along the paths they believe desirable.

Merton L. Dillon, Department of History, Ohio State University, was a doctoral student of Dwight L. Dumond. He is the author of Slavery Attacked: Southern Slaves and their Allies *(1990).*

1. Charles A. Beard and Mary Beard, *The Rise of American Civilization* (1927), 1: 667, 698–99, 710.

2. Merton L. Dillon, *Ulrich Bonnell Phillips: Historian of the Old South* (1985), pp. 45–46, 114–15.

3. William G. McLaughlin skillfully appraises the book and its reception in his introduction to the Harbinger edition of Gilbert Hobbs Barnes, *The Antislavery Impulse, 1830–1844* (1964), pp. vii–xxx.

4. Charles W. Ramsdell, "The Changing Interpretation of the Civil War," *Journal of Southern History* 3 (February 1937): 3–27. See "Hate Mail" folder, Box I, Dwight Lowell Dumond Papers, Bentley Historical Library, University of Michigan, Ann Arbor.

5. Gilbert H. Barnes and Dwight L. Dumond, eds., *Letters of Theodore Dwight Weld, Angelina Grimké Weld, and Sarah Grimké, 1822–1844* (1934), 1: v–xxvi.

6. Eugene H. Roseboom, review, *Mississippi Valley Historical Review* 22 (1935): 103.

7. Charles Willis Thompson, review, *New York Times*, November 29, 1931; James G. de Roulhac Hamilton, review, *Mississippi Valley Historical Review* 19 (December 1932): 430–32.

8. Dumond, undated memorandum (c. February 1965), "Articles and Other Writings: Book Reviews," Box I, Dumond Papers.

9. Frank Owsley, review, *Journal of Southern History* 5 (May 1939): 263–64.

10. Among the most important are Richard H. Sewell, *Ballots for Freedom: Antislavery Politics in the United States, 1837–1860* (1967); and William E. Gienapp, *The Origins of the Republican Party, 1852–1856* (1985). Sewell was an undergraduate student of Dumond's.

11. E. Merton Coulter, review, *Journal of Southern History* 6 (May 1940): 271; Theodore Clarke Smith, review, *American Historical Review* 45 (April 1940): 664; Peter Novick, *That Noble Dream: The "Objectivity Question" and the American Historical Profession* (1988), pp. 269, 289.

12. Dwight L. Dumond, "The Mississippi: Valley of Decision," *Mississippi Valley Historical Review* 36 (June 1949): 3–26, quotation, p. 8.

13. Report of the Annual Meeting, *Mississippi Valley Historical Review* 36 (September 1949): 291; Betty L. Fladeland, "Revisionists vs. Abolitionists: The Historiographical Cold War of the 1930s and 1940s," *Journal of the Early Republic* 6 (Spring 1986): 17–18 (Fladeland attended this meeting).

14. "Dumond's antislavery publications were cited in oral argument by counsel for the plantiffs in the school segregation cases to supplement their written briefs," Sidney Fine, "Recent Deaths," *American Historical Review* 81 (December 1976): 1291.

15. David Potter, review, *American Historical Review* 67 (1962): 1063–65; William W. Freehling, *Road to Disunion: Secessionists at Bay, 1776–1854* (1990), pp. 118, 308, 440. The "Great Slavepower Conspiracy," which Freehling examines, pp. 336ff, is not quite the slave power Dumond had in mind.

16. The charge that Garrison appropriated many of his ideas and much of his rhetoric, without attribution, from George Bourne appears in John W. Christie and Dwight L. Dumond, *George Bourne and The Book and Slavery Irreconcilable* (1969), pp. 83–98; Aileen Kraditor, *Means and Ends in American Abolitionism: Garrison and His Critics on Strategy and Tactics, 1834–1854* (1969), clarifies Garrison's concept of politics.

17. Robert S. Fletcher, *A History of Oberlin College* (1943); Whitney R. Cross, *The Burned-over District: The Social and Intellectual History of Enthusiastic Religion in Western New York, 1800–1850* (1950), pp. 158–59, 177, 217–19; Clifford Griffin, *Their Brothers' Keepers: Moral Stewardship in the United States, 1800–1865* (1960), pp. 275–76.

18. Recent works consistent with Dumond's finding that abolitionism was a response to slavery rather than to northern economic, social, or cultural change are James L. Huston, "The Experiential Basis of the Northern Antislavery Impulse," *Journal of Southern History* 56 (November 1990): 609–40; Herbert Aptheker, *Abolitionism: A Revolutionary Movement* (1989); and Merton L. Dillon, *Slavery Attacked: Southern Slaves and Their Allies, 1619–1865* (1990).

19. Louis Filler, review, *New England Quarterly* 35 (December 1962): 537; Barton Bernstein, *Journal of Negro History* 42 (July 1962): 199–200.

20. Prominent examples are Ronald Walter, *The Antislavery Appeal: American Abolitionism after 1830* (1976); Lawrence J. Friedman, *Gregarious Saints: Self and Community in American Abolitionism, 1830–1870* (1982); Louis Gerteis, *Morality and Utility in Antislavery Reform* (1987); Paul Johnson, *A Shopkeeper's Millennium: Society and Revivals in Rochester, New York, 1825–1837* (1978).

21. Betty L. Fladeland, "Who Were the Abolitionists?" *Journal of Negro History* 40 (April 1964): 99–115. Attempts to identify abolitionists with a particular class or temperament for the most part have been abandoned. For the most recent analysis, see Edward Magdol, *The Antislavery Rank and File: A Social Profile of the Abolitionists' Constituency* (1986).

22. C. Vann Woodward, "The Antislavery Myth," *The American Scholar* 31 (Spring 1962): 320.

23. Herbert Aptheker, review, *Science and Society* 28 (1964): 233.

24. Dumond, undated note, c. 1965, "Personal Material," Box I, Dumond Papers.

NATHAN IRVIN HUGGINS, THE ART OF HISTORY, AND THE IRONY OF THE AMERICAN DREAM

David W. Blight

"I find in the study of history the special discipline which forces me to consider peoples and ages, not my own. . . . It is the most humane of disciplines, and in ways the most humbling. For one cannot ignore those historians of the future who will look back on us in the same way."

—Nathan Irvin Huggins, 1982

"When a boy had come, the friends had said, 'now you have a son and a successor.' But the son was no successor."

—Oscar Handlin, *The Uprooted*, 1951

"Whenever we write history," wrote the late Nathan Huggins in his final work, "we do so with a sense of transcendent meaning. No matter how limited or particular our study, we assume a broader and grander context in which what we say has meaning and makes a difference."[1] In such assumptions is rooted the maligned but enduring vision of history as art, as human story with emplotment and consequences, as narration that matters.

At heart Huggins was a historiographer in the broadest sense of that term, even a philosopher of history, a meditator on the shape and the meanings of American history. He was also, like his teacher Oscar Handlin, a great narrator. Huggins's story-telling, however, resisted closure and avoided endings, happy or otherwise. He was often perceived as a centrist-integrationist on the sensitive issues at the heart of black studies as the field underwent its highly politicized birth and growth from 1970 through the 1980s. But a careful look at his writings reveals a scholar who wrestled in complex ways with the revolution that occurred in the study of Afro-American history and literature from the late 1960s to his death in December 1989. This essay is not a comprehensive appraisal of all of Huggins's work; it assesses his historical and artistic vision by examining primarily his most imaginative book, *Black Odyssey: The African-American Ordeal in Slavery* (1977, 1990) and related essays.

Huggins's first book, a revised dissertation, *Protestants Against Poverty: Boston's Charities, 1870–1900* (1971), was, like all his later work, rich in irony and paradox, and levied a stern critique at the "moralism and self-indulgent mentality" of late-nineteenth-century antipoverty reformers. Although this earliest book did not deal with black history (he avoided, or was urged to avoid, identification with the field early in his career), it did reveal an informed understanding of the social control impulse that motivated "genteel charity reformers." Moreover, *Protestants Against Poverty* carefully demonstrated that, historically, poverty in America was a problem of social, not merely personal values, a theme that has remained at the center of our political culture from the Civil Rights era to the present. This work was written as Americans discovered the "other America," and launched a "war on poverty," the ideas and contexts in which Huggins framed the book. Huggins's essential concern with Americans on the margins, all the while he sought the nature of national history, would remain his scholarly project throughout his life. His *Slave and Citizen: The Life of Frederick Douglass* (1980), written as part of Handlin's Little, Brown series in American biography, is a concise but critical look at the abolitionist turned elder statesman.[2] It richly surveys the stages of Douglass's life, and shows how much the black leader's thought and behavior were rooted, self-consciously, in his own experience—a journey from slavery to freedom to citizenship. Huggins re-created Douglass's story as a reflection of the nation's life in a dramatic era.

Huggins was very much an empirical historian, interested especially in intellectual and social history; but he experimented with forms and style in imaginative ways, insisted on a broad self-consciousness about the craft among fellow historians, and he probably enjoyed writing more than research. Huggins was not a historian's historian in the way, for example, John Hope Franklin or August Meier have been in the same field. He did not open new paths of scholarship with innovative methodologies as, for example, Leon Litwack, Lawrence Levine, or Sterling Stuckey did through folklore. His contribution to the new slavery historiography during the 1970s was an epic history aimed at a broad audience, not a major work of scholarship. He shunned ideology and theory, at the same time he could admire the work of some historians who were innovative in their use. With one compelling exception, *Harlem Renaissance* (1971), he did not produce pioneering monographs that continued to uncover and launch a new field.[3] Huggins entered the field of Afro-American history with, not before, the crest of revolutions in society and scholarship through which that field found extraordinary new growth.

Above all, Huggins may have been at his best as a kind of epistemologist of Afro-American history. He insisted that we could get beyond race as professional scholars at the same time we probe the depths of its meaning in

American experience. He freely acknowledged that for black scholars the black experience is often a matter of personal identification, just as in any other group or national experience. But it was the intersections of multiple experiences that he found the most interesting, and the sheer excitement of history for Huggins may have been the challenge of discovering just what was knowable or unknowable about the past. "Black Americans, like the American nation itself," he wrote in 1983, "will be forever searching into the past to provide a sense of legitimacy and historical purpose, forever bound and frustrated in the effort." Huggins believed that American history, as broadly practiced, is still far too driven by a sense of chosenness, special destiny, or the doctrine of progress. He kept calling for a chastened, more ironic, tragic view of American history, with the Afro-American story brought to the center of a new history evolving from the conceptual and social revolutions of his own time. American dualities and, indeed, the dual character of history itself animated his writing. "We need to know how and why we use history," he said, "to serve both our needs of personal and group identity as well as for the more 'scientific' and humanistic purposes of historical analysis. We should know the differences and not confound them." That notion of what historians do compares well with W. E .B. Du Bois's simple but poignant definition of history as "an art using the results of science." It also squares well with R. G. Collingwood's conception of history as the "science of human nature." Collingwood warned against the underestimation or misunderstanding of the role of imagination in history. "The historical imagination . . . is properly not ornamental but structural," wrote Collingwood. "Without it the historian would have no narrative to adorn. The imagination, that 'blind but indispensable faculty' without which, as Kant has shown, we could never perceive the world around us, is indispensable in the same way to history."[4] The *structures* of historical imagination come from the *questions* we ask of the past. Huggins was one of those narrators who eschewed adornment at the same time he searched for his own voice by exploring into the past. He tried to understand the epic quality of history without being trapped by its formulas.

Huggins loved the big questions. In his 1971 essay, "Afro-American History: Myths, Heroes, and Reality," the lead piece in *Key Issues in the Afro-American Experience*, he tried to capture the meaning of that charged and formative moment in the history of this field. After surveying vast changes in American race relations since World War II, and especially during the sixties, he struck the chord of what was happening: "The crisis of the moment has always given rise to new and pressing questions. Thus, in our time, it is not sentiment, liberalism, humanitarianism, nor sudden enlightenment that has compelled historians to take a new look at the American past, but simply the demands of the American present."[5] Thus could Huggins distrust ideology, as

I think he always did, and still comprehend its force in relation to events. And thus could he in 1971 denounce history that engages in mere fantasy and superficial myth-making, and yet six years later write such a self-described "epic" history of the slave experience, a story that could be felt as much as comprehended. In *Black Odyssey* he told a great tale of human—indeed, mythic—transcendence over evil, his own vision of the destructive unmaking, and yet creative remaking of an African American people, a vision that shares much in outlook with Du Bois and with Ralph Ellison, and was clearly modeled on, and even a provocative response to, Handlin's *The Uprooted* (1951), the epic history of European immigration.[6]

The times were changing, and so were the questions: What did it mean to be a slave? What happens to a culture torn from familiar terrain and ancient values, when it is scattered by an almost unimaginable process of violence into a new epoch? How could something so destructive as slavery produce a "new" people? What did God mean to African American slaves? How do people collectively transcend suffering? How did whole, culturally alive, people walk out of the valley of the dry bones that was slavery? How do we find the right language—in our own voices—to make sense of such bitter ironies and oppositions? How should the scholar with the desire to write self-consciously "epic" history take the fruits of a historiographical revolution and recast it into a broad narrative which both glides and instructs almost exclusively in his own voice (which is what Huggins attempted in *Black Odyssey*)? How, indeed, can we late-twentieth-century scholars best imagine ourselves into the past and understand the "souls" of black folk—or any other folk? Where should we locate the ethnic province of black art within the larger provincialism of American art? Is it or should it be an ethnic province at all? What is it about American history and society that has allowed (or compelled) Americans to always believe that they are "coming of age," that they continually must have a "renaissance" of their culture? What makes Americans re-make themselves, or at least believe that they are? This was one of Alexis de Tocqueville's great observations; it passionately motivated Walt Whitman; Frederick Douglass couldn't live without the faith that he had re-made himself; it informs a great deal of Langston Hughes's poetry; and it was one of the large questions Huggins was trying to test in *Harlem Renaissance*.[7] Big questions.

But there were even more. From the explosion of knowledge, methodology, and particularism of the past thirty years, how do we discern a new picture of the "whole" of American history? Is the whole even knowable anymore? Huggins always answered this question with an emphatic yes. And even broader: What about America as an idea? Is there such a thing? Does—should—America have a "master narrative" of its history? To do this, he answered yes, but not with homilies of American exceptionalism. Black history, wrote Huggins in 1983, "is at once distinguishable, yet necessarily within the fabric." He had the boldness to *generalize* in our age of increasing fragmentation. But he did not want generalizations that would be mere summations or voiceless syntheses. His ambitious hope was that Afro-American history would become one of the "building blocks of a new synthesis, a new American history."[8] Regarding the revolt against the very idea of generalization about America in the 1980s, Huggins seemed to be compelled by the same concern David Hollinger expressed when the latter wrote: "America. If there is such a thing, it would be a shame to miss it." Huggins also seemed to be governed by a maxim that Charles Beard made famous: it is better to risk being wrong about great questions than to be right about trivialities.[9]

If history is a science, Huggins was among those who believed it was a *moral* science. He distrusted determinisms of all kinds, but he surely believed we were bound to levy moral judgments on the past and on ourselves. And, he was profoundly concerned about the relationship of past and present, and with the consequences of how we *use* history. Among the oldest of clichés is that we study the past in order to comprehend the present. In Huggins's work, especially in his essays, one finds the wisdom that the reverse is equally true.

The three essays he published in 1971, 1983, and 1990 respectively serve as a kind of index of the evolution of Afro-American scholarship and especially of his own evolving vision. The 1971 ("Myths, Heroes, Reality") essay had several purposes. He wrote from the position of a scientific historian, describing the craft of history for a general audience, at the same time he tried to introduce a volume (*Key Issues in the Afro-American Experience*) that might open the new teaching field of Afro-American Studies. Then he narrowed in on three targets: black cultural nationalism that sought self-esteem through learning about the black experience in isolation; the early 1970s void of teaching materials on black history; and the American mythology of special destiny and progress. Given the context of 1971, and the cycle we find ourselves in now more than twenty years later, Huggins's observations about the dangers of national myths of origin and hero-worship, whether fashioned by Homer, George Bancroft, or contestants in today's culture and curriculum wars are especially telling. But even as he warned against the dangers of historical mythology, he treated the subject seriously and betrayed a personal fascination for it.[10]

The 1983 essay ("Integrating Afro-American History") acknowledged that the revolution had occurred, and the question was how best to ride its crest into the 1980s. Huggins celebrated the "broad and deep change in American historiography" since the 1960s in relation to the black experience. The 1983 piece joined a preoccupation, indeed virtually a genre among American historians during the eighties: reflections on the fragmentation of the discipline, and calls for a return to "narrative" and "synthesis" in the craft. Such essays, roundtables, and panels at conferences became, and in some ways remain, a staple of historians' increasingly self-conscious introspection about the impact of the new histories. The discipline in crisis, the inaccessibility of the new histories, the loss of audiences: all of these issues animated historians' self-examination in the 1980s, and spilled out of their journals into the popular press. We have earlier heard claims about the end of ideology, and more recently, the end of history. But in the eighties the problem facing thoughtful historians was the end of coherence. In 1981 Herbert Gutman lamented in the *Nation* that the understandable "stress on segments" in the new black, women's, or social histories had led to a "disintegration of coherent synthesis." His jeremiad left a striking impression as he invoked T. S. Eliot's *The Waste Land* in order to describe American history as a "heap of broken images." In a paper delivered in 1984, and one of the most provocative and widely discussed of such essays, Thomas Bender argued that the way to a new narrative was in imagining a new "plot" for American history, rooted in the study of "public culture." Only this way, argued Bender, would all the newly illuminated "parts" find their way into an understanding of the "whole."[11] The "wholes and parts" debate continues to this day—on curriculum committees, school boards, within academic departments, and in national politics. Some postmodernists tell us that the issue of fragmentation does not really matter— all narrative constructions simply struggle against all the others. Some— scholars and the public—jealously protect their "parts" from the conservative tendencies of synthesis, while many others keep seeking coherence within pluralism, a new way of talking about the whole. Jeremiads have always been easier to express than new covenants are to achieve.

In some ways, this was Huggins's favorite conceptual ground. It allowed him to play with ideas, to provoke from a pedagogical pose, or to speak right from the heart about how he perceived History with a capital H. The 1983 essay was full of historiographical optimism about all the new heterogeneity in American history, at the same time it insisted that we all, especially Afro-Americanists, imagine a new synthesis. He played with the metaphor of "latent strands" in a larger fabric, and since all these new, previously hidden, threads had come to the surface, the whole tapestry would now look very different. Such a metaphor may reflect the instincts of a cultural historian, and one who had just taken over the chairmanship of the Afro-American Studies department at Harvard, but it was also precisely—in almost identical language—the same one Handlin employed in his introduction to *The Uprooted*. Writing at the beginning of the age of Reaganism, Huggins recognized that many calls for return to synthesis were coming from "reactionary impulses," but he demanded that we not flinch, not let a new conservatism control the discourse about multiculturalism, and try, hard as it is, to write about a new whole. In a field forever charged with sensitive questions of agency and racial politics, Huggins left this enduring challenge: "In an important way the *story* is what history is about. We all need to be calling for a new narrative, a new synthesis taking into account the new history. It is especially important to Afro-American historians, unless we are content merely to work in an eddy of the larger stream." A serious, pluralistic new narrative of American history— one that can fully integrate race, gender, and class, at the same time that it accepts that nations, as political and cultural systems, still have knowable histories—is just what two generations of historians (in America and abroad) have been trying to construct. The 1983 essay, moreover, contained a confession that since his critique of historical mythology in 1971, he had come to "appreciate better how the mythic can suggest itself into the most scholarly work." What followed was a self-critique of *Black Odyssey*, a book he felt was never fully understood or appreciated.[12]

Black Odyssey is a book that cares deeply about the dead. It was a work with which some reviewers at the time did not know quite what to do. Was it history, or was it literature? Or, was it something in between? Carl Degler refused to consider the work as history, preferring instead the category "emotional re-creation." Robert L. Harris found the book's lack of scholarly apparatus frustrating, but admired its function as a "philosophical . . . excursion into the slaves' interior lives." Lawrence Powell criticized Huggins's lack of concreteness in explicating the dichotomy between tyranny and freedom in American history, but he too admired the author's ability to represent the "emotional truths" of slave experience. In a book so evocatively written, David Donald was, understandably, troubled by the lack of living characters and attention to chronology. Willie Lee Rose, though, admired the way Huggins had found an "honest" place in that marginal land between scholarship and popular history. She honored the way *Black Odyssey* might capture a broad audience at the peak of seventies interest in slavery by asking the "deeper," "harder," "elemental" questions about human bondage.[13] Virtually without quotation or citation, with no scholarly apparatus, Huggins attempted a modern Homeric epic retelling the story of slavery. There are elements of the romantic in the style. The prose is moving and provocative; sometimes it almost sings, and sometimes it is abstract. The story compels attention and reflection, and offers no ultimate resolution or happy ending. He wanted to reach a large reading audience, at the same time he was carefully using the fruits of seventies scholarship in slavery historiography. He wanted to "touch, wherever possible," he said, "the emotional and spiritual essence" of the slaves' experience. His intention was to "reach for the heart of a people whose courage was in their refusal to be brutes, in their insistence on holding themselves together." In such tones one can begin to see the influence of Du Bois on Huggins.

Theodore Rosengarten, among others, picked up on this comparison, suggesting that *Black Odyssey* was written like a "meditation," a story "in the spirit of Du Bois, with a grasp for the whole and for the music in the most trying moments of life." Scholars from all disciplines still argue over which genre or discipline Du Bois's *Souls of Black Folk* (1903) best belongs. The critic William Stanley Braithwaite once called *Souls of Black Folk* "a book of tortured dreams woven into the fabric of the sociologist's document." As a historian's document, *Black Odyssey* might be seen in the same light. Moreover, the literary historian Eric Sundquist has recently argued that Du Bois's *Souls* should be understood for its "bardic function," a work of history as poetic remembrance. With differing degrees of success, Huggins, I think, aspired to the same function in *Black Odyssey*.[14]

The prose style and the epic reach of *Black Odyssey* owes much to *Souls of Black Folk*. Du Bois wrote about a different era than the one Huggins sought to re-create. But when Huggins lays out his argument most directly about black collective heroism and psychological transcendence, his writing sounds very much like Du Bois's poetic renderings of a world of "twoness" and racism that made assertions of "true self-consciousness" so difficult. Both books have a similar spirituality. At stake in Du Bois's most famous work and in *Black Odyssey* were the "souls" of people under enormous pressure and on the wrong side of power. Huggins argued that there were three great challenges to the "souls" of slaves: falling victim to "fear" of their oppressors; having their personalities fully compromised by "deception"; or giving in altogether to "hatred." Du Bois, likewise, had identified "tasteless sycophancy," "silent hatred," and in the most oft-quoted passage in Afro-American letters, "double-consciousness" as the great risks and possible outcomes of the struggle to be black and American, living either under slavery or with its legacy. The sense of tragedy, the probing for legacies, the quest to know just how powerful the hold of the past is on the present, and the critique of "progress," all of which abound in *Souls of Black Folk*, are also dominant themes in *Black Odyssey*. The souls of slaves survived, Huggins argued, because they fashioned an ethical order out of their own humanity, because they learned how to "manage" fear in an unequal power relationship, and because they created a religion in which they found a home.[15]

Huggins's bold effort to capture a "triumph of the human spirit" over oppression was at once the result of his own research and an attempt to turn George Bancroft, Francis Parkman, the Stanley Elkins thesis, Margaret Mitchell, and a host of others on their heads. "To call our society by its proper name," wrote Huggins in the original introduction, "requires a radical reversal of perspective," a phrase, again, identical to that used by Handlin in the introduction of *The Uprooted*. Preoccupied with and determined to subvert the language of the Founding Fathers, the proper name Huggins chose for early America was "tyranny." And in his demonstration of the bitter ironies at the root of American history, he chose words used by John C. Calhoun in his defense of slavery to remind us that (in Huggins's words) "a government is no less a tyranny because a majority finds it convenient." Huggins aimed at the heart in more ways than one: *Black Odyssey* is his own attempt to expose and dissolve the central myth of American history, to seize the language of the Founding Fathers, to reappropriate, revise, indeed rewrite The Story through the eyes, feelings, and experiences of African-American slaves. The first four chapters of the book end with ironic twists and subtle plays on the language of "founders" and "pursuits of happiness." Huggins's story has no sugar coating; at times it is a narrative of bleakness and destruction, slave ships without exits—for the slaves or for the readers. But it is a narrative where those excluded from Jefferson's language in the Declaration of Independence manage to take their fate as a material "resource," and convert that very language into their own moral or natural "resource." In Huggins's narrative, slaves become "immigrants" excluded from "the dream" at the founding, but a people irrepressibly at the center of America's "nation-making."[16] This would not be mere reverse myth-making, or simply a new version of the doctrine of progress, which he had forcefully warned against in 1971. He did, however, take that risk.

Huggins got back to narrative—to words with music and meaning. Listen to the ending of chapter 1, where he tries to capture the "rupture" of West Africans from their known world and their forced transplantation into a new universe:

> As for those who were torn away to America, none would have willed it so. None, beforehand, could have imagined the awful agony to be endured—the separation from all that they were, the voyage into empty space, the trials of adjustment to a new life. Rudely forced, they were, nevertheless, destined to help create a new world, to become the founding fathers and mothers of a new people.

Reaching for the psychological meaning of the African's experience in the slave trade, he tried to give it voice. Personal disasters can simply be part of life, says Huggins.

> But what of that catastrophe that spins one outside the orbit of the known universe, that casts one into circumstances where experience provides neither wisdom nor solace? What if the common ground one shared with the sound and the infirm, the rich and the poor, the clever and the dull, the quick and the dead, fell away and one were left isolated in private pain with no known point of reference? Would not then the pain be the slightest of the miseries?

Huggins's notion of the slave trade as the "rupture" of peoples from one world into a new one borrows from and reconfigures Handlin's "disrupted" and "dislocated" immigrants. Handlin's voice near the end of *The Uprooted* makes an instructive comparison to Huggins's.

> So Europe watched them go—in less than a century and a half, well over thirty-five million of them from every part of the continent. In this common flow were gathered up peoples of the most diverse qualities, people whose rulers had for centuries been enemies, people who had not even known of each other's existence. Now they would share each other's future.

Huggins's narrative is bleaker; his immigrants are not heading for a "refuge." But both authors write a narrative of loss, stories about peasantries on journeys into "strangeness."[17]

Black Odyssey and *The Uprooted* are stories of migrations and transplantations of peoples on an epic scale. Both are concerned with notions of *birthright* and *liberation*, with the severing of Old World ties and the agony of New World beginnings, with dislocation and the alienation between generations, and with the "Americanization" of European and African cultures. In the kind of dialogue between the immigrant father and son with which Handlin concludes *The Uprooted,* one can see at least some of Huggins's inspiration. "America was the land of separated men," Handlin says of his immigrants; they were people both trapped and released by "a cataclysmic plunge into the unknown." Huggins's slaves are forced into a similar plunge, one where questions of degree are the important difference. The immigrant's journey through a sometimes permanent cultural and psychological disorientation becomes the slave's journey through death itself, through hopelessness to survival in a strange new land. The immigrant's fear becomes the slave's terror, the immigrant's "choice" and "opportunity" to venture into the unknown becomes, for Huggins's slaves, the fate of being "instruments of others' opportunity."[18]

Participants in current public debates over "Afrocentric" or "Eurocentric" perspectives on American history might do well to simply begin by reading chapter 1 of *Black Odyssey.* Here they will not find a search for cultural gems of beauty and brilliance to displace an agonizing present, no embrace or invention of roots for their own sake, not even individual heroes or heroines, but a determined attempt to re-create the pastness of the past, a world in which feudalism and pantheism met capitalism and individualism, where ancient tradition and parochialism faced uncontrollable and unimaginable change, worlds being unmade and remade, a story of cultures smashed in a cruel filter but reforged in new forms, a narrative of social death and sometimes rebirth, hopes and dreams we call American seen through the lens of slavery, an unmistakable *uprooting.* Huggins's narrative is not one of adornment, but one of structure and plot. It is frustratingly abstract at times; the lack of chronological moorings and the absence of real historical persons and episodes remain bothersome. But as a narrative of migration, and one that tells the story of individual slaves' interior lives in relation to the national meanings of slavery, it reaches for a new "whole" that links the private and public dimensions of history. The story is hard medicine; it is epic and terrible, but romantic only in the form Huggins chose to tell it.

Less dazzling as literature perhaps than the novels set in slavery by Ismael Reed, Toni Morrison, Shirley Anne Williams, or Charles Johnson, *Black Odyssey* is nevertheless full of literary strategies and instructive metaphors, and it ought to be read with equal care.[19] Today's new narrators would do well to have a look. Huggins's central aim was to represent, or re-create, the psychological and spiritual world views of slaves, which were the resources of their survival. And like the great slave narratives, which he was also in some ways rewriting, *Black Odyssey* is a narrative organized around the tragic doubleness of slaves' lives. Like the tales of Frederick Douglas, Harriet Jacobs, or Solomon Northup, Huggins wrote a story that juxtaposed destruction and creation, life and death, victory and loss, faith and hypocrisy, numbed resignation and peasant stoicism, victimization and transcendence, Africa and America.

Apart from the ways Handlin's *The Uprooted* and Du Bois's *Souls of Black Folk* were models for *Black Odyssey*, there were other influences on the style and substance of Huggins's work. His life itself holds many keys to his approach to American history. Huggins was born in Chicago in 1927, the son of Winston J. Huggins, an African American who worked as a waiter and a railroad worker, and Marie Warsaw, an immigrant Polish American Jew. Huggins later remarked that this mixed racial parentage gave him "a keen sense of race rather early." His father left the family when Nathan was twelve years old. His mother moved the family, including his sister Kathryn who was two years older, to San Francisco, where she died only two years later, leaving the two teenagers on their own. The young Nathan postponed much of his own early education, working as a porter, warehouseman, and longshoreman to support himself and his sister. When he was drafted into the army near the end of World War II, he had not yet completed high school. He finished school in the service, and later went to the University of California at Berkeley on the GI Bill.[20] Once, in a conversation about where, chronologically, one might begin a new course on the Civil Rights Movement that he was organizing at Harvard, Huggins broke into wry laughter and told stories of his service in the war. As a guard for German prisoners of war being transported across the country, Huggins had been denied access, as a black man, to the segregated restaurants in which those German prisoners took meals. The black guard stood outside. To this listener, that story sounded like the perfect place to begin such a course, especially for a historian with his sense of irony. Huggins was a master conversationalist, and such was his favorite terrain: the bitterness of racial ironies in America, processed through metaphors of humor.

During the 1940s and 1950s Huggins learned a great deal about black religion and music from his adopted parents, Howard Thurman and Sue Bailey Thurman. Howard Thurman, a black minister and distinguished early scholar of the spirituals, helped the young man, Huggins later recalled, understand why "in those struggles between Good and Evil, Evil, true to life, triumphed more often than not." Huggins acknowledged Sue Bailey Thurman's "profound influence" on his youth, rearing him, he said, in the acknowledgements of one of his books, "from the subjunctive to the declarative mood." At Berkeley in the mid-fifties, Huggins encountered Kenneth Stampp at the very time the latter was writing his *Peculiar Institution*. In Stampp's lectures, Huggins claimed, he found his first inspiration that there might be a different way to think about slavery and race in America. From these reminiscences we can get a sense of just how far we have come in the study of slavery since the days when, as a schoolboy, Huggins remembered being taught only a "rather sunny picture of slavery . . . about darkies sitting on a plantation, eating watermelons and singing songs."[21] When we talk about historiographical change, are we not really trying to find ways, as well, to help our students read a book like *Black Odyssey* against such a backdrop as the odyssey of Huggins's own life, and that of others like him?

Deep in the well where Huggins gathered his sense of history there remains one further, if more distant, influence: William James. In a piece he wrote for a conference honoring Martin Luther King, Jr., at the United States Capitol in 1986, he asked his fellow historians, as well as the lay public, to take seriously the spiritual power of King's leadership. In assessing King's impact, Huggins wrote, he was struck at how, in our "secular age," scholars are so "poorly equipped to discuss the inner terrain of spirit and mind." In thinking about King, he said he was "drawn again" to a reading of William James's *The Varieties of Religious Experience*. Only by grasping the meaning of King's spiritual appeal, and James's argument for why people need spirituality, Huggins concluded, would we understand the meaning of the civil rights movement itself. James's lectures on religion were so important, he said, (citing three in particular: "The Divided Self," "Conversion," and "Saintliness") because they do "not assume reason to be the norm, and nonrational experience to be in some sense perverse." Surely this was a guiding sensibility in *Black Odyssey*: in order to truly comprehend the travail of the slaves, in their death and rebirth across time and continents, he may have relied heavily on James's masterful, if agonizing, discussion of the "twice-born" soul, the person whose life and faith have been blinded and then sighted, lost and then found. Along with life itself, and an ever closer look at African American history, Huggins may have found in James a further understanding of the persistence of evil in human nature, and a comprehension especially of the consequences of denying evil. There were many guides to understanding slave religion, but James may have helped when he wrote that the "completest religions would . . . seem to be those in which the pessimistic elements are best developed," and that "religions of deliverance" are where one finds such development.[22] It was on this level of consciousness that *Black Odyssey* attempts to speak for and about the slaves.

But James may have had an even wider influence on Huggins's thinking about history and pluralism, his love for the play of ideas and the testing of truths, and his insistent claim that no matter how multiple the parts, a whole story must still be told. The essential ingredients of Pragmatism—a fierce defense of the freedom of the will; the effort through a kind of critical openness to steer a course somewhere between or around all determinisms; and through the study of experience and its consequences, to find not only the links between past and present, but to link nature and the spirit, science with religion—are all prevalent in Huggins's work.[23] He may have found some inspiration in James that allowed him to write with a realism that was not cynical, and a skepticism that was still spiritual.

In the introduction to the new 1990 edition of *Black Odyssey* (the third of Huggins's historiographical essays), one finds perhaps his angriest piece of writing. Written as he was dying, it was a kind of last testament. Although in some ways an uncompleted argument, the piece is a jeremiad about the whole age of Reaganism, the resurgent racism of the 1980s, and the social despair arising from the intractability of racial and economic problems in what he called the "backwash of the so-called Second Reconstruction." Huggins's final essay makes an interesting comparison to John Hope Franklin's recent, *The Color Line: Legacy for the Twentieth-First Century,* a book of three essays characterized by a similar angry tone regarding the persistent racism of the 1980s, and the roles of national leaders in sanctioning that racism. The new introduction to *Black Odyssey* was, moreover, a final broadside at one of Huggins's favorite targets: American historians' enduring attachment to a "master narrative" of providential destiny. Embedded in the middle of this polemic, however, is one of the clearest appraisals of the slavery historiography of the sixties and seventies, a great service indeed to the student and lay readership he was still eager to capture with this book. The essay directs us to works (Edmund Morgan's *American Slavery, American Freedom,* for example) that truly have amended the Bancroftian narrative, that have demonstrated how "American freedom finds its meaning in American slavery, whiteness and white power found their meaning in the debasement of blacks." Huggins may underestimate just how much the Bancroftian paradigm has been dislodged. Eric Foner's new master narrative of Reconstruction synthesizes at least two generations of fundamental revision of a master narrative forged by the Dunning school, *Birth of a Nation, Gone with the Wind,* and decades of textbooks that recycled the

Tragic Legend of the Civil War's aftermath. But, as Huggins suggests, master narratives are not easily reshaped, however "deformed." Any new master narrative we may construct, Huggins challenges, must continue to explain the American paradox from the inside out, and not evade it. Furthermore, Huggins explains why the old master narrative continues to satisfy, how it feeds very real needs of national identity formation, why it continues as an abiding mythology of hope in spite of how reality contradicts it. But he will not let anyone off the hook. Nothing of real importance in American history ought be left in isolation, willfully quarantined, or jealously protected. "The challenge of the paradox is that there can be no white history or black history," he wrote, "nor can there be an integrated history that does not begin to comprehend that slavery and freedom, white and black, are joined at the hip."[24] In this idea of a new or different center, produced by contradiction, made by inclusiveness, and appreciative of deep ironies, new narratives and new textbooks are already being written.

The enigmatic title of this final essay, "The Deforming Mirror of Truth," lends itself to a variety of interpretations. But what seems truly deformed in the mirror Huggins constructed is the idea that history itself is going somewhere, that it has some particular *end* to which it proceeds, that out there on that next hill, just beyond the horizon there may be a national rendezvous at El Dorado. Huggins suggests that the deformed images in the mirror are not the end of mythology or ideology; they are not at all the end of hope either, temporal or spiritual. But they might be images that can help us approach American history as something not only felt, but faced. What he suggests in the unforgettable epilogue of *Black Odyssey* is, in effect, that we need to use our imaginations in order to go back and meet the ghosts of the past, that we should be drawn back to sit in the ugliest corner of the slave ship that landed at Jamestown in 1619, and there read the first two paragraphs of Jefferson's Declaration of Independence. Moreover, in order to understand why generations of immigrants of all colors became attached to something called an "American Dream," we should read Frederick Douglass on the meaning of the Fourth of July to the slaves. And finally, in order to ultimately find our replacement narrative for the Bancroftian paradigm, we will have to root it in contradiction and irony and not flee from them, and we will have to root it in all the uprooted.[25]

David W. Blight, Departments of History and Black Studies, Amherst College, was a colleague of Nathan Huggins at Harvard University, 1987–89. He is the author of Frederick Douglass' Civil War: Keeping Faith in Jubilee *(1989), and is currently researching a book on race and American historical memory of the Civil War.*

This essay is a revised version of a paper delivered at a conference dedicating the Nathan Irvin Huggins Library for American Studies at Palácky University, Olomouc, Czech Republic, March 19–21, 1993. For their criticisms and encouragement, the author wishes to thank Josef Jarab, Rector of Palácky University, Randall Burkett, Christopher Clark, Maria Diedrich, Genevieve Fabre, Jeffrey Ferguson, Henry Louis Gates, Jr., Brenda Huggins, Michael Kammen, Stanley Kutler, Lawrence Levine, Leon Litwack, Berndt Ostendorf, Alesandro Portelli, Richard Sewell, and Werner Sollors. I especially thank Werner Sollors for allowing me access to the original manuscript of Huggins's final work, "The Deforming Mirror of Truth," the introduction of the new edition of *Black Odyssey* (1990), and Larry Levine and Leon Litwack for their inspiration.

1. Nathan Irvin Huggins, *Black Odyssey: The African-American Ordeal in Slavery* (1977, 1990), pp. xvi-xvii. All citations here are from the 1990 edition.

2. Nathan Irvin Huggins, *Protestants Against Poverty: Boston's Charities, 1870–1900* (1971), pp. 3, 201; and *Slave and Citizen: The Life of Frederick Douglass* (1980). *Protestants Against Poverty* was published in the Greenwood series, Contributions in American History, Stanley I. Kutler, ed., and was introduced by Oscar Handlin.

3. Nathan Irvin Huggins, *Harlem Renaissance* (1971). This book is still one of the most original and oft-cited works on that pivotal era in black cultural history. For a critique of *Harlem Renaissance*'s significance, see Lawrence W. Levine, "The Historical Odyssey of Nathan Irvin Huggins," *Radical History Review* 55 (Winter 1993): 113–32. Levine's essay was originally delivered as a lecture in the John Hope Franklin Distinguished Lecture series at Adelphi University, February 5, 1992, and is a source of important information for my own essay. Works Huggins edited or coedited include, with Martin Kilson and Daniel M. Fox, eds., *Key Issues in the Afro-American Experience*, 2 vols. (1971); and *Voices From the Harlem Renaissance* (1976). Huggins's career and scholarship are also discussed in August Meier and Elliott Rudwick, *Black History and the Historical Profession, 1915–1980* (1986), pp. 124, 127–28, 177, 224, 285; and Peter Novick, *That Noble Dream: The "Objectivity Question" and the American Historical Profession* (1988), pp. 490–91.

4. Nathan Irvin Huggins, "Integrating Afro-American History into American History," in Darlene Clark Hine, ed., *The State of Afro-American History: Past, Present, and Future* (1986), p. 166; W. E. B. Du Bois, *Black Reconstruction in America, 1860–1880* (1935), p. 714; R. G. Collingwood, *The Idea of History* (1946), p. 241. For an essay that shares much in content, argument, and mutual influence with Huggins's critique of the myth of American chosenness and the doctrine of progress, see Leon F. Litwack, "Trouble in Mind: The Bicentennial and the Afro-American Experience," *Journal of American History* 74 (September 1987): 315–36.

5. Nathan I. Huggins, "Afro-American History: Myths, Heroes, Reality," in Huggins, Kilson, and Fox, eds., *Key Issues*, 1:8.

6. Oscar Handlin, *The Uprooted: The Epic Story of the Great Migrations that Made the American People* (1951). For recent responses to the new edition of *Black Odyssey*, see Peter H. Wood, Peter Dimock, and Barbara Clark Smith, "Three Responses to Nathan Huggins's "The Deforming Mirror of Truth," *Radical History Review* 49 (Winter 1991): 49–59; and Levine, "The Historical Odyssey of Nathan Irvin Huggins," pp. 121–23. Wood in particular draws attention to the comparison of *Black Odyssey* to *The Uprooted*. For Ellison's historical vision, see the essays in Ralph Ellison, *Going to the Territory* (1986).

7. In the *festschrift* for Oscar Handlin in 1979, Richard Bushman comments at length on how Handlin taught through "the power of his questions," and how a book like *The Uprooted* was infused with the idea that "irony lies at the very heart of history and life." However much Huggins may have come to dislike Handlin's growing conservatism over the years, both of these notions were surely methods or principles by which he taught and wrote. See Richard L. Bushman, Neil Harris, David Rothman, Barbara Miller Solomon, Stephan Thernstrom, eds., *Uprooted Americans: Essays to Honor Oscar Handlin* (1979), pp. xii–xiii.

8. Huggins, "Integrating Afro-American History into American History," p. 159.

9. David A. Hollinger, "American Intellectual History: Some Issues for the 1980s," in David A. Hollinger, *In the American Province: Studies in the History and Historiography of Ideas* (1985), p. 182. Beard is quoted in Michael Kammen, "Vanitas and the Historians Vocation," in *Reviews*

in American History 10 (December 1982), p. 17. The actual quotation is from a letter, Beard to August C. Krey, January 30, 1934, Krey Papers, University of Minnesota: "It is better to be wrong about something important than right about trivialities." On the whole question of generalization and new synthesis, the literature is huge and scattered. But to begin, especially in relation to cultural history, see Michael Kammen, "Extending the Reach of American Cultural History: A Retrospective Glance and a Prospectus," first written in 1983, in Kammen, *Selvages and Biases: The Fabric of History in American Culture* (1987), pp. 118–53.

10. Huggins, "Afro-American History: Myths, Heroes, Reality, pp. 9–16.

11. Huggins, "Integrating Afro-American History," p. 157; Herbert G. Gutman, "The Missing Synthesis: Whatever Happened to History," *Nation*, November 21, 1981, pp. 521, 553–54; Thomas Bender, "Wholes and Parts: The Need for Synthesis in American History," *Journal of American History* 73 (June 1986): 120–36. Discussions of getting back to narrative in the 1980s were many, but see Bernard Bailyn, "The Challenge of Modern Historiography," *American Historical Review* (February 1982): 1–25; Thomas Bender, "The New History—Then and Now," *Reviews in American History* 12 (December 1984): 612–22; Eric H. Monkkonen, "The Dangers of Synthesis," *American Historical Review* (December 1986); "Roundtable on Synthesis," *Journal of American History* (June 1987); "Roundtable: What Has Changed and Not Changed?" *Journal of American History* (September 1989).

12. Huggins, "Integrating Afro-American History," pp. 159–60, 164–65; Handlin, *Uprooted*, p. 3. That self-critique also included an interesting comparison of *Black Odyssey* to Vincent Harding's *There is a River: The Black Struggle for Freedom in America* (1981). On the lack of appreciation for *Black Odyssey*, see Levine, "The Historical Odyssey," p. 121. Huggins's belief that the book had never been fully understood or appreciated is a point he also made to me in conversations after the 1989 Organization of American Historians meeting in St. Louis, where he had just delivered a talk in honor of John Hope Franklin's *From Slavery to Freedom*. I once asked him if he had ever been chided or challenged for using a line from F. Scott Fitzgerald's *The Great Gatsby* to end *Black Odyssey*, one of the rare quotations in the entire book. He answered simply: "No one had ever asked."

13. Carl Degler, "Experiencing Slavery," *Reviews in American History* 6 (September 1978): 277–82; Robert L. Harris, book review, *American Historical Review* 83 (December 1978): 1095–96; Lawrence N. Powell, book review, *Journal of Southern History* 44 (November 1978): 630–31; David Herbert Donald, "A People's Experience," *New York Times Book Review* (December 11, 1977), p. 10; Willie Lee Rose, "A History of Endurance," *New York Review of Books* 24 (January 26, 1978). In her review, Rose made a point of comparing *Black Odyssey* to *The Uprooted*.

14. Huggins, *Black Odyssey*, pp. lxxii, lxxiv; Theodore Rosengarten, book review, *New Republic* 177 (November 5, 1977), p. 33. For Braithwaite and Sundquist quotations see Eric J. Sundquist, *To Wake the Nations: Race in the Making of American Literature* (1993), pp. 482–83.

15. W. E. B. Du Bois, *The Souls of Black Folk* (1903), pp. 44–45, Huggins, *Black Odyssey*, pp. 180–82.

16. Huggins, *Black Odyssey*, pp. lvxv, lxxiii–lxxiv, lxxiii, 24, 56, 84, 113; Handlin, *Uprooted*, p. 3.

17. Huggins, *Black Odyssey*, pp. 24, 26; Handlin, *The Uprooted*, pp. 35–36, 39.

18. Handlin, *The Uprooted*, pp. 304–05; Huggins, *Black Odyssey*, p. 84.

19. Toni Morrison, *Beloved* (1987); Sherley Anne Williams, *Dessa Rose* (1984); Charles Johnson, *The Oxherding Tale* (1982), and *Middle Passage* (1990); and Ismael Reed, *Flight to Canada* (1976). On this trend of black authors to write novels about the slavery period, see Deborah E. McDowell and Arnold Rampersad, eds., *Slavery and the Literary Imagination* (1989). Critic Henry Louis Gates, Jr. has termed this genre the "slave narrative novel." See "The Language of Slavery," introduction to Charles Davis and Henry L. Gates, Jr., eds., *The Slave's Narrative* (1985). In this sense Huggins's *Black Odyssey* might be seen as slave narrative history.

20. These biographical details are taken from George Howe Colt, "Will the Huggins Approach Save Afro-American Studies?" *Harvard Magazine* 43 (September–October 1981): 43–44. On Huggins's biographical background, also see Levine, "The Historical Odyssey," 114–15.

21. Colt, "Will the Huggins approach Save Afro-American Studies?" p. 43. Huggins's *Harlem Renaissance* (1971), is dedicated to Sue Bailey Thurman. In his bibliography for *Black Odyssey*, Huggins makes a special mention of Howard Thurman's *Deep River: Reflections on the Religious Insight of Certain Negro Spirituals* (1945), *The Negro Spiritual Speaks of Life and Death* (1947), and *Jesus and the Disinherited* (1949).

22. Nathan I. Huggins, "Martin Luther King, Jr.: Charisma and Leadership," *Journal of American History* 74 (September 1987): 479–80. William James, "The Divided Self and the Process of its Unification," and "The Sick Soul," in Frederick Burkhardt, gen. ed., *The Works of William James: The Varieties of Religious Experience* (1985), pp. 139–56, 138.

23. See Bruce Kuklick, ed., *Pragmatism* (1981), pp. xii–xiv. Especially important on the question of wholes and parts in history would be William James, "The One and the Many," the fourth lecture on Pragmatism, in Kuklick, ed., *Pragmatism*, pp. 61–74.

24. Huggins, *Black Odyssey*, pp. xlviii, xliii, xliv; John Hope Franklin, *The Color Line: Legacy for the Twenty-First Century* (1993); Edmund Morgan, *American Slavery, American Freedom* (1975); Eric Foner, *Reconstruction: America's Unfinished Revolution* (1988). Huggins's use of the "joined at the hip" metaphor reflects his appreciation of Mark Twain's novel about miscegenation, *Puddin'head Wilson* (1894), a book Huggins insisted belonged in tutorials and introductory courses in Afro-American Studies.

25. Huggins, *Black Odyssey*, Epilogue, pp. 243–46. On the new introduction, "The Deforming Mirror of Truth," see the responses by Wood, Dimock, and Smith, *Radical History Review* 49 (Winter 1991): 49–59. Wood insightfully implies that Huggins's challenge in this essay will make both Postmodernists as well as conservative defenders of national mythology equally nervous.

Library of Congress Cataloging-in-Publication Data

American retrospectives : historians on historians / edited by Stanley I. Kutler.
    p.   cm.
   ISBN 0-8018-5212-9 (h : alk. paper). — ISBN 0-8018-5213-7 (pbk. : alk. paper)
   1. United States—Historiography.   2. United States—History—Book reviews.
I. Kutler, Stanley I.
E175.A455   1995
973'.072—dc20

                                                 95-35208
                                                   CIP